Indexed in

Inventive Minds

Inventive Minds

Creativity in Technology

Edited by

ROBERT J. WEBER
Oklahoma State University

DAVID N. PERKINS
Harvard Graduate School of Education

New York Oxford
OXFORD UNIVERSITY PRESS
1992

Oxford University Press

Oxford   New York   Toronto
Delhi   Bombay   Calcutta   Madras   Karachi
Kuala Lumpur   Singapore   Hong Kong   Tokyo
Nairobi   Dar es Salaam   Cape Town
Melbourne   Auckland

and associated companies in
Berlin   Ibadan

Library of Congress Cataloging-in-Publication Data
Inventive minds : creativity in technology
edited by Robert J. Weber, David N. Perkins.
p. cm.   Papers presented at the Inventive Minds Conference,
held in Tulsa, Okla. Nov. 3–5, 1989.
Includes bibliographical references and index.
ISBN 0-19-507170-0
1. Creative ability in technology—Congresses.
2. Creative thinking—Congresses.
3. Inventions—Congresses.
I. Weber, Robert J. (Robert John), 1936–   .
II. Perkins, David N.
III. Inventive Minds Conference (1989 : Tulsa, Okla.)
T49.5.I6   1992   608—dc20
91-31907

1 2 3 4 5 6 7 8 9

Printed in the United States of America
on acid-free paper

To inventive minds—and to
the men and women of the Patent Office
for their dedication to inventive ideas.

Acknowledgments

The Inventive Minds Conference took place in Tulsa, Oklahoma, November 3–5, 1989. The conference, and now book, had its genesis in conversations between Dave Perkins and Bob Weber over several years. During a propitious dinner conversation, Penny Williams, Oklahoma State Senator, suggested to Bob that the conference would be a fitting tribute to celebrate the centennial of the opening and settlement of the Oklahoma Territory. Just as the opening of the territory was done by "Pioneers of the Land," so would the Inventive Minds Conference celebrate "Pioneers of the Mind" and the quest for new technology in the state.

Ably assisting in this effort were State Senator Bernice Shedrick and State Representative Larry Gish. With special funding from the Oklahoma Legislature, administered by Dr. Carolyn Smith and the Board of the Oklahoma Center for the Advancement of Science and Technology, we moved ahead. Along the way we were helped by many people, including Professor John Campbell, President of Oklahoma State University; Professor Vicki Green; Professor Earl Mitchell; Professor Margaret Ewing; Professor Sydney Ewing; Professor Gloria Valencia-Weber; Dr. John Coyle; Stacey Dixon; Antolin Llorente; Tim McCollum; Lise Patton; and Suzette Anderson.

Diane Downs, office manager for David Perkins, undertook the daunting logistics of getting editors' suggestions to the authors, securing revised and re-revised manuscripts, obtaining permissions for reprinting illustrations, and carrying out related matters in the preparation of this book. Editorial assistance was provided by Manuel Hernandez.

Some of the thinking behind this book was made possible by a grant from the MacArthur Foundation to David Perkins at Project Zero of the Harvard Graduate School of Education to investigate contemporary perspectives on creative and critical thinking. We are grateful for the support of the foundation.

The team at Oxford University Press has been encouraging and helpful. We want to acknowledge the skillful assistance of Joan K. Bossert, Acquisition Editor, Ruth Sandweiss, Manuscript Editor, and Leslie Reindl, Copy Editor.

To all these individuals, and to numerous other people who have helped in many ways, we offer our appreciation and thanks.

Contents

Inventive Minds

INTRODUCTION
The Unphilosopher's Stone

ROBERT J. WEBER AND DAVID N. PERKINS

The Motivation

The alchemists of yore sought nothing less than to remake matter, a cherished objective being the conversion of lead into gold. This might be accomplished by the touch of the "philosopher's stone," a substance that could perform the precious transmutation. Alas, there was no such stone, and, although modern nuclear physics at last gives us ways of transmuting elements, in general the process is nowhere near worth the energy it consumes.

If there is anything like the philosopher's stone, it is as unstony as something can get: It is the human mind. Through the use of the mind (lubricated with a good deal of sweat), human beings have transformed ordinary language into song and sonnet, arithmetic into algebra and the calculus, the Greek atom into quantum physics, geocentric cosmologies into the cosmology of the big bang. Human creativity, ineffable and evanescent as it is generally said to be, is the stone of power.

These allusions to art, mathematics, and science acknowledge three areas of human creativity commonly probed in efforts to disclose something of the workings of the creative mind. However, they leave out another especially central case: invention. Not invention in the general sense of devising the new, but invention in the more particular sense of inventing inventions—clothespins, refrigerators, digital sound, ball-point pens, the Bessemer converter, the McCormack reaper, or, to reach back into the uncalendared past, the flint knife, the bow and arrow, ways of making fire and keeping it alive.

The worldly and ubiquitous character of human invention may in fact have left us too familiar with its products to pay it due attention, because, in studies of creativity, and with a number of exceptions acknowledged, attention generally turns to the arts, sciences, and mathematics. Indeed, inventions (although not inventors) are a dime a dozen. While many of us live in homes fairly well laced with culture—a few paintings or prints, books explaining something of relativity or the Big Bang, others of Shakespeare and Dickens—those homes brim over with human invention—tables, chairs, rugs, mirrors, stairs, plumbing, electricity, air conditioning, central heating. When we step outside, we walk inside inventions (shoes, shirts, skirts), under inventions (hats, umbrellas), on inventions (sidewalks, escalators), by inventions (streetlights, traffic lights, mailboxes, display windows), to inventions (cars, buses, planes) that take us to places full of other inventions.

The whole thing is so wonderfully pervasive. And so pragmatic. If human creativity in general is the true philosopher's stone, one might call human inventiveness specifically the "unphilosopher's stone." Never mind the nature of the universe, the proofs of theorems, the poetic depths of the human soul. Let us find a way to cure smallpox, bridge the river, and dry our wash on rainy days.

Of course, we would not want to suggest that inventors are unphilosophical people. On the contrary, the inventors and other contributors to this volume impress us as quite reflective in thought and deed. A case in point: Robert Wentorf, one of our inventor–participants, a developer of the technology of artificial diamonds, contrived one of his early demonstrations to be the transmutation of peanut butter into diamonds. We take this to be a wry philosophical and artistic act, and not uncharacteristic of our group. Indeed, the poetic reach between peanut butter and diamonds seems greater than that between lead and gold, although the chemically literate will recognize that peanut butter and diamonds are close siblings compared with lead and gold (diamonds are carbon and peanut butter is in good part carbon).

However, whatever its philosophical excursions, certainly human invention is a centrally practical pursuit, a transmutation of matter into directly useful forms, the "unphilosopher's stone." Its job is to devise the thing that gets the job done—kill the mammoth, cultivate the wheat, comb the hair, switch channels, bury the dead, make ice cream. If this pragmatic cast has produced somewhat less attention to human invention than to other forms of creativity, we suggest that the unfortunate trend deserves reversing.

Indeed, invention plainly is a far older and more universal enterprise than science, far more deeply rooted in the human condition. While science in any substantive sense is a very recent phenomenon, all human cultures show inventions in abundance. One might even view invention of things to do jobs as a rough criterion of humanhood. Certainly paleontologists investigating hominid remains constantly look for stone tools as an index of advancement toward the human.

The Occasion

Hence the conference that engendered this volume. It was with full recognition of the fundamental role of human invention in human affairs and the central place of invention in the human condition that eighteen individuals gathered in Oklahoma in the fall of 1989 for three days to explore the nature of invention. We were a calculatedly cross-disciplinary group. There were historians of invention, cognitive psychologists, a retired U.S. Commissioner of Patents and Trademarks, and most important of all, seven world-class inventors. All of the inventors had made important contributions to technology, including some that were familiar if not household words, for instance, the electron microscope, ultrasound, and artificial diamonds.

Our composition deliberately challenged the typical disciplinary boundaries of conferences. Though scholars both, historians and cognitive psychologists do not so commonly share their ideas and puzzlements. And for historians and psychologists of invention alike, inventors are more likely to be seen through documents or the artifice of interviews than as collaborators in a conversation. One might imagine that these groups would spend most of their time yelling to be heard across the disciplinary gulfs that separate them (at least the editors, who also organized the conference, imagined this beforehand with some alarm). But nothing of the sort occurred. Although there was some pointed and useful talk about differences in disciplinary perspective, there were also an easy sharing of mysteries, a merging of vocabularies, and a meeting of minds around the nature of human invention.

We felt one shortcoming that we should acknowledge explicitly: There were no women in the group. Undeniably, both inventors and scholars of invention tend strongly to be male in the present social setting. Uncomfortable with this trend, we had no difficulty including three women of high standing in the original conference list of invitees. But chance conspired against us: none of the three was able to accept our invitation. We very much regret this.

So what did we do? The historians talked about individuals and settings in which invention had thrived: What were the stories? What were the conditions? How did a diversity of factors flow together to allow what happened to happen? The psychologists talked about the mechanisms of invention: How do ideas pop up from or get dug out of the mind? How does expertise figure? Are there strategies that can facilitate invention? The inventors, by request, talked about the ways by which they arrived at some of their most notable inventions: Where the problems came from, how the seeds of solutions emerged, how they grew into viable inventions. And of course, we all had a good deal to say about what one another had said—some arguments, some coalescence, some clear trends, some new puzzles. All in all, it was a rare and fascinating time.

The Themes

Our deliberations were guided by a list of broad questions that poked at various aspects of invention. The questions, an open list extended along the way, gave our presentations and exchanges a broad focus that served the open spirit of the enterprise well. Since the conference, we editors have reviewed the goings-on and sifted out a set of themes admittedly much more organized than those with which we began (after all, now we know what was said!) but with very much the same spirit.

Emphatically we were concerned with what might be called the "front end" of invention—where ideas come from and how they get developed toward functional prototypes. We acknowledge that this front end has an important wider social context. It occurs within and amid social and economic institutions with many other agendas to pursue: marketing, manufacture, production of profit; and within the larger society with its needs, hungers, pressures, and resources. Some contemporary scholars have taken pains to try to see this system of interacting factors whole. We applaud their broad perspective, but that assuredly is not the aim here. We focus on inventors, the inventive process, and the immediate context such as research and development laboratories.

In broadest stroke, our theme is the "how" of invention. We can chunk that how into three questions.

- Descriptively, how does invention happen?
- Comparatively, how does invention contrast with other commonly creative pursuits such as scientific inquiry, musical composition, or painting?
- Normatively, how might invention best happen? That is, what kinds of settings, conditions, strategies, and so on, appear to foster invention?

To give a sample of what these themes mean, consider for instance the role of chance in creativity. A number of scholars have suggested that chance plays a considerable role in creative endeavor. Although chance plainly enters in from time to time, how much it really accounts for is both a puzzle and a debate. So, descriptively, how do we see chance figuring in the inventor–participants' accounts, the historical cases studied, and the psychologists' models? Comparatively, does the story look any different from that in, say, the sciences, where a number of discoveries have occurred with the help of chance, for instance Darwin's reading of Malthus? Normatively, how can we put chance to work in inventive thinking?

For another sample, it is commonplace to note that a great deal of scientific and technological development occurs collaboratively. So descriptively, what sorts of collaborations appear in the cases examined? Comparatively, do these collaborations look like those in the sciences? What about collaborations in the arts? Normatively, do any recommendations emerge toward fruitful patterns of collaboration?

We approach such particular matters not only through the trio of descriptive, comparative, and normative questions but with three broad perspectives in mind. The first, and perhaps least familiar, is the *search perspective.* Invention can be viewed as a process of search through a "space" of possibilities. These possibilities are only potential—they exist as ideas in Plato's heaven, one might say. However, in contemporary cognitive psychology and artificial intelligence, the metaphor of search through a space of possibilities has proved to be a powerful way of conceptualizing problem-solving and invention. Under the rubric of search, we look at the ways inventors search efficiently the vast-in-principal space of possible inventions. The general answer, of course, is that they do not search this vast space but ignore most of it and look in "likely places." But just how? We also look at the ways inventors broaden their searches, getting beyond the limiting assumptions and other boundaries that may hem in invention.

Second is the *psychological perspective.* Granted that in one way or another inventors must search the space of possibilities, what kinds of psychological attributes support this search process—what spirit of playfulness and persistence, sorts of intelligence, technical skills, pattern recognition abilities, strategies for jogging the mind, and so on, appear to figure prominently in the process of invention?

Third is the *social perspective.* The process of search and its embodiment in ingenious minds plays out in a social setting of collaborations, laboratories, available resources, and so on, that may be more or less conducive to invention.

We believe that these themes will be helpful tools for prying open, at least a little ways, the "black box" of inventive process. As we introduce the parts of the book, we will refer back to these questions and perspectives, seeking to keep them on readers' minds. When we come to the concluding chapter, we will revisit them, summarizing and synthesizing what the chapters suggest.

The Organization

We have cast the chapters into a five-part organization. While it might seem sensible to use contrasts like descriptive-comparative-normative or the three perspectives to group the articles, this only works well for a couple of parts, because by and large the chapters speak to several themes at once. Instead, we have opted for an organization reflecting the overt focus of the chapters.

- Part I, *Setting the Stage,* consists of the upcoming chapter by Robert Friedel, which establishes a context for the rest of the book.
- Part II, *Classic Inventors,* looks to the past, with articles from both historians and cognitive psychologists casting light on the inventive thinking of such figures as Faraday, Bell, Edison, and the Wright brothers.
- Part III, *Contemporary Inventors,* contains the seven chapters from our inventor–participants, in which they tell the tales of their own accomplishments with remarkable clarity and insight—and, it may be added, with considerable modesty.
- Part IV, *The Logic of Invention,* includes three chapters representing the search and psychological perspectives on inventive thinking: how ideas develop over time, even millennia; what distinguishes inventive insight from more plodding approaches; what heuristics may aid invention; and more.
- Part V, *The Social Context of Inventions,* deals with the institutional context of inventive thinking, including two case studies of industrial laboratory settings and a thoughtful look at a pivotal institution for fostering invention: the U.S. patent system.

Following Part V, we offer our own concluding chapter.

This, then, is an introductory outline of our exploration of the unphilosopher's stone—human inventive ingenuity—with its power to transform water, sand, wood, and other resources of the wide world into gizmos that will do the jobs we need done. Our first full-fledged chapter is offered by Robert Friedel, professor of history at the University of Maryland, who asks a pivotal question: What really is our conception of invention? How do we as a society see it? How have we romanticized or deromanticized it? Commencing with the well-known quote from Edison about "ninety-nine percent perspiration," Friedel sketches how concepts of invention in the twentieth century have shifted toward a vision of experts sustained by large corporations and laboratories; and questions to what extent this is really so.

SETTING THE STAGE

1 Perspiration in Perspective: Changing Perceptions of Genius and Expertise in American Invention

ROBERT FRIEDEL

"Genius," Thomas Edison is quoted as saying, "is 1 percent inspiration and 99 percent perspiration." The aphorism is often taken as an exhortation to hard work or, possibly, a reference to the cut-and-try approach often associated with America's most famous inventor. It is also a central part of our Edison mythology, a characteristic bit of modest disclaimer from the rough, plainspoken product of the Middle West whom everyone knew really *was* something of a true genius. The aphorism takes on its authority and meaning from the fact that it comes from a genius and therefore, in an important sense, we don't believe it at all. That is to say, we all know that genius is something more than hard work and long hours. Perhaps Edison means to tell us that *invention* is only "1 percent inspiration," and that successful invention entails much more. But, in fact, *genius* is fundamentally associated with inspiration and with invention, especially in nineteenth-century America. This was recognized by our patent law, which the courts interpreted as requiring that a true invention reveal a "flash of genius." There is also a considerable iconography that testifies to this perception, from the dozens of public and academic buildings adorned with the names of Franklin, Fulton, Morse, and others, to the well-known 1862 painting of Christian Schussele, "Men of Progress," depicting the heroes of American invention in the generation before Edison.[1]

For most of the nineteenth century, technical novelty was largely seen as the product of human ingenuity and was closely associated with the "genius" of individuals and of the nation or race. In the twentieth century, by contrast, we have come to look for new technology from institutions and individuals who are characterized not by their creativity, imagination, and brilliance but by their ability to marshal "expertise," specialized knowledge beyond the grasp and understanding of the common person but essential to scientific and technical progress. This may seem merely to restate a truism about the modern world, that we are dependent on a science-based technology, directed by research and development institutions (academic, industrial, and governmental), and that this is distinct from an earlier reliance on empirical technique and craft knowledge. I am going beyond such pat characterizations, however, for I am suggesting that the change in attitudes from the last century to this one is in fact part of a fundamental change in our perceptions of human beings and their capabilities. It also tells us a great deal about how we view technology and the relationship between the technological world and our humanity.

I suggest that this is an appropriate consideration before we embark on careful consideration of both the historical evidence about the workings of inventors and the contemporary testimony of modern research leaders. The significance of this evidence can only be understood against the background of the cultural premises that we bring to the problem. Similarly, we can make informed judgments about the descriptions that we encounter of past inventive activity only if we appreciate the assumptions that guide these descriptions. In the nineteenth century, these assumptions encouraged a view of inventive activity that focused on the role of the individual, and especially on the man or woman who was endowed by nature with special "genius." In our own century, by contrast, it is not only the changing nature of science and industry that leads to a perception of invention as the product of laboratories and other institutions rather than individuals, but there is a changed perception of both the capabilities of individuals to comprehend the complexities of nature and of the importance of special talents or endowments in accounting for individual achievement.

To explore this thesis, I want to take a look at the image and career of a man I believe to be at the very center of this shift in views, Thomas Edison, and at the functioning of his most famous and productive laboratory, Menlo Park. Edison has, of course, been characterized in a number of ways—as the epitome of the hero-inventor, the "Wizard of Menlo Park"; as the organizer of the first modern research and development laboratory; and as an "inventor-entrepreneur," he combined adroitly the functions of master craftsman and savvy salesman. These images are not entirely consistent, and it is part of my intention to reconcile them by suggesting that the multiple images are a product of this broader shifting view of the sources of invention and technical progress. In other words, the Wizard of Menlo Park is one of the last manifestations of a conception of invention and technical creativity that is rooted in the Western notion of genius, especially as it was enunciated in the Enlightenment and modified by nineteenth-century Romantics. And the alternative view of Menlo Park as an R & D lab of the modern type, or at least a team of skilled experts working under Edison's direction and management, is a reflection of a distinctly modern view of technological progress as the product of expertise and special knowledge, rather than of ingenuity and creative imagination.

Genius in Western Thought

The nineteenth century was, in fact, a century of heroes. From Thomas Carlyle, with his assertion that history was really the story of "great men," to Samuel Smiles and his description of the material progress of the eighteenth and nineteenth centuries in terms of the "lives of the engineers," there was accepted to an extent unequaled in history a faith that the individual made a difference in the world and that singular men and women, blessed by Providence (or, in terms more congenial to the late nineteenth century, by heredity) or by a fortuitous combination of nature and upbringing, made the crucial difference in the way the world went. This heroic vision extended beyond the more obvious political and military realms to cultural and intellectual ones. This was, after all, an age when a Fenimore Cooper or Morse might be as much the object of admiration, if not exactly veneration, as a Wellington or Lincoln. To a degree, we can associate this phenomenon with the beginnings of what we know in the twentieth century as the "cult of personality." But this regard for the special individual and the significance of his contributions has much deeper roots, traceable to the Renaissance. In intellectual and artistic life, it is intimately associated with the concept of genius, especially as that concept was shaped in the late eighteenth and early nineteenth centuries.

Genius, in the sense that we use the word here to refer to individuals endowed with special talents and abilities and thus set off from the rest of humankind, has its roots in Greek and Latin culture, but began to take its modern form in the late Italian Renaissance, when men like da Vinci and Vasari began to tout the ideal of the truly creative artist and to associate this ideal with the term *genio*. In the eighteenth century, these notions were extended to refer to the possession by certain individuals of special creative powers, and the term *genius* came to be defined as both a capacity for original creation, discovery, and invention and as an individual having such a special capacity. Genius, in fact, came to be the subject of serious thought and study, and books began to appear reflecting efforts to dissect and explain the phenomenon. The most famous example of these (in English, at least) was Alexander Gerard's 1774 *Essay on Genius.* To Gerard the most essential characteristic of genius was imagination, for this was what made a man "qualified for making new discoveries in science, or for producing original works of art." But, Gerard went on to say, "mere imagination will not constitute genius"; it had to be augmented and disciplined by judgment, sense, and memory. Similar analyses could be found in the writings of Voltaire, Kant, and others. We might call this the "neoclassical" definition of genius (Becker, 1978; Gerard, 1774).

As in much of Western culture, the classical was to give way in the nineteenth century to the romantic. The ideal of the individual genius was, if anything, even more important in this intellectual climate, but it was changed. The primacy of imagination over all other virtues was emphasized in the age of Schiller, Coleridge, and Beethoven. The German Romantics, especially, directed attention to a "mystical" quality of true geniuses. In a sense, the genius was the tool of a greater power, and to interfere with his or her creativity was to disturb the divine order of things. Such a view naturally also directed attention to the eccentricities of the genius. Even in the Renaissance conception, the special intellectual powers of the genius suggested emotional and behavioral peculiarities as well, but these were generally seen to be offset by a certain balance or discipline in the true genius. The Romantics, however, suggested that something was lost if the genius was restrained by ordinary standards of conduct or thought. It was a very short jump from this belief to the "mad genius" of Mary Shelley, Edgar Allan Poe, or Nathaniel Hawthorne. In the mid-nineteenth century, this concept moved from the realm of literary conceit to that of scientific doctrine, albeit a controversial one. It was in this climate that nineteenth-century Americans assessed the contributions of their great inventors.

It is useful to understand that the notion of genius, whether touched with insanity or not, possessed an ambiguity in the American intellectual environment. Where, after all, does the appreciation of genius fit into a social setting fundamentally based on a faith in the equality of persons? One partial answer to this dilemma was a widespread belief in the environmental source of the unequal abilities found among people. Even if people were endowed in similar, if not strictly equal, fashion by their creator, the widely varying circumstances of birth, upbringing, education, moral training, and the like, even in the egalitarian climate of nineteenth-century America, could account for some easily observed differences in the condition and capabilities of free citizens. This sort of solution, however, while always a key part of the American ideology, could hardly explain the favorite American success story—the rise to accomplishment and success of an individual *not* favored by the environment but rather faced with great odds and difficulties, the sort of hero to be so popular in Horatio Alger's dime novels of Edison's day. Another part of the American solution to the problem of inequality was to be seen in the writings of the Transcendentalists. There one can see a commitment to a moral equality that is not necessarily followed by intellectual equality. Ralph Waldo Emerson, for example, was pretty clear in his own mind that whatever the "universal endowment of intuitional and moral qualities" among men, there was a class of individuals whose gifts of character or intellect would always place them on a superior plane (Curti, 1980).

In the mid-nineteenth century, one bit of evidence for the American concern for understanding and explaining the nature of individual differences, and especially the characteristics of exceptional people, was the interest in finding a scientific explanation for genius. One of the earliest published products of this interest was an article in *Graham's Magazine* in 1829 in which one Milford Bard took up the question of genius in a systematic fashion and concluded that the blood supply to the brain was the single most crucial factor. The key and most visible characteristic that linked the world's geniuses was, therefore, red hair. The few non-red-headed geniuses seemed to Bard to simply cement his argument, and the clincher was the easily proven fact that "of all the idiots born, only one in a thousand has red hair" (Kreuter, 1961).

A somewhat more serious and lasting aspect of the American concern with genius was reflected in the popularity of phrenology. The European founders of this field, Franz Gall and Johann Spurzheim, claimed to be building on an ancient tradition of linking the "faculties" of individuals with the development of different portions of their brains and with the consequent differences in the contours of the upper portions of the skull. Given all the trappings of a science, phrenology received widespread attention on its introduction to the United States in the 1830s. Here, some believed, was empirical evidence of the different endowments of talent and character that shaped the life and experience of each man and woman. No less a figure than Walt Whitman reported having "his bumps" read by a phrenologist, with impressive (to the somewhat vain Whitman) results. The materialistic character of phrenology put it in bad odor with clergymen and many other thoughtful individuals, but it possessed a lingering attraction in America for the remainder of the century. Thomas Edison himself would become a subject of phrenology's attentions (Curti, 1980; *Encyclopædia Britannica,* 1911; Kreuter, 1961).[2]

Genius and Invention

Unlike much of the intellectual tradition that defined the American interest in this subject, the linkage between genius and invention was not a European import. In the Romantic view, the peculiar features of the genius might appear in the madness of a Frankenstein, but not in the sober contributions of an engineer or brilliant craftsman. To Americans of the early nineteenth century, however, such an exclusion made no real sense. A good illustration of this early departure from European belief is a parable entitled "Genius and Labor" that appeared in *Graham's Magazine* in January 1837:

> "Of what use is all your studying and your books," said an honest farmer to an ingenious artist. . . . "My Sam does more with his plough in one month than you do with your books and papers in one year."
>
> "What plough does your son use?" said the artist quietly.
>
> "Why he uses ———'s plough. . . . He can do nothing with any other. By using this plough we save half the labor and raise three times as much as we did with the old wooden concern."
>
> The artist, quietly again, turned over one of his sheets and showed the farmer a drawing of the lauded plough, saying, "I am the inventor of your favorite plough." (quoted in Kreuter, 1961)

This is hardly a dramatic episode, but it speaks clearly of a deep-seated American belief that the special gift of genius was not expressed solely through the impractically poetic or artistic, but might also find its outlet in the improvement of the material world. This message was put best by that most American of poets, Walt Whitman, writing in his *Democratic Vistas* that "our republic is, in performance, really enacting to-day the grandest arts, poems, &c., by beating up the wilderness into fertile farms, and in her railroads, ships, machinery, &c. And it may be ask'd, Are these not better, indeed, for America, than any utterances even of great rhapsode, artist, or literatus?" To Whitman, even business, with its sordid preoccupation with money, could be an outlet for genius. To be sure, Whitman sought an American vision that went beyond pure materialism, but the literature that he saw as the responsible and inevitable product of a great people explicitly included "the literature of science" (in which he clearly included applied science) (Whitman, 1948).

Fittingly, perhaps the most explicit statement of this materialistic genius is from an inventor. Writing at the end of the century, when his vision was already being eclipsed, Hudson Maxim, inventor of widely used explosives, spoke of a peculiarly American kind of genius arising in the environment of the New World—"the tinkerer, or inventor, dedicated to the application of useful knowledge to the tasks of human life" (Maxim, 1900, in Kreuter, 1961). At about the same time, that great chronicle of native inventiveness, *Scientific American,* asked its readers to submit essays on "The Progress of Invention During the Past Fifty Years." Edward Byrn, the winner of the magazine's contest, combined patent statistics with an account of the highlights of modern technology and then appended this typical nineteenth-century note:

Looking at this campaign of progress from an anthropological and geographic stand-point, it is interesting to note who are its agents and what its scene of action. It will be found that almost entirely the field lies in a little belt of the civilized world between the 30th and 50th parallels of latitude of the western hemisphere and between the 40th and 60th parallels of the western part of the eastern hemisphere, and the work of a relatively small number of the Caucasian race under the benign influences of a Christian civiliza-tion. (Byrn, 1896)

Thomas Edison—Images of an Inventor

Prominent in both Byrn's patent figures and his descriptions of great inventions was Thomas Edison. It should be no surprise to us that Edison early in his career became a prominent example of the genius–inventor. Indeed, some of the descriptions that appeared of him at work in Menlo Park read like products of the most colorful of the Romantics:

At an open red brick chimney, fitfully outlined from the darkness by the light of fiercely smoking lamps, stands a rough clothed gray-haired man. . . . His eager countenance is lighted up by the yellow glare of the unsteady lamps, as he glances into a heavy old book lying there, while his broad shoulders keep out the gloom that lurks in all the corners and hides among the masses of machinery. He is a fit occupant for this weird scene; a mid-night workman with supernal forces whose mysterious phenomena have taught men their largest idea of elemental power; a modern alchemist, who finds the philosopher's stone to be made of carbon, and with his magnetic wand changes every-day knowledge into the pure gold of new applications and original uses. He is THOMAS A. EDISON, at work in his laboratory, deep in his conjuring of Nature while the world sleeps. (*Har-per's Weekly,* 1879, quoted in Basalla, 1976; Wachhorst, 1981)

There is more in this vein. The newspapers paid a great deal of attention to Edi-son's work on the electric light, and sometimes drew melodramatic pictures for their readers, as illustrated by this piece from the New York *Herald* of January 17, 1879:

Edison himself flits about, first to one bench, then to another, examining here, instructing there; at one place drawing out new fancied designs, at another earnestly watching the progress of some experiment. Sometimes he hastily leaves the busy throng of workmen and for an hour or more is seen by no one. Where he is the general body of assistants do not know or ask, but his few principal men are aware that in a quiet corner upstairs in the old workshop, with a single light to dispel the darkness around, sits the inventor, with pencil and paper, drawing, figuring, pondering. In these moments he is rarely disturbed. If any important question of construction arises on which his advice is necessary the workmen wait. Sometimes they wait for hours in idleness, but at the laboratory such idle-ness is considered far more profitable than any interference with the inventor while he is in the throes of invention (quoted in Friedel & Israel, 1986)

Here we see clearly the picture of the laboratory as the stage for the thought and action of one man—a man whose individual creative activity is so valuable that others must wait for it to play itself out. That phrase, the "throes of invention," is profoundly expressive of the Romantic notion that the creative genius is in some ways held in the thrall of Nature, a tool of greater creative forces. This perception is important, for sometimes the image of Menlo Park as Edison's workshop, rather than as a corporate research establishment, is said to be the product of Edison's own ego and the journalists' naive acceptance of his own boasting and self-centeredness. While the inventor's ego was unquestionably large and loud, it was not the real source of this image. The idea of the individual and his individual talents as central to the creative process was fundamental to nineteenth-century perceptions of invention. To have described Menlo Park in any other terms would have made no sense to the typical reader of the day.

To understand this further, a few other descriptions of Menlo Park will be useful. One of the earliest popular pieces on Edison appeared in the Chicago *Tribune* in 1878 just a few months after he announced the incredible invention of the phonograph. This piece is a wonderful and very clear example of the perception of genius. It is also, it should be noted, a good representation of how Edison's Menlo Park workers were viewed. First, note the headline:

Life of Thomas A. Edison [by Geo. H. Bliss]
Hitherto unpublished Reminiscences of Wonderful Genius
The busy life of one of the greatest of American Inventors
His career as a Newsboy, Amateur Chemist,
Newspaper publisher & Operator

Then, after some descriptions of the laboratory and of Edison's inventions, close attention is given to Edison the individual, indicative of the interest in the characteristics of the unusual genius:

In person he is 5 ft 9-½ inches tall, he wears a 7-⅞ths inch tall hat, his hair is black & worn short & is slightly gray. His complexion is pale and fair, his eyes are gray & piercing, he has a sharp nose & countenance. . . . His chest expansion is 5 inches. His powers of application, patience & endurance are something wonderful. He begins where most people leave off & like a Morphy at chess carries 5 or 6 lines of experiment in totally different divisions, never ceasing any of them till a result is reached or an impossibility proved. (*Chicago Tribune*, 1878, from the Hammer Collection)

In July of that same year, 1878, Edison sat for a phrenological bust, intended to produce a scientific record of the special characteristics (of the head) of an inventive genius. It's hard to see how the results could have revealed anything, and Edison's biographers report that he found the whole experience painful and distressing (the plaster stuck to his hair and stayed in it for days afterward) (Conot, 1979). But he certainly did not normally find such attentions unpleasant. Edison was, in twentieth-century terms, a "media personality," and the full extent of this media attention has been explored at length by Wyn Wachhorst in his study of Edison as "an American myth." Wachhorst observes that the highlighted features of the Edison image changed even over the span of the inventor's life and that this was part of a larger cultural movement: "one shift during this period [1880s to 1930s] was from 'idols of production' (statesmen, industrial leaders, scientists) to 'idols of consumption' (mass media celebrities) . . . from the culture hero, the symbol of shared values, to the celebrity, known only for his 'well knownness'" (Wachhorst, 1981). While

Wachhorst freely associates the complex Edisonian images with a wide range of cultural and social values, he misses one of the key lessons that Edison and his images has for our perception of invention and technological change in the twentieth century. This shift from genius to expert, from the image of wizardry to that of technocratic authority, can be seen in the changing interpretations of Menlo Park's magic. On the one hand, as we have seen, there was a readiness to accept the laboratory as the Wizard's workshop, the apparatus and the apprentices of an exceptional and gifted man, whose creative powers were beyond the complete comprehension of ordinary individuals. On the other hand, we can see emerging an alternative vision, that of invention and creation coming from the concerted application of useful skills and specialized knowledge, possessed and controlled by a number of individuals, endowed not with special genius but with training and particular talents. This alternative vision, dimly perceptible in the Menlo Park years but more insistent as the years followed, was to be the dominant vision of technological change in the twentieth century.

The Importance of the Laboratory

To understand this vision and its sources, one must understand just how the Menlo Park laboratory worked. In particular, we must look at the people with whom Edison surrounded himself there, for it is in large part the nature of their contributions to the great inventions, especially the electric light, that is the subject of changing interpretations. Charles Batchelor, the chief assistant, was an English-trained mechanic who immigrated to America to assist a Newark textile factory in installing its machinery. Recruited to work in Edison's Newark shops, Batchelor distinguished himself by his mechanical ability and cleverness. Despite having no electrical training or experience in telegraphy, by the late 1870s he was clearly seen as the equal of any other in the lab in electrical work. Similar backgrounds characterized most of the others in the lab—they were young men (some, like Francis Jehl or Albert Herrick, were really boys when they came to work for Edison) with little or no "scientific" training. Samuel Mott, the draftsman whose artistic renderings of machines and instruments embellished many of the Menlo Park notebooks in this period, had studied at Lehigh and later acquired his training as a draftsman at the Princeton School of Science (a vocational or mechanics school), but more typical were the Ott brothers, John and Fred, who were machinists recruited in Newark, or Martin Force, who had almost no training or experience before arriving in Edison's shop.

There were individuals with more scientific backgrounds, and these call for closer scrutiny. One or two of the men Edison relied on are often referred to as "chemists," and they were given the tasks of analysis and preparation of the sometimes exotic materials that were pressed into service in the effort to create a workable electric lamp. No doubt these men had specialized training and knowledge, but a look at what they actually did in the laboratory confirms the suspicion that they are no more appropriately called "scientists" than assayers or druggists would be. (Indeed, the term *chemist* in the mid- and late-nineteenth century was generally used as much to refer to a craftsman as to an academic.)

   In late 1879 and in 1880, the Menlo Park lab attracted a large number of new workers, many lured by the fascinating stories of the wonderful new electric light. As Edison began work on developing the capability to manufacture his lamp and install his electric power system, he rapidly expanded his operations, first at Menlo Park and later in New York City. These activities provided places for the new recruits, and among them were men with a wide variety of background and training. For example, Albert Herrick was 19 years old when he started at Menlo Park in August 1879; he attended the Stevens Institute course in mechanical engineering and chemistry a few years later, while still in Edison's employ. William Andrews started work for Edison in December 1879 and worked in John Kruesi's machine shop, despite the fact that he had taught scientific subjects in a British school for ten years. William J. Hammer joined Edison that same month, a 21-year-old with a high-school education and little more than a year's experience working in the electrical shops of Edward Weston in Newark. Edward G. Acheson, who was years later to become famous as the inventor of the abrasive carborundum, came to Menlo Park in September 1880 to work as a draftsman. The 24-year-old Acheson had little schooling, and his experience had largely been as an engineer's assistant (Hammer Collection).

   I describe these individuals and their backgrounds because I want to emphasize that Menlo Park operated very much as Thomas Edison's workshop and not as a modern research and development laboratory. This is an important point, for I wish to show that the changing perceptions of Edison and his work were not in fact based on some clear-cut departure that the Edisonian method or organization of work represented from the general nineteenth-century mode but instead derived from the changing cultural climate in which expert technical knowledge was displacing individual genius as the perceived source of technical progress. Perhaps a couple of references to recent discussions of Menlo Park will make clearer the distinctions I am making. First, from the Gies' popular history of American invention, *The Ingenious Yankees:*

> Yet of all Edison's inventions the most significant was Menlo Park itself. The world's first industrial research laboratory, prototype of all modern research centers, Menlo Park consummated the marriage of technology and science while it institutionalized the future of research. With it, the greatest of the Yankee tinkerers put an end to a century of Yankee tinkering. (Gies & Gies, 1976)

   If this is considered too insubstantial a source to consider, then note George Wise's observation in a 1982 article:

> Like other inventors [of this type] Edison rarely contributed to scientific literature, but carefully read it; he seldom used mathematics or quantitative physical theory in his own work, but hired mathematicians and physicists who did. Edison, the archetypal independent inventor of the 19th century, led a pack of scientists of complementary disciplines. (Wise, 1982)

   Here we have the full picture of Edison and the experts, in contrast to the mystical genius of the nineteenth-century newspapers. To understand the sort of evidence used to support this perception of Menlo Park, we have to look more closely at one or two of the laboratory's workers whom we have not mentioned.

In particular, we need to look at Francis Upton. Upton was a graduate of Bowdoin College and did postgraduate work in physics at Princeton and, briefly, in the laboratory of Hermann von Helmholtz at Berlin. In the fall of 1878 he was recently returned from Germany, having taken no degree, and was apparently at loose ends in a search for work. He approached Howard Butler of the Gold & Stock Telegraph Company in New York, seeking whatever odd jobs he might have for an educated but inexperienced young man. At just this time, Butler was suggested as someone who might be able to help out the electric light research by checking out the patent and scientific literature. He passed the job on to Upton, who so impressed Edison by his thoroughness and earnestness that a position at Menlo Park was quickly offered. There is no evidence that Upton's recruitment owed anything to a conscious effort by Edison to beef up the scientific capabilities of his staff.

Nonetheless, Upton's conspicuously different background, brought into the Menlo Park circle at a crucial stage, does at first glance give credibility to the picture of Edison as an employer of scientists in pursuit of invention. The best illustration of this interpretation of Upton's significance is found in some surprising letters in the Smithsonian's Hammer Collection. In the spring of 1913, Francis Jehl, who came to Menlo Park at the same time as Upton, wrote a letter that came into the hands of William Hammer, another Menlo Park veteran. The letter is a fascinating document, revealing a view of Menlo Park and Edison that is in stark contrast to most others. It is worth quoting at length:

> Those who were at the "round table" in the laboratory in 1879 were comparatively few, and outside of Edison, there were only Batchelor, Upton, Kuesi, Hammer and myself. . . .
>
> The real hero of those days was Mr. Francis R. Upton for his triumphs were silent for himself, and awe commanding for the scientific world and the reputation of Edison. [follows some biography of Upton]. . . .
>
> He not only mastered all the intricate problems in the domains of higher mathematics, but acquired such a routine and versatility in all the complex notions that existed at the time regarding the various branches of advanced philosophy, so that he was most eminently fitted for the work to which he was assigned when he entered the laboratory at Menlo Park in the early part of 1879.
>
> . . . It would be perfectly ridiculous to assume or even conjecture that the work that was executed in Menlo Park at the time was the result of haphazard experimenting without the aid of theoretical insight of the highest order; in fact it was the proficient and eruditive mind of Upton that nailed down the precepts at the time that completely erased the many phantom presumptions that had existed so long, and on account of which an art had laid dormant for so many years. (Hammer Collection)

Jehl makes it very clear that he believed Menlo Park functioned because it allowed the mobilization of expertise. He further decried the fact that others did not recognize this, but instead attributed its accomplishments to the genius of one man. His description of Edison takes on real irony in light of the fact that Francis Jehl was selected by Henry Ford to tend the great shrine built to Edison at Dearborn, Michigan, in 1929:

> It was also Edison's pushing energy as a leader that gave confidence to his financial backers that he would find a way to solve and thaw out the problem that he had contracted to

do in regard to the electric light. There was no fickleness or dilly-dallying about him either, he knew what he wanted and how to get at it from a business standpoint. For that purpose he rigged up his laboratory with various scientific paraphernalia and *most promising human intellects,* [orig. emphasis] and inaugurated thereby a new method of wholesale business researching, that was backed by lots of money and had also the aid of the best routine lawyers. . . . It was a vivid contrast and new departure from the old lines of experimenting by individual minds or limited personal means. (Hammer Collection)

The notion that the presence of men like Francis Upton and his Bowdoin classmate, Charles Clarke, signified that Menlo Park was dependent on scientifically trained experts can be found throughout much of the later Edison literature, beginning early in this century. In 1915, for example, an author wrote in *Science* that Edison's work was "a splendid example of scientific pertinacity." (Maclaurin, 1915; Armytage, 1965). Such a view is not supported either by a broader look at the laboratory and its staff or by the facts of the great inventions of Menlo Park. As we have seen, all but one or two of Edison's associates were men whose training and talents were rooted in the routine and the practical. They were indispensable to the success of Edison's "invention factory," but they were not technical experts in the twentieth-century sense. They did not represent in fact the "promising human intellects" referred to by Jehl. As Bernard Finn has written in describing "the Menlo Park mystique," they were by and large young, enthusiastic, low-paid mechanics, draftsmen, and students who were for the most part thrilled to be working in the most exciting enterprise of their lives. As Francis Upton himself once wrote home, "The strangest thing to me is the $12.00 I get each Saturday, for my labor does not seem like work, but like study and I enjoy it" (Finn, in Friedel & Israel, 1986).

The Rise of the Expert

Elsewhere I have tried to characterize the methods of Menlo Park as exemplified in the invention of the electric light (Friedel & Israel, 1986). As I see it, these methods do not lend themselves to simple or convenient characterization, as "scientific," "systematic," or "empirical." The men at Menlo Park worked in ways that followed from their background, experience, and ambition. Guided always by the ideas and wishes of Edison, these men often had opportunities to use their individual mechanical or technical abilities, solving the problems posed by Edison's ever-changing conceptions of his invention. These contributions were, it can be argued, indispensable to the success of the enterprise. At times, as Jehl suggests, individual workers contributed not only their talents and labor but their knowledge of areas with which Edison was less familiar. But the record is clear that such contributions were generally not at the heart of the effort, but largely sped it along just a bit more smoothly or quickly. Time and again, the records from Menlo Park show, we return to Edison himself to find the source of creation and direction. But whatever weight we give to an individual's ideas or to the talents of his companions, we must conclude that the products of Menlo Park were results of human creativity of the highest order.

If this is true, then we should ask ourselves why such technological creativity is given short shrift, compared with the creativity exemplified by art, music, or even theoretical science.[3] I won't attempt here to demonstrate that this is true, but I simply ask you to think of the ways in which all of us contrast the creative act in the fine arts or literature with the activities we associate with engineering and technology. While no one denies that technical work calls for certain creative energies, there is little question that such creativity is not perceived as being at the heart of modern technology. Certainly, the creative individual is not the central figure in the making and shaping of our technological age. This is what I mean by suggesting that geniuses have been replaced by experts in twentieth-century culture.

To a degree, this replacement was consciously perceived. Take, for example, the remarks of Henry Elsdale, in his 1899 article, "Why Are Our Brains Deteriorating?" While bemoaning the fact that creative genius seemed to be getting scarcer, Elsdale attributed this not to the progressive deterioration of the race but to the great expansion of human knowledge and technological capability for which the nineteenth century was so notable. No individual could learn enough in a lifetime to have the chance to show the kind of genius that had been so important in earlier ages. Continued progress, therefore, would not be the product of exceptional individuals but of groups, each member mastering some little bit of the now gigantic whole of human learning and contributing his or her part to further advancement. Elsdale's sentiments were echoed by others, such as James McKeen Cattell, and they represent clear statements of what we might call the "technocratic ideal" of the twentieth century (Elsdale, 1899).

This ideal, which has been described at length by historians and other students of American life at the dawn of this century, was not, of course, born overnight. Nor did it take hold immediately as the primary vision of technical and material progress. But in the first decades of the twentieth century, under the influence and as part of the spirit of many cultural, intellectual, and political forces and ideas—such as progressivism, conservation, efficiency, management, and the like—there took hold the modern notion of technical change owing more to institutions and less to individuals, of invention as being the province of corporations and not of wizards, of human minds and knowledge making a difference in the way people live and work and die not through creative brilliance but through organization and control (Akin, 1977).[4]

One indicator of this shift in thinking, this growing faith that progress must depend on experts and not geniuses, was the steadily growing investment by industry, from the 1880s on, in the creation of homes for these experts. While laboratories of a cruder sort could be found connected to factories and shops since the early nineteenth century, they were used solely for testing and measurement. Much more sophisticated operations began to appear toward the end of the century. First, well-educated scientists and engineers began to replace laboratory technicians, and testing responsibilities broadened considerably. In some industries, too, the larger and better-equipped laboratories began to be justified in terms of their capacity for not simply ensuring quality, but actually improving products. It was not a long step from this to the expectation that real innovations might emerge from these facilities. The path-breakers in this regard were the German dye manufacturers, who began hiring university-trained chemists in the 1870s to produce new miracles of organic synthesis. Their spectacular success was not lost on other industrialists, especially in the chemical and electrical industries.

In the United States, the creation of modern industrial research and development laboratories is typically traced back to those established by the Pennsylvania Railroad (1875), Du Pont (1881), and Standard Oil (1889). But laboratories directed toward invention, as well as toward providing scientific and technical services, took a little longer to appear. In 1900, the firm that had inherited Edison's electric-light inventions from Menlo Park, General Electric, established a research laboratory at Schenectady, New York, under the direction of a former university professor, Willis Whitney. GE's move in this connection was a particularly telling one, not simply because it was arguably the first industrial laboratory in America where research in basic science was given a prominent place, but also because GE established its laboratory literally next door to its resident "genius," Charles Steinmetz. Steinmetz, who was actively touted by GE as a scientific and inventive genius, was *not* a part of the laboratory—that institution was for organized, systematic research, rather than to provide resources and assistance for individual genius. When, about a decade later, the Bell System set up the Research Branch of its Engineering Department (later to become Bell Laboratories), this too was seen as a means for mobilizing university-trained experts to solve particular technical problems *and* to advance the art and technology of telecommunications (Reich, 1985; Wise, 1985). While these laboratories and similar ones established by such firms as Eastman Kodak, General Motors, and Westinghouse would have well-known and accomplished leaders and researchers, these individuals were clearly valued for their abilities as managers, team-players, and experts.

It is somehow appropriate that one of the most telling episodes of the transition from the old picture of the world to the new should have at its center none other than Thomas Edison. In July of 1915, the U.S. Secretary of the Navy, Josephus Daniels, responding to increasing concern about the implications of the war in Europe for American security, appointed a Naval Consulting Board with the charge "both to originate ideas and to examine those of others, critically and with such a concentration of ability as never has existed before in the personnel of any board." To Secretary Daniels, such a panel, chaired by Edison, was the logical American solution to the pressing needs of modern war:

> I do not expect these celebrated and very busy men personally to devote much time to the questions of the board. But an immense advantage to the nation will accrue if we succeed in planting our most vital problems in these minds.
>
> We know that soil is fertile. We know that, for already it has produced mechanical and scientific marvels which have made us the world's wonder. Then it is not unreasonable, is it, to hope that such seed planted in such soil will grow and presently will fructify in great ideas which will make us so secure against attack that none will ever run the risk of trying to annoy us? (quoted in Marshall, 1915)

In describing the project to a reporter, Daniels went on to refer to expectations that "the inventions of great brains" would be the Board's product.

The results of the Naval Consulting Board were, to say the least, disappointing. Despite the presence of Edison and other distinguished inventors, such as Frank Sprague, Leo Baekeland, and Elmer Sperry, the Board served as little more than a screening committee for the 110,000 or so suggested inventions that poured in from around the country. Only 110 of these merited serious study, and only a single device was finally made.

The same month that Secretary Daniels set up the Board, the ground was being laid for creation of the counterpoint to this mobilization of genius. On July 13, 1915, the astronomer George Ellery Hale communicated with William Welch, the president of the National Academy of Sciences in Washington, urging Welch to consider ways to make the Academy useful to the government in the event of war. A year later President Wilson sanctioned the formation by the Academy of a National Research Council. Over the next couple of years, as the United States moved from peace to war, the NRC became the single most important center for organized innovation. Built around the work of academic scientists and government laboratories, the Council's role was explicitly the mobilization of expertise, as opposed to the harnessing of genius (Dupree, 1957; Hughes, 1989; Noble, 1979). The twentieth-century way was clearly set out for all to see, and Americans' perceptions of technological progress would never be the same.

In his 1925 Lowell lectures at Harvard, Alfred North Whitehead asserted that "the greatest invention of the nineteenth century was the invention of the method of invention." A bit further on, he amplified this remark with special reference to the Germans, pointing out that "in their technological schools and universities progress did not have to wait for the occasional genius, or the occasional lucky thought." Whitehead celebrated the nineteenth century's

self-conscious realisation of the power of professionalism in knowledge in all its departments, and of the way to produce the professionals, and of the importance of knowledge to the advance of technology, and of the methods by which abstract knowledge can be connected with technology, and of the boundless possibilities of technological advance. (Whitehead, 1928)

We are still, at the end of the twentieth century, impressed by "the power of professionalism in knowledge." Indeed, in hindsight it seems remarkable that Whitehead could already see that this was one of the nineteenth century's most powerful and enduring legacies. It is ironic that the century of heroes should ultimately yield a system of change and progress that is seemingly without a place for individual geniuses. But no sooner does one give voice to this conclusion, than the limits of its validity become obvious. Just as the truth of nineteenth-century invention does not lie in a simple picture of individual great minds working alone with their own inspirations, so too does the fact of twentieth-century technological change transcend the image of teams of well-trained and like-minded men and women organized into the systematic production of novelty. We must, in our studies of invention, as in much else in life, always remember the fundamental ambiguities of our images, and be alert to both the power of organized collective action and the central role of individual minds in shaping the past and the future.

Notes

1. For a discussion of Schussele's painting, see Robert C. Post, *American Enterprise* (New York: The Cooper-Hewitt Museum, 1984).

2. For a remarkable late defense of phrenology, see Alfred Russel Wallace, *The Wonderful Century; The Age of New Ideas in Science and Invention* (London: Swan, Sonnenschein & Co., 1903), pp. 405–437.

3. A recent collection of essays, issued under the title *Genius: the History of an Idea,* has not one mention of technology or invention, though pieces are devoted to creativity in poetry, music, and mathematics, among other fields. Weisberg (1986) is another example of a study of creative genius that completely neglects technology; Bach, Picasso, Darwin, and Einstein, among others, are discussed extensively, but one short paragraph on Gutenberg is the only mention of an inventor.

4. While not addressing the question of technical change directly, the linkages discussed here are dealt with in William E. Akin, *Technocracy and the American Dream* (1977), especially p. 3.

References

Akin, William E. (1977). *Technocracy and the American Dream.* Berkeley, Calif.: Univ. of California Press.

Armytage, W. H. G. (1965). *The Rise of the Technocrats: A Social History.* London: Routledge and Kegan Paul.

Bard, Milford (1829). On genius. *Graham's Magazine,* 4 (July), 21.

Basalla, George (1976). Pop science: The depiction of science in popular culture. In *Science and Its Public: The Changing Relationship* (G. Holton and W. A. Blanpied, Eds.). Boston: D. Reidel.

Becker, George (1978). *The Mad Genius Controversy: A Study in the Sociology of Deviance.* Beverly Hills, Calif.: Sage Publications.

Byrn, Edward (1896). The progress of invention during the past fifty years. *Scientific American,* 75 (July 25), 82–83; reprinted in T. P. Hughes (comp.), *Changing Attitudes Toward American Technology.* New York: Harper & Row, 1975, pp. 158–165.

Conot, Robert (1979). *A Streak of Luck.* New York: Seaview Books.

Curti, Merle (1980). *Human Nature in American Thought: A History.* Madison. Wis.: Univ. of Wisconsin Press.

Dupree, A. Hunter (1957). *Science in the Federal Government: A History of Policies and Activities to 1940.* Cambridge, Mass.: Harvard University Press.

Edison in his workshop (1879). *Harper's Weekly,* 23 (Aug. 2), 607.

Elsdale, Henry (1899). Why are our Brains Deteriorating? *Living Age,* 122, 882–890.

Encyclopædia Britannica (1911). "Phrenology," 21, 534–536.

Friedel, Robert & Israel, Paul (1986). *Edison's Electric Light: Biography of an Invention.* New Brunswick, N.J.: Rutgers University Press.

Genius and labor (1837). *Graham's Magazine,* 12 (Jan.), 45.

Gerard, Alexander (1774). *An Essay on Genius.* London: W. Strahan (reprint, New York: Garland Publ., 1970).

Gies, Joseph & Gies, Frances (1976). *The Ingenious Yankees.* New York: T. Y. Crowell.

Hammer Collection. Archives Center, National Museum of American History, Smithsonian Institution, Washington, D.C.

Hughes, Thomas P. (1989). *American Genesis.* New York: Viking.

Kreuter, Gretchen von Loewe (1961). *The American Discussion of Genius in the Nineteenth and Twentieth Centuries.* Ph.D. dissertation, Univ. of Wisconsin (Univ. Micro. #61-3128).

Maclaurin, Richard C. (1915). Mr. Edison's service for science. *Science,* 41, 815.

Marshall, Edward (1915). What is expected of naval board. *The New York Times Magazine* (August 8), 14; quoted in T. P. Hughes, *Changing Attitudes Toward American Technology.* New York: Harper & Row, 1975, pp. 206–207.

Maxim, Hudson (1900). Genius and regeneration. *Arena,* 23 (April), 428–431.

Noble, David F. (1977). *America by Design: Science, Technology, and the Rise of Corporate Capitalism.* New York: Oxford Univ. Press.

Post, Robert C. (1984). *American Enterprise.* New York: Cooper-Hewitt Museum.

Reich, Leonard S. (1985). *The Making of American Industrial Research.* Cambridge: Cambridge Univ. Press.

Wachhorst, Wyn (1981). *Thomas Alva Edison: An American Myth.* Cambridge, Mass.: MIT Press.

Weisberg, Robert (1986). *Creativity: Genius and Other Myths.* New York: W. H. Freeman and Co.

Whitehead, Alfred North (1928). *Science and the Modern World.* Cambridge: Cambridge Univ. Press.

Whitman, Walt (1948). *The Works of Walt Whitman* (the "Deathbed Edition"). New York: Funk & Wagnalls.

Wise, George (1982). Swan's Way: A study in style. *IEEE Spectrum,* 19 (April), 66.

Wise, George (1985). *Willis R. Whitney, General Electric, and the Origins of U.S. Industrial Research.* New York: Columbia Univ. Press.

II | CLASSIC INVENTORS

We begin with classic inventors, individuals whom history recognizes as masters. This approach has several advantages. We are able to see ideas close to their origin, those ideas involve seminal inventions, and they are still simple enough to understand readily. In all, a fertile ground for examining what invention is all about, how searches begin, motives guide, and social forces do their work.

Ryan Tweney introduces us to the work of Michael Faraday, a giant of nineteenth-century science and invention. If today you have come in contact with any kind of electric motor, you have been touched by Faraday's hand. Tweney reveals his methods and tactics in arriving at a wonderful conceptual invention, the electromagnetic field.

Faraday believed in the unity of science, and he was very successful in linking previously disparate fields such as electricity, magnetism, light, and chemistry. In our terms, he was finding bridges between different search spaces and greatly expanding the connections between things and ideas. In fact, his work is a beautiful and seamless integration of science and invention; it is difficult to know where one ends and the other begins. The normative lessons we can learn from Faraday are many. For starters: try to cross boundaries of search spaces, try to work out heuristics for what to combine and how. And whenever a process is working, try to run it backward; if you do so, you may come up with the difference between a motor and a generator of electricity. The social lessons from Faraday also jump out. It is possible to be a great scientist and inventor without any formal education and with little or no mathematical knowledge. All you need is to work closely under one of the best scientists of the day (Humphrey Davy), have a fine intuition for the physical world—and have a large dash of genius.

W. Bernard Carlson and Michael Gorman show us the path to one of your most-or-least-favorite inventions, the telephone. Both Bell and Edison invented somewhat different telephones, leading to patent suits challenging what company would gain the rights to produce telephones. The authors weave this story into the simultaneous tale of the inventive processes of Bell and Edison, as reconstructed from their notes and other accounts.

The telephone can be seen as a generalization of the telegraph, an invention that had already changed the communication patterns of the nineteenth century. While the telegraph sends messages as a series of discrete dots and dashes, the phone transmits a continuous wave form immediately accessible to the human ear without any additional decoding—and the intermediaries required to do it. For the user, phone messages are simpler and more direct. But for the inventor, it is another matter. A simple telegraph requires no more than making and breaking a circuit. A phone must translate speech into a continuously modulating electric signal that can be sent over long distances.

Bell, as a teacher of the deaf, knew this. As he moved beyond his original problem of trying to multiplex many messages over the same wire, he moved ever more closely to the idea of direct speech transmission. The problem and the associated problem space changed dramatically as his incremental choices and decisions piled up. The telephone was not the problem he started with.

The lessons? It's all right to change your goals in mid course. It's good to have a related expertise (teaching the deaf) that other inventors don't have. More information sent more directly is better. The social context is also illuminating. Western Union retained Edison to work around Bell's patents. The scent of money was in the air. Imagine yourself in Bell's position. How would you like an adversary like Edison trying to work around you? The contrasting styles of Bell and Edison are illuminated here.

Tom Crouch tells us the story of wings. At the turn of the century, many inventors were struggling with the problem of heavier-than air flight. He asks, why were Wilbur and Orville Wright, two bicycle mechanics from Dayton, Ohio, ultimately successful? He finds possible answers in certain details of their upbringing, talents, methods, and wonderfully complex partnership.

The Wrights are a study of the right way to go about invention. Early on they parsed the problem of flight into three components: lift, control, and power. This enabled them to shrink dramatically the search space they operated in. To divide a problem into semiindependent components means that one can attack each of the components separately, without much immediate worry of how a solution for control is going to affect a solution for lift or power. The more independent the components, the better this strategy works. Their background as bicycle mechanics presents another case of having an expertise different from most other inventors. They seem to have had a wonderful feeling for mechanism and material. At a social level, one of the most interesting elements is how they worked together. They would have strong disagreements, but evidently their expertise and division of labor brought together exactly the right package of complementary skill and vision to get the job done.

The lessons again are many. Choose an important problem, parse it into independent components, have an expertise off the beaten track, and pick a partner who is strikingly gifted with complementary skills.

2 | Inventing the Field: Michael Faraday and the Creative "Engineering" of Electromagnetic Field Theory

RYAN D. TWENEY

It is a given tenet of folk wisdom that engineering and science are separate endeavors, dependent on each other but driven by inherently different needs and methods. Both fields, however, are seen as dependent (to greater or lesser degree) on certain creative geniuses for their greatest achievements. In the popular view, Edison and Einstein are both geniuses, more alike in this than different in their goals. Einstein "invents" the theory of relativity just as Edison invents the phonograph—by a spectacular leap of insight. In the right frame of mind, any attempt to understand such incidents of insight can be seen as misguided. Creativity is a special term, used only when something *surpasses* understanding: if it's analyzable then it ain't creative, and if it's creative then it ain't analyzable.

Accepting such an impasse is not in the spirit of most traditional studies of creativity, which generally assume (sometimes only for the sake of argument) that at least *some* aspects of creative incidents are understandable; they can be isolated, identified, talked about, generalized, and used to foster other creative incidents. The guiding attitude is, in short, analytic. Put in such stark terms, the creative impasse and the analytic attitude both seem too sharply drawn. We'd like to have both—the mystery of the uniquely creative case *and* an understanding of the general law sort.

Fortunately we are not lacking in ways to approach this problem. Like some of the other contributors to this volume (especially Carlson and Gorman, 1988; Chapter 3; Perkins, Chapter 13), I believe that current cognitive theory permits us to resolve the dilemma and to present scientific inventions in a context that respects the uniqueness of creative events while satisfying our need to explain what is going on. Doing this requires that we follow Simon (1981) and assume that the apparent complexity of cognitive activity reflects the operation of simple processes in complex environments. To use Simon's example, the path in three-dimensional space of an ant traversing a sandy surface may appear exceedingly complex, but the apparent complexity derives from the topography of the environment and not from the motor activity of the ant, activity that is simple in the principles that govern it. In the same fashion, what may appear to be an extraordinary feat of creative insight may well resolve itself into a reflection of a few general cognitive principles mani-festing themselves in a complex cognitive environment (see also Clement, 1989; Tweney & Hoffner, 1987).

Simon's ploy is not reductionistic. He is not claiming that complex cognitive behavior is *nothing but* the effect of a few simple principles. Instead, he is saying that *both* environmental factors *and* the simple principles are necessary for a com-plete understanding, just as we must know about both the ant's behavior and the soil's topography to account for the ant's particular trajectory. Note that this rescues uniqueness for us as well. We would not expect any two ant trajectories to be pre-cisely the same, simply because we recognize the variety of the possible soil topog-raphies. In our context, similarly, we can expect each creative act to be unique given the possible diversity of the cognitive environments.

In contrast to ants (which we may regard as "hard-wired"), a good portion of the complex environment of a thinking person is internal, and consists of the par-ticular "software" routines and data base of the individual. Simon deals with this fact in part by considering the contents of long-term memory as part of the external environment of problem-solving (see Simon, 1981, pp. 63–65). It is external in the sense that it represents part of the complex cognitive topography on which the prob-lem-solving process as such must act. Whether we consider long-term memory to be external or internal seems to me to be a purely semantic issue. What is important is to recognize that it provides us with a way to preserve the uniqueness of the cre-ative person as such (see Wallace & Gruber, 1989); it fully accounts for the idiosyn-cracy so frequently noted in creativity.

In the accounts given by the creative inventors in this volume, there is usually an answer to an implied question: "What makes *you* creative?" Since "modesty forbids" may be at work here, we cannot rely entirely on the answers given. But the answer in every case nevertheless reflects one or another of the two points I am argu-ing: the autobiographical accounts stress either the uniqueness of the external envi-ronment (as when the creative milieu of a research laboratory is credited), or the uniqueness of the individual's internal environment (as when mentors or particular early experiences are described), or some combination of the two. But we do *not* read accounts based on claims of being qualitatively different from others (though some stress quantitative differences—more or less than the average of some trait or characteristic).

Similar considerations have guided my explorations of Michael Faraday's cre-ative scientific thinking (see Tweney, 1989, for an elaboration of the general per-spective and an overview of my broader analysis of Faraday's thought). In the pres-ent context, I will consider specifically his invention of the concept of *field,* a contribution that made him, in some sense, the first of the field theorists in modern physics. Calling field theory an "invention" reflects one of the messages of this chapter, namely, that the underlying creative psychological processes of pure sci-ence and of practical inventing do not differ in important respects. I hope to show that insofar as cognition is concerned, there is no essential gap between science and technology; all that distinguishes the two is the nature of the goal.

The remarkably "thinglike" character of theories supports my point. In partic-ular, there is a close analogy between the dynamic character of Faraday's field the-ory and the dynamic character of an invented device. Thus, Crouch (Chapter 4) has emphasized the fact that Orville and Wilbur Wright succeeded with their airplane design in part because, coming as they did from experience with the dynamic balancing problem of bicycles, they were able to conceptualize the stability problems of flight in dynamic terms. Where others sought ways to achieve a fixed, unvarying stability, the Wrights saw that continuously variable systems were needed to control a flight path dynamically in real time. As we will see later, Faraday's field theory was successful in part because he conceptualized the field as a dynamic entity in which forces were either continuously varying or (even when apparently static) in a state of dynamic equilibrium.

I have said that invention and scientific work differ in their goals—product versus abstract theory, say—however similar they may be in process. Even so, the goals share certain similarities. Both science and invention occur in a social context; the scientist no less than the inventor must succeed in "selling" the object of his or her efforts in a competitive "marketplace." One way to conceptualize the marketing process begins from consideration of the perceptual/cognitive properties of the product on offer.

To sell a theoretical notion to one's peers demands that the notion become *visible* in the sense that it should be apprehensible in a direct way. The preconceptions, assumptions, and chains of argument that support it must be visible to the audience. Since it must account for something in a novel way, a something not previously understood, a theory can be regarded as making the *invisible* visible. From the point of view of invention, however, this order is reversed: ultimately inventions must leave their inner workings hidden, however well known the elements of the mechanism may be. Thus invention proceeds from the visible to the invisible, whereas theory in science reverses this ordering.

Between these two extremes, of course, there are intermediate states that are *transparent*. In science, the invisible must be made visible through a series of steps that are apprehensible by an audience when focused on. The steps are then transparent in the sense that they can be seen when they are the object of attention but do not obscure the view of the visible when not. We "see" phenomena through the intermediary of transparent elements, which can either be taken for granted or singled out for special attention. Something similar occurs in the early phases of invention. In passing from visible elements that work invisibly in the novel device, the inventor must first render the workings transparent to the peer community in a way that reveals the workings when focused on but does not obscure the function of the device when not. Patent applications, for example, seek to do just this.

Thus both science and invention involve a passage between two perceptual/cognitive extremes through intermediary steps collectively known as the transparent. What differs is the ordering:

Science: Invisible → Transparent → Visible
Invention: Visible → Transparent → Invisible

All three stages have a clear cognitive reading (which differs primarily in the role of attention). But all three are also definable in terms of the social context of the activity.

A Case Study

The points made above can be illustrated by Faraday's 1821 discovery of electrical rotations (Faraday, 1821, *ERE,* pp. 127–146[1]), a phenomenon that exploits the force exerted on a current-carrying wire by a nearby magnetic pole to produce a rotational motion. In effect, Faraday invented the first "electric motor." David Gooding (1985) has analyzed Faraday's somewhat cryptic diary notes and replicated the experiments that led Faraday to the discovery (Gooding, 1989, 1990). Using Gooding's analysis, we can quickly see the nature of Faraday's thought processes, while at the same time noting some of the theoretical issues that underlie Faraday's later development of field theory.

In 1820 the Danish scientist Hans Christian Oersted discovered that a current-carrying wire could affect a suspended magnetized needle in its vicinity, that is, Oersted discovered electromagnetism. The discovery was momentous in that it was the first demonstration that electric forces were associated with the production of magnetic forces. Following Oersted's discovery, the inverse question very quickly emerged (though it was not solved until 1831): could magnetic forces similarly be associated with the production of electric currents? If so, then a grand unification of electricity and magnetism would be possible. This was a seemingly easy challenge; one ought to be able to generate electricity from magnetism just by reversing the process—except, of course, that it wasn't easy. The key insight that only *changing* magnetic fields induce currents was an elusive one. Eventually (in 1831) it was Faraday who answered the question by discovering electromagnetic induction (see below). In 1821, however, Faraday directed his efforts toward exploring one of the mysterious aspects of Oersted's discovery, namely, the fact that the magnetic forces generated by a current-carrying wire were not attractive forces directed toward the wire or repulsive forces directed away from the wire (Faraday, *Diary,* September 3, 1821, V. I, pp. 49–50). Instead the forces seemed to be exerted along tangents parallel to the wire's surface. Instead of radial forces like those associated with gravity, static charge, or magnetic poles, Oersted's phenomena produced transverse forces.

Gooding's account shows how Faraday passed from initial representations of these forces in terms of the direction of orientation of a suspended needle (Figure 2.1a), to a reconceptualization of these forces as circular (Figure 2.1b), to a hypothetical apparatus that could utilize the transverse forces continuously to produce rotation (Figure 2.1c), to a demonstration apparatus (Figure 2.1d) that reveals the phenomena to an audience. In my terms, Faraday has taken the *invisible* (the transverse forces) and made them *visible* (the rotations), while refining the apparatus to make it *transparent.*

Faraday has sometimes been credited with the invention of the electric motor for this work, though he made no attempt to turn his apparatus into a practical device. Instead, for him, its significance was theoretical: it revealed a natural phenomenon in a way that allowed it to be used as a building block for further theoretical analysis. As one example, consider Figure 2.2, which is Faraday's diary entry for his successful production of rotations in the earth's magnetic field. At this point, the rotation phenomenon itself becomes part of a transparent system for revealing the invisible.

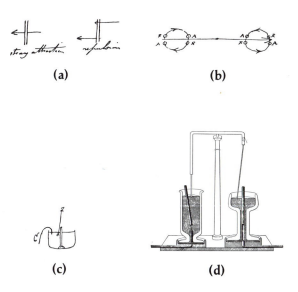

(a) **(b)**

(c) **(d)**

FIGURE 2.1. The progression of Faraday's "invention" of the curvature of electro-magnetic forces. (a) Faraday's initial representation of transverse forces (*Diary*, September 3, 1821, Vol. 1, p. 49). The double lines represent current-carrying wires, the arrows represent magnetized needles held above or below the wire. (b) Faraday's representation of "motions in circles round each pole" (*Diary*, September 3, 1821, Vol. I, p. 49). (c) "Apparatus for revolution of wire and magnet" (*Diary*, September 4, 1821, Vol. I, p. 50). The sketch shows a bar magnet supported in a cup of mercury. A wire is mounted on a swivel above the magnet, with its free end stuck in a cork floating in the mercury. When a current passes into the cup and out through the suspended needle, the needle will revolve around the magnet. (d) Faraday's "electro-magnetic rotation apparatus" (1822 *ERE*, Vol. 2, pp. 147–148 and Plate IV).

1821. DECR. 25TH.

Rotation of a wire by the earth magnetism. In a large glass basin put mercury and a little dilute N. A. Took about 6 inches of wire $\frac{1}{56}$ of inch thick, amalgamated it, formed a hook at top by which it was suspended from another fixed hook as in tube apparatus, put a little bit of cork on the lower end, the wire passing through it, and then held it over and on the mercury so that the wire formed an angle greater than the dip of the needle. Then connecting the mercury with one pole and the wire with the other it began to rotate and continued rotating whilst the connection continued. On changing the connection the direction of the motion changed also.

FIGURE 2.2. The production of rotations in the earth's magnetic field (Faraday, *Diary*, December 25, 1821, Vol. I, p. 63). Faraday's sketch shows a dish of mercury with a wire suspended over it, with one end floating on the surface. The apparatus resembles that of Figure 2.1c, except that the earth, not a bar magnet, is the magnetic source. The text is from Martin's transcription.

The Invention of the Field

The major goal of this chapter is to explicate Faraday's invention of the field concept. This is a much harder task, insofar as the process is spread out over a thirty-five-year span representing literally dozens of papers and thousands of experiments recorded in Faraday's *Diary* (Martin, 1932–1936). The account is thus only a sketch, but it makes, in my opinion, several important points for the goals of the present book.

The sketch of the development of field theory will proceed by first defining what Faraday's concept was in its mature form (as of about 1852), then showing how the separate characteristics of the field were established by Faraday (during the period 1821–1851), and finally discussing the process by which Faraday integrated each of the separate characteristics into a unified conceptual entity. By analogy with the invention process, we will be able to see Faraday "inventing" certain key components, and then will discuss how they were "assembled" into the final theory. With the case study in hand, the last section of the chapter will return explicitly to this theme.

Faraday's Definition of Field

We must first establish just what Faraday's field amounts to, since it differs somewhat from the modern conception (Nersessian, 1984, 1985). Speaking of magnetic forces, Faraday summarized his views in 1852 as follows:

> The magnetic lines of force may be easily recognized and taken account of by the moving wire, both as to *direction* and *intensity,* within metals, iron or magnets, as well as in the space around; and that the wire sums up the action of many lines in one result: That the lines of forces, well represent the *nature, condition, direction,* and *amount* of the magnetic forces: That the effect is directly as the number of lines of force intersected, whether the intersection be direct or oblique: That in a field of equal force, it is directly as the *velocity;* or as the *length* of the moving wire; or as the *mass* of the wire: That the external power of an unchangeable magnet is *definite* yet illimitable in extent; and that any section of all the lines of force is equal to any other section: That the lines of force within the magnet are equal to those without: and that they are continuous with those without, the lines of force being closed curves. (Faraday, 1852, *ERE,* Vol. 3, p. 406, emphasis in original)

In modern terminology, we can summarize by saying that Faraday regarded fields as manifested by lines of force. Each such line is a continuous closed curve having a vectorial character; the ensemble of lines fills all space (including that within a material substance) and can be quantified. Note that there is no ether here; instead, Faraday regarded the lines of force as being immaterial but substancelike. Further, not noted in the quote but pervasive in his work is the notion that electric and magnetic lines of force are similar in nature and always associated together.

The Components of the Field

For the present purpose, I'll first indicate briefly how Faraday established some of the aspects of the lines of force, then consider how he integrated these into a coherent, unitary conception.

Lines of force are curved. This of course is implicit in his 1821 account of electrical rotations, as we saw earlier. Figure 2.1b includes a representation of the curvature, which makes manifest their character as circular lines possessing directionality (though, in 1821, Faraday had not yet clearly articulated lines of force as either vectorial in nature nor as "really" there). Limited though the concept was, however, it possessed great explanatory force; we saw above that Faraday was able to conceptualize the current-carrying wire as bent into a circle and to deduce that many such circles could account for the polar character of electromagnetic coils (a point noted earlier in somewhat different form by Ampére; see Williams, 1965).

Electricity and magnetism are related. The next step, chronologically, was Faraday's momentous discovery, in August 1831, that changing magnetic fields could produce currents in nearby wires—the inverse of Oersted's discovery (Faraday, 1832, *ERE,* Series I, ¶ 1–¶ 139). I've explored the nature of the 1831 discovery elsewhere (Tweney, 1985): in brief, we can see the key aspect as a new focus on transient phenomena in Faraday's thought in the months prior to August. He was thus in a position to notice the key fact, namely, that currents were produced only when the current in an electromagnet was switched on or off or, for the case of a bar magnet, only when the magnet was moving relative to the coil.

Clues to his developing conception of field were given by Faraday in the published report of his discovery. He spoke of the magnetic forces as representable by "curves," which he defined as "the lines of magnetic forces, . . . which would be depicted by iron filings; or those to which a very small magnetic needle would form a tangent" (*ERE,* 1832, Series I, ¶ 114). These are explicitly represented in a figure used to explain "in a popular way" (*ERE,* 1832, Series I, ¶ 116) the relation between polarity of a bar magnet and the direction of an induced current (see Fig. 2.3). In attempting to make his conception further visible to his readers, Faraday suggested that "a little model is easily constructed, by using a cylinder of wood for a magnet, a flat piece for the blade, and a piece of thread connecting one end of the cylinder with the other, and passing through a hole in the blade, for the magnetic curves" (*ERE,* 1832, Series I, ¶ 116).

We need to be careful not to read too much into such accounts. In 1832 Faraday was not willing publicly to claim reality status for the lines of force, though some of his unpublished writings suggest that his thought was heading in that direction (Nersessian, 1985). In fact, after 1832 he seemed to move away from research on what we would call fields as such, exploring instead what looks at first like a different

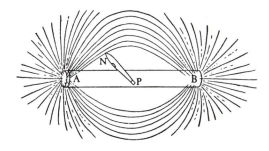

FIGURE 2.3. Faraday's "popular way" to represent direction of induced currents. The bar magnet is AB with north at A. A knife blade, pivoted at P, shows the direction of the induced current from P to N. (From Faraday, *ERE,* 1832, Series I, ¶ 116, Plate 1.)

issue: the electrolytic decomposition of substances by electric currents. This was not *really* a diversion, as has been noted (e.g., Harré, 1981; Tweney, 1989; Williams, 1965), since it amounted to a rejection of action-at-a-distance. One of his central beliefs, that there is no such thing as true action-at-a-distance, was therefore supported. Perhaps this gave him courage to assert later that the lines of force were the agent of the transmission of forces across space.

Lines of force fill all space.   This point was implicit even in 1821 (see Figure 2.2) insofar as terrestrial magnetism was concerned. In fact Faraday was able to show that the earth's magnetic field could be used to generate induced currents (Faraday, 1832, *ERE*, Series II, ¶140–¶264). This "scaling up" of his generalization was an important part of the demonstration. But showing that the lines of force penetrated all *matter* was more difficult. A clue in this direction was Faraday's discovery that the angle of polarization of a light beam would rotate when passed through a glass cube suspended between the poles of a magnet (Faraday, 1846, *ERE*, Series XIX, ¶2146–¶2242). Thus light and magnetism interacted in the presence of a material substance. The next problem was to determine whether magnetic forces directly affected substances other than those few (iron, say) that were attracted or repelled and could be made into permanent magnets. This point was also made in 1846 when Faraday discovered diamagnetism, the complementary property to paramagnetism. If a bar of iron, a paramagnetic substance, is suspended by a thread between the poles of a magnet, it will line up (like a compass needle) north pole to south and south to north. But a suspended bar of bismuth (which is not attracted or repelled by a magnet) will *also* move, except that it will set at right angles to the position taken by an iron bar, as shown in Figure 2.4. The point is general: Faraday showed that all substances set one way or the other, and hence that magnetic forces are affecting them (Faraday, 1846, *ERE*, Series XX, ¶2243–¶2342).[2]

Can it be shown that lines of force penetrate matter? Conceptually, Faraday answered this in 1850 by suggesting that paramagnetics (iron, etc.) act to *concentrate* lines of force whereas diamagnetics (bismuth, etc.) spread them apart (Figure 2.5; Faraday, 1850, *ERE*, Series XXVI, ¶2797–¶2968). Gooding (1981) has explored the empirical and theoretical steps that produced this inference. In brief, Figure 2.5 represents a generalization that can be confirmed by examining the differential tendencies to move shown by a substance as its shape and the surrounding

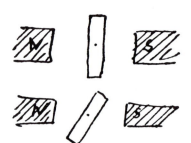

FIGURE 2.4. The equatorial set of a bar of a diamagnetic substance (bismuth or glass, say) suspended in a magnetic field. The bottom figure shows the arrangement when the electromagnet (with poles N and S) is off. When the magnet is turned on, the bar twists to the position shown in the top figure. (From Faraday, *Diary*, November 4, 1845, ¶7902.)

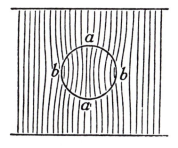

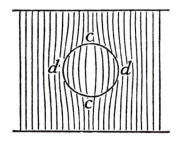

FIGURE 2.5. Lines of force are concentrated by paramagnetics like iron (top) and spread apart by diamagnetics like bismuth (bottom). (From Faraday, *ERE*, 1850, Series XXVI, ¶2807.)

media are varied. Once arrived at, however, it is a representation that is extremely powerful in its ability to capture complex interactions among fields and matter, as Figure 2.6 suggests. At this stage, then, Faraday can claim that lines of force fill *all* space, whether occupied by matter or not.

Lines of force are closed curves. In 1851 Faraday sought to show that the magnetic curves closed in on themselves by investigating the induced currents produced by a rotating magnet (Faraday, 1851, *ERE*, Series XXVIII, ¶3070–¶3176).

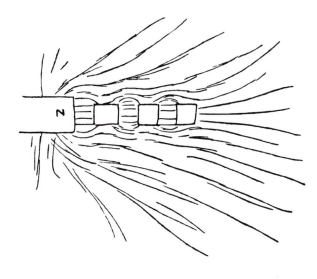

FIGURE 2.6. Lines of force can be traced through very complex field configurations. (From Faraday, *Diary*, November 11, 1851, ¶ 11686.) The squares represent a paramagnetic substance that concentrates the lines of force. At left is the north pole of a bar magnet.

The experimental setup is shown in Figure 2.7a. Faraday mounted a bar magnet on a crank, ran one side of a wire loop through a hollowed slot in the magnet, and connected the internal part of the wire via a commutator to an external galvanometer. Faraday was thus able to rotate the magnet and wire together by turning the crank, or rotate the magnet while keeping the wire stationary, or rotate the wire while keeping the magnet stationary. Further, by dividing the wire into two parts, one running inside the magnet and one outside and making electrical contact via the metal ring, he was able to rotate the inside and outside part of the wire independently. The interested reader is referred to Faraday's original report for all of the details of this remarkable bit of experimental logic, but we can capture the flavor of his demonstration by considering just two of the experimental conditions. If we consider a setup like that in Figure 2.7b and rotate the wire while holding the magnet stationary, then a current is produced in the wire. This is the usual case of electromagnetic induction—the wire loop cuts the lines of force associated with the magnet and a current is generated. Similarly if *both* the magnet *and* the loop are rotated, no current is produced—again, as expected, since the lines of force are carried along with the rotating magnet and loop and are stationary with respect to the wire. Now consider Figure 2.7c. Everything is the same except that the wire now passes through the center of the magnet. Now if the wire is rotated alone (i.e., both its internal and external parts—remember that there is a hole down the center of the magnet and a commutator to complete the circuit), no current is produced. But one *should* be produced, since the external part of the wire is cutting lines of force just as in Figure 2.7b. Faraday reasoned that no effect is found because the internal part of the wire is also cutting lines of force in such a way as to counteract the effect of the rotating external part of the wire. The effects are equal and opposite and cancel each other out. But this can only happen if lines of force exist inside the material substance of the magnet; exactly the claim that Faraday wished to establish!

This finding was a revolutionary one. There could be no better proof that the lines of force were independently existing entities than to show, as in this experi-

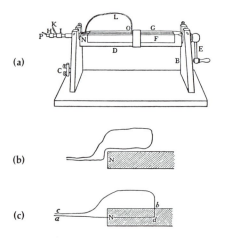

(a)

(b)

(c)

FIGURE 2.7. Faraday's apparatus for the investigation of lines of force within magnetics. (a) The rotating magnet and wire apparatus. (From Faraday, *ERE*, 1851, Series XXVIII, ¶3084.) (b) The wire separated from and entirely on the outside of the magnet (¶3093). (c) The wire run through the inside of the magnet (¶3095).

ment, that they close in on themselves *within* the iron magnet, and that currents are produced whether they are cut within the magnet or outside of it. Williams (1965, pp. 447–449) has argued that this experiment finally undercut the notion of centrally directed magnetic forces, replacing them with the tangentially directed forces that lie along the field lines. Certainly the study was a critical step in that direction, one that gains importance for us insofar as it supports the "thinglike" status of lines of force.

Lines of force can be quantified. An interest in the quantitative specification of the lines of force appeared very early in Faraday's research on electromagnetic induction. Thus in 1832 (Faraday, 1832, *ERE,* Series II, ¶193–¶264), shortly after his initial discovery, Faraday discussed the force and direction of induced currents, linking his discussion to the differential effects of induction on various metallic conductors. Most of the discussion is supportable only in qualitative terms. This paper is of great theoretical significance in the development of Faraday's field theory because it contains his first *supported* claims that lines of force could have an existence independent of matter. But the concept was still a general one; Faraday could specify how the rates of change of induced currents will vary with position and motion, but not in a precisely specifiable way:

> [I]t will require further research, . . . both experimental and mathematical, before the exact mode of action between a magnet and metal moving relatively to each other is ascertained; yet many of the results appear sufficiently clear and simple to allow of expression in a somewhat general manner. (*ERE,* Series II, ¶256)

Faraday did not fully come to grips with the quantification of induced fields until much later. Following a successful series of studies of variations in the earth's magnetic fields (Faraday, 1851, *ERE,* Series XXVII, ¶2969–¶3069; see also Gooding, 1989), Faraday explored the "closed curve" notion we have just discussed (Faraday, 1852, *ERE,* Series XXVIII, ¶3070–¶3176). In the 1852 paper with rotating magnets, he turned to the induced current in a moving wire as an index of the momentary local strength of a magnetic field (previously he had used suspended magnetic needles). In a key passage Faraday noted that "the moving wire can be made to sum up or give the resultant at once of the magnetic action at many different places, i.e., the action due to an area or section of the lines of force" (¶3076). Therefore "a moving wire may be accepted as a correct philosophical indication of the presence of magnetic force" (¶3083).

This was a breakthrough; in effect, Faraday could now measure either the momentary strength of a small portion of the field or the integrated strength of all of the field's lines through a given spatial area. Using this method he could, in a few pages, communicate a series of definitive results that lay to rest a number of uncertainties about magnetic fields, quantifying, for example, the relation between velocity of the magnet and induced current, and the distance of the conductor from the moving magnet. He showed, once and for all, the equivalence of effects when the conductor is moved and the magnet held still, or vice versa. Perhaps most important, he was able to claim "that the quantity of electricity thrown into a current is directly as the amount of curves intersected" (¶3115). Faraday was now ready to make stronger claims about the physical reality of the lines of force. In our terms, perhaps we can say that he had *invented* the lines; if you can count 'em, they must be real!

Linking the Parts

Knowing the various properties of a field is not enough, however. If you've never seen one, knowing that a cat has four legs, fur, and makes purring noises is not enough; you also need to know how it all fits together.

The key to the fitting together of Faraday's field theory is its dynamic character: Faraday's field exists in *time* and it is its time dependency that gives it theoretical power and coherence. Motion (i.e., change of position with time) is implicit in the list of properties, of course, and in the extended summary quoted earlier (p. 36). Currents are generated by moving a wire across the lines of force, and so on. But there is more to the dynamic character of a field than just this. Fields involve a dynamic interplay of forces, continual shifts that balance the "tension" (Faraday's term) in the closed loops of the lines of force.

Faraday described his notion using the diagram shown in Figure 2.8a. In the figure, E and M represent the relation of the electric and magnetic fields. If E is a wire, sending a current around E will produce magnetic lines of force, with polarity indicated by NS on ring M. Similarly, a magnetic line of force through M can induce a current in E. Thus the electric and magnetic fields have a "mutual embrace" (Wise, 1979). But they differ in that two parallel lines of electric current tend to attract each other, as Ampere had shown in 1822, whereas two parallel magnetic lines of force tend to repel each other (Figure 2.8b). This means that any sys-

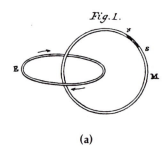

(a)

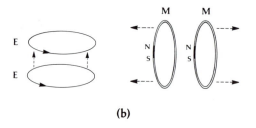

(b)

FIGURE 2.8. The "mutual embrace" of electricity and magnetism. (a) The interlocking curves: E is an electric current and M is a magnetic line of force. (From Faraday, 1852, *ERE*, Vol. 3, Plate IV.) (b) Two rings E of electric current *attract* each other, whereas two rings M of magnetic force *repel* each other.

tem involving both has two contrary tendencies. Now consider each ring as composed of tiny parts ("differentials" in modern terms). Thus the separate elements of a simple magnetic curve can be thought of as a series of tiny bar magnets placed end to end. Since these attract each other, magnetic curves tend to contract. On the other hand, electric currents can be thought of as tiny charged particles of like polarity; hence electric curves should tend to expand. All of these concepts can be fit together by considering Figure 2.9. The top part of the figure represents the lines of force surrounding a bar magnet and the bottom part of the figure shows the corresponding lines of force around a current-carrying helix. Note that the "mutual embrace" in the coil has *attractive* rings of electric force, each of which is trying to *expand,* whereas the magnetic force is in closed curves ("rings"), which are mutually *repulsive* but each of which is trying to *contract.* When the current is on, the magnetic field is dynamically equivalent but contrary in character to the electric

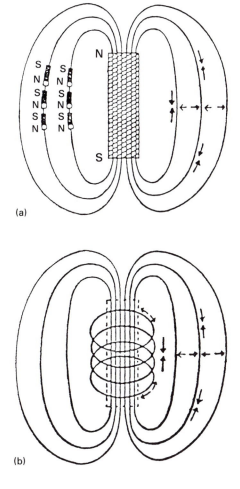

(a)

(b)

FIGURE 2.9. Dynamic equilibria of the lines of force (a) within a bar magnet (top) and (b) within an electromagnet. (From Wise, 1979, p. 1313.)

field. On this view, a bar magnet, like an electromagnet, is a system in dynamic equilibrium. And when a moving conductor cuts across the lines of magnetic force, they introduce a *dis*equilibrium—the whole system shifts, and a current is produced.

In another context, Gooding and I have argued that these relationships were thought about by Faraday in a fashion that constitutes a dynamic, geometrical mathematics (Gooding & Tweney, in preparation), separated from Maxwell's initial representation of fields only by the latter's preference for partial differential equations. What counts for now is that the "aspects" of the field cannot be regarded as independent characteristics in Faraday's version of the field. He has not invented a Rube Goldberg device, but instead a fully functional interdependent system. It is an invention in the best sense: you can "turn it on and watch it run."

Invention and Creativity in Science

The dynamism of Faraday's conception of the field provided him with a theory that went beyond his earlier speculative hypotheses. Indeed, the notion of pervasive forces as the ultimate reality was not new. Boscovich, for one, had postulated that matter was simply a locus of infinitely extended force. In his view, matter consisted of "point atoms," infinitesimally small centers with forces radiating around the central point (Williams, 1966). Similarly, Barlow had represented magnetic "fields" in the form of curving lines long before Faraday (cf. Gooding, 1989; Heilbron, 1981).

But the "thinglike" character of Faraday's field signaled that it was a far more precise and powerful account than the earlier conceptions. Lines of force, to be sure, were still hypothetical entities, but entities that worked just as they should if they are to be models of physical reality. The theory became a concrete, workable idea, elevated from the realm of "mere" analogy to a "physical intuition" rooted in a clear understanding of how nature could *actually* work (Clement, 1989).

It was not a perfect model; gaps remained that needed to be filled. Rather like a new car, bugs remained. Many of these were filled by Maxwell, who saw Faraday's theory as a promising start and sought to extend it. And he found, pursuing our metaphor, that it lacked a crucial part, namely, the so-called displacement current. By adding in a current that accompanied all field manifestations, Maxwell was able to produce a better invention, one that worked better than Faraday's (see, for a clear account, Born, 1962, pp. 175ff; Siegel, 1986).

"Thinglike" theories, like inventions as such, can thus be evaluated by workability criteria. This point is closely related to the cognitive conception of science as a procedurally based enterprise. Scientific thinking, in this view, does not occur in an abstract vacuum. Instead it is a "cut and try" effort involving reciprocal movement between procedural doings *in* the physical world and cognitive doings *about* the physical world (Gooding, 1990). For Faraday, in particular, such doings were a central part of his epistemological assumptions (Tweney, 1987). To know the world was to work with and in the world; one understood something when one could make it do one's bidding. That, ultimately, is why, for Faraday, experimentation was the heart and soul of science. But note too that it is also why, for Faraday, theories were not satisfactory unless and until they could be made to work in the same sense. Successful theories must work as if they were real devices. Ultimately, theories *had* to be inventions.

A common misunderstanding about science can be resolved with this approach. It is often thought that physics has become abstract in modern times, more like mathematics or logic or music, in that the physical referents of theory are far removed from the concrete world of objects, devices, and cut and try experimentation. In fact, the reverse is also the case. Physics has tied itself more closely to the concrete world; its devices work in successively closer approximation to what is "really" there. Like a cubist painting, the goal is greater fidelity to the real, not greater abstractness. But, again like a cubist painting, the greater fidelity places greater demands on the casual outsider.

There has been a shift in physics that makes it look, from the outside, as if it is more abstract. Miller (1984) has shown, for example, that the transition from Maxwell to Einstein was accompanied by a transition in the role of imagery from pictorial representations of reality to pictorial representations of theoretical conceptions. Einstein's world lines, say, are not snapshots of the universe as such, but instead represent constructs of the theory, constructs that let us "see" nature more concretely and more precisely. The meaning of the term *concrete* has shifted, but concreteness is still the touchstone.

In this view, theorizing and inventing are parallel activities, driven by similar goals and carried out by similar cognitive dynamics. To make a better mousetrap and to make a working theory are both reflections of a procedurally based creative process. Neither emerges in a blue flash of insight. Both are processes that must be understood by paying close attention to the microstructure of the cognitive search through a combinatorial space of possibilities (see Kulkarni & Simon, 1988; Langley et al., 1987; Newell & Simon, 1972; Perkins, 1981, Chapter 13 this volume). But it is important to realize that the search process is driven by concreteness. It is not *just* like the search for an anagram solution where the goals are fixed and the combinatorial rules given. At the outset, one does not know what the finished product will look like; in fact, one *cannot* know until prototypes have been built, tried, and learned from.

Invention and science are parallel but not identical. Making the invisible visible is an integral part of the goal of science though it seems, as we noted earlier, to be only a stage of invention, which ultimately seeks the invisibility of the workings of a device. Whereas invention seeks a black box, science wants a lucite box. Both must build the box, however, and both must fill it with workings.

Notes

The research described here was supported in part by the U.S./U.K. Fulbright Commission, which permitted an extended stay at the University of Bath. Discussions with David Gooding at Bath were an integral part of the development of these ideas and are warmly acknowledged.

1. Most of Faraday's papers were published in the scientific journals of his day. For the

most part, his researches on electricity and magnetism appeared in the *Philosophical Transactions of the Royal Society.* Most of the relevant experimental papers were in a numbered series (I–XXX) with continuously numbered paragraphs from ¶1 to ¶3242. Most of these, and other papers, are reprinted in the more easily available Faraday, *Experimental Researches in Electricity* (1839–1855), abbreviated *ERE,* most of which was also reprinted as Volume 45 of the *Great Books of the Western World.* To facilitate access for modern readers (and to minimize the size of this reference list), citations to Faraday's publications rely, where possible, on the series number and paragraph number in Faraday (1839–1855). Thus a reference to Faraday (1850, *ERE,* Series XXV, ¶2762) allows the reader to locate the source in either the three-volume *Experimental Researches in Electricity* or the one-volume *Great Books* collection.

References to Faraday's laboratory diary are to the published version (Martin, 1932–1936). When Faraday numbered the entries (as he did beginning in 1831), these are included in text citations, along with the date and the volume number in Martin's edition.

2. It is interesting to note that, according to Gooding (1981, p. 239n), Faraday here first used the term *field* (Faraday, 1846, *ERE,* Series XX, ¶2247).

References

Born, M. (1962). *Einstein's Theory of Relativity.* New York: Dover (rev. ed., first published 1924).

Carlson, W. B. & Gorman, M. E. (1988). Thinking and doing at Menlo Park: An analysis of Edison's development of the telephone, 1876–1878. In *Thomas Edison and the Menlo Park Experience.* (W. Pretzer, ed.). Dearborn, Mich.: Henry Ford Museum.

Clement, J. (1989). Learning via model construction and criticism: Protocol evidence on sources of creativity in science. In *Handbook of Creativity* (J. A. Glover, R. R. Ronning, & C. R. Reynolds, eds.). New York: Plenum Press, pp. 341–382.

Faraday, M. (1839–1855). *Experimental Researches in Electricity,* 3 vols. London: Taylor and Francis.

Gooding, D. (1981). Final steps to the field theory: Faraday's study of magnetic phenomena, 1845–1850. *Historical Studies in the Physical Sciences,* 11, 231–275.

Gooding, D. (1985). "In nature's school": Faraday as an experimentalist. In *Faraday Rediscovered: Essays on the Life and Work of Michael Faraday, 1791–1867* (D. Gooding & F. James, eds.). New York: Stockton Press.

Gooding, D. (1989). "Magnetic curves" and the magnetic field: Experimentation and representation in the history of a theory. In *The Uses of Experiment: Studies in the Natural Sciences* (D. Gooding, T. Pinch, & S. Schaffer, eds.). Cambridge: Cambridge Univ. Press, pp. 183–224.

Gooding, D. (1990). *Experiment and the Making of Meaning.* Dordrecht: Kluwer Academic.

Gooding, D. & Tweney, R. D. (in preparation). Mathematical Thinking about Experimental Matters: Faraday as a Mathematical Philosopher.

Harré, R. (1981). *Great Scientific Experiments.* Oxford: Oxford University Press.

Heilbron, J. L. (1981). The electrical field before Faraday. In *Conceptions of Ether* (G. N. Cantor & M. J. S. Hodge, eds.). Cambridge: Cambridge University Press, pp. 187–213.

Kulkarni, D. & Simon, H. A. (1988). The processes of scientific discovery: The strategy of experimentation. *Cognitive Science,* 12, 139–176.

Langley, P., Simon, H. A., Bradshaw, G. L., & Zytkow, J. M. (1987). *Scientific Discovery: Computational Explorations of the Creative Processes.* Cambridge, Mass.: MIT Press.

Martin, T. (ed.). (1932–1936). *Faraday's Diary. Being the Various Philosophical Notes of Experimental Investigation Made by Michael Faraday during the years 1820–1862 and Bequeathed by Him to the Royal Institution of Great Britain.* Forward by Sir W. H. Bragg. 7 vols. & index. London: G. Bell and Sons.

Miller, A. I. (1984). *Imagery in Scientific Thought: Creating 20th-Century Physics.* Boston: Birkhauser.

Nersessian, N. J. (1984). *Faraday to Einstein: Constructing Meaning in Scientific Theories.* Dordrecht: Martinus Nijhoff.

Nersessian, N. J. (1985). Faraday's field concept. In *Faraday Rediscovered* (D. Gooding & F. A. J. L. James, eds.). New York/London: Stockton Press/Macmillan, pp. 175–188.

Newell, A. & Simon, H. A. (1972). *Human Problem Solving.* Englewood Cliffs, N.J.: Prentice-Hall.

Perkins, D. (1981). *The Mind's Best Work.* Cambridge, Mass.: Harvard Univ. Press.

Siegel, D. (1986). The origin of the displacement current. *Historical Studies in the Physical and Biological Sciences,* 17, 99–146.

Simon, H. A. (1981). *The Sciences of the Artificial* (2nd ed.). Cambridge, Mass.: MIT Press. (First published 1967.)

Tweney, R. D. (1985). Faraday's discovery of induction: A cognitive approach. In *Faraday Rediscovered: Essays on the Life and Work of Michael Faraday, 1791–1867.* (D. Gooding & F. A. J. L. James, eds.). New York: Stockton Press, pp. 189–210.

Tweney, R. D. (1987). Procedural representation in scientific thinking. In *PSA, 1986, Vol. II.* (A. Fine & P. Machamer, eds.). East Lansing, Mich.: Philosophy of Science Association.

Tweney, R. D. (1989). A framework for the cognitive psychology of science. In *Psychology of Science and Metascience* (B. Gholson, A. Houts, R. A. Neimayer, & W. Shadish, eds.). Cambridge: Cambridge Univ. Press.

Tweney, R. D. & Hoffner, C. E. (1987). Understanding the microstructure of science: An example. In *Proceedings of the Ninth Annual Meeting of the Cognitive Science Society.* Hillsdale, N.J.: Lawrence Erlbaum.

Wallace, D. B. & Gruber, H. E. (eds). (1989). *Creative People at Work.* Oxford: Oxford Univ. Press.

Williams, L. P. (1965). *Michael Faraday: A Biography.* New York: Basic Books.

Williams, L. P. (1966). *The Origins of Field Theory.* New York: Random House.

Wise, M. N. (1979). The mutual embrace of electricity and magnetism. *Science,* 203, 1310–1318.

3 | A Cognitive Framework to Understand Technological Creativity: Bell, Edison, and the Telephone

W. BERNARD CARLSON AND MICHAEL E. GORMAN

The greatest invention of the nineteenth century
was the invention of a method of invention.
Alfred North Whitehead, 1925

While most scholars and laypersons would agree with Whitehead, it has been much more difficult to agree on what constitutes a method of invention. For some, "method of invention" is an oxymoron, for invention (and creativity generally) is the result of mystery, genius, and passion, all of which cannot be neatly analyzed as method. Others would agree with Whitehead that invention became methodical when inventors and engineers applied scientific theories and the experimental method to technology (Constant, 1980, 1983; Layton, 1989). Still other scholars have emphasized that inventors do have a methodology or a style that is not entirely based on science (Hindle, 1983; Hughes, 1971, 1977, 1989; Lubar, 1987). And some sociologists have proposed that invention is not an individualistic but a social process in which negotiations and conflict replace methodology (Gilfillan, 1935; Bjiker, Hughes, & Pinch, 1987; Latour, 1987).

In our research we are adding to this multitude of views about the methods of invention by developing a framework for investigating invention as a mental or cognitive process. Specifically, we view invention as a set of activities in which individuals combine and manipulate the symbolic with the material, a process in which ideas and concepts are manifested in terms of physical objects. To develop this view of invention, we employ three concepts:

- *Mental models*—the ideas and concepts an inventor has about his or her invention. Mental models are often dynamic prototypes an inventor can run in the mind's eye.

- *Mechanical representations*—the physical devices an inventor uses to build inventions. Frequently, inventors have a repertoire of preferred devices that they use repeatedly to secure a specific action.

- *Heuristics*—the strategies and tactics an inventor uses to generate and manipulate mental models and mechanical representations.

Like creativity in art, music, and other fields, inventors succeed by manifesting their mental model in terms of mechanical representations. They are very much like painters who take a vision in their mind's eye and use color and shape to express it.

We are developing a framework—as opposed to a model or theory—because what is needed is a common language or set of concepts for talking about invention. We use the term *framework* here in Tweney's (1989, p. 344) sense:

> I am proposing that we recognize a . . . distinction between claims based on traditional scientific methods, called here *theories,* and claims which attempt to map the complexity of real-world behavior, called here *frameworks.* Truth claims in a theory are based on the familiar strategies of scientific practice, while truth claims in a framework rely on interpretive procedures more akin to the methods of historical scholarship.

To develop our framework, we have undertaken a comparative study of three inventors of the telephone, Alexander Graham Bell, Thomas Edison, and Elisha Gray. By analyzing their notebooks, sketches, legal testimony, and artifacts, we are reconstructing in detail the intellectual path taken by each man to develop a telephone in the 1870s. By comparing their activities, we are identifying and interpreting what appear to be the mental processes these inventors used to create an entirely new technology.

In this chapter we report some of our findings concerning this cognitive framework for invention. To place our research in context, we begin with a discussion of other cognitive approaches to invention and technology. Following this, we illustrate our framework by narrating how Bell and Edison pursued their telephones. (Although essential to our full study, we do not discuss Elisha Gray extensively in this chapter because we have just begun to analyze his patents and artifacts.) In the course of the narrative, we discuss how each inventor's mental model evolved and how each manifested his mental model in terms of mechanical representations. We suggest that it was important for each inventor to develop a mental model as a devicelike image that embodied a complex relationship between sound and electricity. Where appropriate, we identify the heuristics employed by these two inventors, but this chapter focuses on fleshing out the concept of a mental model and its relationship to mechanical representations. We anticipate that in a future publication we will develop more fully our conception of invention heuristics.

Cognitive Approaches to Invention

Although there has been much work in the cognitive psychology of science (see Gholson et al., 1989; Langley et al., 1987; Tweney, Doherty, & Mynatt, 1981; for good reviews), there has been almost no work on the cognitive psychology of invention. A notable exception is the work of Weber and Perkins (1989; Chapter 18 in this volume). In general, they proceed from the view that invention consists of a search through a virtually infinite "problem space" of possible solutions; the challenge for the inventor is to reduce the size of, or find a route through, the problem space.

This view implies that new inventions like the telephone already exist "out there"; it is merely a question of using one's expert knowledge and a few heuristics or strategies to find the right route through a large number of alternatives. We think this approach underestimates the extent to which inventors construct their problem spaces (see Bjiker et al., 1987, for arguments regarding the social construction of technological problems). Inventors seek and define problems in terms of their skills and prior knowledge.

Weber and Perkins have an explicitly normative goal of wanting to "speed up" the process of invention. They seek to accomplish this by providing inventors with a list of heuristics, based on their studies of how inventions such as hand tools *might* have been developed. Weber and Perkins are not concerned with tracing the actual evolution of these tools, but instead reconstruct a probable sequence on the basis of a limited supply of prehistoric artifacts, whose interpretation is problematic even for expert archaeologists. Weber and Dixon (1989) add some experimental evidence that supports their theory regarding the development of the sewing needle. Using experiments and reconstructed sequences is a valid method for generating psychological theories and normative claims about invention. These hypotheses can be tested by further experiments and the norms can be evaluated in a variety of field and laboratory settings.

In contrast, we are not especially concerned with speeding up the process of invention nor do we intend to develop a testable theory or formal model of the invention process, though both are worthwhile goals. Instead, we wish to understand how inventors construct their problem spaces. To accomplish this, we find it crucial to discuss how inventors mentally represent their projects.

Mental Models

Our approach to invention begins with the concept of a mental model. This term is used by cognitive scientists such as Donald A. Norman (1988, p. 17) to describe "the models people have of themselves, others, the environment, and the things with which they interact." Norman (1983, pp. 7–9) further suggests that

> through interaction with a target system, people formulate mental models of that system. These models need not be technically accurate . . . but they must be functional. A person, through interaction with the system, will continue to modify the mental model in order to get a workable result. Mental models will be constrained by various factors such as the user's technical background, previous experience with similar systems, and the structure of the human information processing system.

Although Norman is talking about users of technology, other cognitive scientists have emphasized that mental models are central to how scientists work. For instance, Rouse and Morris (1986) argue that "scientists' conceptualizations of phenomena are almost totally dependent on their own mental models. These models dictate what observations are made and how the resulting data is organized" (p. 359). Rouse and Morris conclude that we can never be sure we have captured an inventor or user's mental model with absolute accuracy, but that this concept provides a useful tool for exploring and improving system design. Therefore, this concept ought to be useful in developing a framework for comparing the cognitive styles of inventors and scientists.[1]

In our research we have found that an inventor's mental model is frequently a dynamic and incomplete devicelike representation that can be manipulated in the imagination. For example, Hoffman (1980) points out that Nikola Tesla visualized and "ran" various models of devices in his mind. For some inventors, the mental model may be directly related to a real object, while for others it may be a construct, as in the case of Faraday's representation of lines of force (Tweney, Chapter 2 in this volume). However, what is important is that the devicelike representation is dynamic; mental models are often unstable or incomplete, which permits the inventor to introduce changes or additions. Also, mental models may function as analogies that allow inventors to anticipate the way in which novel systems might operate (see Clement, 1988; Gentner & Stevens, 1983, for experiments in which mental models function as analogies).

We suspect that inventors may consider several mental models for a particular invention and combine elements from each to create a new device. Similarly, mental models may be linked together. For instance, an inventor may have both a visual representation of how the invention might function and assumptions about how it will be manufactured and used. In the case of his motion picture invention, we found that Edison used his cylinder phonograph as a mental model to guide both the preliminary design and his marketing strategy for the kinetoscope (Carlson & Gorman, 1990). In addition, mental models may also be nested together. As we will see below, both Bell and Edison possessed representations of their overall invention and of specific components.

A useful alternative to mental models is the concept of a frame, as discussed by Robert Weber and David Perkins (1989). They define it as "an entity with slots in which particular values, relations, procedures, or even other frames reside; as such, the frame is a framework or skeletal structure with places in which to put things" (p. 51). To illustrate this concept, Weber and Perkins use simple inventions like the fork. To develop and improve the fork, they propose that an inventor divide the fork into functional slots and attributes and then try different alternatives in the slots.

The concept of a frame was first developed as a way of representing knowledge on a computer. Unfortunately, these attempts led to the "frame problem," in which the computer made a response consistent with the frame but which most people found silly. This problem is part of the reason why recent connectionist approaches to artificial intelligence no longer use frames. Furthermore, it is not clear whether Weber and Perkin's concept of a frame could be applied to a complex artifact such as the telephone. But, as they are careful to point out,

> The frame concept . . . is by no means necessary. The points we make for the most part, hold equally for a semantic network, or some other data structure. We note also that simply to represent an invention by means of a frame or another data structure can itself be a significant act of invention. (1989, p. 53)

In general, we prefer the concept of a mental model because mental models represent a hands-on and intuitive type of knowledge that is hard to reduce to the lists of attributes required of a frame.

Nevertheless, we are intrigued by Weber and Perkin's notion of a slot and we have integrated this notion into our concept of a mental model. Like frames, mental models can have slots or openings in which an inventor can try different arrangements or subassemblies. We suspect that a key skill for inventors is the ability to generate a mental model and then break it into slots that can be manipulated and studied. We believe that inventors create slots in response to personal preferences and their level of craft or "hands-on" knowledge. Yet to appreciate how mental models and slots are linked, we need to look more closely at mechanical representations, the specific technical solutions that can be used to fill a slot.

Mechanical Representations

In addition to mental models and heuristics, we are considering a third aspect of the invention process, mechanical representations. These are the specific working components an inventor uses to construct physical models of his or her invention. Mechanical representations are central to our interpretation of the invention process because they link an inventor's thoughts with the physical devices he or she creates. As Robert Fulton so elegantly described the act of invention,

> the mechanic should sit down among levers, screws, wedges, wheels, etc., like a poet among the letters of the alphabet, considering them as the exhibition of his thoughts in which a new arrangement transmits a new idea to the world. (Quoted in Philip, 1985, p. 47)

To us, the "levers, screws, wedges, [and] wheels" are the basic building blocks of an invention. Although we refer to these building blocks as "mechanical" representations to denote their physical three-dimensional character, they are not necessarily limited to mechanical devices (i.e., gears, pistons, or pulleys) but may also be electrical or electronic circuits, chemical processes, materials, or other components of an invention.

To some extent, mechanical representations resemble the technical structures that Bertrand Gille (1986) defined as the basic tools and elements underlying all of technology. Eugene Ferguson (1977) has described how several technologists identified and catalogued mechanical movements; one example is the mechanical alphabet created in the eighteenth century by the Swedish engineer Christopher Polhem (see also Lindqvist, 1984). A key feature of mechanical representations is that many inventors have a repertoire of them which they use repeatedly. For instance, Reese Jenkins (1984) has observed that Edison frequently employed certain mechanical and electrical components in his inventions—such as a cylinder and stylus, the double-action pawl, and the polar relay—and that these components may be found in his inventions ranging from stock tickers to motion picture projectors.[2] Reflecting on these commonalities, Jenkins concluded, "Any creative technologist possesses a mental set of stock solutions from which he draws in addressing problems" (p. 153). This "mental set of stock solutions" is what we mean by mechanical representations and serves as part of what Giere (1988) calls a scientist or inventor's cognitive resources.

We suspect that mechanical representations not only serve as physical manifestations of an invention but are also central to how inventors think about new inventions. Inventors frequently run mechanical representations as part of an overall mental model of a new invention. They may also try to fill the slots in their mental models with different mechanical representations. Mechanical representations are thus the items inventors use to fill in missing gaps in the analogy that the mental model may embody.

To summarize, we have developed a framework for understanding the cognitive processes of inventors involving three components: mental models, mechanical representations, and heuristics. With this framework, our goal is to facilitate comparisons between different inventors and scientists. Toward this end, let us now consider how mental models and mechanical representations allow us to analyze how Bell and Edison developed their telephones in the mid-1870s.

The Case of the Telephone

The Reis Telephone

To understand the mental models of Bell and Edison, we must begin our story with the first telephonelike device. Invented in Germany by Philipp Reis in 1861, this device consisted of a membrane diaphragm with a metal contact on its surface. If one sang or spoke into the diaphragm, the metal contact moved up and down, touching a needle suspended over the diaphragm. Because the diaphragm contact and the needle were in an electrical circuit, they functioned as a switch and created rapid intermittent pulses. To increase the sensitivity of this switch, Reis added a drop of mercury on the diaphragm contact (Thompson, 1883, pp. 86–87). Reis thought his invention might be able to transmit speech, but he never succeeded and instead concentrated on sending musical tones (Thompson, 1883). Reis was stymied not only by a lack of mechanical skill but by his mental model of the telephone. Drawing on the prevailing practice in telegraphy, Reis assumed that discrete electrical pulses—not continuous current—should be used to transmit messages. As a result, he struggled to improve the on–off characteristics of his invention and failed to see the opportunity for transmitting complex sounds such as the voice. Thus the Reis telephone embodied an important element of the mental model of the telegraph community—that discrete electrical pulses, not a continuous current, should be used to transmit signals (Maver, 1897, p. 50). As David Hounshell (1975, p. 169) has suggested, it took an outsider to this community to reject this mental model and develop an alternative vision.

Bell and the Multiple Telegraph

That outsider was Bell. He was primarily a teacher of the deaf. His father, Alexander Melville, had achieved a reputation for his system of visible speech, a method of teaching the deaf to speak. Anxious to see his father's system come into widespread use and to place it on a scientific basis, Bell began to study speech and acoustics as early as 1865 (Bruce, 1973, pp. 40–51). Initially he conducted experiments to determine how vowel quality related to the resonance tones of the mouth cavity, only to discover that the German physicist, Hermann Von Helmholtz, had already conducted similar experiments. In particular, Helmholtz had demonstrated the compound nature of vowel sounds using a series of tuning forks driven by electromagnets (Helmholtz, 1875). To understand Helmholtz's acoustical work, Bell studied a copy of Helmholtz's experimental apparatus and constructed parts of it himself. Bell later admitted that he never understood the mathematics of Helmholtz's acoustics, but this hands-on work did provide him with insights into how sound waves and electrical currents could be linked (Bell, 1908, p. 289).[3]

Although Bell saw himself as a member of the Boston scientific community (during this time he was professor of elocution at Boston University), he was not interested in Helmholtz solely for scientific reasons. Instead, he saw Helmholtz as a source of ideas for solving a challenging commercial problem, multiple telegraphy (Hounshell, 1976, pp. 1307–1308). During the middle decades of the nineteenth century, inventors and businessmen perfected the electric telegraph and established it as a major form of rapid communication. By the mid-1870s, this technology was largely controlled by Western Union, one of the first corporate monopolies in the United States. Yet in maintaining their nationwide telegraph network, Western Union was hampered by a severe problem: as the volume of messages grew, the cost and complexity of the network grew even more quickly. In response, the telegraph giant encouraged inventors to develop a variety of new devices, including schemes whereby several messages could be sent simultaneously over a single wire. In 1872, Western Union adopted Joseph Stearns' duplex (two-message) system, and it was soon clear that fame and fortune awaited the inventor of a four- or eight-message system (Jenkins et al., 1989, pp. 13, 101; Thompson, 1947, pp. 421–426).

After reading a newspaper story about the Stearns duplex, Bell became convinced that he could devise a multiple-message telegraph using his knowledge of acoustics and Helmholtz's apparatus. In pursuing this invention, Bell was actively encouraged by his future father-in-law, Gardiner Hubbard (Bruce, 1973, pp. 93, 126–127). Hubbard was bitterly opposed to Western Union, which he viewed as a monopolistic giant. Hubbard hoped to slay the giant by having Bell develop a multiple-message system that could be used to create an alternative telegraph network.

Drawing on his work with Helmholtz's apparatus, Bell thought it would be possible to build a multiple telegraph that assigned an acoustic frequency produced by a tuning fork to each message and converted that frequency into a series of electrical pulses by means of a needle on the end of the tuning fork which made or broke contact with a dish of mercury. This pulse could then be sent by wire to a series of duplicate tuning forks on the receiving end. By sending each message at a different frequency, one could theoretically transmit and receive several messages simultaneously on a single wire. While the principle of sending and receiving one message using one acoustic signal had been demonstrated, no one had succeeded in simultaneously sending and receiving several signals.

Bell's Mental Model

Helmholtz had used combinations of tuning forks to reproduce vowel sounds. It occurred to Bell that a sufficiently large number of forks or tuned steel reeds could be used to transmit and receive vowel sounds. Bell visualized a device with numerous individual reeds positioned over a single electromagnet, much like the strings of a harp positioned over a single sounding board (see Figure 3.1). As Bell "ran" this device in his mind, his expert knowledge of speech suggested to him that it could convert a complex sound wave (such as the human voice) into a continuous undulating electric current. According to one telephone historian,

> Although Bell did not have this "harp" apparatus constructed, he had a clear mental picture that if one of the reeds of the harp at one end of the line were caused to vibrate, electrical undulations would be set up in the line and the reed of the corresponding pitch in the harp at the other end of the line would be thrown into vibration, the intensity of its vibration corresponding to the amplitude of vibration of the transmitting reed. . . . His knowledge of Helmholtz's researches told him that when he sang a vowel sound he produced a sound that was composite in character, consisting of a low fundamental tone, with relatively feeble overtone, or partial tones, mingled with it. He saw that, upon singing a vowel sound to the reeds of his harp, the reed corresponding with pitch to the fundamental tone of his voice would be thrown into vigorous vibration; and that other reeds, corresponding in pitch to the overtones characteristic of the vowel sound, would be thrown into feeble vibration; and that all of these vibrations transmitted over the line and reproduced by the receiving harp with the relative loudness of the tone preserved would reproduce his singing of the vowel sound. (Rhodes, 1929, pp. 12–13)

Bell's harp apparatus thus represented a mental model for a new speaking telegraph. Although enthralled by the elegance of this link between sound and electricity, Bell did not build the harp apparatus because he was convinced that it would

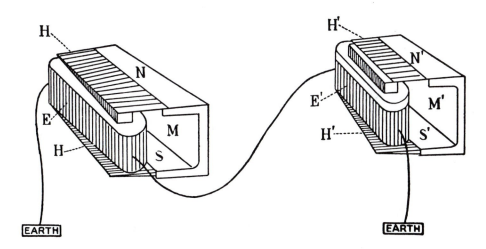

FIGURE 3.1. Diagram illustrating Bell's conception of the harp apparatus. By speaking or singing near one of the two harp relays, one set in motion a number of reeds that captured the complexity of the sound wave. As these reeds vibrated over the electromagnet in the relay, they varied the magnetic field and induced a fluctuating electric current in the circuit. At the receiving relay, this current set the same reeds in motion and thus reproduced the original sound. (From Frederick Leland Rhodes, *Beginnings of Telephony*. New York: Harper & Brothers, 1929.)

require an enormous number of finely tuned reeds. Furthermore, prevailing practice in telegraphy suggested to Bell that a small vibrating reed positioned over a large electromagnet would not induce current sufficient to send a message over a long wire.

But even more important, experiments with the phonautograph, carried on at roughly the same time, helped Bell develop an additional and complementary mental model. The harp apparatus did not solve the problem of translating speech into mechanical motion. To accomplish this, Bell drew on his experience with the phonautograph, which consisted of a diaphragm with a bristle attached. When one spoke or sang into the diaphragm, the bristle traced the sound waves on a piece of smoked glass. Bell was originally interested in this apparatus as a means of teaching his deaf students to recognize speech patterns. However, it also helped him understand how sound could be reproduced as a visible undulating pattern. Bell obtained this "undulating wave" idea from Tyndall's lectures on light (Bruce, 1973, p. 93), but again he sought a practical application of it. Anxious to link the phonautograph directly to his understanding of how individuals hear, Bell built an even more sensitive phonautograph using a human ear. In doing so, he

> was much struck by the disproportion in weight between the membrane and the bones that were moved by it; and it occurred to me that if such a thin and delicate membrane could move bones that were, relatively to it, very massive indeed, why should not a larger and stouter membrane be able to move a piece of steel in the manner I desired? (Bell, 1908, p. 39)

Thus, work with the phonautograph and the human ear provided Bell with a devicelike representation of how sound waves could be converted into mechanical vibrations. The harp apparatus provided him with a mental model of how sound as mechanical vibrations might be converted into an undulating electric current.

From Mental Model to Working Telephone

Bell would later claim that in 1874 he combined these complementary mental models into a "theoretically perfect speaking telephone" (Bell, 1908, p. 61), which suggests that he had developed a new mental model of the telephone. However, it would be a year before this model became a working device. Bell did not directly pursue the telephone because Hubbard and his other backers were pressing him to develop a multiple telegraph. Consequently, Bell and his assistant Thomas Watson tried through the winter and spring of 1875 to construct a multiple telegraph using separate tuned reed relays. These relays served as one of Bell's most important mechanical representations. (For a more detailed account, see Gorman, Mehalik, Carlson, & Oblon, press.)

Although the two men failed repeatedly in their efforts to get these relays to function as a multiple telegraph, it was one of these failures in June 1875 that suggested to Bell how he could convert his mental model into a working telephone. According to Watson,

> I had charge of the transmitter [on the multiple telegraph] as usual, setting them squealing one after the other, while Bell was retuning the receiver springs one by one, pressing

them against his ear as I have described. One of the transmitter springs I was attending to stopped vibrating and I plucked it to start it again. It didn't start and I kept on plucking it, when suddenly I heard a shout from Bell in the next room, and then out he came with a rush, demanding, "What did you do then? Don't change anything. Let me see!" I showed him. . . . The contact screw was screwed down so far that it made permanent contact with the spring, so that when I snapped the spring the current had remained unbroken while that strip of magnetized steel by its vibration over the pole of its magnet was generating that marvelous conception of Bell's—a current of electricity that varied in intensity precisely as the air was varying in density within hearing distance of that spring. That undulatory current had passed through the connecting wire to the distant receiver which, fortunately, was a mechanism that could transform that current back into an extremely faint echo of the sound of the vibrating spring that had generated it, but what was still more fortunate, the right man had that mechanism at his ear during that fleeting moment, and instantly recognized the transcendent importance of that faint sound thus electrically transmitted. (Watson, 1913, pp. 10–11).

When this bit of serendipity occurred, Bell's mental model suggested its significance. The multiple reeds used in the harp were no longer necessary; a single reed could transmit and receive "that marvelous conception of Bell's," an undulating current. This discovery "convinced me that the membrane speaking telephone I had designed in the summer of 1874 would prove a practicable working instrument" (Bell, 1908, p. 61).

With this insight came a new mental model—that a telephone should now be "an instrument modeled after the human ear."[4] To manifest this mental model, Bell had Watson construct such an instrument on June 3, 1875, which became known as his gallows telephone (Figure 3.2).

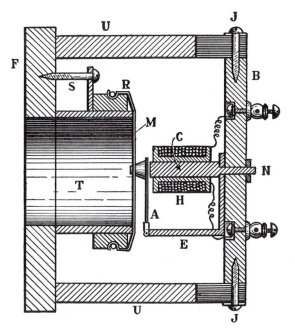

FIGURE 3.2. Bell's gallows telephone of June 1875. Key: T, speaking tube; M, parchment diaphragm; A, reed relay armature; C, core of magnet; H, magnet coil. Note how this device consisted of two basic Bell mechanical representations, the diaphragm and the reed relay. (From Frederick Leland Rhodes, *Beginnings of Telephony*. New York, Harper & Brothers, p. 24.)

This first telephone was essentially a reed relay connected to a parchment diaphragm. As one shouted into the diaphragm, it vibrated the relay's reed armature. As this reed moved through the magnetic field of the relay's coil, it induced a fluctuating electric current in the coil. This current was then transmitted by wire to a receiving relay, which vibrated and was supposed to reproduce the original sounds (Rhodes, 1929, pp. 23–25).

Watson felt that he could hear Bell's voice, but he could not make out the words. Bell heard enough to convince himself that he was on the right track (Bruce, 1973, p. 149). In January 1876, even though Bell had yet to get this telephone to work, he sent a specification to his attorney in Washington and asked him to file a patent application that included a means for electrically transmitting speech. Much of this application was based on Bell's mental model of how sound waves could be converted into an undulating electric current.[5]

Just after filing this application, Bell clarified how the ear formed the basis of his mental model by writing in his notebook, "Make transmitting instrument after the model of the human ear. Make armature (a) the shape of the ossicles [sic]. Follow out the analogy of nature" (Notebook, Vol. I, p. 13).[6] Figure 3.3 shows how the bones of the ear are mounted between a cone and diaphragm and two different arrangements of electromagnets. In the leftmost sketch, the bones serve a role similar to the steel reed and hinge on his familiar relay; in the rightmost sketch, they move an iron core through an induction coil. Thus, Bell saw his telephone as a kind of electro-mechanical ear.

In order to make sense of Bell's subsequent experiments, we divide this mental model into slots. He tried different arrangements of speaking tubes and dia-

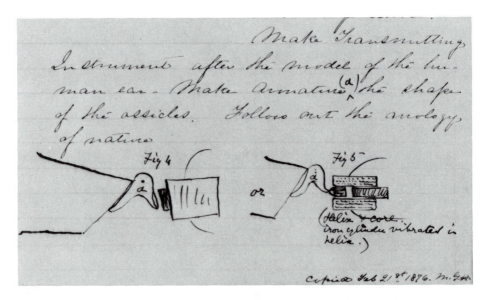

FIGURE 3.3. Bell's sketch of his ear mental model, February 18, 1876. (From "Experiments made by A. Graham Bell, Vol. I," Notebook, p. 13, Box 258, Bell Family Papers, Library of Congress, Washington, D.C.)

phragms, indicating that one of his slots corresponded to the outer ear and eardrum. He varied coils and relays, suggesting that there was a slot corresponding to the bones of the ear. Finally, he conducted experiments in which he tried to alter other parts of the circuit in ways that would magnify the undulating current and facilitate its transmission over long distances. These experiments suggest that Bell had a line transmission slot whose structure was not governed by the ear analogy. (See Figure 3.4 for a picture of Bell's slots sketched on his patent drawing.)

Variable Resistance and Elisha Gray

In March 1876, after returning from Washington, Bell began a different line of experiments focusing initially on the "bones of the ear" slot. He substituted a tuning fork for the transmitting reed, removed the electromagnet from under the tuning fork, and substituted a dish of water into which he dipped the fork (Finn, 1966). Bell was now moving away from a strict analogy to the "bones of the ear." In his later patent testimony, Bell claimed he got this idea from another invention, a spark arrester in which he secured variable resistance by moving a needle in and out of a cup of water (Bell, 1908, p. 85).

Bell may also have gotten the idea from Elisha Gray. Gray, a telegraph inventor from Chicago, filed a preliminary patent application or caveat for a speaking telegraph on February 14, 1876, the same day Bell's application was finally filed. According to his own testimony, Bell learned from a patent examiner that his application conflicted with Gray's caveat on the matter of variable resistance (Bell, 1908, pp. 194–195). In his application, Bell had described how the

> external resistance may also be varied. For instance, let mercury or some other liquid form part of a voltaic circuit, then the more deeply the conducting-wire is immersed in

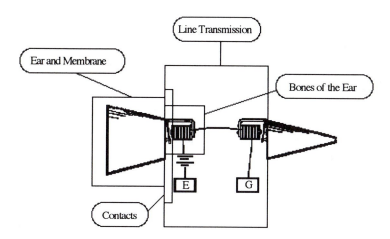

FIGURE 3.4. Slots in Bell's ear mental model. Underlying drawing is from his U.S. patent, "Improvement in Telegraphy," No. 174, 465, (Executed January 20, 1876, granted March 7, 1876).

the mercury or other liquid, the less resistance does the liquid offer to the passage of the current. (p. 194)

Gray's caveat included a transmitter based on the principle of variable resistance (see Figure 3.5), in which a needle attached to a diaphragm vibrated in water; these vibrations increased and decreased the distance between the needle and a contact at the bottom of the cylinder of water. Although the figure does not show it, Gray contemplated

> the use of a series of diaphragms in a common vocalizing chamber, each diaphragm carrying an independent rod, and responding to a vibration of different rapidity and intensity, in which case contact points mounted on other diaphragms may be employed.[7]

This multiple-diaphragm idea suggests that Gray and Bell had different mental models of how speech was to be transmitted. According to Bell, he did not see all of Gray's caveat; the patent examiner merely pointed to the paragraph of Bell's application that conflicted with Gray's.

So Bell may have arrived at the idea of experimenting with variable resistance from Gray. However, he certainly conducted a long chain of original experiments to utilize variable resistance in his telephone. Bell created a new slot in his overall mental model; between the diaphragm and the electromagnet, he inserted a needle that dipped into water or another high-resistance medium. In his first experiments with this arrangement, Bell sought to minimize the surface area of the vibrating contact and maximize that of the contact resting in the medium (Notebook, Vol. I, p. 38). In contrast, Gray had focused on varying the distance between contacts.[8]

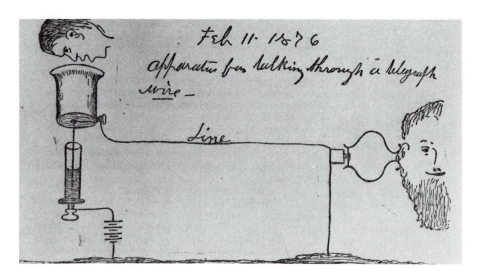

FIGURE 3.5. Gray's sketch of "Apparatus for talking through a telegraph wire," February 11, 1876. A more refined version of this diagram appeared in his patent caveat of February 14, 1876. (From U.S. Supreme Court, *The Telephone Appeals.* Brief for American Bell Telephone Ço. Boston: Alfred Mudge & Son, 1886, p. 441.)

This suggests once again that the two inventors were operating from different mental models. It was in the middle of this sequence of experiments that Watson built the device from which he heard the famous words, "Mr. Watson-come here-I want to see you" (Notebook, Vol. I, pp. 40–41) (see Figure 3.6).

Although he finally succeeded in transmitting intelligible speech on March 10, 1876, the "effect was loud but indistinct and muffled" (Notebook, Vol. I, p. 41), and so Bell continued to experiment. At one point he designed an automatic transmitter to allow him to carry on circuit slot experiments without depending so heavily on Watson to pluck reeds in another room. Using this device, he could try different connections and materials. At another point, following a suggestion from Hubbard, he disconnected all the electrical apparatus and had Watson listen through a tube while he spoke into a diaphragm with a needle vibrating in water. This experiment demonstrated that part of the problem lay in the mouthpiece and diaphragm slot, so he inserted a mechanical representation consisting of the cone and diaphragm from one of his phonautographs into this slot (Notebook, Vol. I, p. 56). Right after this, Bell conducted a series of thought experiments designed to establish "the best way of increasing the amplitude of the electrical undulations so as to admit of the transmission of vocal utterance over long distances" (Notebook,

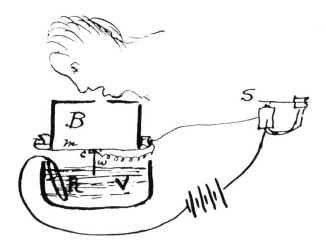

FIGURE 3.6. Bell's sketch for a liquid transmitter, March 9, 1876. By speaking into the opening at the top of the box, one caused the diaphragm at the bottom to vibrate. Attached to the diaphragm was a needle that moved up and down in a small cup of water. Unlike the Reis telephone in which the needle broke contact with the mercury, Bell had his needle stay in the water. By varying the surface area of the needle in contact with the liquid, Bell secured a change in the resistance and hence produced a fluctuating current. (From "Experiments made by A. Graham Bell, Vol. I," Notebook, p. 39, Box 258, Bell Family Papers, Library of Congress, Washington, D.C.)

Vol. I, p. 57). In these imagined experiments, he compared battery power, line resistance, and resistance due to the water. In a final set of experiments on April 7 using two plumbago needles dipping into mercury, he established "that my theory is correct—that musical notes which conflict with one another when transmitted simultaneously by means of an intermittent current will not interfere with one another when an undulatory current is employed" (Notebook, Vol. I, p. 97). Thus for Bell, the end of this long line of experiments was an improvement in his *theoretical* understanding.

Elsewhere we have discussed how confirmation can be a useful heuristic in the pursuit phase of inquiry, when a scientist is trying to determine if a hypothesis is worth an investment of time and effort (Gorman & Carlson, 1989). Bell's variable resistance experiments were an attempt to confirm his hypothesis that an undulating current could reproduce both the pitch and timbre of speech, whereas an intermittent current could only reproduce the pitch. In other words, these experiments confirmed Bell's decision to pursue his original mental model. Consequently, once his variable resistance experiments clarified the difference between intermittent and undulating currents, he went back to using electromagnetic induction to link sound waves and electric currents (Figure 3.7).

It is true, as Bernard S. Finn (1966) observed, that Bell's variable resistance transmitters did not work as well as his induction transmitters. Bell's notebooks, however, suggest that he did not see this difference in performance. In his notebooks, Bell observed that consonants were a particular problem. (Notebook, Vol. I, p. 85). Instead, we suspect that he returned to induction because it was a precise embodiment of his mental model of how sound could be transformed into electricity. Bell's induction design, based on the human ear, was simpler than his liquid

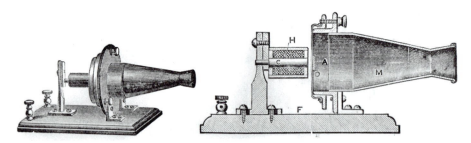

FIGURE 3.7. Bell's magneto telephone from the Centennial Exhibition of 1876. Key for the transmitter: C, core of electromagnetic relay; D, small iron armature on diaphragm; H, coil of relay; M, mouthpiece. By speaking into the transmitter's diaphragm, one caused the small armature to fluctuate above the relay core. This movement generated an electric current in the relay coil. At the receiver, this current created a magnetic field in the other electromagnetic coil, which in turn caused the metal diaphragm to vibrate, thus reproducing the sounds. (From Robert V. Bruce, *Bell: Alexander Graham Bell and the Conquest of Solitude*. Boston: Little, Brown, 1973, p. 196.)

transmitter. This fact may have encouraged him to prefer the induction design to liquid variable resistance.

The Evolution of Bell's Mental Model: An Overview

Figure 3.8 is a simplified overview of the evolution of Bell's telephone. At the top are the harp apparatus, Bell's mental model of how musical tones or speech could

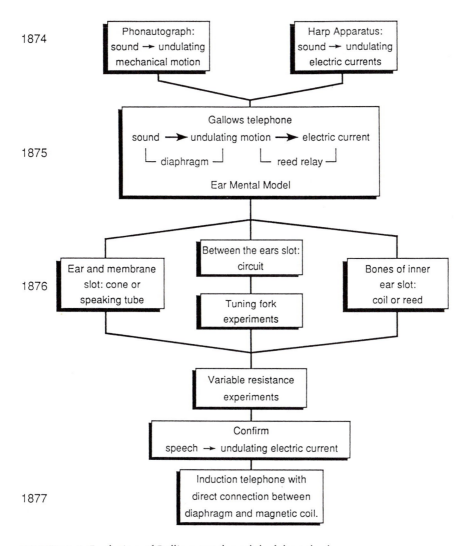

FIGURE 3.8. Evolution of Bell's mental model of the telephone.

be translated into an undulating electrical current, and the phonautograph, which illustrated how speech could be translated into undulating mechanical motion. Bell combined these into a single mental model before building his gallows telephone, in which a diaphragm moved a single reed relay.

After he submitted his famous patent, Bell sketched his ear mental model in his notebook. At this point, it becomes essential to distinguish slots. The cone and diaphragm were varied to serve the role of ear and eardrum, the coil or relay was similarly varied to serve the function of the bones, and the circuit extends beyond the ear analogy to include the batteries, resistances, and wire needed to connect one speaking device with another. When Bell inserted a tuning fork in water to complete a circuit, he opened a new "contacts" slot in the gap between diaphragm and coil. After his initial tuning fork experiments, the lines from the slots converge to indicate that Bell varied more than one at a time in his experiments with variable resistance devices. These experiments confirmed his overall mental model. In January 1877, Bell patented an improved device that was structurally similar to the Gallows telephone, although the slots contained novel mechanical representations.[9]

Bell, Edison, and Western Union

Through the summer of 1876, Bell gave several demonstrations of his telephone, including a highly publicized exhibition at the Philadelphia Centennial. During the fall, Western Union and Hubbard, may have discussed the possible purchase of this invention, but they were unable to reach an agreement (Rhodes, 1929, p. 51; Bruce, 1973, p. 229). In all likelihood, William Orton, president of Western Union, did not wish to negotiate with Hubbard, an outspoken enemy of his company.[10] But beyond this personal animosity, the leaders of Western Union decided that there was no need to buy Bell's patent because the telephone could be easily duplicated and improved by inventors already associated with the company. By the standards of the telegraph industry Bell's first telephones were quite crude, and Western Union managers were probably confident that their inventors could design a better telephone.

Consequently, as Hubbard and Western Union talked about a possible deal, Orton asked Thomas Edison to investigate the telephone. During the previous five years, Edison had offered Western Union a variety of multiple-message telegraphs. Although the telegraph giant did install Edison's four-message or quadruplex telegraph on their lines, it also encouraged Edison to patent as many different designs as possible in order to block rival companies from exploiting the systems of other inventors (Jehl 1937, Vol. I; Jenkins et al., 1989). Because Edison provided innovations that could be used offensively and defensively, Orton had arranged for the company to underwrite Edison's research on a regular basis. With this financial support, Edison withdrew from his telegraph manufacturing enterprises in Newark, New Jersey, and built a new laboratory at Menlo Park in the spring of 1876. Combining technical acumen with a strategic sense of how to patent around rival inventions, Edison was the ideal person to develop a telephone for Western Union.

Edison's Mental Model

Edison was well prepared to begin investigating the telephone. During 1875, he had conducted experiments on an acoustic telegraph, and at Orton's request, he evaluated a Reis telephone. In the fall of 1876 Edison had his assistant, James Adams, experiment with a modified Reis instrument (see Figure 3.9). Instead of using mercury Adams tried different liquids and then sponges, paper, and felting dipped in electrolytic solutions (Prescott, 1884, pp. 114–115). Underlying these tests seems

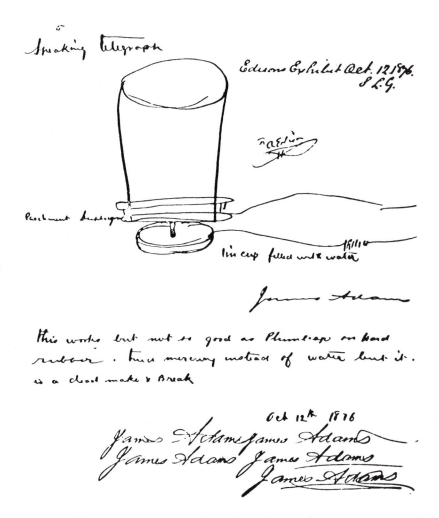

FIGURE 3.9. Sketch by Edison of speaking telegraph, October 12, 1876. From *Thomas A. Edison Papers, A Selective Microfilm Edition, Part I (1850–1878),* Thomas Jeffrey et al. (eds.) (Frederick, Md.: University Publications of America, 1985), reel 11, frame 222.

to have been the goal of learning as much as possible about the electrical transmission of speech. Unfortunately, the liquids evaporated and Edison concluded that a high-resistance liquid was not suitable for a practical telephone. Yet these early experiments with a modified Reis instrument convinced Edison that a successful telephone would be based on variable resistance, not electromagnetic induction. The modified Reis telephone suggested to Edison a mental model of how variable resistance could be secured by having a needle or contact move in a high-resistance medium, and Edison used this devicelike representation in most of his telephones in 1877. Throughout the next few months, Edison periodically returned to this modified Reis telephone to review his mental model and get ideas for new experiments (Edison Microfilm, 1985: 2 April 1877, 11:254[11]).

Edison's Slots and Mechanical Representations

In January 1877, Edison abandoned the problematic liquids and constructed a Reis-like transmitter with three platinum electrodes resting in a dish of loose carbon (see Figure 3.10). He probably chose carbon as his high-resistance medium in this telephone because in 1873 he had used carbon to develop a cheap but compact rheostat for simulating long undersea telegraph cables (Jenkins & Nier, 1984). Here an old invention suggested a mechanical representation (carbon) for use in a new invention.

Although this transmitter did not work very well, it nonetheless helped Edison by serving as a basis for a mental model that he divided into several slots (see Figure 3.11). Each slot constituted a portion of a telephone that Edison could investigate. Edison did sketch two non-Reis telephones using induction coils and capacitors (19 February and 20 March 1877, 11:232, 239), but the rest of his sketches for the spring of 1877 can be classified as modifications on his Reis-like transmitter. Edison appears to have divided each slot into several subslots that were highly specific areas in which he could test different mechanical representations. During the next five months, Edison drew on the extensive stock of mechanical representations he had learned while working on telegraphy and applied them to the telephone through these slots and subslots. Although the accompanying cognitive map might suggest that Edison systematically tested each slot and subslot, the surviving sketches revealed that he jumped from slot to slot and pursued all three simultaneously.

Edison first experimented with modifying the basic design of his Reis-like telephone. Instead of having a platinum needle make contact with loose carbon, he tried having various contacts rub against blocks and rods of a high-resistance material (6 and 20 February 1877, 11:225, 231). Edison also varied the number and shape of needles making contact with a high-resistance liquid, and he made a transmitter consisting of a series of little Reis needle-and-cup arrangements underneath the diaphragm (22 February and 2 April 1877, 11:234, 254, 256). Finally, he sketched a capillary telephone in which a contact fastened to the diaphragm restricted the flow of a high-resistance liquid between two electrodes and hence varied the current in the transmitting circuit (2 April 1877, 11:234).

As a second slot, Edison varied the resistance medium. In place of carbon, he substituted paper soaked in a high-resistance electrolyte (17 February 1877,

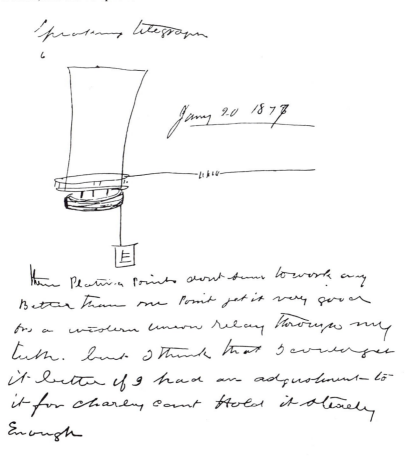

FIGURE 3.10. Edison's sketch from January 20, 1877, of a telephone using three platinum points resting in a dish of loose carbon. (From Edison Microfilm, 1985, reel 11, frame 224.)

11:230). In addition, within this slot he tried blocks of carbon in different shapes and held against the diaphragm by different kinds of springs (9 February, 29 March, and 1 April 1877, 11:226, 248, 252). While Edison later claimed that these carbon experiments were his main line of research, the large number of sketches suggests that this line was just one of several Edison pursued in the spring of 1877.

Indeed, Edison devoted much of his energy to a third slot, varying the contacts between the diaphragm and the resistance medium. In this slot, Edison assumed that the best way to capture the full range of the voice was to use several individual contacts, each of which switched in an additional resistance or battery to the circuit (11 and 17 February, 20; 26 and 29 March; 2, 3, and 5 April 1877, 11:227, 229, 238, 245, 246, 249, 253, 255, 257, 260). (Since Edison was seeking to vary the line current proportional to the voice, he could either impede the current through additional resistances or increase it by adding more batteries.) As a variation, he also

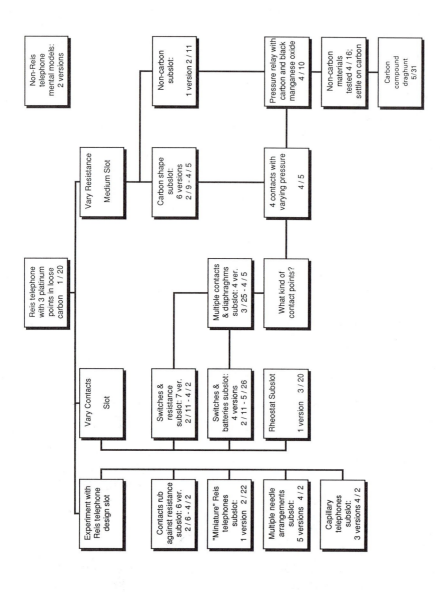

FIGURE 3.11. Evolution of Edison's telephone: January–May 1877.

sketched a rheostat telephone in which a contact rubbed against a coil of german silver (20 March 1877, 11:235–236). As these experiments progressed, Edison added several diaphragms, each of which was sensitive to a different portion of the vocal spectrum and each of which had several contacts (25 and 29 March 1877, 11:243–244, 250).

Edison and his associates experimented with these different telephones, uttering phrases such as "physicists and sphynxes (sic) in majestical mists" to test for the articulation of hissing consonants (quoted in Josephson, 1959, p. 145). Unfortunately, they found that no matter how they arranged the contacts, the movement distorted the sound waves and garbled the transmission.

These difficulties forced Edison to rethink in early April his overall investigation. To focus his thinking, Edison reviewed his mental model by sketching half a dozen variations of the Reis telephone (2 April 1877, 11:254). After doing so, he decided to combine his carbon investigations with his contact investigations. In particular, he decided to place a high-resistance material on the tips of the contacts touching the diaphragm (5 April 1877, 11:259). In doing so, Edison recalled from his carbon rheostat that carbon varied its resistance when placed under mechanical force and so he placed carbon on the tips of several contacts. Subsequently, he devised a pressure relay to investigate how the resistance of carbon changed, and he even mounted a miniature relay on the back of one telephone (see Figure 3.12). While he got positive results with carbon under pressure, Edison was not entirely

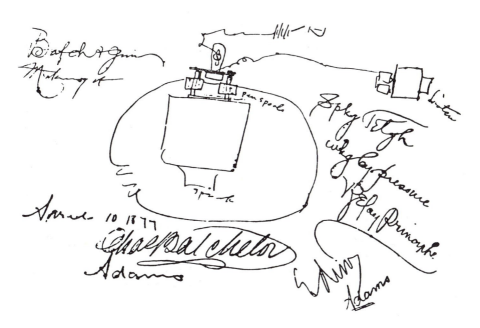

FIGURE 3.12. Edison's sketch of telephone with small pressure relay mounted behind diaphragm, April 10, 1877. To build this miniature relay, Edison borrowed small coils from his electric pen motor. (From Edison Microfilm, 1985, reel 11, frame 261.)

convinced that carbon was the right material and he tested other high-resistance materials in the pressure relay (10 April–10 May 1877, 11:261–271). Eventually, though, Edison concluded that carbon was the best material and that by using it he could simplify the configuration of the contacts.

In late May, as Edison continued to study carbon under pressure as a mechanical representation, he realized that he needed a carbon compound that was very sensitive to physical force. Ideally, a small change in the force on the carbon should produce a large change in the resistance, thus amplifying the signal. The task now became one of finding a carbon compound with this electrical property, and Edison set his associate Charles Batchelor to testing a wide range of carbon compounds and substances. Batchelor tested materials by using a special apparatus in which small samples of carbon could be placed under varying amounts of weight while their resistance could be measured. Starting in June 1877, Batchelor tested hundreds of carbon compounds and mixtures, looking for one with the right electrical characteristics (31 May–24 June 1877, 11:281–329).

The Material Search Heuristic

In testing these materials, Batchelor was employing a material search heuristic. This is a general heuristic used by many inventors and scientists, including those recently searching for a new superconducting material (Lamb, 1987). With this heuristic, the inventor knows that a new material is necessary and has at least a rough idea of what it must accomplish, but his or her stock of mechanical representations does not immediately point to an existing material. The inventor then uses this information to define a search space in the realm of materials and to establish test parameters. In the course of hunting, an inventor may discover new mechanical representations and modify his or her mental model.

Edison's carbon search may seem a wasteful and even silly heuristic, but at this time no one had developed a chemical theory that he could have used to identify a form of carbon with the electrical properties he wanted. This search was hardly a hunt for a needle in a haystack, with Edison randomly trying everything and anything in the hope of finding the right material. Rather, thanks to the accumulation of insight from experimenting with numerous mechanical representations, Edison knew the characteristics of the "needle" he desired. Like Edison, Bell conducted a similar hunt when searching for the right liquid to use in his variable resistance transmitter; Bell's search was far less exhaustive, in part because he sought only an experimental verification of a principle, not a practical device.[12]

In the course of his search, Batchelor eventually found that the soot deposited on the glass mantle of a kerosene lamp possessed a resistance that could be varied under pressure from a fraction of an ohm to 300 ohms. Edison and Batchelor fashioned the lampblack into small carbon buttons that were connected to the speaking diaphragm.

With the right kind of carbon in hand, Edison appears to have again divided his mental model into a new series of slots (see Figure 3.13). During the summer of 1877, Edison varied the carbon carrier, the pressure adjustment mechanism, the

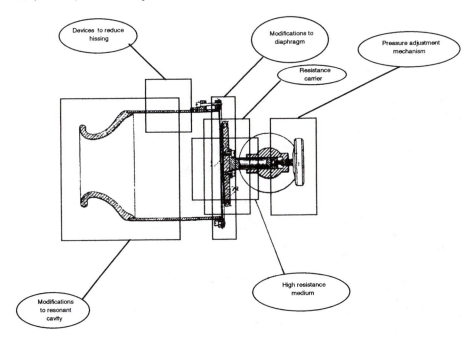

FIGURE 3.13. Diagram depicting slots used by Edison during the summer of 1877. Underlying drawing is from his U.S. patent, "Speaking Telegraph," No. 474,230 (executed April 18, 1877, granted May 3, 1892).

diaphragm, the resonant cavity, and devices to reduce hissing, all with an eye to optimizing the performance of using lampblack carbon. However, to cover his bets, Edison also tested telephones using platinum instead of carbon contacts (28–29 July 1877, 11:396–400).

Modifying the Mental Model

Edison soon discovered that the lampblack buttons were fragile and disintegrated due to the vibration of the diaphragm. To protect the carbon button, Edison placed a small rubber tube between the button and the diaphragm. In doing so, Edison was still being guided by his image of a Reis telephone, for he was assuming that the acoustical vibrations had to be transferred by some means (like a needle or tube) to the resistance medium (carbon). To his dismay, Edison found that the rubber tubing quickly lost its shape and failed to conduct the vibrations. He replaced the rubber tubing with a platinum spring, but even a delicate spring added an extra musical tone to the signal. Consequently, he tried thicker springs, which gave better results (Jehl, 1937, Vol. 1, p. 121). These experiments led Edison to take the spring out altogether and placed an aluminum button and a glass disk between the carbon button and a thick iron diaphragm (Prescott, 1884, p. 118). This new arrangement gave superior results in tests conducted in April 1878 between New York and Philadelphia.[13] It was capable of transmitting even whispers loudly and distinctly, and it became the standard configuration of Edison's carbon telephone transmitter (see Figure 3.14) (Prescott, 1884, pp. 165–168).

By the spring of 1878, both Edison and Western Union were satisfied with the carbon telephone, and the company installed it in several cities. Edison assigned his telephone patents to Western Union for $100,000. Armed with Edison's patents, Western Union attacked the newly formed American Bell Telephone Company through patent litigation. Initially, the courts upheld Bell's basic telephone patent, and moreover, the Bell interests had secured a patent for a carbon transmitter from Emile Berliner. After a year of legal sparring, Western Union and American Bell reached an agreement. Western Union agreed to withdraw from the telephone field and sell its existing telephone exchanges to American Bell; in return Bell agreed to pay Western Union a royalty of 20 percent for seventeen years on the telephone rentals in their former exchanges (Josephson, 1959, pp. 142–149).

This agreement marked the end of the invention of the telephone for both Edison and Bell. With his corporate patron satisfied, Edison turned to the phonograph and electric light. About the same time, Bell lost interest in the telephone as the problems facing the Bell organization came to focus on manufacturing telephones and installing exchanges.

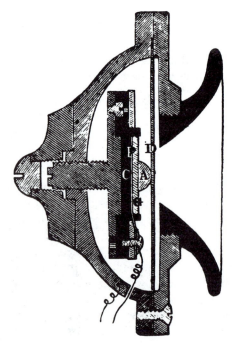

FIGURE 3.14. Final version of Edison's carbon telephone transmitter. Key: D, iron diaphragm; A, aluminum knob; G, glass disk; P, platinum foil that serves as one electrical contact to carbon button; C, carbon button. The other electrical contact is the screw that rests against the carbon button. (From George B. Prescott, *Bell's Electric Speaking Telephone: Its Invention, Construction, Application, Modification, and History.* New York: D. Appleton, 1884; reprinted Arno, 1972, p. 167.)

Conclusion

In this chapter we have interpreted invention as a cognitive process. We have applied the concepts of mental model, heuristics, and mechanical representations to the historical case of the telephone. To review, we see invention as a process in which an individual manipulates both a devicelike conception (mental model) and a set of physical artifacts (mechanical representations) to create a new object. Heuristics are the procedures or strategies by which inventors generate and manipulate mental and mechanical representations. In particular, inventors join mechanical representations with mental models by visualizing their mental models in terms of slots and subslots into which mechanical representations may be inserted and tested. We believe that these concepts provide a common language for comparing the methods of inventors, and in this conclusion we will identify several points of comparison.

Let us begin by comparing the devicelike representations used by Bell and Edison as their mental models. In the case of Bell, we have seen how he combined two complementary devicelike representations based on the human ear into a mental model. Much of Bell's talent lay in working with a limited set of slots and constantly honing his mental model. In contrast, Edison based his mental model on an actual device, the Reis telephone, and his strength lay in being able to divide this mental model in slots and subslots in which numerous mechanical representations could be tried. We suspect that inventors use mental models that are devicelike representations because they find that devices are simple but effective ways of representing complex relationships. Using the Reis telephone as a mental model, Edison was able to think about how sound waves could be converted into a variable current. Likewise, with his ear mental model, Bell was able to picture how sound could be converted into mechanical motion.

But unlike actual devices, mental models are incomplete and unstable, so that inventors may try different arrangements. For example, with the ear mental model, Bell drew an analogy between the bones of the ear and the armature of a relay; however, he left the analogy open in terms of what sort of electromagnetic coil he might use. In effect, Bell converted the bones into a slot he could fill with mechanical representations like the diaphragm and reed relay.

Thus, to gain insight into their mental models, inventors manifest them by using mechanical representations. In the case of the telephone, we have seen that inventors frequently employ familiar mechanical representations. Edison not only borrowed carbon-under-pressure from his 1873 rheostat but he also used a variety of devices he had learned while developing telegraph devices. Similarly, Bell claimed he borrowed the mechanical representation of a needle in water from his spark arrester and applied it to his liquid transmitter. Together, Bell and Edison suggest that inventors possess a set of familiar mechanical representations; without them, an inventor is unable to move his idea from the imagination to the benchtop, and no amount of scientific theory can make up for them.

In talking about mechanical representations, one is implicitly talking about how resources affect the invention process. Clearly, with more money, assistants, and equipment, an inventor can generate more mechanical representations, which is exactly what Edison did. Bankrolled by Western Union and having created an invention factory at Menlo Park, Edison and his staff quickly produced a myriad of alternative telephone designs. To be sure, the process of perfecting an invention for commercial use probably requires numerous mechanical representations, but Bell's contrasting experience shows that the initial conceptualization of a new invention can be done with few resources and mechanical representations. Working on a shoestring budget and with a handful of mechanical representations, Bell created the telephone, an invention that slipped through the fingers of professionals such as Edison and Gray. Bell's strength lay in the originality and simplicity of his mental model.

Yet one must be careful not to be misled by a romantic vision of the heroic inventor struggling against titanic odds to create revolutionary technology. In comparing their stock of mechanical representations and resource base, it would be easy to place Bell in the heroic role and Edison into the corresponding role of corporate hired gun. However, by overemphasizing the material bases of invention, these roles simplify and mask how invention combines ideas with objects. Both Bell and Edison succeeded in developing new telephones because they joined mental models with mechanical representations. What was important was not the number of representations each had but rather that each inventor could work with the representations at hand. We suspect that there is a "fit" between an inventor's mental model and his or her mechanical representations, allowing the inventor to gain insight as he or she moves back and forth from the conceptualization of the invention with its physical manifestation. At the present time we can only hypothesize about the nature of the "fit" between our inventors' mental models and mechanical representations, but we intend to investigate this matter further.

In this chapter we have only mentioned one heuristic explicitly, namely Edison's search to identify a carbon compound with the right electrical properties. We have not discussed heuristics because they only emerge as one has a complete and comparative perspective on the invention process. Heuristics can be reconstructed only when one understands all of the efforts taken by an inventor and one can compare the efforts of one inventor with another. For instance, it is likely that both Bell and Edison had heuristics that guided them in visualizing their mental models in terms of slots and subslots. Both had some kind of informal rules that helped them to decide what portion of the mental model to investigate and how mechanical representations could be tried.

Another general heuristic used by both Bell and Edison is that each man created a "network of enterprises." This term was coined by Howard Gruber (1981, p. 246) to describe the

> groups of activities extended in time and embracing other activities such as projects, problems and tasks. . . . The day-to-day pattern of activities sometimes looks quite chaotic, but when we understand how each act is mapped onto some enterprise, it takes on a more orderly form.

To illustrate this concept, Gruber discussed the creative efforts of Darwin and Piaget.

At first glance, Edison's multiple sketches and devices might appear chaotic, but he was in fact pursuing a network of enterprises. We have seen how he investigated several slots, trying a variety of mechanical representations in the subslots. Edison appears to have pursued this network of enterprises because results from one slot often suggested new experiments to try in other slots. For example, in early April 1877, Edison sketched variations of the basic configuration of the Reis telephone in order to sharpen his understanding of how he might vary the contact slot. Likewise, he combined what he had learned from the contact and resistance medium slots in order to develop the mechanical representation of carbon under pressure. Curiously, once Edison had set up a network of enterprises surrounding the telephone, the network permitted him to generate a number of spinoff inventions in 1878; these included a carbon microphone, the tasimeter, a megaphone, the phonomotor, and of course the phonograph (Carlson, Gorman, 1989). Thus for Edison, one heuristic for invention was to set up a network of enterprises: pursue several lines of investigation at once and freely transfer ideas from one line to another.

Bell's telephone researches were less diverse, but the network idea applies to him as well. Throughout his telephone work, Bell actively investigated several inventions, including both a harmonic multiple telegraph and an autograph or facsimile telegraph. Bell frequently shifted mechanical representations from one project to another. Indeed, as one studies his notebooks, it is often hard to tell whether a particular experiment applies to the telephone or another project. Likewise, Bell also investigated both undulating and intermittent electric currents. Even after confirming the importance of an undulating current in the transmission of speech, Bell continued to experiment with intermittent currents and, following a suggestion from Watson, kept open the possibility that they might eventually be used to transmit speech (Notebook, Vol. II, p. 66). Finally, once in place, Bell's network of enterprises continued to suggest inventions; for example, his photophone sprang directly from his telephone research.

In closing, we hope we have demonstrated our potential framework for interpreting invention as a cognitive process. Yet we wish to emphasize that we are only midway in collecting and analyzing our data. As we undertake more detailed research using the notebooks, sketches, and artifacts produced by our inventors, we intend to expand the analysis we have outlined in this chapter. In particular, we are currently creating detailed maps depicting the paths taken by each inventor. Using these maps as a basis for comparison, we are confident that we will be able to identify heuristics used by each inventor. We are especially concerned with investigating the heuristics that guided the creation of slots. In addition, we expect our maps will reveal patterns and provide insight into how our inventors created a "fit" between their mental models and mechanical representations. To be sure, it will be challenging to draw these comparisons, but only by investigating them can we explain and understand the cognitive functions and patterns that constitute the invention process.

Notes

This chapter is based on research undertaken with support from the Virginia Engineering Foundation, the Spencer Foundation, and the History and Philosophy of Science and Technology Program of the National Science Foundation (Grant Nos. DIR-8722002 and DIR-9012311). We wish to thank Paul Israel, Keith Nier, Ron Overmann, David Perkins, Robert Rosenberg, Ryan Tweney, and Robert Weber for their comments and support. We are also grateful to Nancy Briscoe, Bernard S. Finn, Sheldon Hochheiser, William Pretzer, and Jeff Sturchio for their help in analyzing artifacts and providing photographs. Finally, our work would not have been possible without our student assistants: Ed Barbour, Sanjaya Dharmasena, Klaus Etzold, Tony Fernandez, George Kaczmarskyj, Chip Littlepage, Rich Locke, Dan McKeel, Jeff Martin, Matthew Mehalik, Christy Nilsen, Patrick O'Neill, Mike Oblon, Kristian Simsarian, Eric Sollod, and Paul Vallejo.

1. Recently, mental models have come to play a significant role in efforts to understand the nature of scientific theories. Giere (1988) argues that theories are clusters of mental models. A theory, in this sense, is a set of formal, propositional statements; mental models, in contrast, are representations of objects and/or systems. While Giere appears to imply that mental models precede and underlie theories, Holland et al. (1986) suggest that "theories can be understood as systems of rules furnishing mental models" (p. 327). In other words, for Holland and colleagues, the theory appears to act as a source of mental models. Clearly there is some confusion in cognitive science regarding the relationship between theories and mental models (see also Hoffman, 1985), and we hope our comparative study of inventors can help clear up this confusion.

2. Edison's use of pawls in his telegraph inventions is amply illustrated in Jenkins et al. (1989, especially pp. 171, 203, 238, 323). For a discussion of the pawl in his motion-picture inventions, consult Carlson and Gorman (1990). Lubar (1987) discusses the role of several "stock solutions"—or what we would call mechanical representations—in the nineteenth-century pin industry.

3. One must treat this deposition with some caution, as it was prompted by patent litigation. Bell was trying to establish his priority as the inventor of the telephone; therefore it was in his interest to claim that he had the idea as early as possible. The one advantage of the deposition was that Bell was forced to cite documents and artifacts to corroborate his claims.

4. Bell to Gardiner Hubbard, 30 June 1875, partial letter, Box 80, G. G. Hubbard 1875 fol., Bell Family Papers, Library of Congress, Washington, D.C.

5. Alexander Graham Bell, "Improvement in Telegraphy," U.S. Patent 174,465 (executed 20 January 1876, granted 7 March 1876).

6. Bell's three notebooks for 1876 can be found in boxes 258 and 258A, Bell Family Papers, Library of Congress, Washington, D.C. Hereafter we will refer to these as the Bell notebooks and give the volume and page numbers.

7. Elisha Gray, "Instruments for Transmitting and Receiving Vocal Sounds Telegraphically, Caveat Filed February 14th 1876," Box 4, fol. 4, Elisha Gray Papers, Archives of the National Museum of American History, Washington, D.C.

8. Gray's liquid variable-resistance transmitter varied the *distance* of a needle from a contact at the bottom of a vessel of water; Bell's first variable-resistance transmitter varied the *area* of a needle in contact with water (Bruce, 1973). This suggests that the two inventors had different mental models of how their devices worked. Gray continued to focus primarily on developing a harmonic multiple telegraph, which suggests that he, like other telegraph inventors, did not perceive great commercial potential in the transmission of speech (cf.

Hounshell, 1975). In our ongoing research, we hope to clarify Gray's role in the invention of the telephone.

9. Alexander Graham Bell, "Improvement in Electric Telegraphy," U.S. Patent 186,787 (filed 15 January 1877, granted 30 January 1877).

10. Alexander Graham Bell to Papa & Mama, 22 March 1875, Box 4, A. M. Bell fol., Bell Family Papers.

11. The Edison sketches we have analyzed were entered as evidence in the U.S. Patent Office, *The Speaking Telephone Interferences, Evidence on Behalf of Thomas A. Edison,* Vol. 2. They are available on reel 11 of the Edison Microfilm (Jeffrey et al., 1985). Hereafter in the text we will provide the date, reel number, and frame number of the sketch.

12. During his experiments with his liquid variable-resistance telephone, Bell tried water, cod liver oil, and sulfuric acid in various combinations before settling on mercury. See Finn, 1966, p. 9.

13. "Edison's Carbon Telephone," *Journal of the Telegraph,* April 16, 1878, p. 114.

References

[Bell, Alexander Graham] (1908). *The Bell Telephone: The Deposition of Alexander Graham Bell.* Boston: American Bell Telephone Company.

Bijker, E., Hughes, T. P., & Pinch, T. J. (eds.). (1987). *The Social Construction of Technological Systems: New Directions in the Sociology and History of Technology.* Cambridge, Mass.: MIT Press.

Bruce, R. (1973). *Bell: Alexander Graham Bell and the Conquest of Solitude.* Boston: Little, Brown.

Carlson, W. B. & Gorman, M. E. (1989). Thinking and doing at Menlo Park: Edison's development of the telephone, 1876–1878. In *Working at Inventing: Thomas A. Edison and the Menlo Park Experience* (W. E. Pretzer, ed.). Dearborn, Mich.: Henry Ford Museum and Greenfield Village, pp. 84–99.

Carlson, W. B. & Gorman, M. E. (1990). Understanding invention as a cognitive process: The case of Thomas Edison and early motion pictures, 1888–1891. *Social Studies of Science, 20,* 387–430.

Clement, J. (1988). Observed methods for generating analogies in scientific problem solving. *Cognitive Science, 12,* 563–586.

Constant, E. W. (1980). *The Origins of the Turbojet Revolution.* Baltimore: Johns Hopkins Univ. Press.

Constant, E. W. (1983). Scientific theory and technological testability: Science, dynamometers, and water turbines in the 19th century. *Technology and Culture, 24,* 183–198.

Ferguson, S. (1977). The mind's eye: Nonverbal thought in technology. *Science, 197,* 827–836.

Finn, B. S. (1966). Alexander Graham Bell's experiments with the variable-resistance transmitter. *Smithsonian Journal of History, 1,* 1–16 (Winter).

Gentner, D. & Stevens, A. L. (eds.) (1983). *Mental Models.* Hillsdale, N.J.: Lawrence Erlbaum Associates.

Gholson, B., Shadish, W. R., Neimeyer, R. A., & Houts, A. C. (1989). *Psychology of Science: Contributions to Metascience.* New York: Cambridge Univ. Press.

Giere, R. N. (1988). *Explaining Science: A Cognitive Approach.* Chicago: Univ. of Chicago Press.

Gilfillan, S. C. (1935). *The Sociology of Invention*. Cambridge: MIT Press.

Gille, B. (1986). *The History of Techniques. Vol. 1: Techniques and Civilizations*. New York: Gordon and Breach.

Gorman, M. E. & Carlson, W. B. (1989). Can experiments be used to study science? *Social Epistemology, 3,* 89–106.

Gorman, M. E., Mehalik, M. M., Carlson, W. B., and Oblon, M. (in press). "Alexander Graham Bell, Elisha Gray, and the Speaking Telegraph: A Cognitive Comparison." *History of Technology*.

Gruber, H. E. (1981). *Darwin on Man: A Psychological Study of Scientific Creativity*. Chicago: Univ. of Chicago.

Helmholtz, H. (1875). *On the Sensations of Tone as a Physiological Basis for the Theory of Music*. A. J. Ellis (trans.). London: Longmans, Green.

Hindle, B. (1983). *Emulation and Invention*. New York: W. W. Norton.

Hoffman, R. R. (1980). Metaphor in science. In *Cognition and Figurative Language*. (R. P. Honeck & R. R. Hoffman, eds.) Hillsdale, N.J.: Lawrence Erlbaum, pp. 393–423.

Hoffman, R. R. (1985). Some implications of metaphor for philosophy and psychology of science. From *The Ubiquity of Metaphor* (W. Paprotté & R. Dirven, eds.). Published as Vol. 29 of *Current Issues in Linguistic Theory*. Amsterdam and Philadelphia: John Benjamins.

Holland, J. H., Holyoak, K. J., Nisbett, R. E., & Thagard, P. A. (1986). *Induction: Processes of Inference, Learning and Discovery*. Cambridge, Mass.: MIT Press.

Hounshell, D. A. (1975). Elisha Gray and the telephone: On the disadvantages of being an expert. *Technology and Culture, 16,* 133–161.

Hounshell, D. A. (1976). Bell and Gray: Contrasts in style, politics and etiquette. *Proceedings of the IEEE, 64,* 1305–1314.

Hughes, T. P. (1971). *Elmer Sperry: Inventor and Engineer*. Baltimore: Johns Hopkins Univ. Press.

Hughes, T. P. (1977). Edison's method. In *Technology at the Turning Point* (W. B. Pickett, ed.). San Francisco: San Francisco Press, pp. 5–22.

Hughes, T. P. (1989). *American Genesis: A Century of Invention and Technological Enthusiasm, 1870–1970*. New York: Viking.

Jeffrey, T. E., et al. (1985). *Thomas A. Edison Papers: A Selective Microfilm Edition, Part 1, 1850–1878*. Frederick, Md.: University Publications of America.

Jehl, F. (1937–1941). *Menlo Park Reminiscences* (3 vols.). Dearborn, Mich.: Edison Institute.

Jenkins, R. V. (1984). Elements of style: Continuities in Edison's thinking. *Annals of the New York Academy of Sciences, 424,* 149–162.

Jenkins, R. V. & Nier, K. A. (1984). A record for invention: Thomas Edison and his papers. *IEEE Transactions on Education, E-27,* 191–196.

Jenkins, R. V., et al. (1989). *The Papers of Thomas A. Edison. Vol. 1: The Making of an Inventor. February 1847–June 1873*. Baltimore: Johns Hopkins Univ. Press.

Josephson, M. (1959). *Edison: A Biography*. New York: McGraw-Hill.

Lamb, J. (1987). Industry warms to superconductivity. *New Scientist,* 22 October 1987, 56–61.

Langley, P., Simon, H. A., Bradshaw, G. L., & Zytgow, J. M. (1987). *Scientific Discovery: Computational Explorations of the Creative Processes*. Cambridge, Mass.: MIT Press.

Latour, B. (1987). *Science in Action*. Milton Keynes, England: Open Univ. Press.

Layton, E. T. (1989). Through the looking glass; Or, news from Lake Mirror Image. In *In Context: History and the History of Technology: Essays in Honor of Melvin Kranzberg* (S. H. Cutcliffe & R. C. Post, eds.). Bethlehem, Pa.: Lehigh Univ. Press, 29–41.

Lindqvist, S. (1984). *Technology on Trial: The Introduction of Steam Power Technology into Sweden, 1715–1736.* Stockholm: Almqvist & Wiksell International.

Lubar, S. (1987). Culture and technological design in the 19th-century pin industry: John Howe and the Howe Manufacturing Company. *Technology and Culture, 28,* 253–282.

Maver, William (1897). *American Telegraphy: Systems, Apparatus, Operation.* New York: William Maver & Co.

Norman, D. A. (1983). Some observations on mental models. In Gentner & Stevens (1983), 7–15.

Norman, D. A. (1988). *The Psychology of Everyday Things.* New York: Basic Books.

Perkins, D. (1989). Invention as Search and Insight. Paper presented at Inventive Minds: A conference on Creativity in Technology, Tulsa, November 3–5, 1989.

Philip, C. O. (1985). *Robert Fulton: A Biography.* New York: Franklin Watts.

Prescott, G. B. (1884). *Bell's Electric Speaking Telephone: Its Invention, Construction, Application, Modification and History.* New York: D. Appleton. Reprinted by Arno (1972).

Rhodes, F. L. (1929). *Beginnings of Telephony.* New York: Harper & Brothers. Reprinted by Arno (1974).

Rouse, W. B. & Morris, N. M. (1986). On looking into the black box: Prospects and limits in the search for mental models. *Psychological Bulletin, 100,* 349–363.

Thompson, R. L. (1947). *Wiring a Continent: A History of the Telegraph Industry in the United States, 1832–1866.* Princeton, N.J.: Princeton Univ. Press.

Thompson, S. P. (1883). *Phillipp Reis: Inventor of the Telephone.* London: E. & F. N. Spon.

Tweney, R. D., Doherty, M. E., & Mynatt, C. R. (1981). *On Scientific Thinking.* New York: Columbia Univ. Press.

Tweney, R. D. (1989). A framework for the cognitive psychology of science. In Gholson et al. (1989).

Vincenti, W. G. (1982). Control-volume analysis: A difference in thinking between engineering and physics. *Technology and Culture, 23,* 145–174.

Watson, T. A. (1913). *The Birth and Babyhood of the Telephone.* N.P.: American Telephone and Telegraph Co., 1977. Reprint of an address delivered by Watson to the Third Annual Convention of the Telephone Pioneers of America in 1913.

Weber, R. J. & Dixon, S. (1989). Invention and gain analysis. *Cognitive Psychology, 21,* 1–21.

Weber, R. J. & Perkins, D. N. (1989). How to invent artifacts and ideas. *New Ideas in Psychology, 7,* 49–72.

Whitehead, A. N. (1925). *Science and the Modern World.* New York: MacMillan. Paper reprint: New American Library (1948).

4 | Why Wilbur and Orville?
Some Thoughts on the Wright Brothers
and the Process of Invention

TOM D. CROUCH

Why Wilbur and Orville? That, it seems to me, is the single most interesting and important question we can ask relating to the invention of the airplane. How did these two obscure bicycle makers and mechanics succeed, when some of the world's best-trained and most experienced engineers and scientists had failed?

It was a question the Wrights themselves found difficult to answer. They had kept a meticulous record of the evolution of their technology in diaries, letters, notebooks, and photographs. They knew precisely what they had done, and when. As to why they had done it, and how they had succeeded where so many others had failed, they were far less certain.

Once, when a friend suggested that sheer genius might be the only explanation, Wilbur remarked that he doubted that to be the case.

> Do you not insist too strongly on the single point of mental ability? To me it seems that a thousand other factors, each rather insignificant in itself, in the aggregate influence the event ten times more than mere mental ability or inventiveness. . . . If the wheels of time could be turned back . . . it is not at all probable that we would do again what we have done. . . . It was due to a peculiar combination of circumstances which might never occur again.[1]

Of course Wilbur knew that "sheer mental ability" lay at the core of the Wright achievement. He was simply pointing to the importance of the "peculiar combination of circumstances" that enabled them to exercise their genius to best advantage. Any attempt to understand or explain the success of the Wrights, or that of any other innovators, must include both an assessment of the nature of the talents involved and a consideration of the foundation of life experience enabling the individual to bring his or her gifts to bear on a particular problem.

Wilbur and Orville Wright were, respectively, the third and sixth of seven children born to Milton and Susan Koerner Wright. Separated by the birth of twins who died in infancy, the Wrights had two older brothers, Reuchlin and Lorin, neither of whom played any important role in the invention of the airplane. Their younger sister Katharine, born three years to the day after Orville, was very much a part of their lives and their success.[2]

Most biographers have paid a great deal of attention to the mother, Susan Catherine Koerner Wright. It was from her, we are told, that the brothers inherited their mechanical skills. She kept the house in good repair, designed and built simple household appliances, and produced toys for her children, including a much-cherished sled that was handed down from one youngster to the next.

The father, who by all accounts had difficulty driving a nail straight, is usually portrayed as a shadowy figure, frequently absent from home on church business. In fact he was an extraordinary man who placed the stamp of his own character on the lives and personalities of all his children.

Bishop Milton Wright is remembered, even today, as the most influential, and controversial, figure in the history of the Church of the United Brethren in Christ. In 1889, when Wilbur was 20 and Orville 17, he ended a fifteen-year-old conflict within the church by creating a permanent national schism. He spent the next ten years battling old friends and colleagues for the possession of church property in cases that eventually reached seven state supreme courts. He lost every suit but one.

Having resolved those problems, Bishop Wright proceeded to generate an entirely new conflict within the schismatic branch that he had led away from the original church. A resulting set of new court cases and church disciplinary hearings would continue for another five years, ending with Bishop Wright's retirement in 1905.

Milton Wright was a man who refused to recognize shades of gray. Negotiation and compromise were not in his vocabulary. Once he had decided on a course of action, he would not be moved. He had inherited that strength of will, force of character, and absolute dedication to principle from his father, and he passed it on to his children. He taught them that the world was not a friendly place for honest men and women. Temptations beckoned. Unscrupulous persons lay in wait, eager to take advantage of the weak and unwary. Friends would fall away in times of trial, accepting the easier road of accommodation with error and injustice. Ultimately, the strength of family bonds offered the only real support one could hope for in life.

The lessons of life that Wilbur and Orville learned at their father's knee would serve them well during the years of difficult technical problem-solving that led up to the invention of the airplane. Those same lessons would also make it difficult or impossible for them to deal with the very different problems that they faced as businessmen and public figures during the years after 1905. Their relentless drive and will, their ability to look skeptics and rivals in the eye without blinking, their absolute self-confidence—all were a gift from their father. So, too, were their hard-edged and uncompromising personalities, and their essential distrust of the world beyond their doorstep.

They grew up in a house that was a psychological fortress and a bastion to which their father could retreat from the bitter struggle with church foes. Within that home the children found the love, strength, and support that would sustain them in their own struggles with what they quite literally regarded as the forces of evil and depravity. Late in life it would be Milton's proudest boast that his two famous sons continued to make their home under the paternal roof. Neither of them would ever marry, or find any dearer friends or stauncher supporters than the members of their own family.

The events leading to the invention of the airplane were set in motion in 1884, the year in which the Wright family moved home to Dayton, Ohio, after several years of living in Iowa and Indiana. The move, necessitated by Milton's need to prepare for an upcoming church battle, came so quickly that 18-year-old Wilbur, an excellent student, was unable to complete the course work required for his high-school graduation, then only a month away. Rather than wasting his time on mere formalities, the young man enrolled in a special series of college preparatory courses offered by Dayton's Central High School. His plans to enter Yale were shattered that winter when he was struck in the face by an opponent's stick during a game of "shinny," a kind of free-form ice hockey.

The facial injuries led to a series of more serious complaints, loosely diagnosed as heart palpitations and digestive problems. Almost before he realized what was happening, Wilbur was teetering on the brink of becoming that stock character of Victorian family life, the perpetual invalid. He spent the next three years closeted away at home, sunk in what was, at best, a deep depression, at worst a severe nervous collapse. Even these months were not wasted, however. Wilbur read widely in his father's excellent library; nursed his mother, who was dying of tuberculosis; and kept house for his father, younger brothers, and sister.

Wilbur emerged from his shell rather abruptly during a period of extraordinary family crisis in the spring and summer of 1889. In May of that year, Milton cut the Gordian knot of a thirty-year controversy, leading 10 percent of the national UBC membership away from the majority to establish a new church structure. Two months later, on July 4, Susan Wright died.

Suddenly faced with the collapse of church and family, the twin cornerstones of his life, Milton set about shoring up the foundations. Unable to conceive of his home without a female at its emotional core, he began the process of promoting his 15-year-old daughter Katharine to her mother's role, and enlisting the services of his two youngest sons (Reuchlin and Lorin had left home and married) as allies and assistants in his church battles. Confident that he had a home to return to, Bishop Wright immediately launched a series of lawsuits against the old church while he struggled to establish the new.

It is important to realize that Milton Wright had no desire to limit the intellectual growth of his children. On the contrary, he was a warm and loving father who encouraged his children to stretch their minds and spirits to the fullest extent. He simply saw no reason why they should not be able to do that while remaining at home.

He sent Katharine off for a year at Oberlin Preparatory School, followed by four years at Oberlin College (Class of '98). With that out of the way, however, he was enormously pleased when she returned home to Dayton to begin work as a high school teacher, and to resume her duties as female head of the household.

Milton worked hard to keep his daughter at home. He was delighted when his sons made that decision on their own. Orville did not return for his senior year in high school following his mother's death. Having apprenticed himself for two summers in Dayton printing shops, he was determined to set himself up in business as a job printer. Times were hard. The depression under way since 1893 led to a sudden rise in the number of young adults forced to continue living with their parents, waiting to inherit a home, farm, or business. In Orville's case it was simply cheaper to remain at home while he was establishing himself.

Wilbur, who had spent the last three years closeted away nursing his mother, emerged from his depression during this period, but was still feeling unsure of himself. Old friends had gone off to school, set themselves up in business, and established homes for themselves while he was simply marking time. He feared that college might now be a waste of money, and he did not believe that he had the temperament for success in business.

He observed the problems of his two older brothers with interest and sympathy. Both Reuchlin and Lorin were married and having a very difficult time making ends meet. They were talented men, with some college education, yet both gave the impression of being constantly overwhelmed by responsibility and circumstance. What had gone wrong for them? It was puzzling, and more than a bit frightening, for Wilbur was by no means certain that he could do any better under similar circumstances. Assessing the situation in the late summer of 1889 he recognized that he was fortunate in at least one regard. He was not burdened with the family responsibilities that made life so difficult for his brothers. For the time being, he would be content to work out his destiny within the safety of his father's home.

That destiny would involve a partnership with his brother Orville. Their names had appeared together as the "Wright Brothers" for the first time earlier that year on the cover of a pamphlet entitled "Scenes In the Church Commission." Wilbur was the author of this strident and very professional bit of propaganda in support of his father's position in the church controversy. Orville did the printing. The arrangement proved so successful that the printing operation quickly became a joint venture. Over the next several years they set themselves up as job printers, and issued two short-lived neighborhood newspapers of superior quality.

They branched out in 1892, hiring help for the print shop and establishing a small bicycle sales and repair business. The Wrights continued to enjoy some success with their two businesses, and began manufacturing bicycles on a small scale in 1896.

A friend or neighbor observing the Wrights in the late 1890s would have thought them typical small businessmen—hard-working young fellows, honest to a fault, polite, dutiful brothers, and loving sons. Beneath that placid surface, however, the Wrights were far from satisfied with the routine of their lives. Wilbur, in particular, was afraid that he had somehow "fallen into a corner." He would be 30 years old in 1899, and was still living in his father's home. The enormous reserve of talent and creative energy that he sensed within himself was entirely untapped. Consciously or unconsciously, he was a man in search of a challenge against which to measure himself.

He found it in the airplane. In later years, the Wrights would date their interest in flight to 1878, when their father presented them with a toy helicopter. Perhaps. But thousands of other children must have been just as fascinated as the young Wright boys at the sight of a small rotor climbing toward the ceiling. Wilbur's peculiarly receptive state of mind during the years 1896–1899, and the appearance of one newspaper and magazine article after another chronicling the aeronautical experiments of Otto Lilienthal, Samuel Pierpont Langley, and Octave Chanute during that period, are the real keys to understanding the Wright's entry into the field.

They approached the problem of flight with some important advantages, and a great deal of very useful experience. Close to one another since childhood, business partners for a decade, they knew each other very well and had developed their own effective method of working jointly toward the solution of a technical problem. "Both boys had tempers," Charles Taylor, an assistant at the bicycle shop recalled. "They would shout at one another something terrible. I don't think they really got mad, but they sure got awful hot."[3]

The arguments that shocked Charlie enabled the brothers to explore every facet of a problem. Their ability to defend a point of view with real passion, while at the same time listening to the other fellow's opinion, was an essential part of the process. There were times when they literally argued in a circle, suddenly awakening to the fact that they had switched positions. "I love to scrap with Orv," Wilbur once remarked. "He's such a good scrapper." In the case of the Wright brothers, the whole was greater than the parts.[4]

The Wrights brought considerable mechanical skill and experience to the enterprise. By 1899 they had designed and built printing presses, a special self-oiling bicycle wheel hub, an internal combustion engine, and, of course, several hundred bicycles. They maintained a light machine shop and were reasonably proficient, though by no means professional, machinists.

But this catalogue of advantages is obviously incomplete. While all of these factors represent strengths that the brothers brought to bear on the problems of flight, they are insufficient to account for their final success. Something is still missing.

Looking a bit more closely at the experience of the Wrights prior to 1899, it is clear that they had a considerable local reputation for solving standard mechanical problems in unconventional ways. Take the case of a large printing press that Orville designed and built out of scrap parts with Wilbur's assistance in 1889–1890. Ed Sines, an old friend who helped out around the shop, recalled the reaction of a professional printer who inspected the device.

> E. C. James, I think he was pressman for a Chicago [printing] house, came to the [Wright] shop almost everytime he was in the city. One day he walked into the front office and asked if "that Wright press is running today." When we told him it was running at that time, he said he would like to see it. Well, he went back into the press room, stood by the machine, looked at it, then sat down beside it and finally crawled underneath it. After he had been under the machine some little time he got up and said, "Well, it works, but I certainly don't see how it works."[5]

Obviously, the sort of innovative thinking embodied in the design of that printing press would play a major role in the invention of the airplane. But what was its source? What was there about the Wright brothers that led them to approach a mechanical problem like the design of a printing press from a new and totally unexpected angle?

Expressed in the simplest possible terms, Wilbur and Orville had a genius for visualizing the abstract—a gift for thinking in terms of concrete graphic images.

That was what set them apart. They had an extraordinary ability to visualize the nature and direction of the forces at work in an operating machine and to imagine the way in which those forces might operate in a machine that existed only in their heads. A reconstruction of the chain of ideas leading to the development of an aeronautical control system via the bicycle will shed some light on the basic nature of their talent for innovation.

The basic notions of stability and control are simple enough to grasp. Imagine a flat plate floating in space. The plate is free to revolve around three axes of motion. It can roll to the right or left around an imaginary horizontal axis running along its length fore and aft; pitch its nose up or down around a horizontal axis running across its width; and yaw, or turn its nose to the right or left, around a perpendicular axis running through the center point of the plate.

Most land vehicles are inherently stable in two axes of motion. So long as it has four wheels firmly planted on the ground, a wagon cannot move in the roll or pitch axes. Freedom of motion in a single axis, yaw, can be obtained by allowing the front wheels to swivel to the right or left. Most experimenters who considered the problem of the flying machine prior to the Wrights assumed that the ideal airplane, like a wagon, would be inherently stable in all three axes. The pilot would be provided with controls that would overcome pitch and yaw stability in order to take off, land, and direct the course of his aerial steed. In most schemes, however, roll control was to be completely automatic, usually achieved by setting the wings at a dehedral angle. If everything went as planned, such a machine would be as stable in the air as a wagon moving down a road.

But Wilbur and Orville chose a different, and quite unexpected, model of stability and control—the bicycle. The bicycle differs from all other surface vehicles in that it is unstable both in roll and yaw. Actually, that is not quite true. The spinning wheels and forward motion of the machine do generate a degree of inherent stability. The fact remains, however, that the cyclist must constantly maintain balance by shifting his or her weight, while directing the course of the machine with the handlebars.

There are trade-offs to be made in the area of stability and control. To initiate a control correction with an inherently stable machine, the operator must first overcome the forces of stability. You *can* turn a wagon over, but it is hard to do. The Wrights insisted that the pilot of their machine have absolute control of the craft at all times. They were willing to sacrifice the perfect stability of the wagon for the absolute, precise, and immediate control response of the bicycle.

Other experimenters feared that the operator of a flying machine would be unable to react quickly enough to maintain constant equilibrium. With a flying machine, there would be no opportunity to pull over to the side of the road and think things over. The Wrights, on the other hand, reasoned that a normal person was able to maintain the equilibrium of a cycle with little difficulty. While an airplane would be free to rotate in three axes of motion, rather than two, they assumed that a pilot would be able to maintain constant balance and control as easily as a cyclist. It would be a matter of practice, an acquired skill.

The problem now became one of devising a mechanical control system that would enable a pilot to balance and direct his machine through the air. In this case, the bicycle was of no use to them. They rejected the weight-shifting technique that enabled cyclists, and the hang glider pilots who preceded them, to maintain balance. This technique was dangerous, was imprecise, and limited the size of a flying machine to a wingspan that could be maneuvered by relatively small changes in the center of gravity. Moreover, handlebars would be of no use in directing the course of a machine flying through the sky.

Their attention turned to the only successful model of aerodynamic stability and control available to them, the bird. The brothers spent hours watching birds wheel and turn in the sky, seeking to tease some general principle out of what they observed. "The thought came to me," Wilbur recalled years later, "that possibly it [a bird] adjusted the tips of its wings . . . so as to present one tip at a positive angle and the other at a negative angle, thus . . . turning itself into an animated windmill, and that when its body had revolved . . . as far as it wished, it reversed itself and started turning the other way. The balance was controlled by utilizing the dynamic reactions of the air instead of shifting weight."[6]

Observations of birds in flight had led Wilbur to the notion of aerodynamic control through a differential alteration of the angle of attack of the wing tips. But how could that be accomplished in a flying machine? The answer came to Wilbur while he was working alone in the bicycle shop on a July day in 1899. He was idly toying with a long, thin cardboard box, twisting the ends in opposite directions, when it occurred to him that if just such a helical twist could be induced across the full span of a wing in either direction, the pilot of the machine would be able to raise or lower either wing tip at will to restore balance or bank into a turn.

The Wrights had taken a set of graphic images—a bicycle speeding around a corner, a bird soaring through the air, a cardboard box twisted in the hands—turned them into thought problems, and reassembled the lessons learned into a mechanical system for controlling an airplane in the roll axis. In the simplest terms, they had made use of one gift to visualize the forces operating on the bicycle and the bird, then proceeded to imagine how those forces might be applied in an entirely new way.

It was a process that would be repeated time after time as the Wrights worked their way through the mass of problems that blocked the route to a successful airplane. Most pre-Wright aircraft builders had flown their gliders and models with airfoils shaped like the arc of a circle: that is, with the peak of the camber, or arch, at the centerpoint of the chord line (the midpoint on an imaginary straight line drawn from the leading to the trailing edge of the wing). The Wrights positioned the peak just behind the leading edge as a result of the way in which they visualized the movement of the center of pressure over the wing.

Imagine a flat board held at a 90-degree angle to the airstream. The center of pressure is at the center of the board. Now imagine that the top of the board begins to tip forward into the airstream. As the angle of attack to the airstream decreases, the center of pressure moves closer to the top, until, when the board is parallel to the stream, it rests at the center of the exposed leading edge.

Now imagine the same thought experiment with a wing featuring an arc of a circle airfoil. Long before the chordline is perpendicular to the stream, the center of pressure has passed completely over the leading edge and onto the top of the wing. The Wrights had visualized all of this long before they constructed their first glider, and moved the peak of the camber far forward on the wing to forestall the problem.

The process was clearly at work again during the 1902 glider tests at Kitty Hawk. The Wrights had discovered that their wing-warping lateral control system did not always produce the desired results. When warping was applied for a protracted time to raise a dropping wing tip, the machine would suddenly enter an incipient spin in the direction of the low wing. The brothers visualized what must be happening. In addition to increasing the lift on the low wing, the warping process increased its drag as well, causing it to move more slowly than the high wing. With an understanding of the forces involved, the Wrights came up with an immediate solution, a movable rudder that could be angled to increase the drag on the high side and keep the craft moving straight ahead.

That same genius for reasoning through graphic images was at work when the Wrights struggled with the propellor problem early in 1903. Having demonstrated a successful glider at Kitty Hawk in 1902, they had forged ahead to the design of the world's first powered airplane and the construction of an engine to power it. The brothers had always assumed that when the time came, they would be able to study propellor theory in marine engineering textbooks, and find the basis for the design of an aeronautical propellor. They discovered, however, that there was no such thing as a propellor theory.

Momentarily caught short, the Wrights reasoned that a propellor was nothing more than a rotary wing. The lift of the wing was vectored into thrust in the case of the propellor. A great deal of thinking remained to be done, but the great breakthroughs were behind them. The brothers could calculate the speed at which the blade would be moving at any point along its span at any given revolutions per minute. They drew the appropriate airfoil shape for that condition from the table they had constructed with their wind tunnel, created a series of templates, and carved their blades.

The Wright story is filled with examples of the way in which the brothers were able to make breakthroughs, major and minor, on the basis of their ability to think through a problem by visualizing abstract principles or forces as graphic mental images. The best and most impressive case in point is to be found in their use of the wind tunnel. To understand the importance of the wind tunnel tests, it is necessary to return to the years 1899–1900, when the Wrights first became involved in aeronautics.

When the brothers began their serious course of reading in the spring and summer of 1899, they discovered that what passed for the literature of aeronautics was, for the most part, a mass of confusion, contradiction, and guesswork. They did, however, discover a few bits of information on which to build a foundation for their own work. In the published work of Otto Lilienthal and Octave Chanute, for example, they found two essential equations that would enable them to take the first steps toward the design of an aircraft. The first could be employed to estimate the amount of lift produced by a wing of given size and shape under specific conditions. The other would enable an experimenter to calculate the amount of drag, or air resistance, that would be generated by such a wing.

For the sake of simplicity, we will limit our consideration to the Wright's treatment of the lift equation, which looks a bit daunting to the untrained eye:

$$L = kSV^2C_L$$

Broken down into its components, the equation becomes easier to understand.

L = lift in pounds

k = coefficient of air pressure

S = total area of lifting surface

V^2 = velocity (headwing + airspeed squared)

C_L = coefficient of lift

To solve the equation, the Wrights began by substituting two bits of received information—the numerical values for the coefficients of air pressure and lift. The pressure coefficient was an experimentally derived number expressing the ratio between the velocity of a stream of a particular fluid (air, in this case) and the pressure exerted on a plate immersed in the flow.

Since the mid-eighteenth century, a great many experimenters had produced a variety of values for the coefficient of air pressure, a fact that is not surprising given the difficulty of precision measurement with primitive instruments. The value most generally accepted, however, was .005, a figure based on work presented in a paper by the great English engineer John Smeaton in 1759. Known as Smeaton's coefficient, .005 was the figure employed by both Otto Lilienthal and Octave Chanute, gliding pioneers whom the Wrights much admired. These men had designed successful gliders based on Smeaton's coefficient, and that, initially, was good enough for the Wrights.

The term C_L, usually identified as the coefficient of lift, was quite a different matter. Unlike Smeaton's coefficient, which was a constant, the coefficient of lift varied for every airfoil shape at every angle of attack. Otto Lilienthal had conducted his own airfoil research before building his first glider in 1890, and had included a table of coefficients for lift and drag through a range of angles of attack in an article published in the *Aeronautical Annual* for 1896. Again, the Wrights decided to trust Lilienthal. Referring to his table, they found that the coefficient of lift for an angle of attack of 10 degrees, the highest angle at which they assumed their glider would fly under normal conditions, was .825.

With the two coefficients in hand, solving the equation became a matter of give and take, for the Wrights could use standard procedures to come up with the numerical value of most of the other terms. By consulting a standard table of weights of materials, for example, the brothers estimated that a glider of the approximate size they had in mind would weigh perhaps 50 pounds. Wilbur, who would do most of the flying, weighed 140 pounds. The total weight would, therefore, be in the neighborhood of 190 to 200 pounds.

Next, they chose a reasonable velocity—the speed of the wind in which they would fly. A few trial calculations indicated that they would have to operate in a headwind of 10 to 20 miles per hour. A wind as low as 10 miles per hour would require an enormous wing to generate sufficient lift to fly, while a wind higher than 20 miles per hour sounded positively frightening. They used a compromise figure of 15 miles per hour in their calculations.

With these decisions made, the Wrights could now solve the equation for an estimate of the wing surface required to lift the machine under those conditions:

Step 1 $L = kSV^2C_L$

Step 2 190 (total weight = L) = .005 (Smeaton's coefficient) $\times$ S (total surface area) $\times$ 225 (wind, 15 mph²) $\times$ .825 (lift coefficient from Lilienthal table)

Step 3 190 = .928S

Step 4 S = 190/.928

Step 5 Surface area = 204.74 feet

The use of the equation was only the first step in the design process. The Wrights now had to decide how to arrange 200 square feet of wing area. At the same time, they felt confident that a wing, or wings, of that size, would lift a pilot and machine into the air in a wind of 15 miles per hour.

But there was a problem. When the Wrights took their first two gliders to Kitty Hawk, North Carolina, for testing in 1900 and 1901, they discovered that the lift of these machines fell short of the predicted value by as much as 20 percent. This was enormously discouraging, for it suggested that there was a serious error in the lift calculation. That error could lie only in one of the two coefficients. The brothers now faced the task of identifying and correcting the error.[7]

Their first step was to doublecheck the equation. It was a problem made to order for the Wrights. Their genius for visualizing mechanical solutions to abstract and theoretical puzzles enabled them to devise a simple, yet brilliant, mechanical analogue of the lift equation. According to the equation, solved using Smeaton's value for the pressure coefficient and Lilienthal's value for the lift coefficient, a cambered, or curved, wing with a surface area of 1 square foot, set at a 5-degree angle of attack, should precisely balance a flat plate measuring .66 of a square foot set at a 90-degree angle to the air flow.

The brothers recreated that situation, mounting a bicycle wheel, free to turn, over the handlebars of a bicycle. A cambered Lilienthal airfoil of the correct dimension was fixed to the front of the rim at a 5-degree angle, with a flat plate positioned at a 90-degree angle to the flow, one quarter of the way around the wheel. If everything was in order, the wheel should remain balanced when the bicycle was ridden down the street. The wheel turned, and the Wrights were now certain that there was a problem with one or more of the values used in solving the lift equation. Obviously, there was no possibility of an error in the surface area, actual lift, and velocity figures employed. The Smeaton coefficient, the Lilienthal lift coefficient, or both, had to be incorrect. Moreover, there was yet another complicating factor. The experiments on which Lilienthal had based his lift coefficient had involved measuring the total pressure on a wing surface tested on a whirling-arm device. The nature of the test procedure meant that the coefficient of air pressure was actually embedded in Lilienthal's lift coefficient.

As a first step toward identifying which coefficient was in error, the Wrights assumed that the Lilienthal figure was correct, and, using that value, along with the meticulous data that they had gathered on the actual performance of their 1900 and 1901 gliders when flown as kites, they recalculated the coefficient of air pressure for a number of specific flights. When they averaged the results, they fixed the new value of the coefficient at .033, rather than the .005 suggested by the Smeaton paper.

The brothers were fairly confident, though not absolutely certain, that they had identified the cause of their problems. But the time for guesswork was passed. Wilbur and Orville were determined to find a means of actually measuring the forces that would enable them to calculate a trustworthy value for the two coefficients. The answer was the wind tunnel.

The Wright brothers did not invent the wind tunnel. The English experimenters Frances Herbert Wenham and John Browning had constructed the first such device a quarter of a century before. The Wrights *were,* however, the first to employ a tunnel to take precision measurements of all of the forces operating on a model wing.[8]

The Wrights put their wind tunnel into operation in November 1901. A wooden box 6 feet long and 16 inches square inside, it looked like nothing more than a packing crate resting on two sawhorses. Its sole purpose was to move a smooth, steady stream of air through the box at a constant speed of 27 miles per hour. A sheet-metal hood at one end partially shielded a two-bladed fan that was driven through the gearbox of an abandoned grinder at a speed of 4000 rpm. It would not do for the wind to career off the walls of the tunnel, creating crosscurrents, eddies, and swirls, so the Wrights placed a "straightener," a crosshatch of thin wooden strips covered with wire mesh, just in front of the fan.

A section of the wooden top of the tunnel was replaced by a pane of glass. This window into the heart of the device looked down onto a spindly metal balance bolted into place on the tunnel floor. Carefully crafted of bicycle spokes and hacksaw blades, it was a precision instrument designed to balance (hence the name) lift against drag, just as in the case of the simpler bicycle wheel experiment. This time, however, the Wrights would be making precise measurements of what was occurring as the wind flowed over a small airfoil mounted on the balance.

There were actually three balances. In their first attempt, the brothers sought to devise a single instrument that would provide the data required to calculate both the coefficients of lift and drag. It was a failure. The Wrights then split the functions, and developed separate and distinct balances to calculate the lift and drag forces. They were not much to look at. Each was small enough to fit into a shoe box. The slightest jar would dislodge the many pins on which the various parts rested, reducing the device to an assortment of bits and pieces on the tunnel floor. Reassembly was exasperating, something akin to building a house of cards; one slip and the entire edifice collapsed.

Perhaps because they were so small, fragile, and totally devoid of the aura surrounding the gliders and powered aircraft, it is easy to underestimate the importance of the balances. In fact they were as critical to the ultimate success of the Wright brothers as any of their actual flying machines.

As in the case of the bicycle wheel testing device, the lift balance was a mechanical analog of the now familiar mathematical equation for calculating the lifting force that would be generated by a wing of given shape and dimension in a wind of known velocity. It measured the lift generated by a small model wing as a ratio with the pressure, or drag, exerted on a flat plate (in actual practice, a series of "drag fingers," narrow flat strips with a total known surface area) perpendicular to the flow.

The absolute brilliance of the thing is to be found in the fact that balance enabled the Wrights to calculate the coefficient of lift without making use of Smeaton's coefficient. They had grasped the possibility of devising a mechanical expression of an abstract mathematical equation. They had visualized a way in which the incredibly complex play of forces operating on that machine could be directed so as to produce the *precise* bit of information required. Seen in this light, the lift balance, and the drag balance, must be recognized as intellectual achievements of staggering proportion.

The two months of brilliant achievement at the end of 1901 were a turning point for the Wright brothers. They based a new glider, their 1902 model, on the results of their tests. Unlike its predecessors, it met all of their expectations, and opened the door to the future. Other problems remained to be solved, but the great unknowns were behind them.

Here, at last, is something close to a satisfactory answer to that original question. Why Wilbur and Orville? Why? Because they were the Bishop's boys, a fact that brought them, with their unique gift for visualizing abstraction, to the right place, at the right time, with a drive and will of the sort required to carry them through to the end of a long struggle. As Wilbur had remarked, there was nothing inevitable about it. "If the wheels of time could be turned back . . . it is not at all probable that we would do again what we have done. . . . It was due to a peculiar combination of circumstances which might never occur again."

Notes

1. Wilbur Wright to Octave Chanute, October 28, 1906. In Marvin W. McFarland, *The Papers of Wilbur and Orville Wright* (New York: McGraw-Hill, 1953), Vol. 2, pp. 731–732.

2. For a full examination of the dynamics of the Wright family see Tom D. Crouch, *The Bishop's Boys: A Life of Wilbur and Orville Wright* (New York: W. W. Norton, 1989).

3. Charles E. Taylor, "My story of the Wright brothers," *Colliers* (December 25, 1948), p. 68.

4. Ivonette Wright Miller, "Character Study." In Ivonette Wright Miller, *Wright Reminiscences* (Dayton, Ohio: Privately Printed, 1978), p. 61.

5. Charles J. Bauer, "Ed Sines: Pal of the Wrights," *Popular Aviation* (June, 1938), p. 40.

6. Wilbur Wright, Brief Digest of the Evidence for Complainant on Final Hearing, The Wright Co. vs. Herring-Curtiss Co. and Glenn Curtiss, in Equity, No. 400, pp. 4–25. Plaintiffs copy in Wright State University Archive.

7. For a complete and detailed listing of all Wright glider and powered airplane flights see Arthur Renstrom, *A Chronology Commemorating the One Hundredth Anniversary of the Birth of Orville Wright* (Washington, D.C.: U.S. Government Printing Office, 1975).

8. For a detailed description of the Wright wind tunnel and the experiments conducted with it see Appendix II, 1901 Wind Tunnel, in McFarland, *Papers,* Vol. 1, pp. 547–593. The best secondary description of the wind tunnel experiments is to be found in Peter Jakab, *Visions of a Flying Machine: The Wright Brothers and the Process of Invention* (Washington, D.C.: Smithsonian Institution Press, 1990).

III | CONTEMPORARY INVENTORS

While we can reconstruct some of the thinking of classic inventors from the historical record, contemporary inventors can speak directly to their involvement in important inventions and to the search strategies, motives, and social context that guided their work. We begin with the stories of three instruments, one for disclosing the microstructure of things, another for seeing with sound, and a third that is the integration in a central setting of many instruments in a kind of upside-down observatory. Then we take up four more stories that deal with the manipulation and creation of material worlds: the invention of synthetic diamond, catalysts for petroleum refining, the Kevlar of bullet-resistant vests, and the design of a "wonder drug," ivermectin.

Most of all, we understand by seeing. James Hillier takes us to previously unseen places as he discusses his role in the development of the electron microscope, a fundamental resource for disclosing organic and inorganic structure beyond the reach of optical microscopy. Hillier emphasizes that the theoretical idea of the electron microscope had existed for some time. But he and co-workers required years of painstaking work, as well as some crucial insights, to develop a series of prototypes leading to a fully functional instrument.

Offhand one might not see much relation between the Wright's approach to flight and Hillier's to the electron microscope, but there is indeed a close one. Early on, Hillier found that the resolution and clarity of his images were influenced by a host of variables, any one of which did not make much difference in the overall image—their effects all added together in a mix. So he assumed that these variables were independent of one another and attacked them one at a time. As noted earlier, that assumption drastically reduces the size of the possible search space, if it is correct. In the absence of better information, often it is necessary to make the leap of faith—opposite of Faraday's—that not everything in the world is related to everything else.

Another critical step of Hillier's, adjusting the field irregularity by inserting adjustable iron screws, involves an expansion of the problem space. That expansion comes by way of a linking heuristic: What will distort or shape an electromagnetic field? Now anything that will do this is fair game, and a piece of iron will serve nicely.

The lessons? In the absence of better information, assume that variables are independent in order to reduce the search space. When an effect like distortion occurs, form links to a broader search space to finding nulling methods. On the social front, look for long-term evaluative trends like the ever-increasing power of optical microscopes that seem to hit a wall—here the wavelength of light. When that happens expand the problem space again by hopping to another principle of "seeing" like that afforded by the much smaller wavelength of electrons.

Any woman who has had the anxiety-provoking experience of a mammographic exam or a prenatal examination with ultrasound has been affected by an invention of John Wild's. Ultrasound is an important technology in modern medicine. The idea found its origins in Wild's surgical explorations of bowel problems during World War II in England and a need to develop technical instruments for measuring bowel characteristics. Wild's point of departure was an adaptation of pulse-echo equipment used during the war to detect cracks in armor plate.

The fact that ultrasound's purpose or function can shift so rapidly and so profoundly illustrates a fundamental idea of invention: Deep principles like ultrasound have a reason of their own. No one knows quite what context they will show up in next. On another front, Wild's story also illustrates perhaps more clearly than any other essay in this volume the rollercoaster life and times of the independent inventor. For most of modern invention's history, the inventor has often found himself in litigation; that is certainly true here.

We are all familiar with the idea of an observatory, but this is the story of a different kind of observatory, one underground. James Teeri discusses the development of the Soil Biotron, designed to study organic and inorganic processes below the surface of the soil. Historically, the soil has been rather ignored; but recent research discloses that processes in the soil have an enormous influence on our world above the soil. Here, as in many earlier innovations in science and technology, the right instrument can make all the difference.

To some, the biotron may not seem like an invention; it is just a central place for a number of instruments. But when these instruments come together as building blocks and do their complementary work with their assembly of diverse and mutually supporting expertise, we see a scientific instrument of the highest integration and order. The logic of invention for the biotron is like that of the Swiss Army knife carried to extremes: Put together a package of diverse capability; by doing so, new and emergent capabilities are realized that are well beyond the capacities of the individual instruments and experts working in isolation.

Moving to the material world of diamonds, Robert Wentorf, Jr. ironically notes, "It is interesting to contemplate that enduring love between a man and a woman is signified, in the popular view, by a bit of matter which is inherently thermodynamically unstable." Indeed, the instability of diamonds under many conditions turned out to be a principal challenge to overcome in the synthesis of diamond.

Here we see a search with a precisely defined target: create in the laboratory a crystal with all the properties of a natural diamond. In a sense, the search is a backward one, starting with the target or goal and then trying to backtrack to conditions that will reproduce it. The story tells us of great technique and imagination in recreating the pressures and temperatures that exist deep in the earth where natural diamonds are born.

We all know that gasoline comes from crude oil. But what we may not realize is that one can get much more, or less, out of the same amount of crude oil, depending on the process. Edward Rosinski recounts his and a colleague's development of a catalytic technology now used industry wide, a technology that increased the production of gasoline from a barrel of crude oil by 30 percent.

Along the way, Rosinski gives us a wonderful metaphor for breaking a long petroleum molecule into more useful parts. It's like trapping a snake's head in a rat hole, he says, so you can cut it into parts. The metaphors of our inventors often suggest informal but powerful models to guide the search process through large spaces of possible manipulation and reaction.

The fibers that clothe us differ dramatically from those that covered our ancestors. Paul Morgan reveals important episodes of invention surrounding his and co-workers' development of some contemporary synthetic fibers, descendants of the familiar nylon and Orlon. The process involved not only moments of invention but systematic efforts to probe the molecular mechanisms underlying different fiber properties, as a basis for developing desirable characteristics. One of the fibers, Kevlar, has properties quite distinct from any natural fiber. It is now used for bullet-resistant vests and high-impact environments. Pound for pound, Kevlar is much stronger than steel.

An important lesson here is that the target of a search can vary greatly in specificity. It may be very defined, such as producing a synthetic silk or wool, or very open-ended, such as looking for longer and stronger molecules, with specific applications to come later.

William Campbell recounts the development of the drug ivermectin, used worldwide in keeping cattle healthy and in preventing river blindness, a tropical disease that causes human blindness on a massive scale. You may be familiar with it if you have administered medication to the family dog for the prevention or control of heart worms. Ivermectin's development involved a striking mix of persistent systematic screening, punctuated by key moments where new lines of inquiry emerged.

The story of ivermectin is once more a search for a target that is not too specific, a biologically active product of a bacterium that has the capability of controlling certain parasites, without our knowing ahead of time much of the target's biochemical properties. Along the way, we see a classic search on a grand scale, one that involved more than 40,000 samples and assays.

5 | Electron Microscopy and Microprobe Analysis: Recalling the Ambience of Some Inventions

JAMES HILLIER

Looking back, the period 1935 to 1945 was a most exciting, even spectacular, decade during which a remarkably small group of researchers, scattered throughout Europe and North America, took the magnetic transmission electron microscope (TEM) from a rather quiescent, theoretical concept to a reasonably reliable, practical instrument in serial production. In that decade the same group took the resolving power of the TEM from a doubtful comparison with a light microscope to a value that was routinely 20-fold beyond the limit of the light microscope and, in the hands of experts, 200-fold beyond! It was also in that decade that the electron microprobe analyzer was invented.

In this chapter, I describe the background and environment of two of my own "inventions" and one of another inventor, concluding with some observations derived from this inventive experience and from twenty-five years of managing a large group of professional inventors. Although related, the three inventions would be classified in three quite different categories. The first represents a step-function in the slow and tedious development of a scientific instrument—the transmission electron microscope. The second represents a solution to a major problem associated with the use of the electron microscope. It initiated a completely new series of scientific instruments. The third is an example of the result of a creative individual exploiting his experience in one field (high-energy physics) to make a major breakthrough in another (high-resolution scanning transmission electron microscope, or STEM).

It is interesting to ask why the TEM came into being in the particular decade 1935–1945. The correspondence between the refraction of light rays and the action of fields of force on particles had been elucidated by Hamilton back in 1830 (Conway & Synge, 1931), long before the discovery of the electron. The wave nature of the electron and its small wavelength had been understood for several years (de Broglie, 1924). The theoretical concept of an electron microscope that was the analogue of a light microscope, but with a much greater resolving power, was quite well established by 1930 (Figure 5.1).[1] Without question, Knoll and Ruska (1932) were the first to attempt the construction of an electronic analogue of the light microscope.[2]

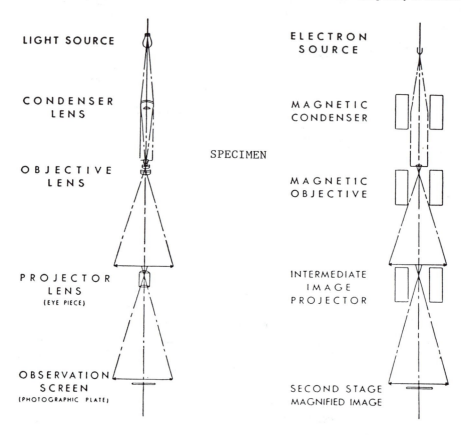

FIGURE 5.1. A comparison between the optical diagrams of light and electron microscopes.

Incidentally, it is interesting that none of the active workers in the field ever claimed to have *invented* the electron microscope.

My answer to the question is that our technological infrastructure appears to be the most significant controlling factor in the *timing* of the transition from a concept to a practical device. This also leads to a conclusion that the person given credit for an invention is determined almost entirely by chance. Certainly, in my own experience with the TEM and microprobe analysis I have two good examples of these points.

I grew up in an environment that was a strange mixture of engineers, craftsmen, and artists. Although I built microscopes, telescopes, and model airplanes as a youngster, I was completely dedicated to becoming a commercial artist. A chance encounter with a high-school geography teacher caused a major shift in my career. He directed my interest to electronics through "ham" radio and engineered a scholarship that practically forced me to go into mathematics and physics in college.

Electron Microscopy

In the early spring of 1937, I was a senior getting ready to graduate from the University of Toronto. In a discussion about my future, the assistant chairman of the physics department mentioned the electron microscope, in which, it appeared, the chairman of the department had some interest. Possibly because of my childhood interests or possibly because I had never heard the words *electron* and *microscope* in the same sentence before, I was immediately intrigued. Thus for a second time, a chance encounter realigned my career.

I did a lot of reading that summer. In the fall I was joined by Al Prebus, another graduate student. We got some practical experience by rejuvenating a couple of emission-type electron microscopes that had been built by another graduate student. By the end of 1937 we had reached the conclusion that the only way we could achieve resolving power better than that of a light microscope was to construct a high-voltage, magnetic transmission instrument similar to one that Knoll and Ruska had described in 1932. Implicit in this decision was our expectation that the technology available to us was adequate for the task or, if not, was close enough so it could be extended.

We spent the Christmas break designing our first instrument. Looking back, I am still amazed. We designed the column and did all the critical drafting in a few eighteen-hour days. Although we made mistakes, it is remarkable that around 80 percent of the design was never changed.

Over the years since then, I have always been impressed by the wisdom of the chairman and assistant chairman of the department in letting two very young, very brash, and zealous graduates undertake such a major project on their own. Remember, at the beginning of 1938, Canada, like the United States, was still in the throes of the Great Depression and the department was seriously strapped for funds. The chairman and his assistant were faced with a Hobson's choice. Should they try to support a large project in an impossibly austere environment, or should they risk deflating two enthusiastic graduate students who might just be bright enough to make a breakthrough? It is to their credit that they approved the project, even though they made it clear that, for the most part, we would have to shift for ourselves.

As an aside, I'd like to point out that the only assistance available to us was the part-time efforts of a glassblower, and a machinist, who was the most recent addition to the machine shop. Fred, the latter, was a willing newcomer whose previous employment was in a locomotive repair shop! He was a delight at the precision machining of very large pieces, but anything that had more than one part per inch completely confounded him. That shook us up but, actually, was one of the more fortunate things that happened to us. Prebus and I quickly realized that if the delicate parts of our instrument were going to be made, we would have to do it ourselves. We did. In later years, for me at least, that experience was invaluable. The many late hours I spent in the machine shop paid off handsomely. They gave me both the ability to communicate with instrument makers and machinists and the experience to screen out the impractical from my designs. Another chance encounter!

That first instrument was a stack of lenses, tubes, a camera, an object chamber, and an electron gun (Figure 5.2). Each piece could be aligned by sliding it transversely relative to the group of segments below it. These junctions were made vacuum tight by very carefully hand-lapping the sliding surfaces and sealing them with a grease that we concocted ourselves by spending many hours stirring pure gum rubber into melted petroleum jelly!

Our electrical components were very primitive. The current supply to our lenses was simply a well-charged group of automobile batteries connected through large, laboratory, sliding variable resistors. We did have a circuit that gave us coarse, fine, and very fine adjustments. We also, very fortunately, had designed water cooling into our lens coil structures so that we could reduce the thermal variations. However these structures took long periods to stabilize. Our high-voltage supply was an unbelievable concoction of parts that we scrounged from various nooks and crannies around the physics department. The only place you could possibly see anything comparable today would be in a very old Frankenstein movie. Miraculously, it worked, although not very well. The instrument showed promise, and because it did support began to dribble in from various interested organizations.

In today's world, it would seem incomprehensible that, in the middle of the 1930s, a few individuals would put enormous effort into the development of a high-resolution electron microscope when the only type of specimen they were sure they could examine was no more exotic than the cutting edge of a razor blade. It was generally assumed that the electron intensity required to make a highly magnified image useful would immediately destroy any but the most refractory specimen. Obviously, our dedication had to be related to the basic challenge of achieving increased resolving power, rather than the ultimate utility of the instrument. About the time in mid-1938 when we began to get some promising pictures, we became aware of a study demonstrating that a film of collodion suspended across a small aperture could be made so thin that very little of the electron energy would be absorbed, thus allowing the film to remain cool. This device immediately became the counterpart of the light microscope slide, opening up the entire field of very fine particles—pigments, colloids, bacteria, viruses, and so on—to electron microscopy.

As we refined the Toronto instrument and our useful pictures became more frequent (Prebus & Hillier, 1939), our reputation began to spread and we had more and more requests for micrographs of materials of interest from an ever-widening spectrum of organizations. It became obvious that a single, homemade, "string and sealing wax" instrument in a university laboratory could not possibly meet the demand. As a result, in February 1940 I found myself at RCA designing a commercial version of the Toronto instrument. I also learned rapidly that the technological infrastructure in the electronics industry was coming together rapidly and was a quantum jump ahead of what we had in the university.

Suddenly we had 50-liter per second oil diffusion pumps, instead of fractional-liter, mercury pumps, and continuously reading electronic vacuum gauges instead of McLeod gauges. We could achieve rapid demountability with synthetic rubber

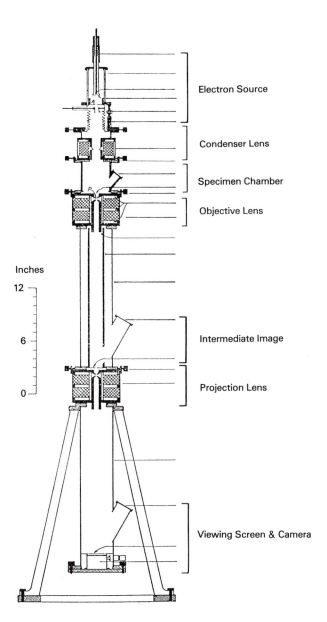

Inches

12

6

0

Electron Source

Condenser Lens

Specimen Chamber

Objective Lens

Intermediate Image

Projection Lens

Viewing Screen & Camera

FIGURE 5.2. A simplified cross section of the Toronto electron microscope drawn to scale. (From Prebub & Hillier, 1939, with permission.)

gaskets and O-rings instead of ground grease joints. We had vacuum-tight flexible metal bellows that gave us new freedom in designing means of manipulating within a vacuum chamber.

On the electrical side, we moved into the electronics age with the newly developed, precision, self-regulating, high-voltage supplies, and similarly, regulated-current supplies that completely eliminated the need for cooling the lens coils (Figure 5.3).

All of these, and other developments, speeded our work by at least an order of magnitude, possibly much more. If you think about that for a moment, you begin to realize that such numbers practically guarantee the historical coincidence of the development of enabling technology and the emergence of a major new development.

The Electron Microscope Matures

Although in 1940 the technological infrastructure that supported the design and construction of TEMs was becoming available, we were still almost two orders of

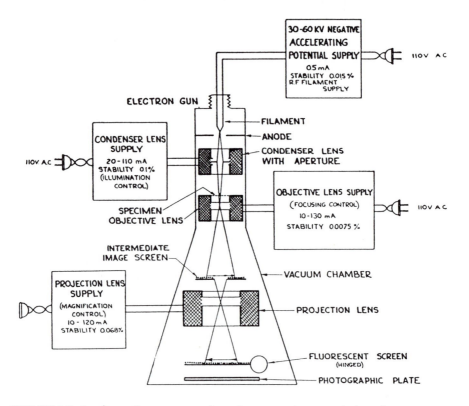

FIGURE 5.3. A schematic representation of a magnetic transmission electron microscope circa 1941.

magnitude from the theoretical limit of our specific design. Unfortunately, the instrumentation needed to analyze the performance of the then-current TEMs at their limits did not exist. Before 1940, few of us appreciated how many external and internal factors were capable of disturbing the TEM image, or of the sensitivity of the image to those factors. Ultimately, the microscope itself, being the only device with sufficient sensitivity, had to become the means for detecting and measuring the effects of the myriads of technical problems that existed in the early instruments. The read-out was, of course, the nature and degree of blurring of the recorded image. Because of the low intensity of the visual images in those days, the necessary sensitivity was achievable only in the recorded image and not in real time. Not only was the read-out very ambiguous, but it related to only those disturbances that happened to occur during the exposure interval and for which we had no independent means of sensing. For example, the effect of a thermal drift of the specimen, which represented a real physical movement of the specimen during the exposure, was indistinguishable from the motion of the image caused by an insulating particle of material, situated near the beam path, that was collecting scattered electrons and becoming charged to sufficient potential to deflect the beam slowly during the exposure. Similarly, the effect of a transient mechanical vibration that happened to occur during the exposure could be indistinguishable from the effect of a small transverse AC magnetic field that had leaked into the path of the beam. In addition, it took a very experienced eye to distinguish between these two sets of examples.

Thus, the development and refinement of the TEM became an unending repetitive series of proposed hypotheses, followed by the designing of experimental tests and then by the actual tests. Because of the variability of many of the defects, their large number, and the absence of real-time observations, the successful identification and removal of a single defect rarely gave an unequivocal signal that anything had been accomplished. However, there is another side to this coin. This same variability prevented the process from becoming completely discouraging. As we were struggling to achieve consistent results at, say, 10 nanometers resolution, making thousands of exposures, there was always the unusual exposure that was several times better. These were the teasers that kept telling us it could be done and gave us the incentive to keep trying.

It is interesting to note that by 1945 the number of defects still present had been whittled down to the point where identifying and removing the remaining ones became relatively simple. As a result, some spectacular improvements in resolving power were made quickly and easily. It was this phenomenon that allowed the implicit asymmetry of the magnetic objective to emerge from the masking effects of other problems and to be corrected by the development of the stigmator; the first of the "inventions" I want to discuss.

Breakthrough 1

It has to be appreciated that the magnetic field, suspended in space between the polepieces that produce it, comprises the critical electron objective lens (Figure 5.4). Using very small round holes in a collodion membrane as our test objects, it became clear we had some asymmetry in the magnetic field of our objective lens and that

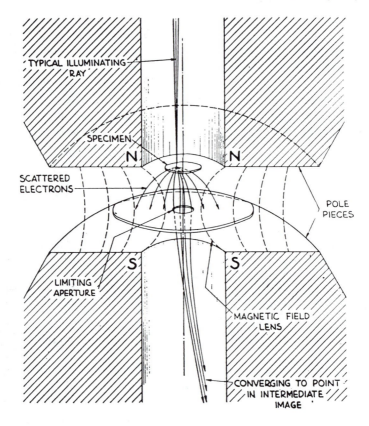

FIGURE 5.4. A close-up schematic representation of the formation, by a magnetic lens, of the image of a single point of the specimen.

asymmetry was a relatively constant characteristic of each set of objective pole-pieces. Obvious assumptions were that the openings of the two polepieces were not round or their alignment was imprecise. We tried lapping the openings in the assembled polepieces with interesting results. Sometimes the lens improved, and sometimes it became worse. Because none of the best polepieces was perfect we tried continuing the lapping. We were surprised to find that, ultimately, the contin-ued lapping always made the lens worse. We began to realize that the asymmetry was due to the relative coarseness of the grain structure of the iron and, frequently, to nonmagnetic inclusions in the iron, probably close to the lens opening. We then went through the exercise of searching for better iron and better annealing pro-cesses. This led only to frustration.

Then came the "eureka." Late one night, my subconscious suddenly made me aware of what immediately became obvious: If crystal structure and impurities were responsible for the distortions of the lens field, why not deliberately introduce a controllable distortion that could be adjusted to counteract the existing distor-tion? Early the next morning I had my machinist make some soft iron screws out of, believe it or not, ordinary welding rod. He then threaded eight of them equally spaced around the polepiece spacer so that they were all pointed at the axis of the lens and could be adjusted in or out (Figure 5.5). It took a few hours to learn how to adjust the screws. Nevertheless, within eighteen hours from the time the idea germinated, we were getting *consistent* results that were better than the average for the day before by a factor of 10 (Hillier & Ramberg, 1947). Economically, it meant that every lens manufactured could be made acceptable instead of a very small percentage. This was the largest step-function improvement that ever occurred in the development of the electron microscope. In the forty-plus years since then, through

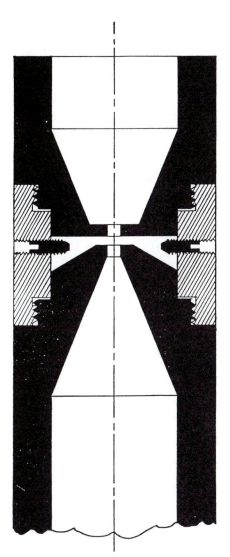

FIGURE 5.5. A scale drawing of the cross section of a magnetic objective provided with screws for correcting lens asymmetries. (From Hillier & Ramberg, 1947, with permission.)

a long series of small incremental improvements, the resolving power of the transmission electron microscope has been improved by an additional factor of only 5.

Interestingly, my reaction to this breakthrough was primarily elation at finally having a solid solution to a persistent problem, but strongly tempered by self-criticism for my stupidity in not having recognized much sooner that I was dealing with the electronic analogue of astigmatism. It was not until the RCA patent department requested a disclosure that the development began to take on the character of an invention (Hillier, 1948).

Although the basic concept of the lens compensation was good, we quickly realized that our implementation was of limited value. This was primarily because our static method of correction was valid for only one field strength in the lens. Because operators often want to use different focal lengths in the objective or different accelerating voltages for the electrons, they ran into a problem. Each set-up required a different compensation. The development engineers quickly solved the problem by introducing a segmented electrostatic lens in the magnetic objective lens field. By adjusting the voltages on the segments it became possible to rotate the axis of correction and its strength. Thus, with good records, an operator could easily compensate the objective for any configuration of his or her system.

I have emphasized in this section the enormous amount of tedious effort that brought the electron microscope into being as a most useful tool for science and technology. Because most of this effort had little, if anything, to do with the basic theory of the electron microscope, very little was ever published. Some form of accepted scientific snobbery, of which I was as guilty as anyone, was at work. Although there was much word-of-mouth exchange of information among the early workers, I feel that our behavior condemned many newcomers, domestically and in particular internationally, to repeat most of our research and many, if not all, of our mistakes.

Electron Microprobe Analysis

In spite of the problems, the TEM did begin to be useful and started providing essential information to an expanding universe of research disciplines, sometimes in spectacular and unexpected ways. Even so, the information the TEM provided was strictly limited to the geometrical structure of the specimen as revealed by differences, sometimes very subtle, in the electron scattering of the different points of the specimen. As soon as the TEM began revealing complex structures, particularly in biological specimens where chemical behavior is the name of the game, it became very obvious that we had to devise some means of determining the point-by-point chemical analysis of those structures. Unfortunately, electron scattering is a very poor indicator of the chemical structure of the specimen. In the very thin specimen it became useless because of the three-way ambiguity among scattering cross-section of the atoms, the thickness of the specimen, and the Fresnel diffraction effects. Staining with heavy metal compounds became useful for enhancing the contrast in images of organic materials. Unfortunately, such stains had very little of the specificity possessed by the stains that became so useful in light microscopy. Any specificity they might have demonstrated would have been of little value. The lack of any counterpart of color in the TEM would have left them the victims of the ambiguities mentioned above.

There was a flurry of activity in our laboratory to explore the potential of electron diffraction as a means of identifying the chemical composition of individual small particles and structures. The effort fizzled rather quickly for a number of technical and physical reasons that are not relevant to this discussion.

While the diffraction approach was not successful, the research did have a payoff. We acquired invaluable experience in the design and operation of an electron probe type of instrument even though, by today's standards, the probe system we had used in the electron diffraction experiments was very primitive (see Figure 5.6). The probe was simply a greatly reduced image of the electron source produced by "running an electron microscope backward." When the probe was focused so that the image of the source was a very small distance from a thin-film specimen, it would cast a magnified shadow of the specimen that could be viewed on a fluorescent screen. The principle was exactly the same as holding one's hand near a candle and getting an enlarged shadow on the wall. The shadow image was magnified by the ratio of the probe–screen distance to the probe–specimen distance, and had unexpectedly good resolution. As the probe was moved closer to the specimen, the magnification rapidly increased, becoming infinite when the probe coincided with the specimen. The point of the image that was observed to expand until it covered the entire field was the point of the specimen being bombarded by the probe. It was somewhat cumbersome but it did enable the operator to select the precise point in the specimen that he or she wanted to analyze.

Breakthrough 2

Sometime around the beginning of 1943, I was browsing in the library and ran across an article by G. Ruthemann (1942) in *Naturwissenschaften,* which is the German counterpart of the British publication *Nature.* Ruthemann had investigated the distribution of electron velocities in the electrons transmitted by thin films of collodion. He showed that the discrete energy losses caused by the excitation of the K-levels of carbon, nitrogen, and oxygen produced observable peaks in the velocity distribution of all the electrons that experienced inelastic collisions.

Let me translate that into experiences without the physics jargon. Many of you know that the X-ray tube that your dentist or doctor uses to look at your teeth or your chest is simply an electron tube in which a high-voltage beam of electrons bombards a target. The electron bombardment causes some of the atoms in the target to absorb energy and thus to be raised to an unstable excited state. Very shortly thereafter the excited atoms return to their normal state. In so doing the absorbed energy is emitted as quanta of radiation, some of which will be X-rays. What is not as well known is that each different type of atom in the target will emit X-rays with a specific set of wavelengths.

Ruthemann was interested in proving that the energy an electron lost when it caused the production of a quantum of X-rays was equal to the energy the quantum of X-rays contained. He could not do the experiment with an ordinary X-ray tube

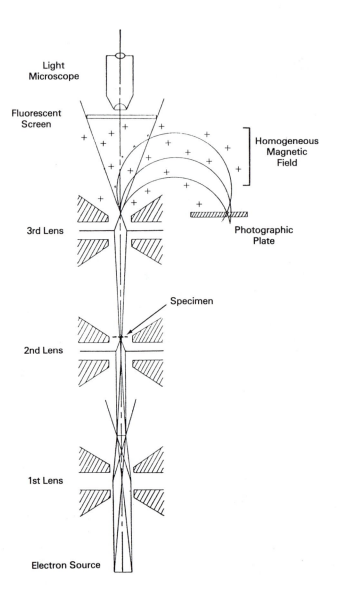

Light
Microscope

Fluorescent
Screen

Homogeneous
Magnetic
Field

3rd Lens

Photographic
Plate

Specimen

2nd Lens

1st Lens

Electron Source

FIGURE 5.6. A ray diagram of the electron microprobe analyzer. The specimen was placed immediately above the second lens close to the position of minimum beam cross section. (From Hillier & Baker, 1944, with permission.)

because the electrons were trapped in the material of the target and he could not measure them. That led him to the very bright idea of using an extremely thin film as the target. He made the target so thin that the electrons did not have an opportunity to interact with more than one atom as they went through. He then measured the energy distribution of the transmitted electrons. As expected, he found a large number of the electrons had lost precisely the amounts of energy that were contained in the quanta of X-rays emitted by the atoms in the target.

Reading that article was an interesting experience in how the human mind works. Ruthemann was interested only in the basic physics, and his article contained no reference to using the observations as a means of analysis. Essentially instantaneously, my brain signaled me that my probe instruments could do the same experiment on a specific point of a specimen and thus, on the basis of my understanding of X-ray physics, I could use the phenomenon for microanalysis. What is even more remarkable is that, in the same instant, essentially the complete design of our first instrument popped into my mind (Hillier, 1943; Hillier, 1945; Hillier & Baker, 1944)! While patent attorneys will quote this as a good example of what they mean when they talk about a "flash of genius" or a "flash of inspiration" and use it to evaluate patentability, I believe that their expression greatly oversimplifies the invention process.

My analysis of the ingredients of this example, in order of importance, is as follows:

1. A long-standing high-priority problem (point-by-point chemical analysis of complex TEM specimens) that had been put on the "back burner".
2. A thorough knowledge of electron probe instrumentation.
3. A good general knowledge of the physics of X-rays acquired as an undergraduate (several years earlier).
4. Some understanding of the methods of measuring the energy distribution in electron beams.
5. An intense interest in any information relating to the interaction of electrons and materials.
6. An element of curiosity coupled with a desire to add to a broad data base.
7. An element of chance in the encounter, but in a situation with very favorable odds.

We quickly constructed a 180-degree magnetic electron spectrometer that we added to one of the probe instruments used in our diffraction experiments. We confirmed Ruthemann's results using much higher voltage electrons and even extended them to some other light elements. We were of course aware that the characteristic X-rays were being produced from the point of the specimen being bombarded by the probe. As a result, we did some work with a crystal X-ray spectrometer in an attempt to detect them. We were able to confirm the theory, but the intensity of the X-rays available was too low to make this approach to microanalysis practical. All of this was good research that we pursued very enthusiastically. Unfortunately, our enthusiasm began to wane as we began to realize that our concepts were running far ahead of the technologies that would be required for their routine application.

Out of many problems, three were particularly intractable. The most annoying was the rapid buildup of contamination when the probe was focused on the specimen. This problem was due to the very-high-intensity electron probe interacting with the residual molecules of organic material in the vacuum of the instrument. As a result, when we tried to analyze a really small particle, the buildup of contamination caused the specimen to become opaque in less time than was required for an adequate photographic exposure to record the spectrum.

The second problem was the cumbersome nature of the state-of-the-art techniques for making quantitative measurements of the X-ray or electron intensities from photographic exposures. Any one who has gone through the exercise of calibrating the exposure on a photographic emulsion, standardizing the development of the photographic material, and then running it through a recording microphotometer will appreciate this. Moreover, to cap it off, all that technology was essentially invalidated by the fact that the situation was rapidly changing during the exposure, as a result of the contamination problem. The third problem was the nature of our probe system already described. It could become very tedious in a routine use.

It was almost three decades before all the necessary technologies came together to make microprobe analysis reasonably practical by either electron energy loss or by emitted X-ray spectra. These technologies involved some major developments such as very-high-resolution scanning transmission electron microscopes; very small, fast, and inexpensive computers; a broad range of very sensitive sensors for direct detection and measurement of X-ray or electron intensities; and finally, the development of instruments with ultra-high vacuum systems. The stories of those developments are exciting but are too complicated and too long for this talk. In any case, they should be told by the individuals involved.

This past July I had the opportunity to attend a conference on microprobe analysis in Asheville, North Carolina. I was impressed by the fact that over 300 workers active in the field presented papers to a considerably larger audience—reasonable evidence that the technique has come of age.

Breakthrough 3

I would like to describe very briefly one of these developments as an example of what can happen when a creative individual from one field happens to switch to another field.

As the resolving power of the electron microscope improved and it could image smaller and smaller structures, we had to make the specimens thinner and thinner. The often-overlooked reason for this is that too many superimposed layers of fine structures make it impossible to interpret the images. As the specimens were made thinner, the contrast in the images decreased because fewer of the electrons were scattered out of the beam. Thus, while the instrument could resolve the smallest structures, the reduced contrast made them impossible to see. We recognized the problem and also understood that we could solve the problem by cutting out the directly transmitted beam and using only the scattered electrons to form the images. This was the counterpart of what is known as "dark field imaging" in light microscopy. In my day, the idea was sound but completely beyond our technology.

Albert Crewe, a high-energy physicist working at the University of Chicago, became involved with high-voltage and high-resolving-power electron microscopy in the early 1970s. The basic culture of high-energy physics is to avoid the main beam and derive all the useful information from the scattered particles. It was completely natural for Crewe to apply that principle to the electron microscope. That led him into scanning electron microscopy, where the beam that scanned the specimen could be produced under ideal conditions with maximum resolving power, while the image signal (the scattered electrons) did not become involved with any lenses.

Thus, while Crewe did not increase the resolving power of electron lenses, he did improve the *useful* resolving power of the instrument by somewhat more than a factor of 2. As a result of his work it became possible, for the first time, to show images of single atoms (Crewe et al., 1975).

Two points should be noted with regard to this development: First, working with the technical culture with which he was comfortable, Crewe recognized and utilized the advantage he had. Second, at the time he became interested, the technology he needed to achieve success was in hand.

Some Personal Conclusions on the Inventive Process

The foregoing covers the first sixteen years of my professional career when I was completely dedicated to the technical development of the electron microscope and its applications. During this period I might have been classed as an "inventor." Those sixteen years have been followed by thirty-six years of involvement in the management of large numbers of professional "inventors," including fifteen years as the hands-on head of RCA's central corporate research laboratory (300 professional inventors), ten years as the functional head of all RCA's research and engineering (5000 professionals), and eleven years of consulting on the management of R&D. During these years, RCA made many important breakthroughs. (Unfortunately, the company was not nearly as successful in translating such inventions into viable businesses.) While I was involved in a great variety of technical developments, the central theme of all of them was the communication and processing of information.

Although my professional activities have dealt largely, but far from exclusively, with technically creative individuals, my personal life has been very much involved with very creative people in many other fields. Because of this broader experience I have come to believe that creativity is a variable but general characteristic and that the inventive mind, particularly the technically inventive mind, is just a special case.

For the purposes of this discussion I shall depart from conventional wisdom and consider the brain to be the equivalent of a very competent work station connected to the analogue of a very large and very sophisticated mainframe—the human computer that is distributed throughout the body. At birth this mainframe is delivered with all its programs operative, taking care of all the chemical, electrical, and mechanical activities necessary for the survival and growth of the body. It is also delivered fully connected to the brain work station, which is to be its interface with the outside world. The brain work station is delivered with a set of very-high-capacity parallel sensors for sight, hearing, touch, taste, and smell, fully connected and ready to feed information to a very large blank memory bank somewhat analogous to the RAM on a PC. It also is delivered with a mysterious, almost blank memory bank, which has a few programs essential for survival but otherwise is ready to be filled with learned programs. This memory bank is already connected, through the mainframe, to all the millions of muscle fibers in the body that constitute the *only* means the body has for communicating to the outside world. It is important to note that, of the astronomical amounts of information processing that must go on in the human body, we are conscious of only the input data, the output results, and the manipulations of certain data we intentionally recall from our memory (the RAM part).

At the time of delivery, the learned program part of the brain has a few instructions that are already active. These are obviously inherited and pertain to survival. They are the primitive beginnings of a program that I shall call "Judgment Call". The continuous flow of packets of input data from our senses is passed by Judgment Call for appraisal and initiation of action if necessary. Each packet is tagged "life threatening" to "safe," "good" to "bad," "pleasing" to "displeasing," or "I'm not sure." At first our reactions to these judgments are instinctive. We recoil from too hot, too sharp, too bright, and so on. Hunger pains stimulate crying, and an offered nipple stimulates sucking—a remarkably complex muscular activity. As time proceeds our Judgment Call program expands as a result of our interaction with our environment. As language develops and we can communicate with other brains, our development accelerates, and Judgment Call expands further to include judgments acquired from them. Through all this, the "I'm not sure" cases are stored in memory until they are resolved or pushed lower and lower in the memory priority. As development of the individual proceeds, judgments of validity and value are added to Judgment Call, and so on. Of course, concurrently, many learned programs—physical or mechanical skills, language skills, mathematical skills—are developed and retained in that part of our memory. Let me move one notch further and assume that the brain was delivered with the beginnings of one other special program in its learned program memory. I'll name it "What If." This is a quite different program. It continually surveys all the data in memory as well as the incoming data, it continually tries different organizations of those data; and it continually uses the data to construct simulated real-world situations. It passes each operation through Judgment Call for evaluation, particularly with regard to validity and value. In the combination of What If and Judgment Call we have the fundamental mechanism for creativity. In this model, the speed of the brain in processing data and the data base available in the environment in which it is embedded, are the major controlling factors of an individual's level of creativity.

A faster processing speed enables the individual to accumulate a broader and deeper data base in a given time and, therefore, provides a higher probability of yielding specific data that might be desired. It also enables the individual to recover needed data faster. Finally, it provides a higher speed of massaging the data in the What If mode. Thus, an increase in the speed of processing data provides a much greater increase in the probability that the What If activity will yield a novel concept or an answer to a problem.

I appreciate that I have indulged in postulating some simplistic hypotheses. However, my conviction that they are worth further consideration comes from the remarkable consistency between the conclusions that can be drawn from these hypotheses and the conclusions drawn directly from my experience.

Here are my conclusions:

1. Creativity is based on a "What If" activity of the brain working in cooperation with a developed judgment.

2. The maximum level of creativity that an individual can possess is determined by the speed with which his or her brain can process data.

3. The individual's speed of processing data is probably an inherited characteristic.

4. The breadth and depth of the data base actually acquired also depends, in a very large part, on the specific data available in the environment in which the individual has been embedded since birth.

5. The field to which an individual's creativity is directed is dependent on the nature of the data base supplied by his or her environment.

6. The way in which "What If" functions is also probably influenced to some extent by adaptation to factors in the environment.

7. The important role of chance in all aspects of individual creativity must not be overlooked.

In other words, I am suggesting that a capability of high-speed processing of data could be the *single* inherited factor that is a necessary, *but not sufficient,* attribute of a highly creative mind. The second necessary (but also not sufficient) attribute is an environment that is rich in data, both in depth and breadth, and that puts a premium on novel concepts, the solving of problems, and the resolving of inconsistencies. Finally, there is the very important role of pure chance, in heredity; in the character of the environment in which the individual finds himself or herself; and in the chance encounters and events that occur during the development of the individual in that environment.[3]

My final thought is that if I were 50 years younger and embarking on a study of creativity, I would definitely attempt to find a way of determining the speed with which the brain processes data and of correlating the results with different demonstrated levels of creativity and the richness of the environment.

Notes

1. The limit of the resolving power of any microscope is set by the wavelength of the radiation used. Because the wavelength of high-voltage electrons could be as short as 1/100,000th of the wavelength of visible light waves, it was anticipated that an electron microscope should be able to image much smaller objects than was possible with a light microscope.

2. For a number of different views of the history of the electron microscope, see the collection of articles by several of the early workers in the field: Peter W. Hawkes (Ed.), (1985), *The Beginnings of Electron Microscopy. Advances in Electronics and Electron Physics, Sup-*

plement 16, New York, Academic Press. See also Reisner, J. H., (1989), An early history of the electron microscope in the United States. In *Advances in Electronics and Electron Physics, Vol. 73,* New York, Academic Press.

3. Permissiveness in our education system, coupled with overemphasis on self-determination by our young people, tends to increase the significance of pure chance in the development of creativity. This raises a question regarding whether America can afford the luxury of having its worldwide competitive position in the technological future so dependent on chance and whether its elementary and high school curricula should contain some required subjects that would assure the emergence of greater numbers of technically creative individuals.

References

Conway, A. E. & Synge, J. L. (Eds.). (1931). *The Mathematical Papers of Sir William Rowan Hamilton. Vol. I.* Cambridge: Cambridge Univ. Press.

Crewe, A. V., Langmore, J. P., & Isaacson, M. S. (1975). In *Physical Aspects of Electron Microscopy and Microbeam Analysis,* B. M. Siegel & D. R. Beaman, Eds. (New York: Wiley), p. 47.

de Broglie, L. (1924). A tentative theory of light quanta. *Philosophical Magazine, 47,* 446–458.

Hillier, J. (1943). On microanalysis by electrons. *Physical Review, 64,* 318–319.

Hillier, J. (1945). Electronic Microanalyzers. *U.S. Patent 2372432*

Hillier, J. (1948). Electron Lens Correcting Devices. *U.S. Patent 2455676.*

Hillier, J. & Baker, R. F. (1944). Microanalysis by means of electrons. *Journal of Applied Physics, 15,* 663–675.

Hillier, J. & Ramberg, E. G. (1947). The magnetic electron microscope objective: Contour phenomenon and the attainment of high resolving power. *Journal of Applied Physics, 18,* 48–71.

Knoll, M. & Ruska, E. (1932). The electron microscope. *Zeitschrift für Physik, 78,* 318–339.

Prebus, A. F. & Hillier, J. (1939). Construction of a magnetic electron microscope of high resolving power. *Canadian Journal of Research, 17,* 49–63.

Ruthemann, G. (1942). *Naturwissenschaften, 30,* 145.

6 | The Origin of Soft-Tissue Ultrasonic Echoing and Early Instrumental Application to Clinical Medicine

JOHN J. WILD

In writing this chapter, intended to convey my motivations and my own peculiar attributes that somehow enabled me to make a unique contribution to our body of scientific medical knowledge, I found it necessary to indulge in a great deal of introspection. My path as an investigative clinical scientist has not been easy, in part because of social restrictions imposed on creative individuals who are sometimes characterized as having overinflated egos. I use the word "inflated" advisedly because of society's leveling propensities. I think I must have come into this world with a propensity for making chaos out of order, since I always seem to be upsetting those concerned with maintaining conventional standards of orderliness and humbleness. I have tried to analyze the reasons people become upset when presented with new concepts, even after the concepts have been proved. In my ultrasonic work I have met many people who do not believe the evidence of their own eyes, even when the miracles of pulse-echo ultrasound are demonstrated to them. Because of the interdisciplinary nature of my discoveries, evaluation has presented many difficulties. Montaigne, the great French essayist who lived from 1533 to 1592 observed:

> Whenever a new discovery is reported in the scientific world they say, first, "It is probably not true." Thereafter when the truth of the new proposition has been demonstrated beyond question, they say, "Yes, it may be true, but it is not important." Finally when sufficient time has elapsed to evidence fully its importance they say, "Yes, surely it is important, but it is no longer new."

In thinking over why and how I have been able to produce new concepts and ideas, I know that intuition, curiosity, an ever-inquiring open mind, and an ability to define a problem, discern its core, and assess the probability of solution are important factors. When these are combined with a broad educational background; continuous, life-long general learning; a natural facility in mechanical engineering; single-mindedness of purpose; and the ability for very hard work, provoked by intense interest in a problem that seems to be solvable, some valuable results are inevitable and may even become prolific.

In addition, I have always had a strong disinclination to being lured into intellectually restricted pigeonholes, which would limit an ongoing, lifetime habit of broad acquisition of knowledge and curtail my love of breaking new ground and looking for new associations and inconsistencies. Specialists know more and more about less and less; integrating generalists know a little about more and more.

Preliminary Events

My application of ultrasound to diagnostic medicine originated in a problem I encountered during World War II, during my service as a surgeon in a London hospital that was receiving thousands of civilian buzz-bomb casualties. Some patients appeared to be unharmed except for pernicious distension of the bowel caused by a bomb blast to the abdomen. My surgical colleagues came to consider this condition hopeless, and patients were left to sink or swim with respect to recovery of bowel function. Most of them died from "progressive deterioration," cause unknown. This high mortality rate awakened in me a lifelong interest in the causes of bowel dysfunction. This interest eventually brought me to the United States and the discovery of ultrasonic pulse-echoing by soft tissues, permitting detection and diagnosis of soft-tissue tumors.

In pursuing during the war the cause of death of bowel failure victims, I observed massive retroperitoneal hemorrhage at the back of the abdominal cavity, presumably as a result of the bomb blast. This process interfered with the vessels and nerves servicing the bowel through the mesentery attached to the back of the abdominal cavity and the bowel and resulted in paralysis of bowel function, with subsequent distension.

I reasoned that the clotted blood mass causing the trouble would naturally resolve, as do the "blood blisters" from pinches familiar to most of us. Resolution takes time, in fact several weeks, depending on how severe the hemorrhage. Abdominal radiographs showed the stomach to be compressed against the diaphragm, which in turn was pushed up into the lung compartment (thorax). This compressed the lower lung, which permitted bacterial invasion progressing to bronchopneumonia and death. It seemed to me that I could construct a long tube with enough drainage capacity that it could efficiently empty the bowel progressively from above by continuous suction.

For such a tube I had to find materials within the hospital, since under war conditions there was little hope of finding them elsewhere. Plastic insulation pulled off electric wiring became the tubes. I fabricated balloons from condoms, to be inflated once in the bowel, for migration. I invented a "gravity director head"—a cut-off finger of a surgical glove, partially filled with mercury and tied to the tip of the tube just distal to the balloon and single suction hole (Wild, 1944). Surgical verve enabled me to carry out my novel next step of inflating the flattened stomach to permit the gravity director head to traverse the stomach to its outlet and into the duodenum. This daring process—that is, pumping up a patient already about to burst—came in for a great deal of criticism from my colleagues. My success justified my conviction as to the safety of this procedure and silenced the criticism. There was even a little bonus: after the gravity director head was placed in the duodenum, patients erupted the gas and expressed great relief. They believed that the gas was a naturally occurring belch from their bowel, when in fact it resulted from my pumping of air. I was able to save many lives by constructing and using these tubes in the hospital.

A post-World War II declaration was made by a member of England's socialist government, Mr. Aneurin Bevin, to the effect that medical research would have no place in the new cradle-to-grave national health care system. He considered that enough medical knowledge was available to operate the system. The problem, as far as he was concerned, was to make this knowledge available in a fair and equitable manner to all who needed it. I may have misunderstood his intention but, since I had lost my place on the academic ladder while serving my country, I thought it time to find more fertile fields in which to seek out and solve problems as a clinical investigator, my chosen vocation.

Armed with Cambridge University degrees in natural sciences, which included zoology, physiology, botany, biochemistry and pathology, and in medicine, together with my wartime surgical experience and research on bowel distension, I wrote to Professor O. H. Wangensteen at the University of Minnesota. He came to mind because I was familiar with his book on intestinal obstructions. I inquired whether I could join his staff and resume my clinical studies on bowel distension, a then common postoperative complication of heroic abdominal surgery. Professor Wangensteen granted me a locally sponsored fellowship to work in the department of surgery at the University of Minnesota, and subsequently I was awarded a two-year postgraduate surgical fellowship by the Public Health Service, which in those days was under the Federal Security Agency.

At Minnesota I worked hard day and night: in the operating rooms by day and in the wards by night, resuscitating patients on the receiving end of the department head's heroic surgery. My only reward for this supplementary night work was free meals provided for the night staff, which helped to augment my meager financial resources.

One such patient with postoperative bowel failure was a VIP of Minneapolis Honeywell Regulator Company. On hearing at his bedside my woes concerning the difficulty of getting research materials in small quantities, he offered me the run of the materials acquisition department at Honeywell, and any other assistance I needed. This introduction and its follow-up were instrumental in my meeting the scientific staff of Honeywell.

My remaining on the staff of the surgery department became uncertain at the end of my two-year fellowship. By then I had manufactured my tubes and supervised their use in 250 patients with bowel failure. My report on the results of these intubations showed the undoubted superiority of this treatment, and detailed the questionable extent of "pioneering" abdominal surgical practices in the surgery department. This latter aspect of my report was deemed an "in house" matter. My magnum opus (Wild & Strickler, 1949), as it was called, was buried, over my protests, in the internal archives of the University's department of surgery. I sensed that my unwillingness to compromise scientific protocol made me suspect. I was not atuned to the unwritten rules of presentation of results for professorial approval. Had I adjusted my findings and personal standards in compliance with those rules, a career in the department of surgery might have been in the offing—had I aspired to such a career. As an independent outsider, I realized it was time to prepare for a possible move.

In the application of my bowel study findings, I had run into other difficulties as well. I had trouble convincing my colleagues as to the proper way to treat the three different types of bowel distension I had found in my studies. Each requires a different approach. In one type, as in the London cases, the bowel is, in effect lifeless, thinned and lengthened. Removal of the contents of the 32-foot-long intestinal tract from the stomach downward by continuous suction can take weeks, and detailed medical attention is required the entire time. Surgeons were notoriously impatient and refused to wait, even though patients were no worse from day to day and were gradually improving. They insisted on reoperation, which only made matters worse, giving me more work in helping patients regain the progress they had been making before the ill-advised surgical interference. In another type of distension the bowel wall gets thicker and shorter in length as it produces more propulsive force to try to overcome blockages of the bowel.* I concluded that clinical measurement of bowel wall thickness would enable more accurate diagnosis, leading to avoidance of unhelpful reoperation; in other words, measurement would help differentiate between thin, paralyzed bowel and thick, hypertrophic bowel. In addition, it seemed possible that other instruments to assess bowel function might be devised. I needed some other arrows in my quiver for my impending move.

By this time I had made friends with the research and development staff at Honeywell. I requested a consultation for the purpose of obtaining help in designing instruments that could be swallowed and then used to measure bowel pressure, bowel diameter, and contractile force in the living, functioning bowel so that these dynamic events could be recorded and studied under various clinical conditions. I left the question of bowel wall measurement until last because of my doubts about the possibility and cost of building such equipment.

I already knew about the pulse-echo equipment used during the war to detect cracks in armor plate, from my friendship with Donald Sproule, one of the inventors of this machine. I also knew that the frequency of such equipment was too low to permit resolution of the few millimeters between the inner and outer surfaces of bowel wall (resolution is a function of wavelength, which is a function of frequency). I asked the Honeywell staff whether any higher frequency pulse-echo equipment could be built and was told, "yes, for a price." Their estimate was $100,000. I had stored my idea for ultrasonic bowel wall measurement in my memory bank once more when Dr. Finn Larsen, a physicist who had been eavesdropping on the conversation, inquired if 15-megacycle frequency would be high enough. I worked out the theoretical resolution with him and said, "That looks good enough—so what?" He replied that he knew of a machine nearby operating at 15 megacycles. He then revealed that during World War II he had been involved with the design and testing of a piece of ultrasonic ordnance navigational gear built to train airborne navigators in recognizing radar images over enemy terrain. I said,

---

*A third type of bowel failure occurs in peritonitis where, at various stages of recovery, both obstructive and paralytic bowel failure can occur.

"That's almost as bad as your $100,000 quote, as far as my chances of ever using such military gear for medicine." He replied, "Not so. I will have a word on your behalf with the naval captain in charge of the Wold-Chamberlain Air Base and ask his permission to give you access to the trainer."

When I arrived at the air base and made my request, Captain E. E. Fickling became very enthusiastic. In the spring of 1949 he introduced me to the personnel in charge of the 15-megacycle navigational trainer—Donald Neal, in charge of the machine, and his naval boss Chief Les Moerhle. Donald explained the operation of the machine. It had two modes of readout of information. A one-dimensional *time-amplitude graphical trace presentation* (now called *A-mode*) and a two-dimensional *imaging presentation* (now called *B-mode*). Commercial fault-finding equipment had not needed this radar-imaging mode to find cracks in armor plate of homogeneous composition. The time-amplitude readout mode of the trainer recorded a graph of echo strength or amplitude arising from a baseline (Figure 6.1D) that recorded time in millionths of a second! I marveled at this fact, and took it on faith.

The time-amplitude graphs were recorded on the face of an oscilloscope continuously at a rate to permit viewing by an observer. The graphs could be represented electronically in another manner. The strength or loudness of the echoes could be recorded as spots of varying brightness or intensity according to their strength (Figure 6.1G). When this intensity-modulated display was presented as a vertical time base on the face of the oscilloscope and moved electronically in unison with the searching soundhead over a relief map in the machine, a two-dimensional radar image could be formed (Figure 6.1H). The piezo-electric quartz soundhead, submerged in a water tank, "flew" over a scale relief map of enemy territory, sending ultrasonic pulses and receiving echoes. The water was necessary to "carry" or transmit the sonic energy, which does not travel in air at the high frequency used. At 15-megacycle ultrasonic frequency, distances were scaled down to about 1 inch to a radar mile. Surrounding the water-filled tank were several "television" monitor screens displaying two-dimensional images of the scanned map contours. Navigators could thus learn to familiarize themselves with radar contour images of enemy territory.

I decided that the simple time-amplitude echographical (i.e., A-mode) function of the machine would be perfect for my purpose. The time for delicate negotiation and persuasion had come. Donald Neal presided over his complex radar machine like a mother hen over her eggs. He was against any interference with the working of his equipment by this crazy medical man—from England yet! With help from Les Moerhle, Donald Neal was persuaded that my request to use only the A-mode function of the machine did not involve modifications, and eventually he agreed to point the soundbeam at an accessible corner of the tank to provide a time-amplitude graphical display of anything I wanted to put into the path of the soundbeam.

Now I had the problem of complying with Donald's limited conditions and devising an experiment that would give the required definitive information for detecting small changes in bowel wall thickness. My knowledge of small-bowel structure served me well in the selection of a suitable experimental specimen. Biological imperatives required the nearest possible thing to living bowel. The next morning I visited the animal experimental lab at the University of Minnesota and

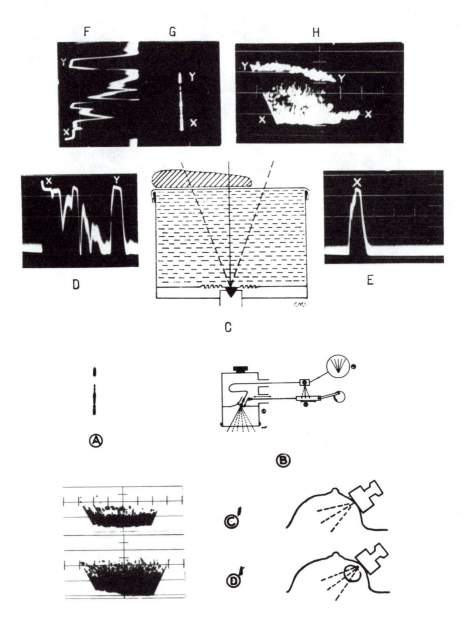

FIGURE 6.1. Representation of a compendium of sector B-mode imaging experiments carried out in the spring and summer of 1951. The B-mode images were in real time and recorded echoes coming from histological structure at 15 megacycles from kidney cortex (H) and from the living, intact breast (D and C). A sectional drawing of the instrument is shown at B and in experimental use at C. The A-mode traces of the kidney tissue are shown at D and F. The time base is horizontal at D and vertical at F. The entry and exist echoes are indicated at X and Y. The intensity-modulated trace of the A-mode trace F is shown at G. Angular motion of this signal mode produced the image at H. The unloaded membrane–air interface is shown at E. The images of a breast cancer (C' and D') visually proved the natural contrast between sonic energy signals coming from the cancer D' compared with the normal breast control C'.

as a surgical staff member removed 6 inches of small bowel from a freshly sacrificed dog. The small bowel is suspended from the back of the abdominal cavity by a sheet of mesentery and is attached along its length at one point of its circumference. The blood and lymphatic vessels and nerves to the small bowel run in the mesentery. As they blend with the bowel wall and pass to the opposite side, the wall thickness gradually lessens imperceptibly as the bulk of the vessels lessens. I made a longitudinal cut along one side of the mesentery and opened the bowel tube, thus forming a sheet of tissue. This sheet was sewn onto a wire frame to form a specimen that was thick at the sides and slightly thinner in the middle. This preparation was taken immediately to the waiting Donald Neal and was submerged in the water in the chosen corner of the naval trainer tank at a distance of 18 inches from the stationary soundbeam. Donald adjusted his controls and announced that he could see two distinct echoes on his A-mode graphical time trace. The distance between these two echoes widened on the time base as the preparation was moved from side to side from its midpoint. This widening on the time base represented distance between the echoes coming from the front and back surfaces of the preparation, and proved that the slight difference in thickness had been detected. Since Donald did not know of the slight thickness difference that he called correctly from his oscilloscope time and time again, the experiment was a success in terms of scientific objectivity. I had found a way to measure the thickness of living intestinal walls for the first time in the history of medical science! My excitement was infectious; from then on Donald became very interested and gave of his spare time and assistance freely.

I was anxious to continue my bowel wall experiments more comfortably on a bench top at a shorter range or distance. This meant construction of a small, self-contained, water-filled chamber. Les Moerhle conducted me to the "morgue," or junk pile, at the navy base and I selected suitable bits and pieces of electronic parts to enable connection with the electronic time-amplitude section of Donald's machine. The Navy had a supply of soundhead parts containing a piezo-quartz crystal plate that produced and received the pulse-echo system. Each cost about $100. With Chief Moerhle's intervention, Donald reluctantly released this part from their stockpile.

Very excited, I rushed home to my quarters in which I had installed a small portable lathe purchased in spite of my meager resources, and I produced the first self-contained "echoscope," so named in analogy with the stethoscope. Whether the soundbeam would emerge from the water column, and whether the chamber could be sealed with a sound-permeable membrane, were the next questions. In other words, would the sound energy coming from the quartz crystal plate get all confused and rattle around inside the chamber and fail to emerge usefully? No help was forthcoming from my technical advisor, Donald. The answers had to come from scientific experiment.

I have since learned how lucky I was in knowing nothing about ultrasonic acoustics. Where ignorance is bliss, it is folly to be wise. When I decided to enclose the soundbeam at a greatly reduced range, I was indeed tempting providence. As it happened, the operation of the air-backed quartz transducer plate was close to acoustical perfection for this application. I had unwittingly operated in the near-field with lots of diffuse backscatter of sonic energy and almost no side lobes.

The water-filled chamber was set up vertically and filled with tap water to the top. Layers of fresh dog bowel were placed in contact with the water. With range adjustment it became possible to obtain definitive echoes from one, two, and three layers of the bowel. Through-transmission of the soundbeam was confirmed by placing a small sheet of metal on top of the bowel and observing the disappearance of its echo on removal. I found that tiny air bubbles were being released from the tap water and obscuring the echoes, so sensitive was the equipment. Henceforth, boiled distilled water was used to transmit the sonic beam in the chamber. It only remained to seal the chamber with a membrane permeable to sonic energy. Since I had in mind introducing a soundhead into the bowel clinically to measure and follow changes in thickness of bowel wall, a special rubber latex balloon would have to be inflated with water after introduction. I made a pilgrimage to Akron, Ohio, to learn the then arcane art of latex balloon dipping, having been first sworn to technical secrecy. Condom-thin rubber worked marvelously and did not affect the layered dog bowel experiments when repeated with the membrane in place. Thus I had succeeded in my objective of measuring thickness changes in fresh dog bowel and had convincing photographic records that it would be possible to carry out measurements clinically.

Proof of Echo-Reflection by Soft Tissues

At this time Donald requested a standard biological specimen with which to adjust his equipment quickly from its normal training range in the tank to that of my experimental echoscope. My response was to carry out a series of experiments, coincidentally proving sonic reflection by both gross anatomical and histological tissue structure. No such proofs had been recorded in the literature to that time: sound scientific procedure required experimental proof of an a priori assumption that soft tissue reflected ultrasound. The need for a biological standard turned out to be the acorn from which the mighty tree of diagnostic pulse-echo ultrasound grew.

Fresh beef muscle was cut and sliced into small sections of various thickness and placed on the echoscope. As a biologist I was amazed at the myriads of echoes coming from the meat. As a physician I immediately realized the significance of the tissue echoing—a new noninvasive medical tool had been found. Better yet, a new vacant field lay before me, challenging my skills. By trial and error, I confirmed through-transmission by resting a sheet of metal on top of the specimens and identifying the echo from the metal–air interface by its disappearance on removal. I found that the sound beam traversed a much greater thickness of structural fat than of beef muscle. Beef structural fat returned almost no echoes compared with beef muscle at the same range setting of the machine. In scientific terms, the sonic energy was attenuated to a much greater extent by the beef muscle than by the beef fat.

I found that a preparation of 1 centimeter total thickness with approximately 1 millimeter of beef muscle naturally attached to 9 millimeters of beef fat could be sonically traversed. The A-mode trace of this specimen on the oscilloscope showed a wide (time) baseline echoless gap and a shorter one with echoes. The wide echoless gap was recognized as coming from the 9 millimeters of fat, and the short echoing section as coming probably from the 1 millimeter of beef muscle. This was proven by turning the preparation through 180 degrees—the trace was reversed in terms of the echoless part and the echo section.

This experiment proved that the fat–muscle interface was resolved, that echoes were coming from within the beef muscle, and that beef muscle attenuated or diminished sonic energy per distance penetrated much more than did structural fat. From then on a 1-centimeter cube of beef muscle was found to be a satisfactory and convenient means of adjusting the range of the soundbeam when the incident soundbeam crossed the meat fibers. It was also found that no echoes were produced when the soundbeam was parallel to the meat fibers. This property—*anisotrophy*—was destroyed when hamburger meat was substituted. My need to produce a standard biological specimen had led to the proof of echo production both by gross anatomical structure, such as between fat and beef muscle, and, more important, by histological beef muscle structure.

The dog bowel experiments required one more confirmatory test using human bowel. In carrying this out, a serendipitous discovery was made: *the differential sonic properties of tumors.*

Discovery of Differential Acoustic Properties of Soft-Tissue Tumors

Human bowel was not available at a time convenient to Donald, but a slice of human stomach containing a carcinomatous ulcer was offered from the operating room and rushed still warm to the navy base. Normal stomach wall of the specimen was draped over the echoscope. The entering and leaving echoes were identified. Between these two echoes was an asymmetric echo, which was transposed when the preparation was turned over (see A_1 and A_2 in Figure 6.2). The stomach contains a sheet of muscle, called the lamella muscularis mucosae, that adjusts the digestive lining independent of the main stomach wall. The asymmetrical echo was considered to come from this structure, giving further proof of echo reflection from within tissues. Ultrasonic gastroscopy had now been made possible. However, many years were to pass before this experimental work was applied clinically.

Natural curiosity prompted examination of the cancerous portion of the stomach wall, using the biological technique of control of multiple variables. The specimen (Figure 6.2, Center A–E) was draped over the echoscope at positions progressively toward the ulcer from the normal stomach wall. The settings of the controls of the machine were not altered between each specimen position. Thus, conditions of experimentation were unchanged except for the position of the stomach wall. The electronic gear had been first checked for "drift" and found to be stable over long periods. The stomach wall was all one thickness except for the ulcer protruding from it. But the cancer cells had grown from the ulcer into the adjacent stomach wall to produce a stiffening that could be felt (Figure 6.2, sectional drawing, B)

As the specimen was moved across the echoscope, a widening of the time base of the oscilloscope trace occurred and the echo content of the trace figures increased

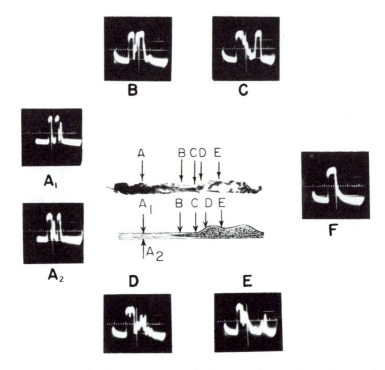

FIGURE 6.2. Empirical experiments on a fresh operative section of stomach cancer (carcinoma) carried out in October 1949 at 15-megacycle frequency. The records are of the time-amplitude A-mode type. The baseline is time; echoes rise vertically from the baseline in varying heights depending on their strength or amplitude. The echo from the condom-rubber membrane–air junction (interface) is shown at F. The slice of stomach wall containing the cancerous ulcer is placed centrally above a sectional drawing. Proof of echo reflection from within the stomach wall is shown at A_1 and A_2 by transposition of a low-amplitude echo group associated with a muscle sheet within the stomach wall. Widening of the time base can be seen at B and C as the sound-beam was directed through the stomach wall infiltrated with cancer cells, as indicated in the sectional drawing. In addition, multiple echoes can be seen coming from the stomach wall and ulcer (B–E).

(Figure 6.2 B–E). This demonstrated that cancerous tissue of this type not only delayed passage of sonic energy but also produced multiple echoes. The records, obtained in October 1949, proved an historical landmark in direct cancer detection and diagnosis by pulse-echo ultrasound.

This discovery raised the immediate, most urgent hope in my mind of making a very great advance in the direct detection and diagnosis of cancerous tumors at least at the most common sites of incidence, the breast and colon. The importance of this breakthrough to medicine demanded my full dedication in following it up. The bowel function studies were put on hold. At that time, chances of curing tumorous cancers looked extremely bleak, and today's mortality figures show little improvement. The greatest hope of cure is still early detection. The object of cancer surgery then seemed to be to cut away from the cancer as much of the patient as would survive. I had always felt that with my faith in following my nose and sticking to my values and ideals, I would do something important in my life. As a young man I had developed a growing sense of destiny as I went on learning and gaining wide experience.

A paper on the work up to this stage was submitted for publication on November 15, 1949. My primary (much-ignored) reference in the field of pulse-echo ultrasound was published the following year in *Surgery* (Wild, 1950).

The need to move on to confirmation and proving of my cancer discovery right up to testing on the living, intact patient became imperative. It was quite a challenge, since my equipment was not portable and I was dependent on the continued support of the personnel at the navy base, situated 7 miles from my base at the department of surgery in the University of Minnesota Medical School. The University Medical School showed little interest in my work. The coming winter also promised to hinder my meager travel capabilities, since I had been without income for several months when my surgical fellowship ended.

I formulated a modus operandi. First, I needed a source of fresh cancerous material to confirm my stomach cancer findings. To this end I succeeded in interesting individuals in the University departments of neurosurgery and medical physics. The representative of the medical physics department decided to determine the feasibility of detecting brain tumors with an experiment of his own design. He arrived at the navy base with a dry skull and a small balloon filled with gelatin to represent a tumor. He expected results with this totally inadequate model. At 15 megacycles the sonic beam would not penetrate the dry bone of the skull. On failing to find evidence of feasibility for brain tumor detection, he lost interest. I suspect that there are many examples of this kind of "peer" inquiry which, when taken seriously by funding agencies, has quashed potentially promising ideas. A similar instance of woolly peer-reviewer thinking will be described later.

Examination of fresh, warm neural tissue obtainable from the operating room seemed to me a more practical approach to my experimental ultrasonic techniques. At this point—as in the case with the stomach cancer experiments—the biological technique of controlling for multiple variables was once more used. With this technique one can compare the properties of one complex system, such as tissue, with another equally complex system. In my case, the sonic echo response of normal brain tissue, the control, was compared with that of the tumorous brain tissue, the variable. The setting of the acoustic system was not changed after acoustic gain adjustment, to allow visual demonstration of a maximum difference in the traces of normal control tissue and that of the tumor tissue. The only variable was the tumorous tissue. Under these conditions of experimentation, no *physical* acoustic properties of the tissues were necessary to find out whether tumorous tissue differed in its response to pulsed sonic energy from normal tissue of the same origin.

This biological technique was heavily criticized by "hard" scientists as "subjective knob-twiddling"; my findings were termed "preposterous" in spite of their multiple reproducibility. I did not think it practical to get hard, scientific numbers from complex, living biological systems and was thankful for my biological training, which provided this path through the darkness.

Fresh, warm, operatively excised brain tumors were found to have differential sonic reflection properties when compared with normal brain tissue under these biologically controlled conditions. Success with these specimens prompted examination of whole brains of patients who died from brain tumor. This was no problem for a surgeon. Permission was obtained from relatives, and I awaited the *instant* of death at the bedside: I examined the retinal arteries with an ophthalmoscope to determine cessation of blood flow, apparent by the formation of blood beads within the retinal arteries. Immediately the scalp was incised and turned back over the face, the top of the skull was sawn through and removed, the brain stem was cut, and the brain was received into a warm saline-soaked cloth. The brain was transported immediately by ambulance to the air base where Donald Neal was waiting with his machine warmed up and ready to go.

The first brain to be tested, examined within twenty minutes of death, contained a large tumor on the surface on one side. The other side of the brain was normal. Differential sonic return was again demonstrated between the tumor and normal tissue of the same origin. Another brain containing a different type of tumor was examined with the same result. This time, in addition to the surface tumor, signals indicated a tumor buried deep in the brain. Donald suggested plotting the returning echoes to obtain a graph of the deep tumor echoes; reluctantly I decided that such an experiment would be invalid since the brain was already digesting itself. And, I had promised to return the brain to its owner for the mortician's art. Upon sectioning the brain I confirmed the presence of a tumor deep within.

About this time a rumor emerged from the University surgery department that ultrasound was potentially damaging. Apparently the source was ignorant of the very slight amount of power in each pulse of my equipment and was thinking of continuous therapeutic ultrasound, which would, indeed, fry tissue with enough power. However, I carried on with my program directed toward clinical application. I began exposing live rabbit brains (the skull was removed) to ultrasound for about thirty minutes and then the skullcap was replaced. One rabbit so treated was observed to copulate. On sacrifice of the animals at varying times, no damage was seen microscopically. I also insonated my left arm (I was right-handed) for thirty minutes. I still have a left arm with no signs of damage, nearly forty years later. On the other hand, nails of both my hands show damage due to setting World War II casualty fractures under X-ray fluoroscopy without the protection of lead gloves.

(In days gone by, the level of responsibility for doing no harm to a patient was very high. The punishment for infraction was ostracization by one's colleagues. There was little fear of sophistic arguments in a law court proving that doctors were at fault for normal statistical accidents and poor results beyond their control.)

The way was now cleared ethically to apply ultrasound to the living patient. The Navy was very accommodating and provided a suitable private changing room and a facility for examination of the female breast, a common source of tumor. Two patients were examined: one with a small, clinically benign breast tumor and one with a similar clinically malignant tumor. The biological technique of adjusting the gain control for maximum visual contrast of sonic response between the tumor and comparable normal tissue was again used. Inspection of the trace pairs showed differences in the two breast tumors, of two sorts. In the benign case, *less* sonic energy in terms of echo response was returned compared with its normal control. In the case of the malignant tumor, *more* sonic energy was returned. This experiment brought to a close the usefulness of the naval radar instrument. It was not possible, without interfering with its routine training function, to adapt the B-mode imaging part of the trainer, which I now had in mind for use with the clinical instruments.

The period of fifteen months from the spring of 1949 to June 30, 1950, had been a productive and crucial time in the beginning field of diagnostic pulse-echo ultrasound. I had had an experimental field day with my new toy! During this period I demonstrated the possibility of linear measurement of tissues, the production of echoes and other acoustic parameters by various types of soft tissue, the differential acoustic properties of tumors in fresh brains, the detection of an unsuspected brain tumor, the harmlessness of my use of ultrasound, and finally, the diagnosis of one small benign tumor and one small cancerous tumor in the living breast. I had also observed signals in real time synchronous with the beating of my radial and femoral arteries and moving signals associated with tonic activities of muscles. All this work was accomplished without formal financial support; it necessitated a frugal lifestyle and was dependent on the goodwill and unstinting support of, and accommodation by, the Wold-Chamberlain Naval Air Base in Minneapolis and its personnel—in particular, Donald Neal and Les Moerhle. It was, nevertheless, a scientifically exhilarating time for me.

With the now somewhat diffident sponsorship of the University department of surgery I had applied for a grant in 1949 to the National Cancer Institute, in time for activation early in 1950, if successful. The millstones of the new post-war bureaucracy ground extremely fine, however, and fault was found with insignificant details of the application, which delayed any grant-awarding activity until June 30, 1950. In the meantime, reporting on further progress of the brain and breast work in the early part of 1950 jerked loose at least enough money for salaries for myself and an electrical engineer from the National Cancer Institute. A highly recommended friend of Donald Neal, Jack Reid, who had just finished his B.S. degree, accepted the job on my terms and concepts of research between clinical science and technology.

I explained to Jack that the task before us was not simply to work in formal isolation from each other, but to interact intimately in clinic and laboratory. Within the clinic he would supervise the operation of the instrumentation he would design, build, and test with me. I explained the limitations, time-consuming nature, and disciplines of clinical work with its requisite respect for patients' needs. Together we would assess the scientific results of our work and discuss indicated improvements. We would publish jointly, the one most involved with content being the primary author.

Jack Reid proved to be one in a million. He never flinched at some of the medical things we did together. I thought he might not be able to take removal of the skull plate in our brain tumor diagnosis effort, and had a nurse keep an eye on him. He survived and did his job.

Jack and I formed possibly one of the first high-tech interdisciplinary teams for intimate co-working in clinic and laboratory. We started work in the department of surgery on August 1, 1950. No suitable space or facilities were provided by the department, although they had contracted to do so in the grant application. The surgery department declined to publish my paper on breast cancer detection in the living patient, reporting on studies carried out at the Navy base in May 1950, suggesting delay until more work was done. Another departmental group had now decided that pulse-echo ultrasound could be used safely. This group, well funded by the Atomic Energy Commission, conducted research in 1952 and 1953 and reached negative conclusions about the potential value of pulse-echo ultrasound for tumor detection (U.S. Atomic Energy Commission, 1955). In the meantime, my landmark paper on breast tumor detection was published in the *Lancet* in England (Wild & Neal, 1951).

By this time I had set up a workshop in the basement of my new home. During the winter of 1950–1951 Jack and I designed and built a portable "echograph" on wheels. We wheeled the echograph around University Hospital early in 1951 for clinical testing. A series of A-mode traces was taken from breast tumors, and various other clinical tests were made on blood clotting, arteries, arterial flow, arterial pulsation, and pediatric brains. After a week the hospital administrator ordered us out of the hospital.

The Beginning of Soft-Tissue Pulse-Echo Imaging

Jack Reid continued to incorporate technical improvements into the echograph in our basement workshop. He had become familiar with Donald Neal's radar technology and suggested that we build a two-dimensional sector-scan imager to try to see tumors directly. I built such an instrument (Figure 6.1B) over a weekend to await Jack's electronic modifications of our Tektronix oscilloscope the following week. At the time my wife had some fresh kidneys in the refrigerator, preparatory to making the English dish, steak and kidney pie. I "borrowed" a slice of the kidney and placed it on my new self-contained imaging instrument (Figure 6.1, C-top), to produce a two-dimensional scanning representation of histological kidney structure (Figure 6.1H). The first direct image of soft tissue, and *in real time!* This means without delay in processing: you put the kidney on the instrument and the image materializes instantly!

It was now early May 1951. The next problem was how to get back into University Hospital unnoticed, to conduct further clinical trials. The head of the obstetrics department, a Canadian friend, gave us space for storage and examination of ambulatory patients. Friends in the admissions department shunted breast tumor patients on their way to surgery through the obstetrics department. The surgical pathology department routinely entered a diagnosis at biopsy in the patients' records. My project's sponsor, the now unfriendly department of surgery, knew nothing of this sub-rosa activity. In addition, when the "coast was clear" (after the hospital administrator left at 5 pm), my work on clinical material in the wards continued.

The first real-time sector-scan images of gross anatomical structure (my forearm) were obtained at this time (Figure 6.3), in addition to images of a recurrent tumor of the knee and a malignant breast tumor (Figure 6.1C', D'). The images of the knee tumor were selected for publication in the *1952 Yearbook of Pathology.* Twenty unselected breast lump cases were collected using the time-amplitude A-

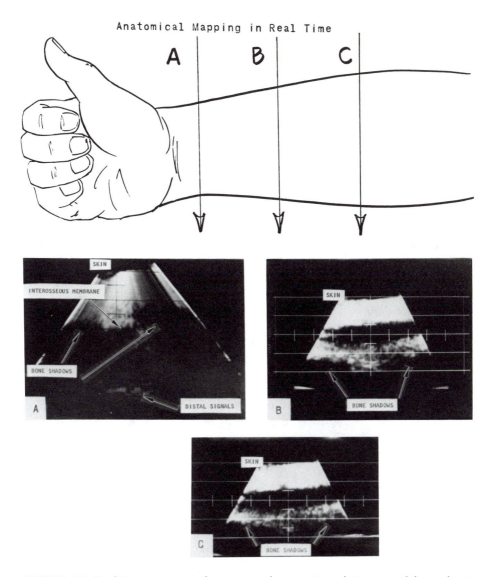

FIGURE 6.3. Real-time anatomical mapping of sector B-mode images of the author's left forearm from the wrist to mid-forearm carried out in the summer of 1951. The instrument was placed on the front of the arm. The wrist image is shown at A. The two bone shadows are clearly outlined with the joining membrane between them. No echoes are seen beyond the bone shadows but the interosseous membrane was traversed by the beam to produce a deeper group of signals. Signals in synchrony with the radial artery pulse were identified by their rapid movement on the monitor face. The value of real-time operation was apparent. At positions B and C, the bone interfaces are less distinct and the scatter pattern of echoes from the muscles is more evident. The muscle scatter pattern was seen to change with movement of the fingers with which the muscles of the forearm are involved, again revealing the value of real-time imaging.

mode trace, maximum contrast comparison technique (as mentioned, referred to by some as "knob-twiddling"). I had now demonstrated the use of pulse-echo ultrasound for both anatomical mapping and tissue characterization in real time.

Using the A-mode technique, on June 30, 1951 a malignant tumor of the living brain was correctly diagnosed *instantly in real time* in the operating room after removal of the portion of the skull over the tumor. The clinical diagnosis had been that it was nonmalignant (Wild & Reid, 1953). This application has only recently come into use in operating rooms.

Shortly after this landmark clinical experiment, pressure by the surgery department to shut my work down took the form of refusal to sponsor renewal of my National Cancer Institute grant. Opposition from the University of Minnesota Medical School was to continue thenceforth, culminating in the appearance of an amazing array of my old Medical School associates in civil court in 1972 to badmouth me—to no avail, in terms of a successful outcome in my favor.

My first encounter with professorial hegemony had been Prof. Wangensteen's suppression of my work on intestinal distension (Wild & Strickler, 1949) (mentioned earlier). In another instance Prof. Wangensteen ordered me to delay publication of my 1950 breast tumor diagnosis paper. With his finger he tattooed the order on my chest: "I'm not *asking* you, Wild, I'm *telling* you!" Since publication was my career life-line, I went ahead and published in the *Lancet* (Wild & Neal, 1951). In my case it was not a question of "publish *or* perish," but rather "publish *and* perish." Prof. Wangensteen's final public opinion concerning my work, delivered under oath in a court of law nearly two decades after I had left the University, was that while I worked very hard in his surgery department, "there was no real accomplishment."[1] Apparently, the old dictum to destroy what cannot be controlled remains true to this day.

After a lot of "ad hoc" investigation of the situation in 1951, the National Cancer Institute decided to carry my project without funds until October 1951. In August 1951 I was successful in transferring my basement laboratory to the department of electrical engineering at the University of Minnesota under the direct sponsorship of the University's Board of Regents, against considerable opposition now from the whole Medical School. Jack Reid loyally stuck with me as our small stipend came to an end, pending renewal of a grant emanating from the department of electrical engineering for two years from October 1951 to October 1953. The atmosphere in this department became much more friendly and conducive to the hard job of continuing applied research.

The two-dimensional real-time imaging work that we had done up to that time was published by *Science* as a lead article in February 1952 (Wild & Reid, 1952a). This was the primary publication on pulse-echo imaging. I now had under control the technology for designing and building imaging equipment for specific objectives; but clinical testing had been reduced to hollow assurances to the National Cancer Institute representatives about its availability in the Medical School. The problem was circumvented by installation of the A-mode part of the echograph instrument at Saint Barnabas Hospital, Minneapolis, a nearby private hospital whose medical staff enthusiastically referred patients to me for clinical diagnosis of breast tumors. At last I could legitimately work full time at research.

In today's plethora of electronic instrumentation it is hard to conceive of what a formidable task was the building of the first dedicated imaging monitor in 1951. The machine had to be built from the ground up. Jack Reid did a magnificent job of designing and building the multiple-use monitor that was necessary for use of the various examining instruments I was designing and building.

The basic limitations of ultrasound had now been determined, in terms of specific application. The exciting advantage of this new, noninvasive approach to medical diagnosis was its potential versatility and safety compared with X-radiography. This potential has still not been fully exploited. One of the most important applications I can envisage is the rapid interrogation of tissues with instantaneous visual and/or numerical readout to produce efficient screening techniques for early detection of tumors of the breast and colon—the most common sites of tumorous cancer. Direct application to suspect tissue at high frequency circumvents the basic frequency-range limitation. The higher the frequency, the less penetration but the greater the resolution of small volumes of cellular tissue. The higher the resolution, the greater the target sensitivity to cancer cell volumes.

The Area Ratio

In 1951 and for many years following, I faced the problem of scientific acceptance of my work by clinicians, physicists, and technologists, each field having its own rules and protocols for assessment and evaluation. Like the blind men describing an elephant in terms of whatever part they had grasped, each of these specialized groups assessed my work according to which part of it came within its limited area of expertise. The "hard" sciences at the time were almost derisive of my valid, qualitative biological methods. Acoustic and electroacoustic knowledge—in terms of practical application of pulse-echo ultrasound to nonlinear, heterogeneous tissue systems—was nonexistent. (The technical mysteries of the electrocardiograph have still not been explained, in hard technical terms.) Clinicians, of course, wanted clinical statistics and their own instruments, which were barely in the prototype stage; they had little understanding or interest in the technology involved in this newly evolving field of medicine. My task was to educate scientists and workers in related and/or contributory fields in order to gain acceptance of my novel results by these individuals. Or, as Oscar Wilde wrote in his poem "Helas," I had to "strike one clear chord to reach the ears of God." An image of a living, intact cancer should do the trick. In addition, wide publication in the language of each field would be necessary.

What could I do with the trace pairs of breast lumps so far accumulated in order to justify the expense of building imaging equipment? Interpretations of the traces had been subjective, based on adjustment of the controls to produce the maximum visual contrast between normal and tumor (A-mode) traces. Subjective data are always suspect. I had to have objective numbers. Obtaining hard science "numbers" was considered impossible because of nonlinearity and inhomogeneity and the dynamic nature of living, functioning biological tissue. Fourier analysis of the trace wave forms was far too slow with equipment available at the time. Accordingly, empirical analysis of the traces in terms of possible correlative features was attempted throughout one long night in my new campus laboratory. The pairs of traces were transferred onto paper ruled in squares. Squares subtended by the A-mode trace pairs were laboriously counted and compared. A significant ratio of comparison emerged that correlated well with the pathological diagnosis. The area beneath the A-mode traces is a measure of the total amount of sonic energy returned. I had discovered a possible clinical index for diagnosing the histological nature of growths and for comparison from case to case. I called this number the "area ratio". The area ratio was to provide the key to my subsequent effort to develop automatic, instantaneous, objective readout for tumor detection and diagnosis in the screening mode. This work was published in the *American Journal of Pathology* in March 1952 (Wild & Reid, 1952b).

In applying the area ratio to my collected breast tumor A-mode traces, I showed that a natural contrast existed with a high statistical probability between the amount of sonic energy return of tumors compared with return of the surrounding tissue of origin. In the first series of twenty cases the contrast was of two kinds: *positive,* where the tumor was malignant, and *negative,* where the tumor was benign. This meant that tumors could be delineated directly in real time by sweeping a sound beam in a linear motion to "slice" completely through the tumor and surrounding tissue.

The necessary self-contained, hand-held, linear B-mode instrument was operational by May 22, 1953, in the electrical engineering department (Wild & Reid, 1954). A call went out to my supporting medical colleagues for a breast lump to examine, but nary a breast lump was available. Instead, an "inflamed nipple" was offered, with apologies. Both of the patient's nipples were examined with the new linear B-mode instrument. It recorded an image of a group of echoes, estimated at about 7 mm wide, within the inflamed nipple (Figure 6.4). The A-mode trace integration gave an area ratio of 1.34, which was in the malignant range. The equipment was then rushed to the St. Paul Auditorium to be set up in the scientific section of the Centennial Meeting of the Minnesota State Medical Association. Records were rapidly processed by Jack, who brought them to the exhibit the next day, hastily assembled on a piece of building material. They were exhibited with a public declaration of "a malignant tumor of about 7 mm." Following the meeting, biopsy of the diseased nipple confirmed our diagnosis. A medical miracle, equal to Roentgen's first radiograph, had occurred. This is the stuff that drives scientists.

In retrospect, it was incredible that we should have examined a rarely occurring tumor in the nipple instead of a more common glandular breast tumor, since the nipple, unlike the glandular breast, produced a high visual contrast between the nonechoing background and the tumor signal because of the parallel arrangement of the milk ducts—a structural arrangement similar to that in the beef in the original navy experiment demonstrating anisotropy. The tumor was revealed in positive contrast, shining like a planet in the night sky: it could not be missed. My basic work on area ratios had provided the knowledge that permitted interpretation of this first soft-tissue image and the confidence publicly to proclaim the diagnosis.

I now began to envisage the possibility of detecting tumors on an efficient screening basis early enough to alter the dismal statistics of breast tumor mortality. I had the necessary black-on-white instantaneous visual readout for the central nipple-areola area of the breast, which is the site of 25 percent of breast malignancies. But the technology necessary to process my area ratio instantly in the rest of the

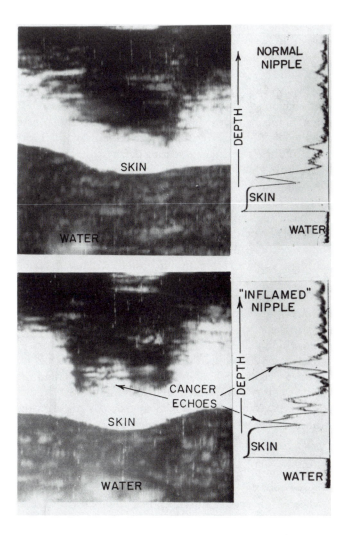

FIGURE 6.4. This first image of a cancer in the living breast was recorded on May 22, 1953, in the department of electrical engineering, University of Minnesota, by Wild and Reid. At top is the outline of the normal nipple outline (pointing downward). Below this image is that of the contralateral, diseased nipple. The images were obtained at 15-megacycle frequency in linear B-mode. A correct diagnosis of malignancy was made from the A-mode trace pair at the right. The greater amount of sonic energy beneath the lower trace of the tumor compared with that of the normal control nipple under comparable setting of the gain control can be seen. The computed areas were expressed as a ratio of 1.34 and enabled the histological diagnosis to be publicly declared with complete confidence.

breast, in which the contrasting background had to be visually adjusted, was not yet available. Breasts vary greatly in texture. This vision was stored in mind from thenceforth. I continued to collect clinical data that confirmed my previous work on breast tumors, and I began work on the detection of colon tumors. By September 1953 the first breast cyst had been visualized. This capability was of great use clinically, since cysts, which feel like hard tumors, are a common source of doubt and worry for women. In the meantime, the University of Minnesota Institute of Technology informed me that because of increasing pressure from the Medical School, I had to move out of the electrical engineering department by October 1954.

Saint Barnabas Hospital received my laboratory and offered space for an expanded operation, including clinical testing. Following this transfer I returned briefly to England to carry news of my discoveries and lectured in London in October 1954. At this meeting I met a young physician, Dr. Ian Donald, who became very excited by my vision of ultrasound's use in medicine, including obstetrics, and went on to produce obstetrical ultrasound applications. I had mentioned the potential importance of ultrasonic examination in obstetrics in my first paper on medical ultrasound (Wild, 1950), and in 1957 Sir MacFarlane Burnet (a Nobel Laureate of 1960) congratulated me on my work leading to eliminating the need for ionizing radiation in medical diagnosis, especially in obstetrics.

I stayed at Saint Barnabas until 1960, once more able in peaceful surroundings to concentrate on the clinical follow-up of the diagnostic breast work. A breast lump clinic was established. At 117 cases it became apparent that we had reached a technical limit with our original echographic equipment. We could diagnose small breast tumors with a yet-to-be-matched, high degree of positive predictive accuracy for malignancy (Reid & Wild, 1956). The diagnosis was based on the presence in front of the tumor image of increased speckle density. This speckle density was thought to be due to the high concentration of malignant cells, which produced more *diffuse* backscatter, especially at our high-frequency, near-field operation. The diagnostic function of our clinic had encouraged referral from medical practitioners, but this was not the primary scientific objective. The primary purpose was to determine whether all types of breast tumors could be visualized at a size of 1 centimeter and smaller. Tumors in this size range cannot be easily felt, and detection and removal carries a very good prognosis. All types of small tumor were indeed imaged.

The fundamental range limitations at 15-megacycle frequency limited tumor detection to superficial sites, such as breast and thyroid, examined from outside the body; and to those sites accessible from body orifices. Work on instruments to allow access to the vagina and the lower and upper gastrointestinal tract, other common sites of cancer, had been started in 1952 and continued.

The Beginning of Cancer Detection and Screening

The first images of normal bowel wall and prostate histology in the living subject were obtained in 1955 (Reid & Wild, 1956; Wild & Reid, 1957). The advantage of close co-working in clinic and laboratory is illustrated by the first attempt to determine whether images of the walls of the colon and prostate could be obtained. Jack designed and built the electronic components, and I incorporated them into the instrument. Jack also designed the sequential recording equipment. I built the camera. Early flexible probe designs had proved technically unsuitable, and thus I designed and fabricated a rigid instrument.

An enthusiastic friend volunteered for examination. Insertion of the instrument was carried out by the standard procedure of advancing a colonoscope with direct vision and bowel inflation ahead of the instrument. Once the colonoscope was in position, the rigid instrument was passed into the colonoscope, followed by withdrawal of the colonoscope. The soundhead now within the subject was designed to rotate while being withdrawn on a screw system. Jack was adjusting the display monitor to establish visual contact with the unknown. I was steadying the long rigid instrument within my friend's vitals, somewhat distracted by the amazing images of the histological structure of the colon being automatically produced and recorded sequentially on film as the soundhead was being extracted, when I was awakened from my scientific reverie by a loud anguished howl from my friend. I pressed the crash button to stop the instrument's rotation and started to sweat as I imagined the extremely unlikely possibility of his colon being twisted up on the spindle of the instrument. I had not provided reverse rotation when constructing the instrument. In reality, I knew that this fear was unfounded, since the interior of the bowel is without direct pain sensors. I needed to know the location of the subject's pain and learned from him that it was in the anal area which, incidentally, is quite sensitive to pain. I examined the polished shaft of the instrument and saw that some anal hairs had stuck to the vaseline on the shaft and had wound around to pull on their attachment, thus producing pain. The wound-up hairs were cut and rotation extraction resumed without further comment from my friend.

This experiment produced the first serial images of the structure of the colon walls and prostate. The colon images showed a square-shaped colon!—not due to genetic abnormality of my friend but to a minor technical fault in the resolver of the instrument. We learned much from this clinical research experiment about designing and building a system more suitable to my objective of colon tumor screening. By 1956 a technically adequate flexible instrument was ready for testing (Reid & Wild, 1956). In this design the separate "business end" of the instrument was attached to a recording-extraction section after "blind" insertion. The feasibility of automatic colon cancer detection in the screening mode was demonstrated, and serial pictures of cancer of the bowel were obtained. Such automatic detection has yet to be clinically applied.

The year 1956 saw the beginning of the building of a huge instrument designed to carry out serial ultrasonic sectioning of the breast for detection of lumps within the breast. This was a very large undertaking with my meager resources, and I had to get additional space in the linen room of the nurses' quarters at Saint Barnabas Hospital for assembly and testing of this machine. In 1957 the breast-imaging machine was operational, and a film record of automatic tomographic—serial—sweeps of the breast was obtained. (Eventually this makeshift laboratory was totaled when the nurses' building was torn down to make space for a parking lot. However, I did get some films of this equipment in use. The hope was that this film record would call forth a far greater amount of enthusiasm by the National Cancer Institute, but to no avail. I have often wondered why the denizens in this institute failed to get behind my fundamental work on tumor imaging.)

Independent confirmation of my basic work on echo reflection by soft tissues came from Japan in 1956 and encouraged a small amount of bonus money from the National Cancer Institute, to continue basic exploration, and from the National Heart Institute, to pursue cardiovascular applications (Wild, Reid, & Crawford, 1957). Jack did a great deal of acoustic system development at this time.

At Saint Barnabas in 1958 we witnessed another first in the development of medical ultrasound: the first through-transmission of heart and lungs at 1-megacycle frequency (Crawford et al., 1959). This project also illustrated the value of close interdisciplinary cooperation. The project's resident physicist, who (against my orders) had risked his life by driving continuous 1-megacycle ultrasound through his heart over the weekend, dumped a huge pile of paper recording tape on my desk the following Monday morning, challenging me to find something useful in the records. I set to work and after a while a pattern emerged that correlated with the heart rate and the size of the heart in terms of Doppler frequency shifts. This analysis met with the approval of my physicist colleague—Doppler signals from the beating heart had been demonstrated. In addition, we found that, unlike the clinical finding that ultrasound in tissues was stopped by air, ultrasound did indeed go through lungs partially inflated with air. In other words, as the lungs were emptied, the sound eventually would find a tissue path through the lungs. This work has not been followed up and applied clinically. It has great potential for determining the state of health of people with lung problems.

In 1960 there apparently had been some moves by Saint Barnabas' administration to set up a teaching and training department. It was suggested that the head of this department could easily take over my research department as well. The National Cancer Institute had been clamoring for me to produce large-scale clinical trials, without having provided enough funding to make the necessary number of instruments. Collusion between the hospital and the National Cancer Institute resulted in my receiving a veiled ultimatum whereby large-scale clinical trials were to be undertaken despite lack of proper funding. I felt I was to be relegated to a corner, there to remain until asked to contribute help and new ideas. As far as I could tell, my grant money was to be controlled by others and I was to surrender control over my project and research to a newly created research program director. I elected to leave Saint Barnabas. I had finished the diagnostic breast tumor stage of my screening objective, and I didn't see how I could continue directing my work with outside limiting control of my research program. The significance of my demonstrated automatic breast-screening equipment had been lost in the confusion of clinical trials to be targeted at demonstrating the *diagnostic* potential of pulse-echo ultrasound. This application was, in my opinion, irrelevant compared with the public health, mass-screening potential for *detecting* tumors at an early stage.

Sponsorship of my projects was transferred from Saint Barnabas to the Minnesota Foundation, to which I had been recommended by a local foundation that had been following my work since the prize-winning 1953 exhibit. My laboratory was stored in the basement of a friendly doctor's clinic for two years under the aegis of the Minnesota Foundation before funding was once more found. During this interim nonfunded period, a definitive report was written by me with the approval of Mr. Sidney Colbert, chairman of my scientific advisory committee for the consideration of Senator Hubert Humphrey. This report discussed the interactions of myself with Public Health Service officials and brought attention to the inadequacy of support for my broad-based research by specific disease-oriented government agencies (Colbert, 1962). In my case, the Public Health Service directly interfered with my scientific project objective of breast and colon cancer screening in their insistence on large-scale clinical trials of the diagnostic potential of pulse-echo ultrasound. I like to think that this "nothing-to-lose" report was influential in inaugurating a new broad type of grant, the Program-Project grant, offered by a new agency, the General Medical Sciences Institute of the Public Health Service, which came into being about this time. My application for one of their grants brought an award of $500,000 to run for four years beginning August 1, 1962, with possible extension for an additional three years. At the time, this was a record grant to a single medical worker and was given for "scientific excellence." My work had at last earned adequate funding levels.

I was given the franchise to set up and head an interdisciplinary facility in Minneapolis. This facility was to build a laboratory complete with machine shop and clinical testing facility, to continue development of existing projects, and to find new applications for the detection, diagnosis, and assessment of health and deteriorative processes such as aging. Some of the new scientific studies to be undertaken by my interdisciplinary groups were:

- The assessment of physical fitness of individuals in terms of the kinetics and visualization of the cardiovascular system and other possible indices of malfunction such as the lungs and muscle tonus.
- The assessment of the physiological age and the rate of aging of individuals, natural or after unusual radiation, based on elasticity of skin, leukocyte fragility, cardiovascular kinetics, acoustic absorption of lungs, and so on.
- The detection, diagnosis, and biogenesis of neoplasms and the effects of treatment in situ.
- Ultrasonic plethysmography.
- Monitoring of vital functions, such as peripheral vascular resistance, before, during, and after surgery.
- Measurement of the dynamic acoustic properties of blood and of tissues at sites such as the thumb web, penis, and ear lobe, which may provide significant data on liquid content of tissues and capillary blood flow.

By December 1963 I was again out of business. My engineering staff felt they could run the project without me, and colluded with my sponsor to this end. I had taken precautions, after the Saint Barnabas attempts to take me over and put me in a cupboard, to draw up a contract, contained in the program-project grant application, which precluded any negotiations among the contracting parties behind my back. My disloyal staff was surreptitiously used by my sponsoring foundation's executive administrator (a lawyer, yet!) to support pejorative claims against my leadership. Ultimately these claims could not be substantiated in a court of law.[2]

Close to the impending dissolution of my laboratory in late 1963, I replaced the disloyal engineering marplots with two very competent graduate engineering students trained in electronics and experienced in radar who rapidly repaired lab equipment maliciously sabotaged by the departing staff. Their skill, augmented by good humor and dedication, resulted in the creation of the necessary circuitry for numerical computation of area ratios at a speed of 1/2000th of a second—fast enough to follow my searching soundheads. By December 30, 1963, I had produced instrumentation that would enable cancer detection of the breast and colon on an efficient screening basis. I called this application *echometry*—echo measurement. I had reached my objective, technically.

In justification of the destruction of my laboratory, the sponsor's representative defensively opined in the press that nothing of value to humanity had been lost. In the subsequent lawsuit (see note 2 at end of chapter), a world-famous academic member of my Advisory Committee described the December 30th achievement of instantaneous computation of the area ratio as a "medical breakthrough."

Following this well-orchestrated destruction of my research career, a nonprofit foundation was formed to enable me to resume my work. An application with modest objectives for work on the colon was made to the National Institutes of Health. This brought another visit from an NIH ad hoc peer review group to assess my proposal. On seeing my serial images of the normal and the cancerous colon, several reviewers became very excited and impressed. The senior reviewer, a radiologist, apparently did not comprehend that the serial images had been taken in real time from within a living subject; he felt that ultrasound would not penetrate feces (which it would). In spite of my assurances that this was no more a problem in my ultrasonic imaging practice than in his radiological practice, my application was rejected as not worth pursuing. This was a final example in my experience of the selection of myopic medical peer reviewers steeped in conventional practices who, of necessity, could not be at the "cutting edge" of totally novel concepts. It takes a broad mind not to turn down something new that threatens a specialist's livelihood.

After a hiatus of eighteen years, by 1981 I was able to resume my work, as in its beginning, alone with my thoughts. Like Rip Van Winkle awakening, I found electronics had made many advances of value to my ongoing work. The potential that I demonstrated by sound scientific steps nearly forty years previously had been applied in many marvelous ways for medical diagnostics.

The acoustic design used in today's medical ultrasonic advances is mainly based on tissue-structure imaging in the radiological paradigm to produce images that radiologists can learn to interpret in terms of subjective experience. On a case-by-case basis, present-day ultrasonic equipment is proving useful for diagnosis of overt tumors, especially cysts. For mass screening, today's breast tumor detection systems, whether by ultrasonic or X-ray imaging, are far too labor intensive to be economically feasible on a tumor-found-per-cases-examined basis. For these reasons, I decided to pursue my mass screening objective. Echometry has the potential for safe mass screening of populations at risk for common early breast, colon, and cervical tumors on an economical basis. X-ray mammography, which uses ionizing radiation, requires costly subjective interpretation. My echometric system is far more operationally efficient because of its potential for automatic, objective, instantaneous readout for tumor detection. Only abnormal tissue, when found by the interrogating echometric probe, requires registration. The operator is alerted by an objective signal when a tumor is found. At this point images can be made for detailed interpretation. It follows that if no tumor is found, image or graphic records are unnecessary, which eliminates the costly labor-intensive problem of interpreting large masses of normal records.

As found from my clinical work on breast tumors, the echometric function that continuously compares the sonic energy return of normal and abnormal tissue will, obviously, show no response unless the area ratio readout varies from its zero setting, to indicate the presence of a tumor. In addition to detecting a tumor, the readout indicates malignancy (a ratio greater than unity) or benignancy (a ratio less than unity). Echometric systems will not only detect tumors, but will diagnose them at the same time.

The acoustics system design for echometry is significantly different from that of tissue-structure mapping in that *diffuse* backscatter is essential. The acoustic design of current equipment for tissue mapping suppresses backscatter in order to produce maximum possible image structural clarity, in terms of tissue structure, for subjective visual interpretation. In other words, in attempting to produce maximally clear images, the baby (diffuse backscatter) has been thrown out with the bath water.

The delineation of all types of tumors, used at first as an essential scientific step toward development of the electronic integration and the area ratio, has served its purpose. Thus, the ultrasonic imaging of tumors that I pioneered and used on my scientific path to tumor detection has now been assigned by me to a position adjunctive to echometry in my anticipatory tumor screening applications. In my thinking, diagnostic imaging is secondary to the prerequisite of finding tumors in the populations at risk. No doubt, these innovative concepts will be resisted by current practitioners and teachers of the imaging-producing, imaging-interpreting arts, and by the manufacturers of current digital imaging systems.

The need for such innovations exists. Present day X-ray and ultrasonic systems have serious deficiencies. Recently, I have succeeded in greatly improving the acoustic diffuse backscatter target sensitivity of my transducers for cancerous tissue. The problems of rapid, systematic interrogation with instantaneous readout of the breast and placement of instruments "blind" within the colon have reached prototype stage in my laboratory. These technical developments should ensure the success of echometry for mass screening.

Throughout this chapter, I have indicated a number of ideas and promising leads for development of ultrasonic medical instrumentation to fuel future ultrasonic applications. Medical ultrasonic technology is still in its youth, providing many opportunities for future invention.

Thank you for traveling with me down the thorny and challenging path of innovation and finally acceptance of diagnostic ultrasonic medical instrumentation.

Notes

1. Wangensteen, O. H. (1972). Transcript in *Wild* v. *Ravig* et al., p. 2499, lines 23–24. 4th Judicial District, Hennepin County, Mn.

2. In 1972 my lawsuit against my sponsoring foundation, its executive officers, and par-

ent foundation for defamation and malicious breach of contract came to trial in Hennepin County district court. At the trial some of the University of Minnesota Medical School department heads who had hounded me out of the University turned up for the kill. After weighing their gratuitous opinions against my documented accomplishments, the jury, which had no difficulty comprehending the significance of my research, disregarded their paid testimony and awarded me a record-setting verdict for defamation, which is recorded in the *Guiness Book of World Records.* Although the Public Health Service had also breached its contract with me, I chose not to litigate against them because ethically I felt that one should not bite the hand that feeds it. This gesture on my part has not yet moved the Public Health Service to assist in any way replacing my dismembered laboratory or facilitating resumption of my interrupted research.

References

Colbert, S. (1962). Report in explanation of misunderstandings between Dr. J. J. Wild and the N. I. H. which have arisen as a result of his scientific activities during the ten years under the sponsorship of the N.C.I. and N.H.I., 1950–1960. Presented by Sidney Colbert, Chairman of Dr. Wild's Interdisciplinary Committee to the Minnesota Foundation. In collaboration with Dr. J. J. Wild. Minneapolis, MN May 1962.

Crawford, H. D., Wild, J. J., Wolf, P., & Fink, J. (1959). Transmission of ultrasound through living human thorax. *IRE Transactions on Medical Electronics, ME-6,* 141–146.

Reid, J. M. & Wild, J. J. (1956). Current developments in ultrasonic equipment for medical diagnosis. *Proceedings of the National Electronics Conference, XII.* Hotel Sherman, Chicago, Illinois, Oct 1–3, 1956.

U.S. Atomic Energy Commission. (1955). Studies in methods in instruments to improve the localization of radioactive materials in the body with special reference to the diagnosis of brain tumors and the use of ultrasonic techniques. Final Progress Report July 1, 1952 to June 30, 1953. AECU-3012. Aug. 1955 [TIS Issuance Date] University of Minnesota, Minneapolis. Technical Information Service, Oak Ridge, Tennessee.

Wild, J. J. (1944). Intestinal aspiration apparatus. *British Medical Journal,* I, 815.

Wild, J. J. (1950). The use of ultrasonic pulses for the measurement of biologic tissues and the detection of tissue density changes. *Surgery, 27,* 183–188.

Wild, J. J. & Neal, D. (1951). The use of high frequency ultrasonic waves for detecting changes of texture in living tissues. *Lancet,* 1, 655–657.

Wild, J. J. & Reid, J. M. (1952a). The application of echo ranging techniques to the detection of structure of biological tissues. *Science,* 115, 226–230.

Wild, J. J. & Reid, J. M. (1952b). Further pilot echographic studies on the histological structure of tumors of the living intact human breast. *American Journal of Pathology, 28,* 839–861.

Wild, J. J. & Reid, J. M. (1953). The effects of biological tissues on 15-mc pulsed ultrasound. *Acoustical Society of America Journal, 25*(2), 270–280.

Wild, J. J. & Reid, J. M. (1954). Echographic visualization of lesions of the living intact human breast. *Cancer Research, 14*(4), 277–283.

Wild, J. J. & Reid, J. M. (1957). Progress in the techniques of soft tissue examination by 15 megacycle pulsed ultrasound. In *Ultrasound in Biology and Medicine,* Elizabeth Kelly (Ed). Washington, D.C.: American Institute of Biological Sciences, Publication No. 3.

Wild, J. J., Reid, J. M., & Crawford, H. (1957). Visualization of the excised human heart by means of reflected ultrasound or echography. *American Heart Journal, 54*(6), 903–906.

Wild, J. J. & Strickler, J. (1949). Clinical results of the use of a long intestinal tube of improved design. *Bulletin of University of Minnesota Hospital and Minnesota Medical Foundation, XX*(27), 1–40.

7 | The Soil Biotron: An Underground Research Laboratory

JAMES A. TEERI

The concept of a special-purpose research facility that provides many investigators with a unique observational ability is well established. In earlier centuries deep-ocean sailing ships provided natural scientists with the means to collect and inventory the plants, animals, and geology of the earth. Today submersible vessels continue to make this process of discovery possible in environments that were previously inaccessible. The discovery of the undersea thermal vents and their associated unanticipated biota is a recent example of the new information gained from such facilities. Satellites for observations of deep space, particle accelerators in the physical sciences, special-purpose aircraft, and large-scale controlled environment growth chambers are additional examples.

The Soil Biotron at the University of Michigan is an underground laboratory that is designed to facilitate the study of life processes in the soil. From the beginning, the Biotron was intended to be a special-purpose research facility that would provide the opportunity for a broad range of interdisciplinary investigations and manipulative studies in the soil. The Biotron was also an attempt to improve the ability to use statistically appropriate replication in soil studies. Traditional methods of studying soil processes have often had associated large measurement errors.

The original idea and most of the ongoing motivation for developing the Biotron came from Dr. Robert Fogel of the herbarium at the University of Michigan, and much of the information that I report here was obtained in discussions with Dr. Fogel and his colleagues.

The Problem

The processes by which energy and nutrients are exchanged by green plants and the abiotic environment remain incompletely understood. The processes by which energy and nutrients are transferred from green plants to herbivores, carnivores, and decomposer organisms are even less well understood.

Photosynthesis results in the conversion of the energy of sunlight to chemical energy contained in the organic compounds that green plants synthesize. Photosynthesis also results in the conversion of carbon dioxide (CO_2) from the atmosphere into organic compounds. These reactions usually occur in the leaves of plants. The newly synthesized organic compounds, and the chemical energy they contain, can be used for the growth and development of the leaf, or these compounds can be transported to other parts of the plant to be involved in the growth and development of flowers, fruits, stems, or roots. Eventually many of these organic compounds are consumed by animals or shed from the plant to be broken down by decomposer organisms such as fungi and bacteria.

A major uncertainty is both the nature and the magnitudes of transfers of energy and nutrients that take place in the soil beneath terrestrial ecosystems. As will be described below, a lack of appropriate study methods is to a large degree the cause of this uncertainty.

In 1971 Dr. Fogel began his Ph.D. research in fungal systematics. The fungal genus he studied (*Leucogaster*) is mycorrhizal—the underground hyphae (the threadlike strands of fungal tissue) are in intimate contact with the fine roots of trees such as pines and Douglas fir. The hyphae encapsulate the surface of the roots, with hyphal strands extending into the soil. This symbiosis benefits the tree because the hyphae greatly increase the ability of the roots to gain nutrients such as phosphorus from the soil, permitting enhanced growth of the tree. The nongreen fungus benefits from obtaining organic compounds and chemical energy derived from the photosynthesis of the tree.

In the early 1970s Dr. Fogel was one of many investigators attempting to determine the ultimate fate of all of the organic matter produced by the annual total photosynthesis (primary production) of a forest stand. The study was carried out in a moist coniferous forest near the Pacific coast of Oregon. Fogel made the surprising observation that over 70 percent of the primary production was transferred below ground for the growth of roots and their associated mycorrhizal fungi (Table 7.1). In fact nearly one-half of the forest's primary production was used for one process, the growth of mycorrhizal fungi (Table 7.1). There is not good agreement whether this figure is representative of other moist coniferous forests, or other ecosystems.

TABLE 7.1. Ultimate allocation of organic matter captured by the total annual photosynthesis in a coniferous forest[a]

Structures to Which Organic Matter Was Allocated	*Amount Allocated as % of Annual Total Organic Matter Uptake*	
Foliage	12.5	
Wood	14.1	
Mycorrhizae	49.0	below ground total = 73.4%
Roots	24.4	
Total	100.0	

[a]Data from 1977–1978 (12 months) at Dinner Creek, Oregon (Fogel & Hunt, 1983; R. Fogel, personal communication).

Intuitively, 70 percent of the annual production moving below ground seems to be high. Estimates in other ecosystems range from values near this level to values of 40 to 90 percent of annual production. The lack of agreement is a reflection of the lack of fundamental information about soil biology. The apparent magnitude of this process suggested to Fogel that fungi may be extremely important in the transfers of nutrients and energy in forest ecosystems. He began a program of research to study the role of mycorrhizal fungi in the cycling of nutrients and energy in forests.

In his first funded project he used the traditional method of soil cores to estimate the mass of fungi in the soil. This method presented several serious impediments. The process of extracting and examining a soil core disrupts the spatial organization in the sample. It is difficult to obtain accurate estimates of which fungi, roots, and other organisms were originally associated with each other. Because of the destructive process of sampling, it is not possible to observe continuously a particular hyphal strand or root over a growing season.

Continuous observation is important because very little is known about the life span and ultimate fate of individual roots of trees. The same is true of the mycorrhizal fungi that are symbionts of those roots. Improving the understanding of the transfers of nutrients and energy in the soil will require knowing when roots and fungi appear, how long they live, and what changes occur in their nutrient and energy content over their life span. We will need to know what nutrients and energy exchanges occur between the root and its living and nonliving environment. Dr. Fogel recognized that continuous observation needed to be coupled with the ability to subsample roots and their fungi repeatedly to determine their contents of nutrients and energy. Similarly it will be necessary to observe soil animals continuously to objectively quantify their role in removing nutrients and energy from roots and fungi. It will also be necessary to subsample the soil animals and their waste products repeatedly for determination of nutrient and energy contents.

Because such a large fraction of the annual primary production was moving below ground, the temporal dynamics of the process were of great interest. Dr. Fogel was dissatisfied with the limitations of the soil core method. This method had permitted him to identify an important problem. Now he needed better methods to study the problem.

He tried inserting permanent long glass cylinders, "minirhizotrons," into the soil and at regular intervals using a fiberoptics probe to observe the soil through the glass cylinder. This method permitted repeated observations of the same locations. However, the total surface area of soil available for study was not large and, apart from adding water and nutrients from above, manipulative studies of the soil were not feasible. In addition, the light source used to illuminate the soil caused unwanted reflections resulting in poor-quality photographs.

These deficiencies led to consideration of building an underground laboratory—the Soil Biotron. Over the past century open trenches, trenches with glass walls, and soil-filled boxes with glass sidewalls have been used by numerous investigators to study plant root systems, mainly of agriculturally important crops. Beginning about fifty years ago, a series of underground laboratories termed "rhizotrons" were constructed for the study of crop root systems. The rhizotrons were tunnels in the soil with glass windows on the sidewalls for viewing the soil and plant roots. The focus of these studies was usually the development of roots of one or two crop species in relation to moisture and nutrient availability. Manipulative studies were not common, nor was a whole ecosystem approach.

In the early 1980s Fogel visited an existing rhizotron in an apple orchard at the East Malling Research Station at East Malling, Maidstone, Kent, England. At that rhizotron, with the exception of radiotracer studies the underground lab was not used to directly access roots, other soil organisms, or the soil from the tunnel. However, the investigators had made time lapse photographs of growing roots. The photographs clearly documented the sudden appearance and disappearance of nematodes (miniscule wormlike soil animals) in the vicinity of roots that were shedding large amounts of tissue. The photographs convinced Fogel of the value of this approach in his research. It also reinforced his belief in the need to use a multidisciplinary approach and to design a facility in which direct manipulative studies of the soil would be possible.

The biotron (Figure 7.1) is a tunnel embedded in the soil of a northern hardwood forest at the University of Michigan Biological Station near Pellston, Michigan. The tunnel is about 120 feet in length, 10 feet deep, and 10 feet wide. It has cinderblock walls and a cement pad for a floor. The roof of the tunnel is just above the surface of the forest floor. Along both sides of the tunnel are thirty-four window bays, which extend vertically from the soil surface to a depth of 4 feet. The vast majority of plant roots and soil animals are thought to be found within this zone in this forest. Each window bay is approximately 4 feet by 4 feet in height and width and contains sixteen removable glass windows. The windows are constructed of 1/4-inch plate glass that is reinforced with embedded wire. The windows are attached by clips to a gridlike metal frame in the window bay. The joints between the margins of adjacent window panes are sealed with a silicone caulking compound.

Unique Capabilities of the Soil Biotron

The Soil Biotron can be thought of as an observation platform on which many kinds of tools may be mounted. Already we have found that each new tool multiplies the uses of the others. There are a number of unique construction features in the biotron.

No other facility allows observation of such a large amount of native soil (544 square feet of viewing surface) with such resolution. Windows look out onto a soil that is about 98 percent sand, so biota are clearly visible up to 2.5 millimeters from the windows. Windows may be removed and replaced for manipulative experiments. Other kinds of facilities for observing below-ground processes include minirhizotrons and fiberoptics probes, neither of which allow views of as large an area with as much resolution as do the biotron windows. Investigators are in the unique position of being able to compare these three methods of viewing the soil because each is in use at the Soil Biotron. Video photography allows recording of short- and long-term events. Examples from our studies range from the feeding movements of a mite over one minute to continuous time-lapse recording of the same root for

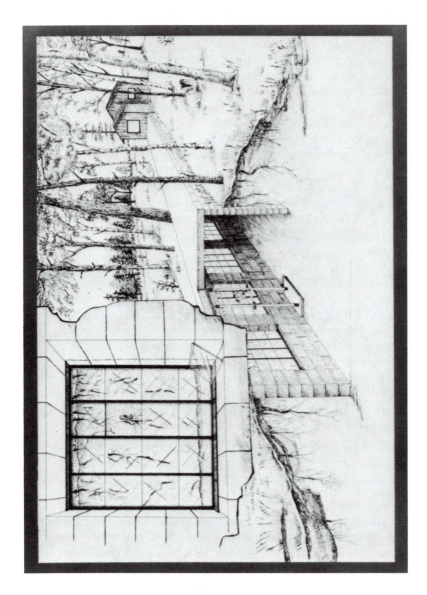

FIGURE 7.1. Artist's rendering of the Soil Biotron located at the University of Michigan Biological Station illustrating the window bays that are on both sides of the 120-foot-long tunnel. The inset (upper left) illustrates one of the window bays containing 16 removable glass panes.

seven months. Two cameras are being used in the Soil Biotron. One camera has a resolut'on of 50 microns (larger fungal hyphae can be resolved), the other has a resolution of about 15 microns (most fungal hyphae can be resolved). Both of these cameras have greater resolution than is available in minirhizotrons or fiberoptics probes, which can only resolve roots and larger invertebrates. Additional cameras will be added in the near future.

If quartz windows are used, the natural autofluorescence of endomycorrhizal roots will allow their quantification. The important point is that nowhere else is there a facility for direct observation of all the soil biota.

There has been an increasing degree of social interaction among scientists involved with the biotron. The initial decision to attempt to build it was Fogel's. Early in the project Dr. Fogel discussed with Dr. John Lussenhop of the University of Illinois at Chicago his possible participation. Lussenhop is a specialist on soil invertebrates, and Fogel felt that a multidisciplinary team would be essential to developing the project and convincing potential sources of funds to support the project. Invitations to consider working in the proposed biotron were sent to specialists in a number of related disciplines. All of these individuals were listed in an appendix to the National Science Foundation proposal describing how the Biotron could benefit their research. Dr. Fogel also approached Dr. Kurt Pregitzer of Michigan State University. Pregitzer specializes in soil nutrients and root growth. He had spent several years developing the software necessary for digitizing video images of plant roots. It was clear that continuous recording of the soil over time spans ranging from seconds to years would produce monumental amounts of information on the videotapes. Dr. Pregitzer's software is a modified Geographic Information System (GIS) originally developed for digitizing information to be displayed as maps with numerous overlays. The combination of automated time-lapse photography, the ability to digitize and store the video image, and the ability to analyze the image with GIS software permits the acquisition and reduction of large amounts of data. Computer-aided analysis of video records vastly increases the rate and accuracy with which we can analyze videotapes. This is the newest, most unique capability of the biotron, because the software was specially written for video analysis of root data. Using this software we are able to rapidly quantify areas, lengths, and widths of objects on video records. Recordings made at different times can be compared, allowing calculation of growth rates. In essence, information on video tapes can either be abstracted as outlines or diagrams or be put in quantitative form suitable for further computer analysis. Computer-aided analysis will allow more accurate measurement of variables like root growth and area, which we intend to measure. But it will also open up new areas of study by allowing us to quantify short-term root and hyphal turnover and the second-to-second feeding behavior of invertebrates. The spatial and temporal patterns of movement and aggregation of invertebrates were readily quantified using these analytical tools this past summer. All of the observational tools, the computer hardware and software, and the other facilities discussed above are dedicated to the Soil Biotron and are permanently available in that facility. An accurate accounting of the annual transfers of nutrients and energy among soil organisms would not be possible without these complementary technologies.

The construction of the biotron cost about $70,000. However, the equipment necessary for making observations will ultimately be a much larger figure. The equipment used to date in the early work in the biotron has a total value of about $100,000. This figure includes microscopes, video cameras, several computers and GIS software, infrared gas analyzers to measure and control CO_2 levels, soil moisture detection probes, soil temperature probes, light meters, and other items.

Observations through the glass are made by viewing the soil with the unaided eye, by hanging microscopes mounted on movable trolleys, and by the time-lapse videocameras. The image from the videotape can be displayed in full color on a computer screen. Using the GIS software the image on the screen can be digitized and stored in the computer's memory. The investigator can accurately estimate the length, width, and volume of roots and fungi. It is also possible to identify species of soil animals, most of which are tiny invertebrates. Patterns of animal movement and aggregation are easily quantified. The amounts of root and fungal tissue that are consumed by the animals over time can also be measured.

Manipulative studies are made possible by removing individual windowpanes and exposing the vertical soil surface to the investigator. When a pane is removed the soil remains in place because the root hairs, fungal hyphae, and organic compounds in the soil all act as cementing agents attaching adjacent soil particles together. When the first pane was removed (not without trepidation), less than a teaspoon volume of soil fell from the exposed surface. Removal of the windows provides the opportunity to remove subsamples of the soil and soil organisms to determine nutrient and energy contents. It will be possible to manipulate organism abundances, nutrient levels, moisture levels, soil gas composition, and many other properties of the soil ecosystem.

The Soil Biotron and Global Climate Change

The biotron is an important new tool for research on the ecological consequences of global atmospheric changes. When Teeri moved to the Biological Station in 1987 he learned of the imminent construction of the biotron. He had previously been studying how green plants adapt to variation in climate and weather. These studies mainly were concerned with the physiology of leaves. The biotron presented the opportunity to extend his work to the physiology of roots, which have been inadequately studied. In the summer of 1988 Dr. Peter Curtis visited the Biological Station. He was in the process of moving to Ohio State University and was curious about opportunities for conducting long-term research at the station. For the previous several years Curtis had been conducting research on the effects of elevated atmospheric CO_2 levels on plant growth in natural ecosystems. A frustration in that work was the inability to adequately study the response of the below-ground parts of the plants. After a brief discussion it became clear that the biotron presented an unusually promising opportunity for investigating the below-ground consequences of elevated levels of atmospheric CO_2. We have initiated a long-term research project focusing on the response of the below-ground processes in a northern forest ecosystem to elevated atmospheric CO_2. This is a multiinvestigator project, drawing on the talents of plant physiological ecologists, foresters, mycologists, and soil scientists. Results of this work will advance our knowledge of the relationships between above-ground and below-ground ecological processes as well as improve our understanding of the implications of global climate change.

Background

As a consequence of the anticipated global increases in atmospheric CO_2 content and air temperature, it is not known whether forest soils (including litter, which comprises decaying leaves and other plant parts on the soil surface) will act as a sink or a source in the net exchange of CO_2 with the atmosphere. This is important because it is estimated that two-thirds of the labile carbon in terrestrial ecosystems is in soils, with a third of that total in forest ecosystems (Post et al., 1982).

Recent studies conducted in growth chambers and field settings have demonstrated that both woody and nonwoody plants can exhibit a wide range of growth and developmental responses to elevated atmospheric CO_2 (e.g., Curtis, Drake, & Whigham, 1989a; Curtis et al., 1989b; Fajer, Bowers, & Bazzaz, 1989; Fetcher et al., 1988; Drake et al., 1989; Oberbauer, Strain, & Fetcher, 1985; Strain, 1987; Tissue & Oechel, 1987; Tolley & Strain, 1984a, b, 1985).

In growth chambers many tree species have higher photosynthetic rates when exposed to elevated levels of atmospheric CO_2. However, it is not clear that such an increase in photosynthesis (and subsequent carbon storage in wood and roots) will occur in natural forests. Global warming of the atmosphere will be accompanied by warming of the upper layers of the soil and the overlying litter. The resulting increased soil and litter temperatures and longer frost-free periods could result in higher rates of decomposition and higher rates of respiration by soil organisms including roots, and release of increased amounts of CO_2 to the atmosphere. This release of CO_2 from the soil could result in an accelerated accumulation of CO_2 in the atmosphere, further exacerbating the rate of global change. Conversely, in many forest soils it is thought that low levels of soil nitrogen, phosphorus, or other essential nutrients may prevent any potential CO_2-caused increase in net photosynthesis. The availability of these nutrients is controlled by soil processes.

Observations suggest that the below-ground organs of plants can exhibit growth responses to elevated atmospheric CO_2 ranging from no detectable change to highly significant changes in below-ground growth and/or carbon allocation. The differences in response have been attributed to biological differences among species as well as to interactions with other environmental variables including soil organisms, soil moisture availability, nutrient uptake, levels of solar irradiance, and both soil and air temperature.

There are a few reports that mycorrhizae may exhibit responses to elevated atmospheric CO_2 levels. These responses also range from no detectable change to statistically significant changes.

Very little information is available concerning the extent to which elevated atmospheric CO_2 will perturb the interactions between green plants and herbivores

(Strain, 1987). Recent experiments (e.g., Fajer et al., 1989) have demonstrated that elevated atmospheric CO_2 can alter the growth and mortality rates of herbivorous insects feeding above ground on plants grown at high CO_2.

Below ground, the overall effects of elevated atmospheric CO_2 are unknown. Turnover of soil organic matter may increase proportionally more than above ground, resulting in loss of litter and soil organic matter. This is suggested by strong effects of temperature and moisture on forest organic matter (Post et al., 1982), and by loss of soil organic matter in experimentally thinned forests. Possible mechanisms for these effects may include the high-temperature-stimulated increase in the metabolism of soil microorganisms and invertebrates, as well as the stimulating effect of slightly elevated CO_2 on fungal growth and invertebrate activity.

Because the potential CO_2-mediated response of soil organisms and soil processes is conditioned by many interacting environmental variables, it is important to document responses in natural ecosystems with as little disturbance as possible caused by the process of investigation. Virtually all studies belowground are hampered by the inherent spatial heterogeneity of most soils and the great difficulty of performing repeated observations of a particular organism or process. These difficulties are exacerbated by inherent spatial and temporal variation in the growth of soil organisms and below-ground plant organs as well as often large experimental errors associated with the destructive sampling of soil organisms and organs. As a result, in many published studies, elevated-CO_2 treatment effects that are substantial frequently fail to be statistically significant. For example, CO_2-induced differences of about 30 percent in mean root weight between treatments are often not statistically significant due to a combination of measurement variance and inadequate sample size, yet such a mean difference could have profound importance to the tree, to soil organisms, and on nutrient dynamics. It is clear that future advances in our understanding of the effects of global changes on soil processes will require an improved opportunity for continuous observation and the statistically appropriate replication necessary to detect small but biologically meaningful treatment differences. Increasingly investigators are using glass-sided rhizotron boxes or video recording via soil periscopes (minirhizotrons) in an attempt to overcome soil measurement problems.

Immediate research on these questions is needed, and the research must be done in natural settings. The existing greenhouse and growth chamber research approaches do not completely address these problems. In many ways the Soil Biotron is the ideal facility in which to conduct this research. The soil is a homogeneous well-drained coarse sand with extremely low nitrogen (and other nutrient) levels. We will be able to achieve experimentally any nutrient level we wish by fertilization. The Soil Biotron also provides the opportunity to manipulate soil temperature and soil water content.

We are now beginning to study the effects of elevated levels of CO_2 and their interaction with changes in soil fertility, on a relatively undisturbed forest soil ecosystem. Open top chambers placed over existing natural vegetation alongside the biotron windows serve to increase atmospheric CO_2 levels to twice ambient concentrations (~ 700 ppm). Nested within each chamber will be a drip irrigation system delivering additional nitrogen. Treatments will be isolated from each other and from the surrounding forest by soil partitions. At least four replicates of each treatment, including chambers at ambient CO_2 ($\sim$350 ppm) and unchambered controls, will be used. This system may be complemented by similar experiments within large root boxes to be constructed in a nearby facility.

Areas of Interest and Preliminary Hypotheses

Root growth.   Elevated CO_2 should increase root growth relative to shoot growth, particularly on nutrient-poor soils. This in turn will result in a greater rooting volume per plant and an increase in root sink strength. Production, longevity, and senescence of fine roots may also be affected.

Root physiology and nutrient acquisition.   Translocation of photosynthate to fine roots will increase at high CO_2, as will allocation to storage carbohydrate in older root tissue and loss to the soil via root deposition. Root respiration will increase, both on a whole root basis, reflecting the greater mass, and on a per unit fine root length basis, reflecting increased translocation and turnover and greater mycorrhizal biomass. Nutrient acquisition may be affected by changes in total root mass, rate and efficiency of fine root production, uptake kinetics, and mycorrhizal association.

Soil organisms.   Increased root growth, carbohydrate content, and root deposition should promote increased mycorrhizal infection and activity on roots of plants grown at high CO_2. Free-living microorganisms and soil invertebrates should also increase in response to increased rhizodeposition with consequent changes in the trophic interations among these organisms.

Decomposition and nutrient availability.   The carbon/nitrogen ratio of leaf litter and senescent roots will increase at high CO_2 level, possibly leading to decreases in decomposition and mineralization rates.

Leaf gas exchange and primary production.   Photosynthetic adjustment to high CO_2 has been observed in a number of species, presumably due to accumulation of photosynthate (both starch and sugars) in leaves. We expect such acclimation responses to decline as root sink strength develops. In addition to increased maximum photosynthetic rates under high CO_2, we expect less midday stomatal closure under high CO_2 and significantly greater net twenty-four-hour carbon gains. Delayed leaf senescence and reduced dark respiration may further contribute to increases in net primary production.

Nutrient dynamics.   The low fertility of the soils at the biotron may limit the magnitude of the CO_2 response, but we expect this negative feedback to be modified by long-term changes in root growth and mycorrhizal associations. Experimentally increasing soil nitrogen content will allow us to assess the degree of such limitations and to extrapolate our results to areas of higher fertility.

Timetable.   We are primarily concerned with long-term ecosystem responses to rising CO_2 levels and we expect our treatments to remain in place for several years at a minimum. Preliminary results obtained at the Biotron in 1989 (Peter Curtis, personal communication) show a rapid growth response to elevated CO_2 by both red maple (*Acer rubrum*) and white pine (*Pinus strobus*), which are naturally occurring species along the Biotron and to be introduced into the chambers.

The difference between the earlier rhizotrons and the Soil Biotron is the purpose of the facility. The term *rhizotron* (rhizo = root) reflects the main purpose of studying roots. In the biotron (bio = life), the emphasis is the study of all life processes that occur in the soil. As is stated elsewhere, the biotron has been designed for multidisciplinary, manipulative studies of the soil and its biota.

Dr. Fogel has an unusually diverse combination of interests and expertise that facilitated the development of this project. His formal training is in classical, descriptive systematics, specializing in fungi. However, during his graduate training he worked as a technician on a whole-ecosystem study of energy flow in a coniferous forest. As a youth his family had a blacksmith shop and he learned welding and other mechanical skills at an early age and has considerable experience in this area. As a college student he worked part-time as a welder. He feels that these experiences helped him to develop the ability to conceptualize in a spatial context.

Dr. Fogel considers the process of scientific inquiry to be an ongoing series of approximations. When he approaches a problem he considers and discusses many different methods of inquiry. If a method appears promising he attempts to employ it quantitatively. He uses a trial-and-error approach. For example, he tried building small soil windows early in this project. Later he spent considerable time attempting to modify the minirhizotrons to suit his purpose. Standing in the East Malling rhizotron convinced him to abandon that approach and scale up to the biotron approach. As a part of the search process he feels it is very important to know when to abandon a particular approach and when to seek information in other disciplines.

·   The team of scientists currently working at the biotron consists of individuals who think and work across the traditional boundaries of disciplines. Their work is already multidisciplinary and cross-disciplinary. Approaches being used at present come from such traditionally identified disciplines as soil science, agriculture, forestry, plant and animal ecology, meteorology, climatology, physics, plant physiology, biochemistry, geography, molecular biology, genetics, systematics, and microbiology.

Like Dr. Fogel I am very conscious of the conventional boundaries of disciplines and I view such boundaries as impediments to progress. These boundaries are artificial and scientists need to cross freely them. It can be difficult to secure funding for attempts to work across boundaries. However, the biotron team is currently preparing funding proposals to support broadly interdisciplinary investigations. The group is convinced that any significant advances in understanding require closely coordinated cross-discipline research.

ACKNOWLEDGMENTS

I thank the following individuals for contributing ideas and stimulating discussion about the Soil Biotron: D. Atkinson, P. Curtis, R. Fogel, J. Lussenhop, M. Paddock, K. Pregitzer, and D. Zak. Financial support for the biotron was provided in part by NSF grant BSR 8906666 (to R. Fogel and J. Lussenhop), the University of Michigan, and the UMBS Alumni Fund.

References

Curtis, P. S., Drake, B. G., & Whigham, D. F. (1989a). Nitrogen and carbon dynamics of C_3 and C_4 estuarine marsh plants grown under elevated CO_2 *in situ*. *Oecologia, 78,* 297–301.

Curtis, P. S., Drake, B. G., Leadley, P. W., Arp, W. J., & Whigham, D. F. (1989b). Growth and senescence on an estuarine marsh exposed to elevated CO_2 concentrations. *Oecologia, 78,* 20–26.

Drake, B. G., Leadley, P. W., Arp, W. J., Nassiry, D., & Curtis, P. S. (1989). An open top chamber for field studies of elevated atmospheric CO_2 concentration on salt marsh vegetation. *Functional Ecology, 3,* 363–371.

Fajer, E. D., Bowers, M. D., & Bazzaz, F. A. (1989). The effects of enriched carbon dioxide atmospheres on plant-insect herbivore interactions. *Science, 243,* 1198–1200.

Fetcher, N., Jaeger, C. H., Strain, B. R., & Sionit, N. (1988). Long-term elevation of atmospheric CO_2 concentration and the carbon exchange rates of saplings of *Pinus taeda* L. and *Liquidambar styraciflua* L. *Tree Physiology, 4,* 2550–2562.

Fogel, R., & Hunt, G. (1983). Contribution of mycorrhizae and soil fungi to nutrient cycling in a Douglas-fir ecosystem. *Canadian Journal of Forest Research, 13,* 219–232.

Oberbauer, S. F., Strain, B. R., & Fetcher, N. (1985). Effect of CO_2-enrichment on seedling physiology and growth of two tropical tree species. *Physiology of Plants, 65,* 352–356.

Post, W. M., Emanuel, W. R., Zinke, P. J., & Stangenberger, A. G. (1982). Soil carbon pools and world life zones. *Nature, 298,* 156–159.

Strain, B. R. (1987). Direct effects of increasing atmospheric CO_2 on plants and ecosystems. *Tree, 2,* 18–21.

Tissue, D. T. & Oechel, W. C. (1987). Response of *Eriophorum vaginatum* to elevated CO_2 and temperature in the Alaskan tussock tundra. *Ecology, 68,* 401–410.

Tolley, L. C. & Strain, B. R. (1984a). Effects of CO_2 enrichment and water stress on growth of *Liquidambar styraciflua* and *Pinus taeda* seedlings. *Canadian Journal of Botany, 62,* 2135–2139.

Tolley, L. C. & Strain, B. R. (1984b). Effects of CO_2 enrichment on growth of *Liquidambar styraciflua* and *Pinus taeda* seedlings under different irradiance levels. *Canadian Journal of Forest Research, 14,* 343–350.

Tolley, L. C. & Strain, B. R. (1985). Effects of CO_2 enrichment and water stress on gas exchange of *Liquidambar styraciflua* and *Pinus taeda* seedlings grown under different irradiance levels. *Oecologia, 65,* 166–172.

8 | The Synthesis of Diamonds

ROBERT H. WENTORF, JR.

This story is about some inventions, or discoveries, that took place at General Electric in a lab that was working on synthesis of diamonds at very high pressures. I hope that it will show how, in research, one thing leads to another in ways that are hard to foresee. In this case the path led from the synthesis of small grains of abrasive diamond, to large single diamond crystals or gems, and thence to large pieces of sintered diamond for cutting tools and wire-drawing dies.

By "high pressures" I mean pressures around 50,000 atmospheres, or 50 kilobars, or 750,000 pounds per square inch. These are far higher than those at the bottom of the ocean. Now most of us may at some time work under high pressure, but 50 kilobars is going a little far, and so a brief introduction to the world of high pressure and diamond synthesis, a world corresponding to depths in the earth of about 100 miles, may be helpful here. High pressures of this magnitude are called for because of the nature of carbon. (Actually, high pressures are not needed to make some kinds of diamond, but that is another story.)

The Background of the Problem

Figure 8.1 shows ball-and-stick models of the crystal structures of diamond and graphite. The graphite structure has widely separated sheets of atoms, which makes graphite soft and slippery (graphite is the main ingredient of pencil lead). In diamond the atoms are tightly linked in all directions. Diamond thus is the hardest known material and is especially prized for cutting and grinding work. Ever since Lavoisier showed that diamond was simply carbon, people have tried to make valuable diamonds from cheaper forms of carbon, like charcoal or graphite, and often this strong desire resulted in claims of success that were simply not true.

The higher packing density of diamond means that this structure will be favored at high pressures, and various measurements and calculations provide a good guide to the pressures required at different temperatures. Thus we find that graphite is the stable phase at pressures below about 16 kilobars at very low temperatures. "Stable" means that if you leave it alone, it will tend to remain as graphite for what we call

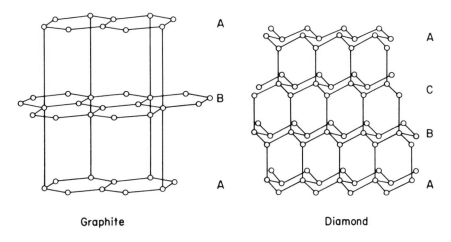

Graphite	Diamond

FIGURE 8.1. Models of the crystal structures of graphite (left) and diamond (right).

"forever," which I suppose is a very long time. Diamond is the stable phase at pressures of 16 kilobars and above; the pressure required for stability increases with temperature. However, the carbon atoms in these two kinds of crystals are very strongly bonded together, and so if the temperature is not too high (say below a red heat), graphite can persist at high pressures and diamond can persist at low pressures, indefinitely, as we all know. Indeed, it is interesting to contemplate that enduring love between a man and a woman is signified, in the popular view, by a bit of matter that is inherently thermodynamically unstable.

To generate the pressures and temperatures required for diamond synthesis, say 50 kilobars and 1500°C (a temperature about the melting point of steel), special apparatus is necessary. Such pressures are way beyond the strengths of most materials except a few very hard and brittle things, like diamond. But by using the strongest, yet slightly ductile, materials, like cemented tungsten carbide, and by backing these parts up with the strongest available steel, all the while using the principle that it is not the stress itself that is destructive but rather the gradient of the stress, one can contrive suitable apparatus. One form, named "the belt" by its inventor, H. T. Hall, is shown in Figure 8.2 (Hall, 1960).

In "the belt," two opposing conical pistons, pushed by a sturdy hydraulic press, compress the material trapped inside a strong doughnut. A compressible, extrudable gasket made mostly of a special kind of stone supports the flanks of the pistons and the doughnut to provide a sufficiently gradual reduction of pressure from the inside outward. The gaskets also serve as electrical insulation, and heavy heating currents can be passed through the pistons to heat a small insulated furnace in the central high-pressure region.

This apparatus has a major shortcoming: there is no way to watch what is happening inside. Merely trying to measure the temperature inside by thermocouple wires is tricky. Hence one does not know exactly what is happening during an experiment. Instead one looks at the evidence to be found in the little pile of debris

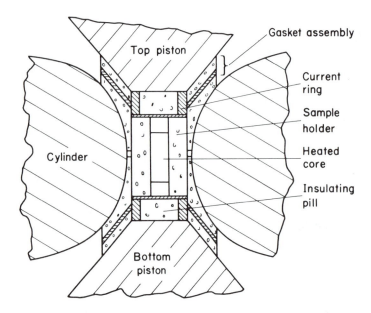

FIGURE 8.2. Cross section of the inner, high-pressure region of "the belt" high-pressure, high-temperature apparatus (see text).

pushed out of the doughnut after the experiment is over, and then tries to guess what happened. A second experiment designed to check this guess may be required, and so on. Careful observation and an open mind are helpful here as life becomes a series of hypotheses. Not everybody likes this kind of work.

In a typical diamond-making experiment, one begins with some lumps of graphite lying against some catalyst metal, say nickel. After a suitable pressure has been applied, the system is heated until the nickel starts to melt and dissolve carbon from the graphite. Because diamond is the stable form under these conditions, it is slightly less soluble than graphite in the molten nickel, and so diamond crystals form and grow out of one side of a thin nickel film while graphite dissolves into the other side of the film. The film thereby works its way through the graphite and leaves a pile of diamonds behind, as if it were Rumplestiltskin spinning straw into gold. If the system is cooled off suddenly early in the game, one finds a layer of diamond crystals, all covered by a thin film of nickel, stuck to the nickel chunk. It is easy to clean off the nickel in acid and recover the diamond crystals. (For more details, see Wentorf, 1971, 1986; Wentorf & DeVries, 1987.)

The crystals made by this general method tend to be small, rarely over 1 millimeter in size, but they are well suited for use in abrasive wheels for cutting and grinding all kinds of hard materials like glass, stone, concrete, and cemented carbides. Dozens of tons of diamonds synthesized in this way are used in industry every year. Some of these crystals are shown in Figure 8.3.

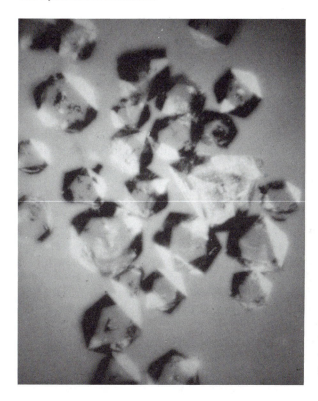

FIGURE 8.3. Small diamond crystals for use as abrasive. The crystals are about 0.3 millimeter or .012 inch in average size.

Obviously a lot of invention was required to come this far, and we—meaning Bundy, Hall, Strong, Cheney, Bovenkerk, and Wentorf—were helped by a lot of dumb luck, or doing the right thing for the wrong reason. Still, as Pasteur observed, "Chance favors the mind that is prepared," and after some three years of work on the problem, our minds were prepared. We succeeded where many others had failed because we combined sufficiently high pressures and temperatures with the right chemical conditions. We were guided by, and our choices were limited by, the most basic principles we knew plus the scanty data and hints from physics, chemistry, and geology. Lastly, we knew the problem had a solution because diamonds existed.

With this general background in mind, let's look at some particular inventions or discoveries with which I was closely connected.

Mechanisms of Diamond Formation

In the picture painted above, diamond formation is driven by the extra free energy of graphite compared with diamond at the pressures and temperatures involved. Experiments showed that if the pressure were too low, diamond could change back to graphite in the presence of molten catalyst metals such as iron, nickel, cobalt, manganese, platinum, and so on. However, a simple dissolving-and-crystallizing picture did not quite fit all the facts—some catalyst or "mystery" action was involved (Wentorf, 1966). So there were some unanswered questions.

Why did we consider such questions? Partly out of curiosity and partly because General Electric and De Beers were engaged in a long patent litigation on diamond synthesis. It was ultimately resolved in favor of General Electric, and the documents involved made a stack over 3 feet high. Expert witnesses were called in by both sides to give learned opinions. One of the issues in question was whether the action of iron, nickel, and other metals was catalytic or simply that of a solvent. Because of the magnitude of the potential business involved and because we diamond-makers at GE were given a lot of free rein, we had opportunities to pursue a number of subtle questions.

In this pursuit we were guided and nagged by an extraordinary manager, Tony Nerad. He had no Ph.D., but he had grown up in the Research Laboratory under the influence of men like Langmuir and Whitney, men who had active spirits of inquiry. And Tony loved to debate, often taking the opposite side for the fun of argument and uncovering the truth. Several times a week he would drop into each of our offices and spend half an hour or more talking about some idea. He often consulted the library beforehand. He felt, and I think rightly, that talking with his people was far more important than handling administrative paperwork.

In this atmosphere we discovered that graphite, not diamond, could crystallize from solution even though the pressure was high enough for diamond stability, for example, from decomposing iron or nickel carbides, or from seemingly unlikely solvents like silver chloride or cadmium oxide. On the other hand, experiments with highly crystalline natural graphite, like that which we had gathered from near Ticonderoga, New York, showed that in some obscure way the diamond crystals grown from this graphite remembered the orientation in space of their graphite crystal forbears. So the idea of catalytic action seemed pretty convincing.

But Tony was not satisfied. He argued that diamond could form only from graphite. He used Ostwald's rule as his gospel here. Ostwald's rule is based on sound thermodynamic principles and says that if two different phases or crystal forms of the same substance can crystallize, the more unstable one forms first—in this case, graphite before diamond. (Actually Tony usually said "Oswald's rule," not out of ignorance but exalting, in fun, his dog Oswald, a Kerry Blue who bit me once, sort of experimentally.)

Tony's argument was a tricky one. It's like arguing that all rain begins as ice crystals which melt as they fall. I finally thought of an experiment to test Tony's argument. This experiment grew out of one I did for Hub Horn, to crystallize boron out of a platinum melt at high pressure. The diamond experiment was to find the answer to the following question: If diamond were the only form of carbon present and it were caused to dissolve in liquid nickel at high pressure, would the carbon that precipitated from a cooler part of the melt crystallize as diamond, or as graphite? If only diamond formed, Tony's argument would be shot down in flames.

By this time we had a pretty good grasp of the temperature conditions inside the high-pressure chamber, and it was fairly easy to arrange diamonds and nickel so as to perform the experiment. Even though the experiment was counterproductive in that some diamonds would be destroyed, it might produce some information that was more valuable than the lost diamonds.

The experiment worked fine again and again, and showed that diamonds could dissolve in a hot nickel melt and re-form as diamond in a cooler part of the same melt. Apparently graphite was not a necessary part of the diamond-forming process. Even Tony was convinced. He did not mind if his ideas were shot down—they were just vehicles for approaching the truth.

The influence of this experiment did not stop there. It formed a root in my mind from which grew a tree of several branches, among them large diamond crystals, and sintered diamond tools.

Large Single Diamond Crystals (Gems)

When most people think of diamonds, they think of large colorless crystals around 1 carat or a fifth of a gram in weight. The General Electric management was no exception. We diamond-makers could always feel an undercurrent of desire from them for the Big Bauble. Bundy, Strong, and I sort of took turns at the problem. I recall I even dreamed about making a gem diamond. It was green and nearly an inch across. In real life we tried other interesting activities like synthesizing semi-conducting diamonds or cubic boron nitride, or the melting of carbon, or geophysics.

Finally it was informally my turn again for big diamonds and I remembered the experiment on growing diamond from diamond across a temperature difference, as described above, and I decided to examine it more. This was about six years later, and we had refined our pressure cell construction, thanks to the insights of Bundy and Strong and Tuft, so that larger working volumes and closer control of the conditions in the experiment were possible. Part of the high-pressure cell could now be made out of salt for greater uniformity of pressure in both space and time.

So after a few warm-up experiments to get a feel for the experimental conditions, I was able to allow new diamond to grow onto seed crystals, as indicated in Figure 8.4. Here diamond dissolves in the hotter bath at the middle and diamond grows on seeds in the bottom cool end. Only the bottom cool end is practical for

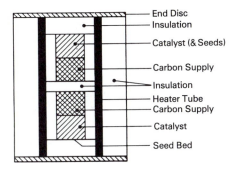

End Disc
Insulation
Catalyst (& Seeds)
Carbon Supply
Insulation
Heater Tube
Carbon Supply
Catalyst
Seed Bed

FIGURE 8.4. Cross section of a cylindrical reaction cell, about 1 inch high, to fit inside "the belt" for studying the growth of diamonds on seed crystals. The mid-length is maintained at about 1500°C while the seed bed is about 30 degrees cooler.

large crystals because diamond floats in the liquid metal. A cool seedbed at the top of the cell accumulates many tiny seeds that float up from the hot central carbon source as it dissolves, and many tiny seeds lead to the growth of many tiny crystals instead of one large one. Down in the bottom end the seed crystals grew to a respectable size, if slowly, and I had a lot of fun puting various foreign elements into the metal bath to see how they affected diamond growth. With some nitrogen, the crystals were yellow; with more, they were green; with still more, they didn't grow at all. Traces of boron made blue semiconducting crystals. Aluminum apparently gathered up the nitrogen and made the crystals colorless. Other elements seemed to favor dark inclusions of carbides, or else had no detectable effect.

In one sense some of these experiments were frustrating because usually I knew exactly what conditions would be best for growing nice crystals, but actually attaining these conditions was a matter of changing and adjusting this and that part of the apparatus way down inside where you couldn't see what went on until it was all over. It was like trying to practice a piano piece while wearing earmuffs and mittens—you made plenty of mistakes and you had to listen to a recording of the session to learn what they were.

About this time, seeing my results, Strong and Tuft wanted to carry on similar work aimed at growing the Big Bauble. So they ostensibly tried to repeat some of my experiments. But no diamond grew for them! Therefore my method had apparently failed the first test of scientific truth, namely, that an honest skeptic can find what you did.

I asked Roy Tuft: "Did you dry the salt?"

He replied: "No, we didn't think it was necessary."

Then I told him about the many small details that I had found were important, among them drying the salt of the reaction chamber, and so he dried the salt. And it worked! After a couple of years of development we were able to extend the growing time to a week and the single crystal size to 1 carat, and there we stopped. That was big enough. Some of these crystals are shown in Figure 8.5 (Strong & Wentorf, 1972) The colorless ones turned out to have extraordinary crystalline perfection, greater than that of any natural diamond, and the general science of diamonds grew a little bit as the result of this work.

So you see, the gem diamonds really came out of our curiosity about how diamonds grew on a detailed, microscopic level. It just took about ten years to go from knowing that principles of growth were OK to actually growing the 1-carat gem. Part of the delay was learning how to use seed crystals so that only one big crystal grew instead of a mess of smaller ones. But that's another story.

Diamond Compacts

As the source of carbon for the gem diamond crystals, we used industrial diamond grit mixed with a little graphite to fill in the chinks for a denser mixture. After the gem crystal had grown, some of the source diamond was left as a hard little pill. I was always intrigued with these little pills because they were almost strong enough to use as cutting tools. Almost.

FIGURE 8.5. High-quality single crystals of diamond, about five millimeters or 0.20 inch in size, grown on diamond seed crystals.

One day Bill Rocco and I were offered the opportunity to try to make strong sintered diamond masses out of diamond powder. There was a large industrial need for such things, and several respected workers in other places had tried to sinter diamonds before we started, but their results were never quite good enough to be practical. There already existed natural polycrystalline diamond pieces called "carbonado" and "ballas," which were relatively scarce but in great demand because of their toughness or resistance to splitting. They are found in Brazil and Africa where the two continents were once joined. Some people had theories about how they were formed but we had never had much luck in the lab trying to verify such theories.

There is a fundamental problem involved in sintering diamond, which at first seems insurmountable. It is simply that diamond is the hardest substance known and has nearly the highest melting point. If you want to sinter it, you must put it inside some kind of a container, but what material can you use that won't be distorted or melted? The answer is that you have to use chemistry as well as physics. You have to find out what keeps the diamond grains from sticking or growing together.

I spent many hours lying awake thinking about this problem. This was not so unusual; if you really care about your work, it is with you all the time. So-called working hours of 8 to 5 have nothing to do with solving the more difficult problems, and I think the GE management knew this and fostered an attitude of devotion to problems instead of devotion to a time clock.

Finally, out of a swarm of ideas that sort of buzzed around the problem in seemingly random ways, a crucial idea came along, based in part perhaps on my experiences in making concrete. For good concrete you must wash the mud out of the sand and gravel beforehand. So one part of my idea was to equate mud with dirt on diamond surfaces and allow molten catalyst metal to sweep through the mass of diamonds and carry the mud off so that the clean surfaces could grow together freely. Ah, but there was a hitch here. The sweep had to be arranged so that no stable arches or shells could form out of sintered diamond and shield the remaining diamonds from the pressure applied to them. If they were shielded, they would not only fail to grow together; they would also partly turn to graphite, a real no-no. It took a few experiments and some thought about them to understand this.

About a year and a half later, after hundreds of experiments and grinding tests, we found a process that produced a well-bonded mass of sintered diamond. We were held back some because the analysis of an experiment took a few days. We had to determine whether a change in experimental conditions increased hardness or toughness, and this had to be measured by some sort of a severe grinding test that took several days to schedule and perform. In the absence of current immediate test results we could make blind foray experiments in which we tried something different, just to keep going, and hope that a particular blind experiment would lead to a mini-breakthrough in a slightly different, useful direction. Our motto was "Make mistakes as fast as possible but don't make the same mistake twice." Over all this activity hung the awareness that to climb the highest hill, you have to know when you are on it; the hill you are currently climbing, though difficult, may not be the highest one. So we tried all the hills in sight, that is, all the possible processes we could think of. Viewed from the goal end, the route seems almost obvious, but viewed from the starting end, it is just one of myriads of routes that may lead anywhere or nowhere.

The process looks simple but it embodies several subtle factors. The need is for clean diamond surfaces so that their carbon atoms are free to move and join. It is nearly impossible to handle diamonds, even in high vacuum, without their surfaces becoming contaminated, usually with oxygen. So the final cleaning of the surfaces has to be done in the reaction cell in the press. This is accomplished in two steps in the following way: The diamonds are contained in a zirconium cup that is sealed at the open end by a block of cobalt-cemented tungsten carbide. At high pressure, during heat-up, the diamond mass is full of pores because diamond is so strong. Much of the foreign atom dirt on the diamond surfaces can depart in gaseous form, meander through the pores, and be chemically absorbed by the zirconium, a very active metal. Then as the temperature increases further, the cobalt in the cemented carbide begins to ooze into the pores. It is a diamond-forming catalyst and it allows diamond to dissolve from regions of high local stress and deposit in regions of lower local stress. As a fluid, it ensures that the local pressures are high enough for diamond to be stable. It sweeps its way through the mass, pushing away more dirt and consolidating diamond as it goes along.

In this way the entire mass of diamonds becomes about 93-percent diamond by volume and it is well bonded internally by diamond-to-diamond joints. This is crucial because no metallic bonding agent or glue can come close to the strength and thermal conductivity of diamond, and the mass would behave more like the glue than like diamond. A good analogy would be like trying to make concrete with a binder of mud in place of portland cement—the resulting solid would be more like mud. So what is needed for a good tool is a mass of diamonds stuck together like the raisins in a squished box of raisins, not like the raisins in cookies, which are bonded by dough. Obviously 100-percent diamond would be even better than 93 percent, but those last few percent remain an extremely difficult goal, perhaps to be reached by some new method.

Usually diamonds are somewhat difficult to hang on to, not because somebody might steal them, but because they are not easily wetted by most metals, and special solders are necessary to stick them down. But in these tools the mass of diamonds is firmly stuck to a cemented tungsten carbide block which facilitates holding the diamond masses as tools in various devices.

Another incidental benefit from this discovery was that the diamond-making factory then had a use for the considerable quantities of what might be loosely called diamond dust or unwanted sizes of diamond grains that were generated as an inevitable by-product of manufacturing diamonds—these leftovers can now be made into something extremely useful.

These sintered diamond compacts have been very successful as cutting tools and wire-drawing dies, where they are simply much better than anything else. (Bundy, DeVries, & Wentorf, 1980). They will withstand considerable pounding. Figure 8.6 shows a cutting tool made by this method; the diamond part is the thin dark layer. They are widely used for cutting rock and other abrasive materials. The same high-pressure process can be used to make wire-drawing dies. Here the diamond part is a core inside a cemented carbide jacket. The strength and uniformity of the polycrystalline diamond plus the availability of the die in large sizes at relatively low cost has made the dies very popular.

FIGURE 8.6. The small block on the bottom is a sintered diamond-cutting tool made at high pressure and temperature. The thin, dark top layer is diamond; the bulk of the block is cemented tungsten carbide. This block is clamped in a pocket in the large tool-holder just above the block.

Cubic boron nitride grains can also be sintered, at high pressures, into cutting tools like the diamond ones, but the chemistry of boron nitride is a little different, the sintering techniques are different (it took us another year to learn how to do it), and the tools are used for hard ferrous and nickel-based alloys where diamond tools are a flop, but that is another story also.

Closing Remarks

This chapter sketches out what seems to me to be an unbroken chain of insights, discoveries, and inventions that all began with discussions of the mechanisms of diamond formation. The helping forces were patent contests, a search for understanding, and considerable freedom of inquiry.

Many good ideas occurred to me while showering, or swimming with H. M. Strong, or lying awake at night. Often new ideas popped up in discussions as if they had lives of their own. Another excellent source of ideas and insights was the experiment that "failed," and there were plenty of those. Not all new ideas are worthwhile, but they can serve as driving forces for doing experiments, the results of which are often astonishing and enlightening. At times it turned out that I was not even testing the idea I had planned to test. Ha. Every experiment has a story to tell you! And for the complete, true story, you usually have to do the experiment yourself, so that the reported results are uncolored by someone else's interpretation.

It seems to me that the successful inventors I know all work with their own hands on things. Thus they obtain a direct connection with, a sort of feeling for, the way the physical world works. Such experiences enable me to imagine in three dimensions in a feeling way that is not a visual way—there are no visual images involved and yet the spatial relationships, the relative sizes, the fitting-togethers, are all evident and can be called out as needed. Like many other important things in life, there are no substitutes for actual "hands-on" experiences, beautiful though theories may be.

Where do ideas come from? From considerations of older ideas previously unassociated. From guesses, analogies, and intuition. One could easily become sort of metaphysical here. I have had dreams in which abstract concepts like logarithms or orthogonality or purity are given concrete physical forms and then manipulated. I sometimes create jokes, and they arrive, complete with introduction and punch line, in a fraction of a second. Many of you must have written stories and found that the story grew far beyond your original idea as you actually put the words on paper. Our minds can be wonderfully creative things, restrained, but not too much, by what seems to be reality. Luckily, everyone looks at things differently.

Another thing about inventing is the novelty or unforeseen nature of a true invention. It simply had not been thought of or known before. We are used to thinking about things that we have thought about or known previously. To say this in another way, I quote from a conversation between Raj and Paul Tuttle in the latter's book (Tuttle, 1985, p. 216) Raj: "There is no reason for you to feel that you must be able to understand the new view before you see it. There is no way for Revelation to mean the revealing of what you already know, except in the Absolute sense."

Thus the new thing comes like a rock dropped at your feet out of a clear sky. If you could have foretold it, it would not have been much of an invention. If you are lucky, you will recognize it for what it is.

References

Hall, H. T. (1960). Ultra-high-pressure, high temperature apparatus: The Belt. Review of Scientific Instruments, *31,* 125–131.

Strong, H. M. & Wentorf, R. H. (1972). Single crystal diamond synthesis. *Naturwissenschaften, 59,* 1–7.

Tuttle, P. N. (1985). "You are the answer." Kairos, Inc., P.O. Box 71280, Seattle, WA 98107.

Wentorf, R. H. (1966). Solutions of carbon at high pressure. *Berichte der Bunsengesellschaft fur Physiche Chemie, 70,* 975–982.

Wentorf, R. H. (1971). Diamond synthesis. In *Kirk-Othmer Encyclopedia of Chemical Technology,* 2nd ed., Vol. 4. New York, Wiley, pp. 294–313.

Wentorf, R. H. (1986). Diamond. In *Encyclopedia of Materials Science and Technology,* M. B. Bever (Ed.). London, Pergamon Press, pp. 1139–42.

Wentorf, R. H. & DeVries, R. C. (1987). High pressure synthesis (chemistry). In *Encyclopedia of Physical Sciences and Technology,* Vol. 6, New York, Academic Press, pp. 491–506.

Wentorf, R. H., DeVries, R. C., & Bundy, F. P. (1980). Sintered superhard materials. *Science, 208,* 873–880.

9 | The Origin and Development of the First Zeolite Catalyst for Petroleum Cracking

EDWARD J. ROSINSKI

The Initial Idea, and How It Led to Others

This chapter presents the circumstances surrounding the development of a new catalyst that would enhance the catalytic cracking of crude petroleum. The catalytic cracking process, one of the petroleum refiner's most important technologies, upgrades low-value petroleum fractions with high molecular weights to lower-weight, higher-value products such as gasoline and fuel oil (diesel). We received U.S. Patent 3,140,249, for our invention.

The historical value of catalytic cracking of petroleum crude fractions is well known. In World War II it made possible generation of a sufficient amount of the high-octane gasoline necessary to fuel all the aircraft participating in the European campaign. Prior to the advent of catalytic cracking, reduction in molecular weights was achieved in distillation units known as "stills," where the high-molecular-weight petroleum fractions were raised to a high temperature, a process known as "thermal cracking." Catalytic cracking was pioneered by Eugene Houdry in the late 1920s; improvements in the cracking catalysts followed through the mid-1930s.

A statement often made and still valid about the origin of technical inventions is that necessity is the mother of invention. It is understandable how a need can motivate people and corporations to spend considerable time and money on meeting the need, particularly if this can yield a profit along the way. For instance, extracting 4 percent more C5 + gasoline from a unit volume of crude oil can save $80 million per year at retail or 110 million barrels of crude annually.

Understanding the magnitude of this saving led us to the search for a more efficient cracking process for the conversion of crudes to useful products such as gasoline and fuel oil. It was widely understood that a more efficient catalyst was needed, one that could generate more useful products than could conventional processes of the time, which yielded much waste coke and dry gas. This understanding eventually led to our concept and the preparation of the first zeolite cracking catalyst.

Figure 9.1 describes the crude processing, with subsequent catalytic cracking,

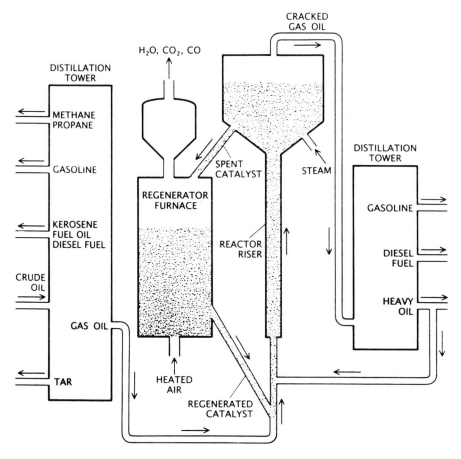

FIGURE 9.1. *Catalytic cracking,* or breaking, of hydrocarbons by zeolite crystals to produce gasoline and other products is done after crude petroleum is separated by distillation into a range of products from methane (which has small molecules) to tar (which has large ones). Some of the products are listed at the left. The gas-oil fraction is vaporized by contact with hot particles *(dots)* containing the zeolite Linde Y. Together with the particles, the vapor moves up a tube called a riser, where the hydrocarbons (which diffuse into the zeolite's pores) are cracked. Above the riser the vapor is passed into a distillation tower that separates the resulting fragments by size; smaller molecules form gasoline, and heavier ones form diesel fuel and what is called heavy oil, some of which is recycled. Meanwhile, the catalytic particles themselves are prepared for recycling. They are steam-treated to remove hydrocarbons and passed to a regenerator, where hot air burns off a carbonaceous deposit called coke. (From Kerr, George T., "Synthetic Zeolites," © 1989 by Scientific American, Inc. All rights reserved.)

of gas oil (Kerr, 1989). It is a good representation of the commercial crude distillation process generally. As it shows, the crude is fractionated into methane, pro-
pane, gasoline, kerosene, and fuel oil; the residue, or bottoms gas oil, is contacted
with hot regenerated catalyst to yield (in the catalytic cracking process) additional
gasoline and diesel fuel. The heavy oil here is recycled to the cracking unit.

By the early 1950s it became apparent to us that crude limitations would have
a significant effect on our national economic health. Although catalyst manufacturers and petroleum companies had done continued research prior to the mid-
1950s to find a more efficient cracking catalyst, only minor gains were realized. We
formulated a new approach to the problem. This approach was based on a new concept: use of a catalyst having uniform internal pores approximately the size of the
molecules of the desired distillates. We assumed that the uniform pores would allow
the absorption of molecules or parts of molecules into the small pores, increasing
catalytic surface contact and interaction.

Our first test of this concept, in 1956, involved forming a conventional amorphous silica–alumina matrix catalyst by incorporating a C6 and a C16 amine in the
amorphous structure. This was achieved by inducing the C6 or C16 amine to react
with an acidic silica–alumina sol (which comprised the reaction mix prior to gel-
ation) to form a hydrogel, a precursor to the final solid catalyst particle. The amine
was occluded in the solid, then removed on calcination to leave a residual cavity
equal to the size of the starting amine. Figure 9.2 shows the molecular framework
for zeolites (Kerr, 1989).

In our research, we evaluated experimental catalysts in a small laboratory unit
consisting of a feed preheater, a fixed-bed reactor, and connected product-collec-
tion attachments for dry gas and liquid products.

The laboratory evaluating conditions were as follows:

Temperature	900°F
Liquid hourly space velocity (LHSV)	2
Catalyst/oil ratio vol. (C/O)	3
On-stream time	10 min.

Initial catalytic evaluation, at catalytic-cracking conditions, of the solid calcined
catalyst particles did show catalytic advantages in selectivity over a conventional
silica–alumina catalyst used as a reference. The selectivity advantage was manifested as an increase in C5+ gasoline yield with a corresponding decrease in production of dry gas and coke waste products.

Unfortunately, cracking catalysts in a commercial petroleum distillation application have to function in the presence of a high-temperature steam atmosphere.
Our test of the first experimental catalysts involved a simulation of actual use, that
is, prolonged and repeated exposure to steam at elevated temperatures (1200°F) and
steam at atmospheric pressure. The initial-concept catalyst, which had been selec-

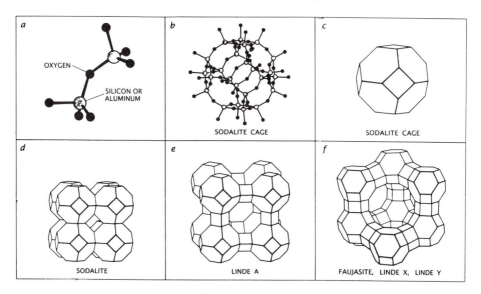

FIGURE 9.2. *Framework* of zeolites is constructed of tetrahedral building blocks; in some cases there is a characteristic "sodalite cage." The four tetrahedral vertexes are filled by oxygen atoms *(orange),* and a silicon or aluminum atom *(blue)* lies at the center (a); each oxygen is shared by two tetrahedrons. In representations of the sodalite cage (b), which consists of 24 tetrahedrons, and of zeolites in general, the ball-shaped atoms are usually omitted (c): straight lines join the centers of two tetrahedrons, so that each vertex represents an aluminum or silicon atom and the midpoint of each line represents an oxygen atom. Sodalite cages are found in all of the structures depicted here: sodalite itself (d), the synthetic crystal Linde A (e) and a group of like-structured crystals, namely the mineral faujasite and the synthetic zeolites Linde X and Linde Y (f). (From Kerr, George T., "Synthetic Zeolites," © 1989 by Scientific American, Inc. All rights reserved.)

tive after calcination, was evaluated after steam treatment at 1200°F and was, to our disappointment, no longer selective. We concluded that the concept was valid but that we still lacked a method to achieve uniform pores that were stable to the steam atmosphere.

To evaluate the experimental product, we varied temperature, LHSV, and catalyst to obtain different degrees of conversion in the range of 35 to 65 percent. This experimental catalyst was much better than the conventional catalyst. These advantages are presented as delta values in all our tabulated data.

The gains in selectivity from our generating uniform pores in the silica–alumina matrix material by incorporating C6 or C16 amines were transient, disappearing after steam treatment; the process was promising but unsuccessful. We had to seek an alternative source of stable, uniformly porous materials. During the period of this research it happened that Union Carbide's Linde division had synthesized new materials that X-rays revealed to be crystalline, unlike the amorphous conventional catalyst. These crystalline, uniformly porous solids were known as zeolites X and Y. The use of these crystalline solids led us to the development of materials covered in U.S. Patent 3,140,249.

Hoping that the crystalline source of uniform pores would be more stable to steam than was the amine, we incorporated a calcium and a calcium–NH_4, exchanging Linde X into silica and silica–alumina matrices, in U.S. Patent 3,140,249.

In the formation of zeolites, silica and alumina ions combine with oxygen to form tetrahedra, with the silica and alumina in the center and the oxygens at the apices (Figure 9.2). These tetrahedra are grouped to form building blocks known as sodalite cages, which can arrange to form larger sodalite groupings such as crystalline zeolite Linde A and faujasites Linde X or Linde Y. It can be seen from the respective groupings how they form uniform pore systems. Pore systems in zeolite crystals adjoin to form microscopic channels; in Linde X and Y, these are characterized as being 6 to 15 angstroms in size.

As synthesized, these zeolites contain ions of alkali metal, which serve to balance the charges of the alumina tetrahedra. This alkali can be exchanged out of the tetrahedra with cations such as calcium, manganese, or rare earths, as well as with combinations of cations with proton precursors. Products with metal cations and proton precursors are known as metal acid catalysts. We found metal acid catalysts to be more active, more selective, and more steam stable than the catalysts prepared with strictly metal cations.

Patent 3,140,249 describes a composite catalyst consisting of a silica–alumina or silica matrix and a zeolite component, the composite having a residual alkali content of less than 1 percent alkali by weight. The zeolite is described as an X zeolite, finely divided, highly dispersed, having pores of 6 to 16 angstroms, and substantially free of alkali. Exchange cations covered here were Ca^+, Ca^+ $^+NH_4^+$, and RE^{+++}. The matrix used was silica or silica–alumina, of which silica–alumina was favored because the product gasoline had a higher octane. While the level of zeolite addition can be as high as 90 percent, the levels we evaluated were 10, 25, and 40 percent by weight. Catalyst activity varies directly and substantially with zeolite addition (higher zeolite content, higher activity) [see Figure 9.3 (Plank & Rosinski, 1964]. Lowering the level of alkali also contributes to higher activity, particularly after steam treatment. Most of the catalysts covered in patent 3,140,249 were evaluated after a steam treatment of at least twenty hours at 1225°F in 100-percent steam at atmospheric pressure, conditions that exist in commercial units, where the used catalyst is subjected to steam stripping to remove any residual hydrocarbons prior to high-temperature regeneration.

In the process of developing the scope of coverage for the zeolite cracking catalysts in patent 3,140,249, we found a number of leads that allowed detailed coverage of some aspects of the zeolite catalyst. For instance, we found in this investigation that zeolite composites base-exchanged with solutions containing both rare earth and ammonium cations were not only more active and more stable to steam treatment but also more selective to the production of the desired liquid products, namely gasoline and fuel oil.

The specific advantages shown for some of the examples in patent 3,140,249 became subjects for coverage in additional patents.

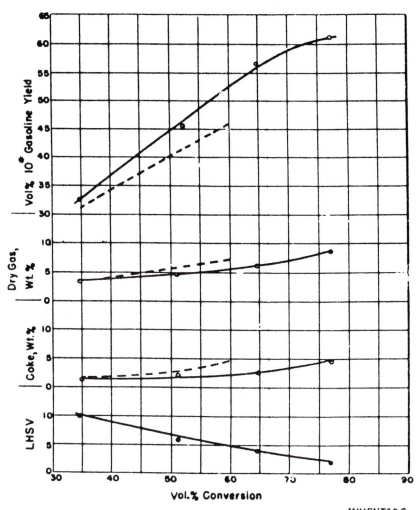

—— Catalyst of Example 3

- - - - Standard Silica-Alumina Cracking Catalyst

INVENTORS
Charles J. Plank
BY   Edward J. Rosinski

Raymond W. Barclay

ATTORNEY

FIGURE 9.3. Catalytic cracking of hydrocarbons with a crystalline zeolite catalyst composite (Plank & Rosinski, 1964).

It can be understood, starting from patent 3,140,249, how the composite of a crystalline zeolite and a siliceous matrix might be varied to yield new and improved catalyst compositions. The zeolite described in the patent was limited to finely divided crystalline alkali metal aluminosilicate having uniform openings between 6 and 16 angstroms; the process covered by the patent was limited to base-exchanging the resulting product, that is, treating it with a solution having a pH in excess of 4.5 and containing an ion capable of replacing said alkali metal, thereby reducing the alkali metal content of the resulting product to less than 1 percent by weight.

The references to other patents that follow will show how experiments done in the course of developing patent 3,140,249 led to new ideas and other patents. These patents show that in some cases it was possible to disperse alkali type and either subject the final particle to cationic exchange to reduced the alkali to less than 1 percent by weight or, in one case using a clay matrix, to cause the alkali to migrate from the dispersed zeolite to the clay and to interact with it in the presence of steam. The result in this case was formation of an irreversible alkali aluminosilicate in which the alkali became inert. This process was described as a solid–solid exchange process and does take place in commercial units, a fact allowing zeolites to function despite their initially higher content of alkali.

Clearly, varying or modifying each of the components contributing to the composite could lead to different properties in the material—and, we hoped, to new and improved catalysts with more desirable properties. For instance, the zeolite could have different characteristics, being for example Linde Y instead of Linde X— Linde Y having a higher molar ratio of silica to alumina in its composition. Here the silica–alumina matrix was favored due to its contribution to the gasoline octane number. A silica-only matrix gives lower-octane gasoline.

The role of the crystalline zeolite was to provide high catalyst activity and selectivity; different cations could give different results such as more selectivity and stability, while alkali exchange contributed to a catalyst's thermal and steam stability. The level of added zeolite also controlled overall activity. It was essential to make sure the zeolite was highly dispersed in the matrix. One objective of making the composite was to achieve the best relationship between the matrix and the zeolite. The matrix had roles of its own, particularly with heavy charges: its pores would precrack the heavier molecules, reducing them to a size that could interact with the zeolite component. It was also realized that some of the coke precursors could migrate from the zeolite to the matrix. Matrix preparation and processing conditions could be modified to give large or small pore matrix by controlling the pH of the interaction mix. The matrix was formed by reacting an acid alum solution with a soluble sodium silicate solution (water glass). A high pH of reaction gave a larger-pore matrix.

It is notable that the zeolite-containing catalysts as prepared prior to steaming were superactive, forming high conversions and high yields of dry gas and coke. As a normal practice we subjected all experimental catalysts to a steam treatment to cut their sharp initial activity and render their performance more selective. Commercially, it was not necessary to presteam fresh catalysts, since steam selectivation would take place in the unit during the cyclic process of cracking, steam stripping, and regeneration.

Highlights of U.S. Patent 3,140,249

Basic Scope

This invention relates to the catalytic conversion of hydrocarbon oils into lower-density, normally liquid and gaseous products and to improved catalysts for effecting that conversion. More specifically, the invention relates to catalytic cracking of hydrocarbon oil in the presence of a new and improved catalyst.

One aspect of the invention concerns the creation of an improved aluminosilicate-siliceous gel cracking catalyst characterized by unusually high attrition resistance, capacity to be cycled without loss of activity, selectivity, and stability to deactivation by steam. Loss of activity means less feed can be converted. Loss of selectivity means a less desirable product, for instance fuel oil. Another aspect of the invention involves a method for preparing the aforementioned catalyst for use in catalytic cracking of heavy petroleum fractions into lighter fractions with boiling points in the gasoline range.

As presented in patent language, the catalyst consists of a composite of two major components: crystalline aluminosilicate and a siliceous gel matrix. The limitations applied to each were as follows:

Crystalline Aluminosilicate

- Pore diameter 6–15 Å
- Finely divided, with mean particle size $< 10\mu$
- Composing 5–90% of composite's weight
- In bead form, at preferred level of 10–50% by weight

Siliceous Gel Matrix

- Cogel of silica and oxide of at least one metal selected from groups IIA, IIB, IVA of periodic table (e.g., silica–alumina, silica–magnesia, silica–zirconia, silica–thoria, silica–beryllia, silica–titania; silica–alumina–thoria, silica–alumina–magnesia, silica–magnesia–zirconia). Particularly preferred are silica–alumina and silica–alumina–zirconia. Silica generally presented as major component in range of 55–100% by weight.
- Possibly a chemically treated clay

The composites could be in any form—spheres, extrudate, or spray-dried microspheres.

The crystalline alkali metal aluminosilicate may be base-exchanged either before or after intimate admixture with the siliceous matrix material. Base-exchange removal of the alkali is effected by treatment with a solution essentially characterized by a pH of at least 4.5 and preferably in the range of 5 to 10, containing an ion capable of replacing the alkali metal. The alkali-metal content of the finished catalyst should be less than 1 percent by weight and preferably less than 0.5 percent by weight. The base-exchange solution may be brought into contact with the crystalline aluminosilicate in the form of finely divided powder, compressed pellet, extruded pellet, spheroidal bead, or any other suitable particle shape.

A silica–alumina matrix composite containing 25 weight-percent zeolite can be processed to exchange its alkali metals with

$CaCl_2$

NH_4Cl

$ZrOCl_2$

$CaCl_2–AlCl_3$

$CaCl_2–NH_4$

$CaCl_2–ZrOCl_2$

$CaCl_2–MgCl_2$

Acetic acid

Rare-earth chlorides

to give good results in most cases. However, catalysts exchanged with NH_4Cl, $ZrOCl_2$, and acetic acid gave much lower conversions and much poorer selectivities, that is, a low C5+ advantage over the standard silica–alumina. It is possible that these exchanges generate acid-X specie, which is unstable to steam and should be avoided.

Data presented in U.S. Patent 3,140,249 show that silica–zirconia matrix could be used as the matrix for the zeolite and would give excellent results.

From the evaluation of catalysts prepared using rare-earth metal exchange in Patent 3,140,249, it became apparent that rare-earth-exchanged catalysts were more active and more stable than the calcium-exchanged catalysts. The idea to use rare earths for the exchange process originated with others at Mobil experimenting on the pure zeolite. U.S. Patent 3,140,253, covered rare-earth-exchanged catalysts either in powdered or matrix form. The degree of alkali exchange is defined as resulting in a catalyst having no more than 0.25 equivalents per gram atom of aluminum of alkali. These catalysts had enhanced selectivity because they had associated with them both rare earth and ions selected from the group consisting of hydrogen, hydrogen precursors, and mixtures thereof. These catalysts are identified as rare-earth acid (REH).

Rare-earth acid (REHX) catalyst offers certain advantages over one prepared by base-exchanging the alkali X with rare-earth salts only (REX) catalyst. There is an apparent steam-stability advantage of the rare-earth-exchanged catalysts over the standard silica–alumina catalyst. Also evident is that the REHX catalysts were more selective.

Rare earth salts as available may be divided into cerium or cerium-free forms. Some rare earths give more selective catalysts. Particularly, La, Sm, and Gd salts resulted in more selective catalysts. Of these, however, catalysts using pure La proved uneconomical because of the higher cost of pure La salt.

U.S. Patent 3,368,981

From our understanding of the composition and technology disclosed in patent 3,140,249, we found it logical that other modifications in the catalyst's composition might yield improved catalysts.

In U.S. Patent 3,368,981 we described a new technique wherein a conventional silica–alumina catalyst in bead form for use in moving-bed units could be surface coated with powdered crystalline aluminosilicate that had had its alkali component exchanged with a rare-earth ion, identified as REY. Coating was achieved by the addition of a binder (such as brytes or powdered aluminum metal) to the powdered active zeolite. The bead catalyst was rolled at high temperature with the powdered zeolite and binder, causing the zeolite to stick to the surface of bead particles. The significance here is that pure zeolite (plus binder) could be added to a commercial unit while the unit was on-stream, giving immediately the advantages of the zeolite function. This technique could enable a refiner to adjust a unit's selectivity perfor-mance while the unit remained in operation and without changing all the catalyst.

U.S. Patent 3,391,075

It was pointed out above, in the description of patent 3,140,249, that two types of crystalline aluminosilicates, Linde X and Linde Y, were available from the Linde Corporation. The Linde X had a molar ratio of silica to alumina of 2.5:1, while Linde X had a ratio of from 3:1 to 6:1. Each of these catalysts was ion-exchanged with NH_4pl. We found that 5.1-percent Y was more active and more selective than 4.6-percent Y. Catalysts exchanged with ammonium chloride (a proton precursor) are known as acid catalysts. We also evaluated an acid Y versus an acid X, and found the Y catalyst to be more stable and more selective. Thus the catalysts pre-pared with the Linde Y zeolite are to be preferred because of their selectivity and stability.

U.S. Patent 3,442,795

Since it was apparent that crystalline aluminosilicates having a high molar ratio of SiO_2 to Al_2O_3 were more active and more selective, it was logical to evaluate zeolites with still higher ratios. These were not then available to us, but we found that alu-mina could be extracted from the crystalline aluminosilicate without destroying the structure. The alumina removal was achieved by contacting the Linde Y with a che-lating agent. EDTA (ethylenediaminetetraacetic acid) was found to be an effective agent. As much as 50 percent of the alumina could be removed and still leave a good catalyst. Research attempting to synthesize zeolites with higher molar ratios of SiO_2/Al_2O_3 continues.

U.S. Patent 3,431,218

The zeolites used in the above preparation were, as we have noted, synthetic fau-jasites obtained from Union Carbide Corporation's Linde Division. It became apparent early in our research that we needed to develop our own zeolite synthesis process. U.S. Patent 3,431,218 covers a method we developed for converting a nat-ural clay, a source of both silica and alumina, to a crystalline aluminosilicate of the faujasite type. Here clay was contacted with caustic sodium hydroxide and soluble sodium silicate (water glass) at temperatures of 600 to 1200°F for reaction. The powdered product was then contacted with a limited amount of water and reacted at 210°F, forming a crystalline product characterized by a high capacity for cyclohexane absorption. An important relationship holds between cyclohexane absorption and product crystallinity. Products were prepared that had high degrees of crystallinity and cyclohexane absorption. Pure Linde X or Y had a cyclohexane capacity of about 18 weight-percent. This process yielded products with equivalent capacities, and we considered that an excellent result.

U.S. Patent 3,391,088

We note above that in some cases the alkali form of crystalline aluminosilicate could also be incorporated into a matrix. On subsequent cyclic use, the alkali would migrate out of the zeolite and react with the matrix, neutralizing the alkali's tendency to interfere with the desired catalysis of petroleum cracking. After seventy cycles the catalyst had a selectivity advantage over standard silica–alumina catalyst in producing C5+ gasoline. This catalyst continued to improve as it was cycled further. After 344 cycles the advantage was 10.6 percent C5+ gasoline. The data show that any residual alkali in a final catalyst composite would migrate to the matrix. This solid–solid exchange process reduces the need for an extensive exchange process to reduce the alkali metal to low levels in the initial catalyst.

U.S. Patent 3,493,490

During use, the crystalline aluminosilicate catalysts are subjected to steam at elevated temperature. Actually, the catalyst becomes more selective. We found that the deactivated selectivated catalysts could be regenerated to their original nonselective state. A REHX catalyst was selectivated with steam at 1200°F, giving a C5+ gasoline yield of +7.5. Treating this catalyst with an aqueous solution of ammonium hydroxide, it was possible to cause the steamed catalyst to revert to its original unsteamed performance and a −4.8 C5+ gasoline yield. The selectivity was restored on resteaming. The ability to reactivate used catalysts is of particular interest in commercial applications. Currently, deactivated catalysts are withdrawn from the units and must be replaced with fresh catalysts.

U.S. Patent 3,758,403

The catalysts presented and covered in patent 3,140,249 were prepared employing only one type of crystalline aluminosilicate, either Linde X or Linde Y. We reasoned further that some of the straight components in the gasoline contribute to low octane: normal heptane, for instance, is a C7 carbon fraction with a very low octane. A catalyst that could crack out this fraction would increase the octane of the remaining gasoline. Accordingly, we reasoned that a combination of crystalline zeolites like a large-pore and small-pore 4- to 5-angstrom zeolite like ZSM 5 or Erionite could result in octane advantages, since the small-pore zeolites would crack out the low-octane straight-chain components. We showed that catalyst containing the large-pore REY yielded a C5+ gasoline having a 93.7 research octane number, while the combination of REY and ZSM gave 97.2 and 98.6. High-octane gasolines are desirable and competitively sought after in current refinery processes.

U.S. Patent 3,769,202

It is apparent that many combinations of zeolites could be used in making cracking catalysts for the octane application. This patent lists numerous possible combinations that could be functional. The components are categorized as greater than 8 angstroms or less than 7 angstroms. Various matrix compositions are also identified.

The concept of subterranean catalytic cracking was considered in our research as a logical extension for an application of the new superactive catalysts. These, particularly in colloidal form, could be injected into a depleted crude reservoir to react with the residual hydrocarbons and generate low-molecular-weight molecules, which could act as solvent for the residual heavy crude components. At the same time, gaseous components of this "passive" cracking would pressurize the reservoir and help recover more of the crude. Some crude deposits are currently hot enough themselves to drive the catalytic reaction. In others, heat could be generated through partial oxidation by in-situ combustion. Porosity of the reservoir would be a limiting factor.

References

Kerr, G. (July, 1989). Synthetic zeolites. *Scientific American,* 100–105.

Kerr, G. T., Plank, C. J., & Rosinski, E. J. (1969). Method for preparing highly siliceous zeolite-type materials and materials resulting therefrom. U.S. Patent 3,442,795.

Plank, C. J. & Rosinski, E. J. (1964). Catalytic cracking of hydrocarbons with a crystaline zeolite catalyst composite. U.S. Patent 3,140,249.

Plank, C. J. & Rosinski, E. J. (1964). Catalytic hydrocarbon conversion with a crystalline zeolite composite catalyst. U.S. Patent 3,140,253.

Plank, C. J. & Rosinski, E. J. (1968). Catalytic conversion of hydrocarbons with the use of a steam treated Y type of crystalline aluminosilicate. U.S. Patent 3,391,075.

Plank, C. J. & Rosinski, E. J. (1968). Utilization of superactive catalytic materials. U.S. Patent 3,368,981.

Plank, C. J. & Rosinski, E. J. (1969). Conversion of clays to crystalline aluminosilicates and catalysts therefrom. U.S. Patent 3,431,218.

Plank, C. J. & Rosinski, E. J. (1970). Regeneration of aluminosilicate catalysts. U.S. Patent 3,493,490.

Rosinski, E. J. Plank, C. J., & Schwartz, A. B. (1973). Catalytic cracking of Hydrocarbons with mixture of ZSM-5 and other zeolites. U.S. Patent 3,758,403.

10 | Discovery and Invention in Polymer Chemistry

PAUL W. MORGAN

This chapter describes discovery and invention in an industrial laboratory whose purpose is to seek new products for a synthetic fibers business. Here the search may be for fundamental information and understanding or for a specific practical goal. The searcher may be an individual working alone or a member of a team. The researcher may work on more than one project at a time, and assignments often are changed in midstream to serve the manpower needs of the laboratory.

The laboratory where the research described here took place was the Pioneering Research Laboratory of the Textile Fibers Department of the Du Pont Company. The history of this laboratory to 1950 has been reviewed by Hounshell (1989). The laboratory was formed in 1935 under the directorship of W. Hale Charch at a rayon plant in Tonawanda, New York. Personnel grew from a few chemists and engineers to around 100 first-line people and their supporting teams of analytical services, physical testing laboratory, machine shop and building maintenance, semiworks, library, and secretarial staff shortly after 1950, the year in which it became a unit of the company Experimental Station in Wilmington, Delaware.

The assignment of the laboratory was, and is, to discover or invent new products and processes for use by the Textile Fibers Department. It is a very productive research group and is the point of origin of such products as Orlon® acrylic fiber, Dacron® polyester fiber, and Lycra® spandex fibers. While the primary focus was always on new fibers, the goals were broadly interpreted and included at some time such products as nonwoven fabrics, synthetic leathers, synthetic polymer papers, filter pads, and sanitary napkins, and processes such as improved dyeing procedures, innovative fiber-forming methods, and small-scale preparation of starting materials for polymer synthesis.

Naturally, discoveries were made of products not within the goals of the department. Information on these materials was transferred to other company departments in various ways.

The development of a product to commercial scale requires the cooperative efforts and expertise of many segments of a large department or company. Some of these are planning, safety, finance, scale-up adaptation and equipment development, engineering assistance, market evaluation, procurement or production of chemical intermediates, plant construction or adaptation, and advertising.

With this background, let us turn to some of the constraints and motivation factors in the activities of a first-line researcher.

Disciplines of an Industrial Laboratory

In the Pioneering Research Laboratory, a number of goals and constraints determined the range of activity and freedom of the research worker. These varied somewhat for individuals, depending on their position in the advancement ladder, greater freedom and responsibility being given to those with more advanced positions in the hierarchy. Here are some of the goals and constraints.

Goals

- Company goal: to make money for the stockholder.
- Departmental goal: to find new or improved products and processes for the Textile Fibers Department.
- Laboratory goal: to find new products and processes for the Textile Fibers Department.

Constraints

- Funding: individuals or small groups submit Project Proposal for approval by Research Management which:

  Outlines goal or problem

  Tells background and benefits of solution

  Proposes methods of solution

  Tells how many researchers are needed

  States how long work will take and what expenditure is expected to be
- Duties of individual researcher:

  To work on problem and report to supervisor

  To keep research notebook

  To contribute items on research progress to monthly newsletter

  To present oral research reviews to laboratory personnel 2–4 times a year

  To write two or more formal research reports each year

  To write proposals for patent action

  To do "bootleg" research to discover new areas for future research projects
- All employees given formal, yearly performance reviews by their immediate supervisor

These goals and constraints were not in a written document but came to be known by the researcher through supervisory instruction. They were a means of managing a research laboratory and the research budget. The list shows that the research worker was required to be a good communicator as well as a good investigator.

Qualifications of a Researcher

The researcher should have appropriate training in problem solving, a background of information and experience (not necessarily on the problem at hand), curiosity, an open mind (not misled by prejudices), optimism, self-confidence, integrity, persistence, and a sense of urgency. The researcher must also be motivated.

Individuals are motivated to strive industriously at their work by a variety of factors, usually by a combination of factors. Some of those affecting industrial researchers are listed below. The order of importance is a personal matter and might change with time. For the most part, I was motivated by factors toward the upper part of the list, although I certainly was glad to get paid for work that was usually fun to do. Publication of the research work became an abiding secondary interest, which had a positive effect on the quality of the research. By this I mean that in product research one may jump by intuition or experience to the next step, whereas publication often requires a more detailed proof and analysis of the product or phenomenon.

Factors Motivating Performance

Challenge and curiosity

Self-esteem and personal triumph

Regard of peers and supervision

Competition, local and outside

Requirement to meet goals and deadlines

Patents and publications

Travel to professional meetings

Desire for continued employment

Money and bonuses

Pay for inventorship

Promotion

Awards

Approach to Problem Solving

An important requirement for a productive research program is that there be a defined objective or problem as a starting point. The goal should appeal to workers in the program as worthwhile and should be a challenge to the best of their abilities. Here are some of the steps in setting up and carrying out a research program.

Setting of goals

Definition of problems to be solved

Search for background information

Thinking about possible solutions to problem

Assembly of equipment and materials

Active and diligent experimentation
    Planned variation of experiments
    Reassessment in response to results
    Indirect approaches
    Alternate solutions
    Thinking while relaxing
    Consultation with others
  Serendipity

One starts a program with what B. J. Luberoff (1989) calls *"the ultimate assumption,* that for this problem a solution does exist." My usual approach to a research program was to do some planned scouting experiments as soon as possible, using past experience and judgment in selecting the conditions and materials. Such experiments may or may not yield promising results, but they help define the problem. Frequently, these experiments would have been done prior to preparation of a research proposal.

A brief literature survey may be made before or during the research. Care must be taken not to be deterred by past reports of failure, but rather to analyze why there was a failure. As the program progresses and as needed, all available technology and ideas are applied toward reaching a solution. If the problem does not yield to a head-on approach, one may make gains by first working out a closely related but less difficult problem.

Examples of Polymer Research

Three research programs that resulted in patents will be described. Two were applied commercially. All three involved the preparation and/or use of condensation polymers.

My part in these programs, and that of associates in my group, was to make discoveries and inventions, to do small-scale evaluation of the products and processes, to provide aid and consultation to others who might carry on or develop the technology, and to support the preparation and prosecution of patents. The programs often included the assembly and/or use of fiber-spinning equipment and making arrangements for fabric sample preparation.

Let me digress further and explain a bit about the nature of condensation polymers and their preparation.

Condensation polymers (Figure 10.1) are commonly made by reaction of two or more bifunctional complementary intermediates in chemically equivalent amounts. The formulas are chemists' shorthand for the structure of chemical compounds: C stands for carbon, H for hydrogen, N for nitrogen, and O for oxygen. The connecting lines are bonds between the atoms. The terminal $-NH_2$ groups are called amine or amino groups; the terminal $-C-O-H$ group is a carboxyl or acid
                                          O
group. In the formula for the polymer, hydrogen-substituted carbon chains have been shortened by indicating only the number of $-CH_2-$ groups. *n* stands for the

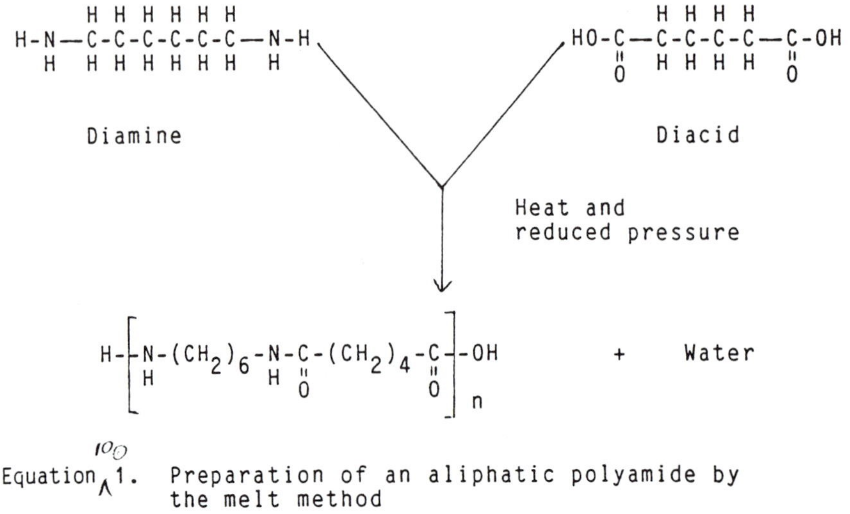

$$H-N—\overset{\overset{\displaystyle H}{|}}{\underset{\underset{\displaystyle H}{|}}{C}}-\overset{\overset{\displaystyle H}{|}}{\underset{\underset{\displaystyle H}{|}}{C}}-\overset{\overset{\displaystyle H}{|}}{\underset{\underset{\displaystyle H}{|}}{C}}-\overset{\overset{\displaystyle H}{|}}{\underset{\underset{\displaystyle H}{|}}{C}}-\overset{\overset{\displaystyle H}{|}}{\underset{\underset{\displaystyle H}{|}}{C}}-\overset{\overset{\displaystyle H}{|}}{\underset{\underset{\displaystyle H}{|}}{C}}—N-H$$

Diamine

$$HO-\overset{\overset{\displaystyle H}{}}{\underset{\underset{\displaystyle O}{||}}{C}}—\overset{\overset{\displaystyle H}{|}}{\underset{\underset{\displaystyle H}{|}}{C}}-\overset{\overset{\displaystyle H}{|}}{\underset{\underset{\displaystyle H}{|}}{C}}-\overset{\overset{\displaystyle H}{|}}{\underset{\underset{\displaystyle H}{|}}{C}}-\overset{\overset{\displaystyle H}{|}}{\underset{\underset{\displaystyle H}{|}}{C}}—\overset{}{\underset{\underset{\displaystyle O}{||}}{C}}-OH$$

Diacid

Heat and
reduced pressure

$$H-\left[\overset{}{\underset{\underset{\displaystyle H}{|}}{N}}-(CH_2)_6-\overset{}{\underset{\underset{\displaystyle H}{|}}{N}}-\overset{}{\underset{\underset{\displaystyle O}{||}}{C}}-(CH_2)_4-\overset{}{\underset{\underset{\displaystyle O}{||}}{C}}\right]_n-OH \qquad + \qquad Water$$

10

Equation 1.   Preparation of an aliphatic polyamide by
                  the melt method

FIGURE 10.1. Preparation of an aliphatic polyamide by the melt method.

average number of repeat units in a polymer molecule and might be as much as 50 to 100 or more.

In this example the diamine and a diacid react at elevated temperature and under vacuum, with the elimination of water to form a polyamide. This is the procedure of Carothers, the originator of nylon. The word *condensation* indicates the process of combining the materials with the elimination of a simple molecule, water (H_2O) in this case. You will note that the components alternate in the product to form long chains. The product is called a polymer, meaning *many units,* or more specifically, a *polyamide* because the linking units are known by the name *amide.*

In addition to using a shorthand of symbols to describe their chemistry, chemists use space models of varying degrees of sophistication to help them visualize molecules in three dimensions. The latest and most precise method is computer imagery.

A crude model (Morgan, 1960) that I have used in school classrooms to convey the idea of a forming chain of a two-component condensation polymer, such as nylon, is illustrated in Figure 10.2. It consists of an imaginary reactor (a paper bag) in which one puts equal quantities of the two ingredients (represented by elliptical blocks of balsa with small bar magnets inserted in the ends), one type colored black and the other white. Since the magnets are oriented in such a way that black combines only with white, a chain of alternating units is formed. This is a mechanical depiction of the simple chemistry outlined in Figure 10.1 but without the elimination of a by-product. The three investigations in the following discussion use similar simple chemistry for polymer preparation.

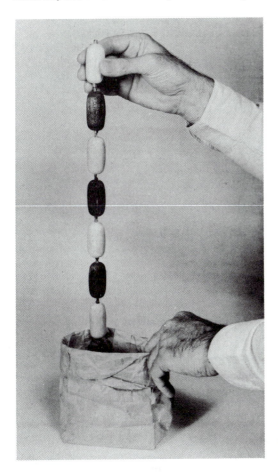

FIGURE 10.2. Demonstration model for condensation polymerization.

Interfacial Polycondensation

The first example resulted by chance within another program with an entirely different goal. In 1950 Emerson Wittbecker in our laboratory, with a lead from German patents, started a program on polymer preparation by a low-temperature procedure that became known as interfacial polycondensation (Figure 10.3). This is a process in which a water solution of a diamine and an inorganic base, such as sodium carbonate (washing soda), is rapidly stirred with a solution of the complementary reactant in a solvent that does not mix with the water. You might think of mixing up an oil and water salad dressing and carrying out a chemical reaction at the interface of the two liquids. High reaction speed is attained by replacing the hydrogen–oxygen group of the acid intermediate with a chlorine group. In the presence of soda the by-products are salt and carbon dioxide. The polyamide is obtained as a granular precipitate.

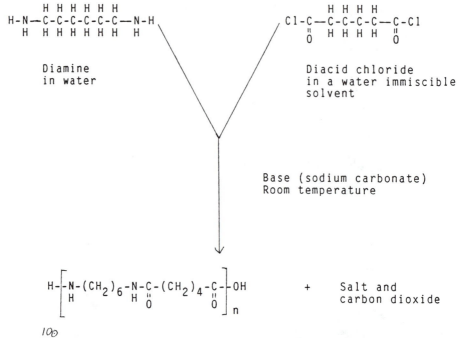

Equation ∧ 2.   Preparation of an aliphatic polyamide by
                 the interfacial method

FIGURE 10.3. Preparation of an aliphatic polyamide by the interfacial method.

It was soon realized that the interfacial process might have broad applicability, especially for the preparation of unmeltable or thermally unstable polymers and for use with thermally unstable starting materials. A group of chemists took up the preparation of various classes of polymers.

I undertook an investigation of the mechanism and process variables of interfacial polycondensation. Up to this point all preparations had been carried out with high-speed stirring. One of the first experiments was to look at an unstirred system, that is, to place a solution of a diamine, hexamethylenediamine (six carbon atoms), in water on a solution of sebacyl chloride (ten carbon atoms) in carbon tetrachloride in a beaker (Figure 10.4). A coherent film of a polyamide, a nylon, formed at once and, when the film was pushed aside or grasped with tweezers and pulled upward, more film formed and followed continuously. This was an exciting discovery in itself and we later studied it extensively. The experiment became known as the "nylon rope trick" (Morgan, 1965, 1980; Morgan & Kwolek, 1959) and has been widely used as a dramatic demonstration of condensation polymerization. In fact, the experiment is currently part of the chemistry exhibit at the Smithsonian Institution in Washington, D.C.

The invention to be discussed was derived from this experiment. To prepare the

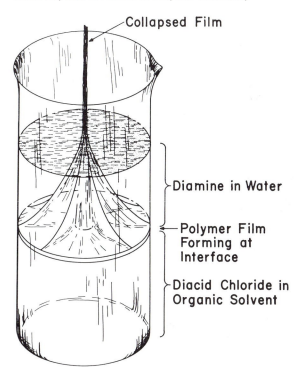

Collapsed Film

Diamine in Water

Polymer Film
Forming at
Interface

Diacid Chloride in
Organic Solvent

FIGURE 10.4. Preparation of
6–10 polyamide by interfacial
polycondensation.

rope of polymer film for analysis, the polymer was placed in a blender with water and shredded to a fibrous pulp. When the pulp was collected on a sintered glass filter, a small sheet of paper was formed. This product was recognized as potentially useful as a synthetic polymer paper. I then did some experiments in which pre-formed polymers were dissolved in solvents and caused to precipitate in fibrous form by being poured into nonsolvents with rapid stirring. These, too, formed papers. The results were recorded and communicated by discussion and by letter to others who had some interest in papers. Two years passed before a full-scale program on papermaking from synthetic polymers was established. This was due partly to the fact that much of the early research was directed toward the formation of a suedelike sheet material. Today, papers from Nomex® aramid, an aromatic ring-containing polyamide to be discussed later, are manufactured by DuPont for use in electrical insulation and for the preparation of heat-resistant honeycomb panels. The fibrous particles are called "fibrids" and may be used alone or combined as a binding material for chopped synthetic fiber.

The patent on these fibrids and their papers, U.S. Patent 2,999,788, has 184 examples and 92 claims (Hounshell & Smith, 1988; Moreman, 1961). It contains much work by other chemists, although I spent six months helping to define the range of suitable polymers and processing conditions. I did not participate in the development of a paper product. The Patent Office considered this patent for issue as number 3,000,000, but decided it was too bulky to be a suitable choice.

*Aromatic Polyamides and Solution
Polycondensation (Forney, 1988; Hounshell &
Smith, 1988; Morgan, 1979, 1985)*

After the development of interfacial polycondensation, Pioneering Research chemists made literally thousands of new polymers. During this period of several years, the discovery of a high-temperature-resistant polymer was considered a goal, but none was found with wholly satisfactory properties. Aromatic diamines and diacid chlorides, which contain carbon ring structures, were expected to provide the desired high melting points and probably the desired thermal stability (Figure 10.5). However, only low-molecular-weight products were obtained by interfacial polycondensation. Long polymer chains, or what I am going to call loosely "high molecular weights," are essential for the formation of tough, strong products such as fibers and films. It was thought that aromatic diamines lacked sufficient reactivity or that there were some interfering side reactions.

The term *aromatic* and the ring symbols in Figure 10.5 require an explanation. The hexagonal rings represent a ring of six carbon atoms. Each carbon atom bears a hydrogen atom, not shown, or an amino or acid chloride group. The inner circle represents a system of bonding forces of varying position. The compound, benzene, is represented by a hydrogen-substituted, six-carbon ring. Substances in this class are called aromatic, originally because of the odors associated with some of them.

I had continued the study of the interfacial polymerization process in detail, and in 1952, because of the challenge, took on an additional project to examine polymer preparation from aromatic intermediates. Now it would be nice to be able to say

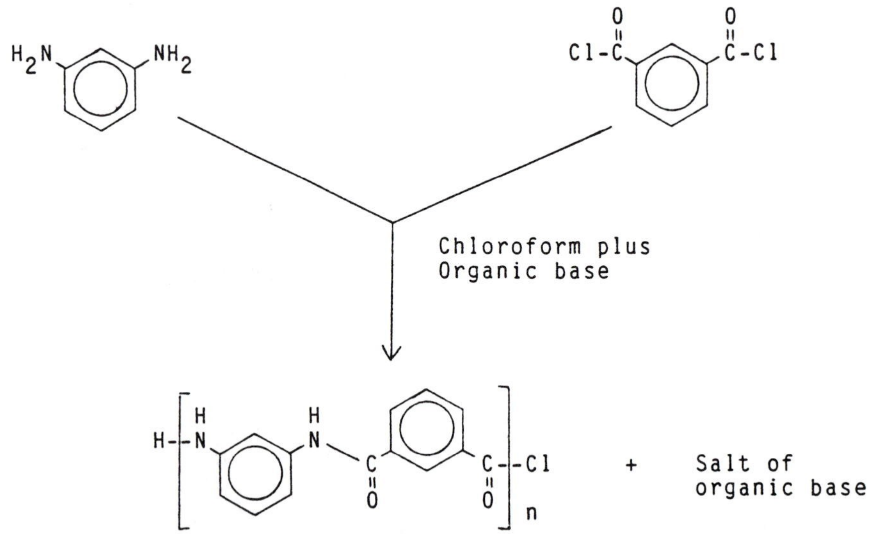

FIGURE 10.5. Preparation of a 1,3-linked, semiflexible aromatic polyamide.

that the problem was quickly and brilliantly solved, but the evolution of useful products and processes took more than a year and contributions by chemists from several groups.

That reactivity of the starting materials was adequate was shown by reaction rate measurements. High purity was indicated by analysis and by the formation of high-molecular-weight polymers when the aromatic components were allowed to react with nonaromatic intermediates.

In late 1953 I started experiments to determine if condensation polymers could be made in a single organic solvent without the water phase. I found as a result of a fortunate choice of materials that in many cases the liquid interface was not needed.

The first experiments were with a polymer that was soluble in the organic solvent and with an added organic base, a tertiary amine, as the neutralizer for the by-product acid. The lore of interfacial polycondensation was so firmly established that we had to demonstrate that polymer was truly formed in solution and not in the isolation step. I must add that I enjoy making discoveries that are contrary to what I, myself, and others believe at the time. The single liquid process was called "solution polycondensation" regardless of whether the polymeric product remained in solution or precipitated.

An important concept developed during the work on interfacial and solution polycondensation was that the longer the growing polymer chains remained swollen or dissolved by the solvent medium, the higher the molecular weight could be. In hindsight that thought seems rather obvious. However, considerable experimentation was required to classify solvents according to solubility potential, to take into account an accompanying effect of solvent polarity on reaction rate, and to relate these data to actual degrees of polymerization.

Solution polycondensation was the key to the successful preparation of high-molecular-weight, wholly aromatic polyamides. Among the first high-molecular-weight polymers was the one shown in Figure 10.5 prepared in the liquid, chloroform, with added triethylamine $[(C_2H_5)_3N]$. An accompanying discovery was that the triethylamine hydrochloride $[(C_2H_5)_3N.HCl]$, formed in the reaction or added to the chloroform, enhanced the solubility of the polymer and was essential for attaining high molecular weight (Morgan, 1979b).

The discovery of the salt effect was made in a backhanded way. The available high-quality diamine was in the form of a hydrochloride salt. This diamine salt was used with extra triethylamine to yield the free reactive diamine, at the same time forming more triethylamine hydrochloride. When pure diamine in the nonsalt form was used in subsequent experiments, the polymer was much lower in molecular weight. Chloroform did not yield high-molecular-weight polymer in interfacial polycondensation because the salt effect was absent.

Later on, amide solvents, with or without added salts, were found to be useful polymerization media. A good example is dimethylacetamide

$$[(CH_3)_2N - \overset{C}{\underset{O}{||}} - CH_3]$$ plus lithium chloride. These solvents are slightly basic and act as both a polymerization medium and an acid neutralizer. From here on media of this type will simply be called "amide solvents."

The final outcome of this program was the development of a polymerization-spinning system without polymer isolation. The polymer structure shown in Figure 10.5 is that of Nomex® aramid. Nomex® aramid fiber was introduced commercially in 1961. The term *aramid* is defined as a polyamide in which at least 85 percent of the amide groups connect aromatic rings. Nomex fibers are used in flame- and heat-resistant fabrics used in protective clothing, fire hoses, and smokestack filter bags and as papers for electrical insulation and in high-strength honeycomb paneling.

This summary touches only a few highlights of the beginning of a complex interaction among chemists in different research groups and laboratories; it does not touch at all on the additional research and engineering that go into preparing for manufacture of a new product.

Liquid Crystalline Aromatic Polyamides (Morgan, 1979a; Hounshell & Smith, 1988)

The polymer shown in Figure 10.5 has aromatic rings that are linked to amide units at the 1,3- or meta positions. Although the rings are rigid and planar, the 1,3- linkage allows the chains to be appreciably flexible.

During this research on aromatic polyamides, 1,4- or paralinked polymers were prepared, such as those illustrated in Figure 10.6. They were somewhat low in molecular weight and were set aside after the selection of the Nomex® composition as a heat-resistant fiber candidate.

In 1964 as a result of writing a review book (Morgan, 1965) on condensation polymers, and with the appearance of a Monsanto patent on a paralinked aromatic polyamide, we became more aware that this was a neglected area of study that might yield some new products with superior properties, particularly greater thermal stability. Stephanie Kwolek was assigned the work of examining poly(1,4-benzamide), represented by the top formula in Figure 10.6. This polymer is derived from a single

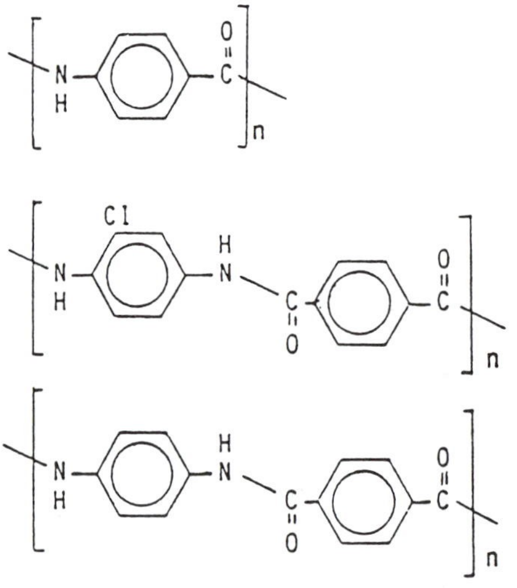

FIGURE 10.6. 1,4- or paralinked polymers. Top, 1,4-benzamide. Middle, chlorine substituent on diamino unit of paralinked polyamide. Bottom, unsubstituted paralinked polyamide.

starting material. Polymers can be made from molecules with both interactive groups in one intermediate by masking one group, in this case the amine group, and then unmasking it in the polymerization medium.

By careful experimentation and unusual persistence, Kwolek succeeded in making high-molecular-weight polymer samples and preparing spinnable solutions in amide–salt solvents. The solutions had a pearly, turbid appearance, which was enhanced by stirring, and were less viscous than the usual spinning solution. Because of these unusual characteristics, Kwolek had some trouble convincing the technician in charge of the spinning service that the solution should be spun. We later recognized that the solutions were *liquid crystalline,* which means that the polymer molecules, which are rodlike, were organized into parallel arrays in microscopic regions. The importance of this property is that, when the solutions are spun, the as-extruded fibers have a high degree of alignment of the polymer molecules in the direction of the long fiber axis. The result is unusually high strength (tenacity) and elastic modulus in the as-spun fiber.[1] These properties are further improved by heat treatment under tension. Normally the production of useful fibers requires an expensive drawing step after the spinning to align the polymer chains and yield a strong, stable product.

The first high-quality solutions and fibers were nearly a year in the making. The fibers were recognized at once as exceptional materials. Scale-up, testing for applications, and exploration for alternate compositions were begun. After the initial discovery I prepared a memorandum outlining polymer structures that should yield similar results. Later research showed that many of these did indeed form liquid crystalline solutions and high-strength, high-modulus fibers. Some did not because we did not fully understand the structural requirements for liquid crystalline solutions and adequate solubility.

Thomas Bair, a newly employed chemist in my group, was assigned the work of preparing solutions and fibers from the polyamide from 1,4-phenylenediamine and terephthaloyl chloride (Figure 10.7) that we had previously examined in a limited way during the Nomex® development.

Bair first worked out the conditions for synthesizing the 1,4-linked polymer having a chlorine substituent on the diamine ring (middle formula, Figure 10.6), which was more soluble (Bair & Morgan, 1974; Bair, Morgan, & Killian, 1977). The polymer formed liquid crystalline solutions in amide–salt solvents. High-tenacity, high-modulus fibers were prepared. This represents a stepwise approach to a problem. Instead of tackling a tough problem head on, one works out the conditions for managing a related, more tractable material. Sometimes chemists work with low-molecular-weight materials as models to simulate the behavior of high-molecular-weight polymers. We did this in determining solvent effects in the Nomex® studies.

With further experiments Bair discovered how to prepare the unsubstituted polymer (Figure 10.7) in high molecular weight and found that it would form stable liquid crystalline solutions in very concentrated sulfuric acid. High-tenacity stiff fibers were obtained by extruding these solutions into water, a process called wet-spinning (Bair & Morgan, 1974; Bair, Morgan, & Killian, 1977). After other critical improvements by other chemists, this polymer was selected for full-scale development as Kevlar® aramid fiber and was introduced commercially in 1972. The fibers

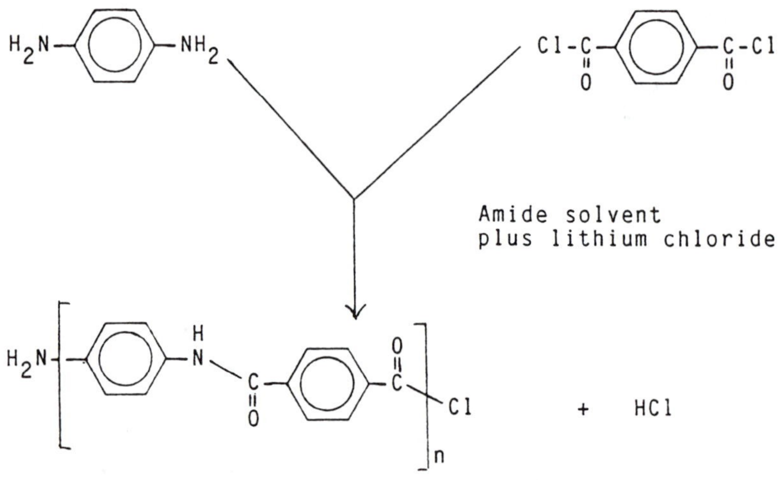

FIGURE 10.7. Preparation of a 1,4-linked aromatic polyamide.

are five times or more stronger than steel on an equal weight basis and have a modulus (stiffness) greater than glass fibers. They have many uses, such as in reinforcement of plastics and rubber, ropes, and cables; in bullet-resistant vests; in cut-resistant clothing; and in asbestos replacement in brake and clutch linings.

The introduction of Kevlar fibers, the liquid crystalline behavior of paralinked, aromatic polyamides, and more recent work on liquid-crystalline melts of polyesters (by J. R. Schaefgen and others) has stimulated worldwide research activity and the production of competitive fibers and some specialized plastics.

Polyazomethines

The third example illustrates the application of a technique developed for polyesters to a hitherto intractable class of polymers.

The work of Kwolek, Bair, myself, and others established the ability of polyamides with rodlike, extended polymer chains to form liquid crystalline solutions, which, when spun, yielded highly oriented, high-tenacity fibers. Therefore, along with this research we studied other classes of condensation polymers that we believed had similar potential. Some of these have been described since in patents and publications.

I examined published lists of low-molecular-weight compounds that were reported to form liquid–crystalline melts. Among them were paralinked aromatic azomethines. Here was a possible class of polymers to serve our purpose. The advantage of spinning a polymer from a melt is that no solvent in needed and the step of solvent recovery is eliminated.

Polyazomethines (Morgan, 1977, 1978; Morgan, Kwolek, & Pletcher, 1987) should be formed by the simple condensation of an aromatic diamine and an aro-

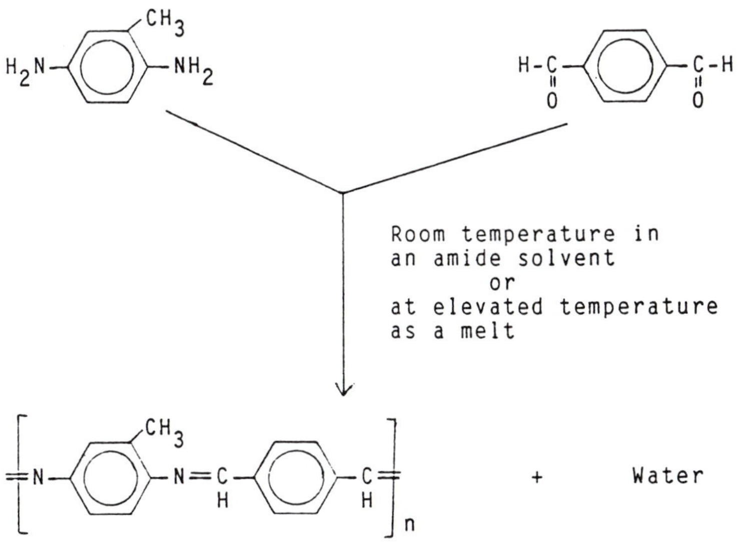

FIGURE 10.8. Preparation of a 1,4-linked aromatic polyazomethine.

matic dialdehyde with the elimination of water (Figure 10.8). In this Figure there are two new groups, the $-\overset{C}{\underset{H}{|}}=O$, which is an aldehyde function, and the ring-linking group $-\overset{N}{\underset{H}{|}}=C-$, which is called "azomethine."

Reports in the literature of attempts to make aromatic polyazomethines described the products as low in molecular weight, brick-dustlike powders, and black unmeltable masses. Two problems needed solution: a process for attaining high molecular weight and a means of lowering the melting point to a practical range for melt spinning, 350°C or less.

John Schaefgen, in our laboratory, had demonstrated that paralinked aromatic polyesters could be made meltable in a useful range by placing a substituent on the ring of one of the intermediates. By applying this method of structure modification to polyazomethines and using a solution polymerization procedure in amide solvents to which lithium chloride was added to absorb the by-product water, I was able to synthesize high-molecular-weight polyazomethines that formed liquid crystalline melts and were melt-spinnable (Figure 10.9).

The first example shown in the table was among the earliest to be prepared and one of the most promising. The substituent, CH_3-, is called a "methyl group." Other useful intermediates show chlorine (Cl-) substituents. The fibers had exceptionally high tenacity and stiffness. Two broad patents were obtained (Morgan, 1977, 1978).

Other synthetic methods were found useful and appreciable scale-up work was done, but the fibers were not commercially produced. Several factors contributed to this decision. Among them were the cost of intermediates and the existence of other high-tenacity fibers, such as Kevlar® aramid fibers.

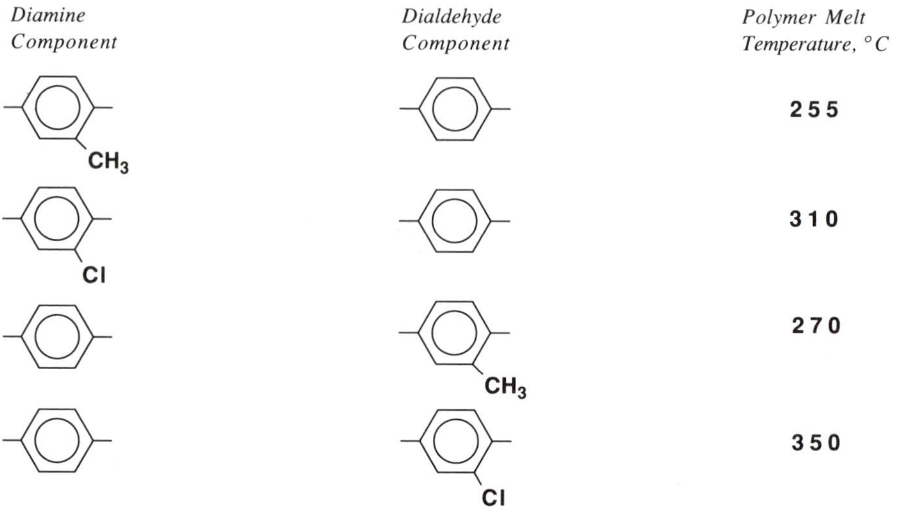

Diamine Component	Dialdehyde Component	Polymer Melt Temperature, °C

FIGURE 10.9. Aromatic polyazomethines

Concluding Note

In the foregoing review we have progressed from the aliphatic polyamides, nylons, with their very flexible polymer molecules through the 1,3-linked aromatic poly-amides, which are semiflexible, to the 1,4-linked aromatic polyamides and poly-azomethines, which have extended rodlike molecules. The discussion illustrates how often serendipity plays a part in solving a problem or yields a new discovery. The three examples also show how one research program can lead to and support a following investigation. After checking patents in my name, I find that only about 15 percent are based on chance discoveries; the rest were the result of solutions to planned objectives. Serendipity sometimes played a part in reaching that solution.

    Not all discoveries or inventions are patented or are patentable. Even though unpatented, they add to the fund of information available to the researcher and his or her colleagues. They may be useful, too, in manufacturing developments and may provide a basis for worthwhile publications.

Notes

    1. Tenacity is the force required to break a fiber divided by its cross-sectional area or by a factor that expresses its weight per unit of length. The modulus referred to is known as the *elastic modulus*. This is the slope of a plot of tensile force versus the amount of fiber extension or elongation (stress vs. strain). It represents the resistance of the fiber to extension and is a factor in stiffness. This modulus is often measured near the beginning of the stress-strain plot because for many fibers the plot is appreciably curved. High tenacity is important in rein-forcing fibers because they then have higher load-bearing capacity and less fiber may be used for attainment of a given strength than with a lower tenacity fiber. A high elastic modulus provides resistance to deformation under load or sudden impact.

References

Bair, T. I. & Morgan, P. W. (1974, June 18). Wholly aromatic carbocyclic polycarbonamide fiber. *U. S. Patent 3,817,941* (assigned to DuPont Co.).

Bair, T. I., Morgan, P. W., & Killian, F. L. (1977). Poly(1,4-phenylene-terephthalamides): Polymerization and novel liquid-crystalline solutions. *Macromolecules, 10*(6), 1396.

Forney, R. C. (1988). Advanced materials and technological innovation. *Chemtech, 18*(3), 178–183.

Hounshell, D. A. (1989). Invention at Du Pont: From individual act to collective process. Paper presented at *The Inventing Mind: A Conference on Creativity in Technology.* Tulsa, Okla., November 2–5.

Hounshell, D. A. & Smith, J. K. (1988). *Science and Corporate Strategy.* New York: Cambridge Univ. Press, pp. 374, 426–433.

Luberoff, B. J. (1989). The ultimate assumption. *Chemtech, 19*(10), 577.

Morgan, P. W. (1960). Models for linear polymers. *Journal of Chemical Education, 37,* 206.

Morgan, P. W. (1961, September 12). Synthetic polymer fibrid paper. *U. S. Patent 2,999,788* (assigned to DuPont Co.).

Morgan, P. W. (1965). *Condensation Polymers: By Interfacial and Solution Processes.* New York: Interscience.

Morgan, P. W. (1977, September 13). Polyazomethine fibers and films. *U. S. Patent 4,048,148* (assigned to DuPont Co.).

Morgan, P. W. (1978, October 24). Fibers and anisotropic melts of polyazomethines. *U. S. Patent 4,122,070* (assigned to DuPont Co.).

Morgan, P. W. (1979a). High performance fibres: development and uses. *Plastics and Rubber: Materials & Applications,* (2), 1–7.

Morgan, P. W. (1979b). Aromatic polyamides. *Chemtech, 18*(5), 316–326.

Morgan, P. W. (1980). A short autobiography in *Modern Scientists and Engineers.* New York: McGraw-Hill, *2,* 324.

Morgan, P. W. (1985). Development of low temperature polycondensation processes and aromatic polyamides. *Journal of Polymer Science: Polymer Symposia,* 27–37.

Morgan, P. W. & Kwolek, S. L. (1959). The nylon rope trick. *Journal of Chemical Education, 36,* 182–184, 530.

Morgan, P. W., Kwolek, S. L., & Pletcher, T. C. (1987). Aromatic azomethine polymers and fibers. *Macromolecules, 20,* 729–739.

11 | The Genesis
of the Antiparasitic Drug
Ivermectin

WILLIAM C. CAMPBELL

Enter, with Flourishes and Caveats

It was not a neat event; it is not a "gee whiz" story. No cerebral light bulb flashed the form and function of ivermectin on anybody's mental screen. Nor was the discovery of this new drug the result of an industrial research team's deciding to take existing scientific knowledge at point A and develop it to point B, where it would yield a product to be sold. Nor, yet again, was it a matter of chance, in which some industrial Princes of Serendipe sailed to an antiparasitic landing while bound for other therapeutic territory. No, it was a complicated and unglamorous mixture of all of these. That is not as trite as it may seem, for all of those kinds of discovery do happen in the context of modern industrial research. I have been asked to tell the story, despite my warnings about its intrinsically untidy nature, and am emboldened by assurances that an examination of any such real-life situation would be, if not pleasing, at least edifying. My excuse for accepting the invitation to tell the story myself is that I was, in Dean Acheson's sense of the phrase, "present at the creation." I speak as a parasitologist; and the parasitology effort, after all, provided as good a vantage point as any from which to observe the emergence of what was to become a major antiparasitic drug.

The new drug was actually one of a family of new antiparasitic substances, and these were found as a result of a deliberate effort to find such things. The research was conducted in an industrial laboratory. In that setting it is not enough to find new compounds that are active against parasites, but to find new active compounds that can be made into successful products. The present account, therefore, while not directly addressing the process of drug development, must deal not only with a moment of discovery but also with a complex process of assessment. The goal, more specifically, was to find an anthelmintic, that is, a drug that is effective against worm parasites (helminths). The goal furthermore was to find an anthelmintic that was not just a bit more potent than existing drugs, or a bit safer, or a bit broader in therapeutic spectrum, but to find one that was radically different. From the outset we avoided the temptation to base our research on the chemical structure or biochemical action of known anthelmintics. We wanted new structures that would do new things to parasites.

Before plunging into a more or less chronological account, it is well to sound a warning or two. In the ten years following the discovery of the avermectins, scientists of the Merck Sharp & Dohme Research Laboratories published more than seventy scientific papers on the subject. My list of these publications proved too much even for the most tolerant of editors, but the names of the authors are listed in Acknowledgments. Other papers were published during that period by scientists at other institutions. The papers cited in this chapter necessarily represent only a portion of those published from our own or other laboratories. In many cases I have linked specific contributions to specific investigators or publications, but it has not always been feasible to do so. It is often surprisingly difficult to pinpoint the contributions of individual workers, and attempts to do so by consulting those involved are fraught with problems of fading memory, wishful thinking, and excessive intradisciplinary loyalty.

Even a complete listing of scientific papers would overlook an important element of the discovery process—the role of the executive. J. B. S. Haldane once explained that his only contribution to an important discovery (for which he got much of the credit) was that he did not stop a junior colleague from doing an experiment that Haldane considered ill-advised (Clark, 1984). In a hierarchical situation, that is an important sort of contribution. In an industrial setting, even before a candidate drug is selected from its analogues to be moved from "basic" to "developmental" research, grave decisions must be made. A bench biologist will not be able to spend tens of thousands of dollars to test a compound in cattle if his or her colleagues in other disciplines believe the compound to be unstable or to have an unfavorable tissue–residue profile. A bench toxicologist will not be able to initiate a chronic safety study in rats, costing perhaps a quarter of a million dollars, to test a compound that his or her microbiological or chemical colleagues consider too difficult or too expensive to produce commercially. Such decisions are invariably discussed by committees or task forces, but the final responsibility rests with the ranking executive scientists, and these individuals deserve much of the credit for the scientific advances being made.

Of even greater importance in the present context is the role of the executive in determining the direction or focus, or even the existence, of a particular research program. (Lest this seem self-serving, I hasten to point out that I am referring to those who occupy more elevated positions in the scheme of things.) The program that led to ivermectin was one in which the emphasis had shifted from the empirical testing of synthetic chemicals to the empirical testing of fermentation products (Campbell et al., 1983). That was a decision involving several scientific disciplines and several institutional departments, which therefore had to be made at a high level of management. It will be pointed out below that the ivermectin discovery came about because of a formal collaboration between the Merck Sharp & Dohme Research Laboratories in New Jersey and the Kitasato Institute in Japan; and regardless of whether that was the brainchild of one person or many, the decision to act on it was a crucial executive event—one of far-reaching scientific consequences, but not one that is reflected in the scientific literature. It would be rash indeed to try to compensate for this literary neglect by compiling a list of the executive scientists whose authority (seen in retrospect to have been used wisely) made possible the discovery and development of ivermectin. How would one accommodate the changes in executive portfolio? Where would one draw the line, in terms of year, rank, discipline, and geography? One can, however, call attention to the importance, if not the identity, of these individuals.

Ivermectin was the product of a goal-oriented scientific project. A project of this type is, naturally, more likely to succeed if the science is good than if it is bad. I like to think that in this case the science in the various departments was good—but it is important to keep in mind that we are dealing here, not with the quality of the science, but with the process of discovery.

Discovery of an Active Fermentation Product

The anthelmintic program at MSDRL began in 1955 and continues to this day. From it emerged thiabendazole, the first of the benzimidazole anthelmintics, as well as cambendazole, rafoxanide, and clorsulon. There were, of course, other active compounds, but they did not reach the marketplace; and by the early 1970s it was evident that the empirical testing of synthetic chemicals was reaching a point of diminishing returns. The history of antibiotics, however, suggested that microorganisms, unencumbered by the constraints of human knowledge, were capable of producing wildly exotic chemical structures. Novelty, after all, would be the key to success. New analogues of existing anthelmintics, or even moderately adventurous departures from known structures, might provide better products—but only a truly novel structure, with a truly novel mode of action, would yield a real breakthrough.

The problem, as always, was how to test the substances that needed to be "screened" for anthelmintic activity. After the discovery of thiabendazole, we abandoned the assay used for its discovery (and after the discovery of ivermectin we were to abandon the assay that discovered it) and we were constantly developing new assays. One of several assays initiated at about this time was an assay for detecting coccidiostatic compounds in mice infected with a murine species of *Eimeria.* Early in 1973 this assay was installed in our fermentation screening operation in Spain, now known as Centro de Investigacion Basica Espana. In January 1974 the coccidian parasite was supplemented with the parasitic nematode *Nematospiroides dubius,* and in August 1974 this "tandem assay" was installed also at our Rahway, New Jersey, laboratories. For several years we had been testing fermentation products against larval parasitic worms or adult free-living worms in vitro. The results had been so discouraging that we very much wanted to test our materials in vivo. The new assay was not our only in vivo anthelmintic assay, but it was the one developed by Dr. J. R. Egerton to serve specifically as our primary assay for fermentation products. It had the advantage of utilizing a small host species, thereby conserving animal-maintenance resources and requiring only small amounts of test substance to produce a putative effective concentration of that substance in the blood or tissues of the host.

Another important decision had been made independently but more or less concurrently. It was a remarkable adventure in international collaboration in the applied sciences. In March 1973, MSDRL (represented primarily by Dr. Boyd H. Woodruff) and the Kitasato Institute in Japan (represented primarily by Dr. Satoshi Omura) reached agreement on a plan to look jointly for new antibiotics. In January 1974, the agreement specified that microorganisms isolated in Japan should be shipped to our laboratories in New Jersey for testing in the various assays being run there. The objective of the project was not the selection of microorganisms that seemed likely, on the basis of existing knowledge, to be of value in any particular chemotherapeutic or pharmacologic application. Rather the objective was to select microorganisms that were unusual in appearance or in culture characteristics, and that might therefore be a source of unusual chemical structures—which might be useful in unexpected ways. With the new assay being set up in Rahway later that year, it was decided that the Kitasato cultures would be tested for antiparasitic activity and that the "tandem assay" would be used for that purpose.

The Kitasato Institute had some 4000 microbial cultures already on hand, and these were sent to Rahway as the forerunners of many that were to follow in subsequent years. One batch of fifty-four was received in March 1974. About a year later they were inoculated into flasks of microbiological medium and allowed to grow for three days (that is, the medium was allowed to "ferment"). The resultant "broths" were then harvested and sent to the tandem (coccidiosis-helminthiasis) assay. In May 1975, each broth was mixed into the feed of an infected mouse, and the mouse was allowed to eat it ad libitum for six days. When the feces of the mice were subsequently examined for worm eggs, and the small intestines were examined for worms, only one mouse was found to be free of worms. It was not in great shape—it had eaten only half of its food and had lost weight—but it was worm-free! Subsequent experiments were soon to indicate that the absence of worms in that mouse was not a coincidence or a failure of inoculation or anything like that. Rather it was due to the ingested broth, which had been produced by the growth of microbial culture OS3153, which had been isolated at the Kitasato Institute from a scoopful of soil, which had been dug up at a golf course near the Japanese city of Ito!

Mention has been made of the contributions, often unheralded, made to a scientific project by executives. Perhaps this is the time to mention, not those workers near the summit of the hierarchy, but those who work on the front line—the assistants and technicians who cajole microorganisms to multiply abundantly, who train their microscopes on mouse droppings, and who (physically and metaphorically) grapple daily with the blood and guts of a project. In the case of the ivermectin project, the names of most of them appear as authors of scientific publications; but, since a line had to be drawn somewhere, a few of them appear only under Acknowledgments. A famous tale tells us that "for want of a nail a kingdom was lost." In the present instance, had a particular mouse not been examined properly, and had the follow-up procedures not been carried out conscientiously, a major new drug might have been missed.

It will have struck some readers as singular that I have referred to the test animal in the singular—but the truth is that the avermectins were discovered in one particular individual mouse. This brings up an important concept in primary screening. In the case of synthetic organic chemicals, many compounds are available in amounts so small that even with a host animal as small as a mouse, the usual sort of experimental groups of, say, five to ten animals cannot be used—because a small test sample of compound would have to be subdivided into extremely small amounts and the test dosage on a body-weight basis would therefore be unreasonably small. Such compounds tend to remain untested in the in vivo assays. There is, however, an alternative. In the case of a schistosomiasis-mouse assay developed in the late 1950s (Campbell, Bartels, & Cuckler, 1978), studies conducted in the mid-1960s showed that a single animal could be used for each test compound with no real danger of missing active compounds (D. A. Ostlind, private communication). In a given assay, if the experimental infection is highly uniform, "false positives" (compounds exhibiting spurious activity) will be recorded only rarely. In the case of fermentation products, the amount of available test substance (the amount of putative active principle per unit of volume of test fermentation broth) is unknown, but assumed to be extremely small. The objective then becomes to administer, in principle, the largest possible quantity of fermentation material to the smallest possible biomass. Under the circumstances of routine fermentation operations, this can best be done by using one mouse to test each microbial culture. It is after, not during, the detection of activity that statistical validation is needed. This was the basis of the "tandem assay" that was developed in these laboratories (J. R. Egerton, J. Di Netta, unpublished data) and that was being operated as a routine bioassay at the time of the new discovery (B. M. Miller, R. K. Hartman, G. Wilks, unpublished data). Secondary assays were also used to evaluate the new materials (Ostlind & Cifelli, 1981).

Perhaps this is also the time to mention the importance of picking up the right soil sample and knowing what to do with it. One cannot predict which soil sample will yield a new microorganism, or which new microorganism will yield a new biodynamic substance, but those skilled in the art know how to increase the probabilities. The investigators at the Kitasato Institute are such experts (Stapley & Woodruff, 1982), and two of them (Dr. Oiwa and Dr. Omura) are listed as co-authors of the paper describing the isolation and characterization of the bacterium that produced the new-found antiparasitic activity (Burg et al., 1979).

Within a few months after that initial observation of anthelmintic efficacy, broths obtained from culture OS3153 had been shown to be active against *N. dubius* in mice over an eight-fold range of dosages, although some of these dosages were toxic to the mice. The culture was given the MSDRL code number C-076, and work proceeded immediately on a number of fronts.

Isolation and Identification of an Active Principle

The time has long gone when one could bottle a batch of crude gunk and sell it in the international marketplace, no matter how plentiful, efficacious, or safe the stuff might be. The first order of business, then, was to isolate from culture C-076 a pure active ingredient.

The crude broth of that actinomycete culture was a potent toxin. The only thing more striking than its toxicity for mice was its even greater toxicity for worms. Fortunately, the toxic component turned out to be unrelated to the antiparasitic components. The isolation chemists prepared various fractions and extracts, and used the *N. dubius* mouse assay to determine whether a given preparation retained antiparasitic activity. It was quickly shown that the activity resided in the mycelium, not in the surrounding broth fluid, and could be extracted by organic solvents. Thin-layer chromatography (TLC) using silica gel plates showed that the extracted material consisted of two pairs of components, arbitrarily designated A_1, A_2, B_1, and B_2 (Miller et al., 1979). When viewed under ultraviolet light, these materials in the chromatographic plate absorbed the light in a characteristic pattern (appearing as "quenched" nonfluorescing spots in an otherwise fluorescent surface, or registering as peaks on a line graphed by a "densitometer"). This led to one of the most important discoveries in the development of the new drug—one that is not mentioned in any of the published research papers! The reason for its omission is that it did not constitute "new science." The reason for its importance is that it greatly speeded up the isolation and characterization of the active components—for it was found (by Mr. Tom Miller and Mr. Bob Ormond) that these UV-absorbent areas, when eluted from the silica gel and administered to mice, were active against *N. dubius.* This meant that in subsequent isolation studies it was no longer necessary to wait for a couple of weeks to find out if a particular fraction of broth was active against *N. dubius* in the mouse. Instead one could, in a couple of hours, determine its UV absorbence on a TLC plate and use the results as an indication of efficacy or lack of efficacy.

The technique of mass spectrometric analysis revealed that each of the four components of the active principle consisted of a major and a minor subcomponent that could be separated by reverse-phase high-pressure liquid chromatography (HPLC). The major components were designated A_{1a}, A_{2a}, B_{1a}, and B_{2a}, while the minor components were designated A_{1b}, A_{2b}, B_{1b}, and B_{2b} (Albers-Schonberg et al., 1981).

New techniques were devised to isolate the new complex of materials from fermentation broth. In one operation, some 8000 liters of broth were subjected to various extractions and concentrations and yielded 2.3 kilograms of an oily substance containing all of the active components. Chromatographic techniques for separating and measuring the components were refined (Miller et al., 1979).

As we shall see, some of the purified components were extraordinarily effective against worms in laboratory animals, but nothing was known about their chemical identity. This mystery was solved by the application of two sophisticated analytic techniques—mass spectrometry and nuclear magnetic resonance (NMR) spectroscopy. The components of the C-076 active principle were found to be glycosidic derivatives of pentacyclic sixteen-membered lactones (Figure 11.1). The process of structure determination was hastened by the realization that the new compounds were similar in structure to the milbemycin compounds that had recently been discovered in Japan and that were known to be toxic to free-living mites (but which were not then known to be toxic to parasitic worms). The milbemycins, however, did not have a carbohydrate moiety, whereas the new material had two sugars attached to the lactone structure.

A new name was needed. I proposed *avermectin,* the ending "-icin" indicat-

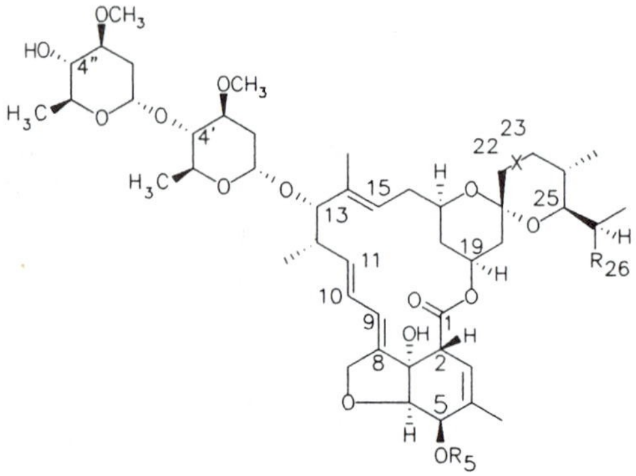

AVERMECTIN	R_5	R_{26}	$C_{22}-X-C_{23}$
A_{1a}	CH_3	C_2H_5	$-CH=CH-$
A_{1b}	CH_3	CH_3	$-CH=CH-$
B_{1a}	H	C_2H_5	$-CH=CH-$
B_{1b}	H	CH_3	$-CH=CH-$
A_{2a}	CH_3	C_2H_5	$-CH_2-\overset{OH}{CH}-$
A_2b	CH_3	CH_3	$-CH_2-\overset{OH}{CH}-$
B_{2a}	H	C_2H_5	$-CH_2-\overset{OH}{CH}-$
B_{2b}	H	CH_3	$-CH_2-\overset{OH}{CH}-$
IVERMECTIN	H	>80% C_2H_5 <20% CH_3	$-CH_2-CH_2-$

FIGURE 11.1. The chemical structure of ivermectin and the natural avermectins. (From Fisher and Mrozik, 1989.)

ing, by convention, an actinomycete origin, and the rest of the word suggesting antagonism toward worms (vermes) and ectoparasites. Dr. Jerry Birnbaum proposed that the name be trimmed to *avermectin,* and that name was accepted by the United States Adopted Names committee on new drugs. The family of closely related compounds is known collectively as the *avermectins.* In the singular, the word is best used only in adjectival form (although it has occasionally and imprecisely been equated with the B_1 component). The organism that gave rise to these compounds also deserved a new name, for it was found to be a streptomycete bacterium of some distinction. It had a spore mass of brownish-gray color and smooth spore surface, and had helical sporophores forming side branches on an aerial mycelium. Quite coincidentally, Mrs. S. Currie of MSDRL drew upon similar latinity in naming it *Streptomyces avermitilis*—the streptomycete that helps to create an averminous condition. *S. avermitilis* has a distinction that is not entirely biological. Scrutiny of the list of authors of one particular paper (Miwa et al., 1982) reveals what is either an unusual example of hominid whimsy or an unusual degree of microbial scholarship!

Identification of the active principle not only permitted all kinds of studies (toxicological, pharmacological, parasitological, etc.) to be conducted in a more precise and meaningful way, but also opened up an opportunity for molecular manipulation.

Molecular Theme and Variations

My chemist colleagues appear to take the view that, while nature can make a truly novel compound, only a chemist can make it right! The A series of avermectins (Figure 11.1) was not considered potent enough against worm parasites. The B compounds were better, but B_1 was imperfect because it lacked effectiveness (especially against cooperid worms) when injected into cattle instead of being given orally. The B_2 compound was imperfect because it was mysteriously ineffective against adult *Haemonchus*, while being highly effective against the immature stage and against the other important worm species. We wanted, of course, the best of both worlds, and we seriously considered developing a combination of the two compounds. The chemists, however, took a more elegant approach. Structurally, avermectin B_1 has an olefin linkage between carbons 22 and 23, whereas B_2 has a hydrated linkage, with the hydroxyl group at carbon 23. The difference is important from the stereochemical point of view, because the fully saturated ring is chairshaped whereas the olefin-bearing ring is somewhat flat. The chemists decided to make a derivative that would retain the chair-shaped ring of avermectin B_2 but from which the hydroxyl group would be removed from the 23 position. They were encouraged in this objective by the fact that the milbemycins had a saturated 22-23 linkage, without substitution. The milbemycins (see above) were known to be active against arthropod pests, and we had recently discovered that they were also active against parasitic nematodes.

Making the compound was not easy. Of the five olefins in the avermectin molecule, only the 22,23 olefin had to be hydrogenated. Fortunately that was the only one of the olefins that was cis-substituted and thus likely to be amenable to the use of Wilkinson's homogeneous catalyst. The catalyst was tried. It did not work—at first. But persistence eventually led to its successful use in the preparation of 22,23-dihydroavermectin B_1 (Chabala et al., 1980). And it *was* active against adult *Haemonchus* as well as the other nematode species, whether given orally or by subcutaneous injection! At the time, it was only one of many modified avermectins, but as time went on that compound became, as we shall see, of great potential value and so it had to have a name of its own. The obvious choice for this hydrogenated avermectin was *hyvermectin,* but this was overruled by those of our number who protect our global respectability. Apparently that name would sound slightly naughty to certain eastern European ears, and so it was amended to *ivermectin.* [This is a process that can work in either direction. Halasz (1963) relates that Hungarian Nobel Laureate Szent-Gyorgyi developed a commercial health food and gave it a name that reflected both its high content of vitamin C and the fact that it was made from paprika. But it did not do well in English-speaking countries until he changed the name—which was originally Vita-prik.]

Ivermectin was not more potent in antiparasitic activity than its natural precursor, avermectin B_1. Indeed it was slightly less potent; and now that more than a dozen years have elapsed and more than 1000 derivatives have been made and tested in our laboratories, it can be said that, in terms of potency, very few of them surpassed the natural precursor and none surpassed it by much. A great deal has been learned, however, about the chemistry and structure–activity relationships of the series (Fisher, 1985; Mrozik et al., 1982, 1983, 1986, 1988; and see reviews by Fisher and Mrozik, 1984, 1989).

Parasites Inside and Out

Even before the new family of compounds had been separated into its component parts, the parasitologists were busy with the crude, oily concentrates of active material that were being provided by the isolation chemists. The stuff was active against *N. dubius* in mice when fed in the diet at a concentration of 0.0001 percent. That, as Dr. Johnson said in a different context, was enough to "concentrate the mind wonderfully."

The *N. dubius* assays that confirmed the activity of culture OS3153 were completed in September 1975. Only a few people were taking notice (probably for the good reason that empirical screening occasionally throws up tantalizing evidence of activity that turns out to have been spurious for one reason or another). By the end of the year, a great many people were paying attention. Enough data had then been accumulated to warrant review, and our first formal interdisciplinary meeting on the subject was held in January 1976. It was reported at that meeting that C-076 (as it was then called) had been given orally to laboratory animals, dogs, and sheep and had been highly active against the following roundworm parasites: *N. dubius, Syphacia obvelata, Aspiculuris tetraptera, Trichinella spiralis, H. contortus, Ostertagia circumcincta, Trichostrongylus axei, T. colubriformis, Cooperia oncophora,* and *Oesophagostomum columbianum.* It was thus active against parasitic nematodes occupying all the major segments of the gastrointestinal tract. In addition, it had been found active against nematode strains known to be resistant to benzimidazole anthelmintics. It had been active against the notoriously refractory inhibited L_4 stage of *Ostertagia* in sheep. Further, it had been found active against extraintestinal nematodes: oral treatment of a dog, and parenteral treatment of a jird, had shown efficacy against the microfilariae of *Dirofilaria immitis* and *Brugia pahangi.* It had been found *inactive* when tested intraperitoneally or subcutaneously against cystic larval tapeworms (*Taenia crassiceps*) in mice; when tested orally against adult strobilate tapeworms (*Hymenolepis nana*) in mice, and when tested orally against the adult filarial parasite, *Brugia pahangi,* in the jird. Its efficacy against inhibited *Ostertagia* larvae had been demonstrated with a single oral dose at 10 milligrams per kilogram, and efficacy against the intestinal stage of *Trichinella* had been observed at 2.0 mg/kg—yet the preparation used was estimated to contain about 1 percent (later shown to be 0.75 %) of active principle! In short, we knew then that this new entity, without any molecular modification or formulation work, was the most potent anthelmintic known; it acted orally and parenterally; it had an unusually broad spectrum of activity; it apparently had a wide therapeutic index; and it probably had a novel mode of action. To link this information with some of the foregoing sections, it may be noted that thirty-five fermentation batches of the organism had by then been produced, and the association between efficacy and ultraviolet-absorbent TLC spots had been discovered.

Within another quarter-year (by the end of March 1976), broad-spectrum activity had been demonstrated in cattle. Fermentation batches of 400 liters were being produced every week, and a 4000-liter batch was planned. The chemical structure had been determined in almost every detail. The activity against heartworm microfilariae had been confirmed, and an extraordinary lucky break had come our way. If one had to choose a worm species against which a new broad-spectrum anthelmintic should fail, one would unhesitatingly pick the dog heartworm (adult stage). Killing adult heartworms in dogs is sometimes desirable, but it involves grave risk of causing pulmonary embolism and killing the infected dog—so one does not want to do it inadvertently as the incidental effect of giving the drug for other purposes. Our new drug, regardless of which component was tested, was totally inactive against adult heartworm!

We had been looking for an anthelmintic and we had found one. We found something else as well—an insecticide–acaricide. It was not the first time that anthelmintic and insecticide–acaricide activities had been found in the same chemical class. Phenothiazine and the organophosphates had both kinds of activity, but rarely did a given compound have a useful degree of clout against both targets. The similarity between the chemical structures of avermectins and milbemycins has been mentioned. The milbemycins were known to be active against various free-living arthropods, and as early as February 1976 we had a hint that the avermectins might share that property. A concentrated preparation of *Streptomyces avermitilis* broth was dissolved in sesame oil and given orally to a horse—which soon expelled a large number of stomach bots (and worms) in its feces (Dr. J. R. Egerton, unpublished data). The bots were fly larvae of the species *Gastrophilus haemorrhoidalis* and *G. intestinalis,* and they normally remain securely anchored to the stomach lining until development is complete. In March 1976, one of our number (Dr. R. F. Riek) took a few milligrams of B_1 to our laboratory in Australia where larvae of the blowfly *Lucilia cuprina* were routinely used for assay purposes. The drug was duly incorporated, at 0.0005 parts per million, into the serum on which the test larvae were fed. Even before that test was done, one of our New Jersey crew (Dr. D. A. Ostlind), who always kept some flour beetles on hand (for use in tapeworm transmission) decided to add the new drug to some flour and turn the beetles loose in it. The beetles died. The *Lucilia* larvae in Australia also died. We had unequivocally demonstrated the efficacy of the avermectins against free-living insect pests and against parasitic insects (James, Picton, & Riek, 1980; Ostlind, Cifelli, & Lang, 1979). Later that year (summer of 1976) some of our rabbits obligingly developed severe infestations of ear mites; and topical application of C-076 worked like magic in curing them (J. R. Egerton, unpublished data; P. Malatesta, unpublished data). It was of interest that components A_1 and A_2 were even better than B_1 and B_2. These observations were later confirmed in our laboratories and extended to other acarine parasites (Wilkins et al., 1980, 1981). The discovery of activity against arthropods changed the scientific and commercial prospects dramatically. When ivermectin was eventually launched as a product for cattle, it was offered not as an anthelmintic but as an antiparasitic agent for the control of various endoparasites and ectoparasites. Inevitably, someone coined the term *endectocide* for such a product and the name seems to have caught on. (People do not seem to have been alarmed at the prospect of having their cattle killed both on the inside and the outside.)

By this time the parasitological emphasis was on the individual components and the new derivatives that the synthetic chemists were already turning out. The thrust of the work was, on the one hand, to compare the efficacy of particular structures against a small set of representative nematode species (D. A. Ostlind, unpublished data) and, on the other hand, to broaden the range of parasites against which selected compounds were tested (see references). Thus, by September 1976, marked differences had been recorded in the anthelmintic potency and spectrum of the naturally occurring components and various derivatives, and efficacy had been observed against mange mites and sucking lice (but not biting lice or fleas). Efficacy against certain gastrointestinal nematodes had even been observed following application of the drug (at high dosages) to the skin of infected sheep (J. R. Egerton, unpublished data). By March 1977, numerous trials, many conducted by our "developmental research" colleagues, had shown that component B_1, given orally at 0.1 or 0.2 mg/kg, was highly effective against virtually all of the important immature and mature nematode parasites of sheep and cattle (Egerton et al., 1979; W. D. H. Leaning, personal communication). It was, at that point, under serious consideration as a candidate for a formal "development" program. By September it was running neck and neck with one of the chemically modified candidates—the 22,23-dihydro derivative of component B_1 (later named ivermectin), which similarly was active against the important nematodes of ruminants at dosages of 0.1 to 0.2 mg/kg (Egerton et al., 1980; Leaning, 1984). As will be described briefly below, ivermectin won by a head.

Once ivermectin had been selected for development, parasitological testing expanded, with both the "basic" and the "development" teams examining all sorts of formulations against all sorts of parasites in all sorts of animals (for a comprehensive list of susceptible nematode species, see Stretton, Campbell, & Babu, 1987). The process quickly moved beyond the scope of this review, and mention will be made only of a couple of special instances. Ivermectin, like avermectin B_1, was active (fortunately) against the microfilariae of dog heartworm but was inactive (fortunately) against the adult stage. It turned out also to be active (fortunately) against the preadult stage developing in the tissues of the dog prior to invasion of the heart. The result was not only a successful commercial product for heartworm prevention (and a widely used but unapproved treatment for microfilaremia) but also a salutary and dramatic example of stage specificity in chemotherapy. For while the adult heartworm is not susceptible to even the highest possible dosage, the preadult stage is perhaps the nematode organism that is most sensitive to the drug—with single dosages as low as 0.002 mg/kg (and in some cases even 0.001 mg/kg) giving a high degree of efficacy (for a review see Campbell, 1989).

The discovery of ivermectin's potential for the prevention of heartworm disease illustrates the value of maintaining a wide-ranging exploratory type of research within a goal-oriented project. Usually a new anthelmintic is not tested against the preadult stage of the heartworm (*Dirofilaria immitis*) until long after the discovery of the drug. Only a few laboratories, industrial or academic, work on the parasite. Prophylactic experiments take some eight to twelve months to complete, and require the funds and physical resources necessary to maintain dogs under experimental conditions for such long periods. In research unrelated to the avermectins, however, we had found that the ferret is an admirable substitute for the dog in such studies, and the prophylactic activity of the avermectins was demonstrated in that host species before it was demonstrated in dogs (Blair & Campbell, 1978, 1980a,b; Campbell & Blair 1978a,b).

Another observation that had far-reaching consequences was again a matter of the filarial group of worms. In April 1978, ivermectin was about to be tested against gastrointestinal nematodes in horses. At the last minute a decision was made (prompted by a suggestion from Ms. Lyndia Slayton Blair) to examine pieces of skin from the treated and untreated horses to detect a possible effect on the microfilariae (microscopic larvae) of *Onchocerca cervicalis*—should those horses happen to be infected with that parasite. The horses did happen to be infected, and an effect on the microfilariae was clearly evident (Egerton et al., 1981). The significance of the observation lay not in the importance of the parasite in horses, for it is an obscure parasite that was then considered of no importance whatever, but rather in the relationship of the parasite to an important pathogen of humans. To those of us who were actively interested in human parasitology, the potential utility of the finding was clear. In the summer of 1978 I sent the drug (and relayed our results) to an investigator in Australia who was conducting antifilarial drug tests under the sponsorship of the World Health Organization. The investigator, Dr. Bruce Copeman, quickly showed that ivermectin was active also against the microfilariae of *Onchocerca* spp. in cattle. The information from horses and cattle, together with the toxicological data that had by then been gathered, served as the basis for recommending the testing of ivermectin in humans. The subsequent clinical trials directed by Dr. Mohammed Aziz and conducted by a number of independent clinicians demonstrated that ivermectin was similarly effective against the microfilariae that live in the skin and eyes of people in the tropics and which cause severe skin disease and "river blindness." Ivermectin is now being distributed to people in endemic areas to prevent the disfiguring and blinding effects of the infection (Aziz et al., 1982; Greene, Brown, & Taylor, 1986). The collaboration between WHO and Merck & Company, Inc., in evaluating and distributing the drug has been reported in the press (Eckholm, 1989).

The Way It Works

Work on the mode of action of the avermectins began almost as soon as they were discovered. The actions of known anthelmintics served to guide early experiments, and there is a memo on record indicating that C-076 acts by blockade of cholinergic nerve transmission. This was an error due to miscommunication, and it soon became evident that the action of the new drug was new. Almost from the beginning, the work included collaboration with academic biochemists; by April 1977 a collaboration between Dr. C. C. Wang in our laboratories and scientists at Rockefeller University had indicated that the drug might paralyze organisms by inducing an influx of negatively charged ions into nerve and muscle cells. (For parasites, paralysis is generally just as good—or, rather, just as bad—as being killed outright.) In certain invertebrates, chloride ions can enter cells through membrane channels that are opened by the action of the neurotransmitter gamma-aminobutyric acid (GABA); and it was proposed that the avermectins cause such channels to open, thereby decreasing the electrical resistance of the membrane and disrupting cell function (Fritz, Wang, & Gorio, 1979; see Wang & Pong, 1982). Subsequent studies, using cell membranes from rat brain, demonstrated that avermectins can stimulate the release of GABA and can enhance its binding to the receptor (Wang & Pong, 1982). Intensive further investigation in other laboratories has confirmed and extended those observations. Now, however, it is thought that the drug increases the influx of chloride ions even through channels that are not governed by GABA (Turner & Schaeffer, 1989).

The action of the drug on the nervous system of susceptible invertebrates operates at extraordinarily low concentrations. Antiparasitic agents have hitherto been administered in dosages of milligrams or tens of milligrams of drug per kilogram of host body weight. Ivermectin is used commercially as a broad-spectrum agent at 0.2 or 0.3 mg/kg, and is active against certain species at even lower dosages. The immature dog heartworm, *D. immitis,* is affected when the host dog is given a single oral dose of ivermectin at 0.002 mg/kg (McCall et al., 1986); and the cattle grub, *Hypoderma* spp., is affected when host cattle are given a single injection at 0.0002 mg/kg (Drummond, 1984). One cannot help wondering how close one can approximate the point at which efficacy can be achieved without giving any drug at all! Readers were astonished when Professor Terada's group in Japan reported that ivermectin paralyzed worms in vitro at a concentration of 3.6×10^{-18}M (Sano et al., 1981) and some concluded that it might now become possible to calculate the number of molecules of the drug required to cause the death of a worm.

Many mysteries remain about the mode of action of ivermectin. Why, for example, is it active against heartworm microfilariae but not against the adult, despite the fact that both dwell in host blood? Even when the drug gets into the tissues of the adult worm, as it does in vitro, the worm is neither paralyzed nor killed

(R. E. Howells, unpublished data). Why does it take the adult *Onchocerca* several months to resume its output of microfilariae? Opinions differ as to how the drug shuts down the production of filarial progeny in the first place, and this phenomenon is now being studied in several laboratories. Why are some individual animals more susceptible to avermectin toxicity than others of the same species and same breed or strain? Such questions are important, but lie outside the scope of this discussion.

Safety for Humans and Animals

They say there is safety in numbers; and in demonstrating the safety of ivermectin, large numbers of numbers were generated. Much of the effort can be considered "developmental" research, but for any new drug the early phases of safety assessment are part and parcel of the discovery process. Without a therapeutic index one has merely discovered an active compound.

As soon as C-076 was separated into its four major components, it was clear that the two with pronounced anthelmintic activity (B_1 and B_2) enjoyed a clear margin of safety when given to mice as a single oral dose. As tests were carried forward into sheep, cattle, dogs, and other animals, it was comforting to find efficacy without signs of overt toxicity. We were very conscious, however, that this was only the beginning of a very long road. Specters of mutagenicity, teratogenicity, and unacceptable tissue residues always confront those who wish to introduce a drug for use in food animals. By June 1976, component B_1 had passed successfully through the "Ames test" with no signs of having a potential for mutagenesis. That was good news. Less reassuring were reports that mice had exhibited marked individual variation in susceptibility to avermectin toxicity (Lankas & Gordon, 1989). It was later to be discovered that certain dogs, especially some individuals of the collie breed, also had an unexpectedly high susceptibility to avermectin toxicity (Paul et al., 1987). (The phenomenon has not been a problem in practice—the dosage of ivermectin used for heartworm prevention in dogs is well tolerated even in sensitive collies.)

By September 1976, component B_1 had passed a teratogenicity test in rabbits with flying colors; but by December it was known that when the drug was given daily to pregnant mice (days 6–15 of gestation), the fetal mice developed cleft palate! This, however, happened only at dosages high enough to be toxic to the dams. Further studies were to show that ivermectin caused fetal abnormality in rabbits, but again only when the drug was administered daily at maternotoxic dosages (Lankas & Gordon, 1989). These avermectins thus did not appear to be selectively fetotoxic. In the subsequent development program, ivermectin (at twice the recommended dosage) was given to cattle, dogs, and horses at various intervals during gestation with no signs of toxicity to the fetus (Pulliam & Preston, 1989).

Safety is a complex issue. It involves safety for the people or animals destined to be treated; but it also involves safety for the people who manufacture the drug, safety for the people who administer the drug to thousands of animals under farm conditions and who might therefore get it on their hands or into their eyes, safety for the people who eat the meat obtained from treated animals, and safety for the flora and fauna of the environment which will be exposed to the drug as it is excreted from treated animals. These issues cannot be addressed here in any detail, but brief comment might be made on the question of meat safety. As early as 1976, studies were being done on the metabolism of the drug and the distribution of the drug or its metabolites in the tissues of the mammalian body. In the United States, the Food and Drug Administration establishes the amount of drug residue considered safe for human ingestion (and therefore the length of time that must elapse between treatment and slaughter) and these calculations are based, not on the edible tissue likely to be ingested in largest amount, but on the edible tissue having the highest concentration of drug residue. In the case of cattle treated with ivermectin, the highest concentration was found in liver (and the lowest in brain), and the drug therefore had to meet a standard of safety based on the assumption that someone might eat large amounts of liver from treated animals every day for a prolonged period. In fact the drug residue in muscle was found to be thirty-four times lower than in liver, so that consumers of beef enjoy an even greater margin of safety than the already acceptable margin of safety enjoyed by the hypothetical consumers of liver. The associated research required the development of methods for isolating and measuring drug residues, and was accompanied by intensive investigation of the absorption, metabolism, and excretion of the drug in various animal species (Lo et al., 1985; Chiu & Lu, 1989).

Decisions and Processes

It is not easy to identify "decision points" along the road from discovery to the marketplace. They are too numerous, too ill-defined, and often insignificant in themselves. The decision to make the 22,23-dihydro derivative of avermectin B_1 was one of enormous consequence, but it was one of the many everyday decisions, not a "decision point." That is not, of course, to suggest that the idea of doing it was ordinary, or that the doing of it was ordinary, but rather to suggest that no one would have lost sleep over making the *decision* to do it. Similarly, the decision to add *N. dubius* to a mouse coccidiosis assay was of critical importance—but it was only one of a number of things that were tried, and its importance is apparent only in retrospect. The decision to examine skin samples (instead of just the gut) of treated horses led eventually to a new means of preventing a blinding disease in humans—but that was opportunism at its best, not an element of strategy. Some anticipated decisions took care of themselves or simply did not arise; for example, the new drug would be produced by fermentation and chemical modification because total chemical synthesis would have been technically and economically impracticable.

There were, however, a couple of decision points that can be identified clearly, even if they can no longer be described precisely. They were decisions that are fashionably called "go/no-go" decisions—those that had the potential for stopping the project or at least diverting it. For example, answers had to be found to the following linked questions: Should an avermectin be moved from "basic" research into the vastly expensive process of "developmental" research, and, if so, which one? The constant aggregation of data from various departments made development of an avermectin more and more likely. At a meeting in February 1977, the chief objective was to decide (1) whether to develop an unrelated but highly promising anthelmintic on which we had been working for some years, and (2) whether to develop avermectin B_1 or avermectin B_2, or a mixture of the two. By September of that year the competing candidates were the natural product, avermectin B_1, and its 22,23-dihydro derivative. The selection of the latter (later named ivermectin) was made at a particular "task force" meeting. It was recognized that the potency and spectrum of activity of the two compounds were not very different. The toxicological data on ivermectin were a little more favorable, so it won the nomination! That is an extreme simplification of the proceedings, but I believe it captures the essence. (The rejected avermectin candidate, B_1, was later developed for use in certain segments of the antiparasitic market, but that is another story.)

Choosing a particular avermectin in 1977 would have been difficult enough if we had been faced merely with the then existing array of derivatives and accompanying test data. But we were faced with the prospect of more derivatives. One of the most difficult problems in the conduct of a chemical derivatization program is knowing when to stop. No compound is perfect—but the next one just might be! In the case of the avermectins, we chose to select our candidate early in the program because we had a compound that looked like a winner. (In fact, of course, the derivatization process continues to this day, but that is for the discovery of "second generation" compounds.) The decision to pick ivermectin and the decision to drop our non-avermectin candidate may seem in retrospect to have been easy decisions, but the outcome was by no means obvious and a great deal of time, effort, and money was at stake.

A decision that was crucial to the success of the project was to continue the project when some 40,000 microorganisms from around the world had been tested but no promising antiparasitic activity had been discovered. That is perhaps a tougher issue than the problem of deciding when to stop testing derivatives of a promising lead compound. There is no question that some were discouraged by the failure of the new fermentation screening assay (tandem assay) to yield exciting clues in the period January 1974 to May 1975. Scientists running a routine assay are generally optimistic about their assay, otherwise they would not engage in that pursuit. Others, removed from the day-to-day screening operation, must decide whether that optimism is well founded. In the case of the tandem assay, it was, as I recall, a close call. Well-designed assays invariably turn up "actives" fairly often, and although they almost always turn out to be useless for one reason or another (e.g., toxicity) their occurrence is an important motivator. They not only give hope for better things in the future, but also provide tools for basic research—and a great deal of fun. Ordinarily one would conclude that if we had not discovered the avermectins, some other person or group would soon have done so; or that if we had not discovered them when we did, we would have discovered them later. That is because a drug produced by a particular isolate of a particular species of microorganism is generally produced by other isolates or other species. We, and others, proceeded to test hundreds of thousands of microorganisms from all over the world, but an avermectin-producing organism has never again been found!

In bringing a drug to the clinic or the marketplace, the "developmental" processes are as crucial to success as the discovery of an active compound. Nevertheless, in the present context it is the "basic" research that is of principal interest. The line between the two, while of administrative importance, needs to have a degree of elasticity. It would be a great mistake to suppose that topics such as mutagenicity, target-animal safety, tissue residues, production methods, and so on are addressed only when a candidate product moves into "developmental" research. That is an important turning point to be sure, and the commitment to the expenditure of money and manpower is of a different order of magnitude. But in several scientific disciplines there is a gradual escalation of research activity rather than a new beginning. In the case of ivermectin, the antiparasitic efficacy trials moved with unusual rapidity, due in part to the fact that we had been planning to evaluate another promising anthelmintic candidate. Arrangements had been made to test that compound in our research farms in several parts of the world, so that when the superiority of the avermectins became evident, those resources were brought to bear on the newer project even while it was still in the "basic" mode.

Had improvement in fermentation techniques not been achieved at the outset, there would have been precious little test material and correspondingly little basic research. Early fermentation technology paved the way for developmental research. *S. avermitilis* was isolated from nature, but the organism that now supplies the industrial output of ivermectin is hardly natural. It is a carefully nurtured mutant that produces, if treated with proper consideration, 100 times as much avermectin B_1 (the ivermectin precursor) as was produced by the ancestral strain under the original conditions (Nallin-Omstead, Kaplan, & Buckland, 1989).

To reduce this enormous accomplishment, and similar accomplishments in other areas, to a few words is to risk being misunderstood. It is patently unjust to leave out the patent experts. To ignore the field trials is to be unfair on an international scale. I should inject a congratulatory account of how the formulation experts (Mr. George Blodinger and colleagues) modestly proposed three vehicles (designated A, B, and C) as a place to start in the development of a formulation suitable for injecting ivermectin into cattle—and how one of these (a mixture of glycerol formal and propylene glycol, still known around here as "Formulation B") gave a highly desirable rate of absorption and excretion of the active principle and went on to become the vehicle used in commerce. But I must be brief, and the reader may get some hint of the scope of these other activities by consulting the literature citations at the ends of the chapters that make up a recent monograph (Campbell, 1989).

Exit, with Banners and Sighs

Ivermectin is a commercial and clinical success. The sales of the cattle-injectable product are greater than those of any other product used in animal health. The heartworm prevention product for dogs is the largest selling product in small-animal medicine. It is making steady (noncommercial) progress as a drug for the prevention of skin disease and blindness in human onchocerciasis. Drug resistance can occur (Egerton, Suhayda, & Eary, 1988) but is not now a practical problem. Related compounds, "second generation avermectins," are under development in other laboratories and in our own laboratories.

As in any such large and long endeavor, there were strains and stresses along the way. Parenthetically, however, it might be noted that when the stakes of the game are high (professionally, not financially), cooperation among players is also high. There were failures as well as successes in the day-to-day operations. None of them seems traumatic, or even memorable, in retrospect. Had the process been thwarted at some point by inept management, faulty science, or plain bad luck, that would have been memorable.

The discovery and development of ivermectin was *in essence* fairly typical of the way in which modern drugs have emerged for the treatment of infectious diseases (Campbell, 1983). Other approaches to discovery are actively being pursued in our own and other laboratories, and perhaps future accounts of drug discovery will provide quite a different perspective. The traditional approach, however, has not been abandoned, and the story of ivermectin provides a good example of how it works. In its specific characteristics, the story is not typical. The potency and spectrum of the avermectins were immediately seen to be far superior to anything that had gone before. Excitement, in the early days, was constrained only by awareness that practical utility depended on so many other factors, especially the economics of production and the manifold aspects of safety. Each step of the process was filled with suspense, and it hardly seemed possible that all of the obstacles would be overcome. But as obstacles fell, optimism expanded—as did the commitment and financial risk. Interdisciplinary research was the key to success from beginning to end. In a project of this type diverse talents and personalities must work as a team; and the organizational framework must make that happen—or rather *allow* it to happen, for the professional allure and excitement of such an enterprise is hard to beat.

ACKNOWLEDGMENTS

The following scientists (listed alphabetically) of the Merck Sharp & Dohme Laboratories were authors of more than seventy papers that dealt with the avermectins and that were published within ten years of the discovery of the compounds. Their contributions thus form the basis of the present discussion.

G. Albers-Schonberg, B. H. Arison, M. A. Aziz, E. E. Baker, D. Barth, G. W. Benz, J. Birnbaum, L. S. Blair, J. Blodinger, E. S. Brokken, R. P. Buhs, R. W. Burg, R. D. Bush, W. C. Campbell, T. Capizzi, I. H. Carmichael, J. C. Chabala, L. Chaiet, S. H. L. Chiu, S. Cifelli, J. D. Cole, L. J. Cole, J. Conroy, S. A. Currie, A. W. Douglas, G. V. Downing, R. A. Dybas, C. H. Eary, J. R. Egerton, P. Eskola, D. V. Ewanciw, D. W. Fink, M. H. Fisher, J. E. Flor, A. G. Foster, R. T. Goegelman, V. P. Gullo, R. Hartman, O. D. Hensens, P. Ho, I. K. Hotson, R. K. Isensee, L. Jacob, T. A. Jacob, P. S. James, H. Joshua, L. Kaplan, A. J. Kempf, R. L. Kilgore, Y. L. Kong, W. R. Krellwitz, R. Lang, W. H. D. Leaning, P. A. Lo, V. J. Lotti, A. Y. H. Lu, A. Lusi, P. F. Malatesta, A. Matzuk, P. A. McCann-McCormick, E. C. McManus, T. N. Mellin, B. M. Miller, T. W. Miller, G. T. Miwa, R. L. Monaghan, H. Mrozik, M. Nallin, G. Olson, J. C. Onishi, R. E. Ormond, W. J. O'Shanny, D.

A. Ostlind, L. H. Peterson, J. Picton, R. E. Plue, S. S. Pong, D. G. Pope, M. Porta, J. M. Preston, J. D. Pulliam, I. Putter, R. F. Riek, B. Robin, R. A. Roncalli, A. Rosegay, C. Ruby, D. Schneider, J. Schroder, M. D. Schulman, E. Sestokas, R. L. Seward, J. L. Smith, M. D. Soll, E. O. Stapley, D. Suhayda, I. H. Sutherland, G. E. Swan, R. Taub, J. W. Tolan, R. L. Tolman, J. B. Tunac, P. C. Tway, D. Valentino, W. J. A. VandenHeuvel, R. Visser, F. Waksmunski, R. W. Walker, D. H. Wallace, H. Wallick, J. S. Walsh, M. A. R. Walsh, C. C. Wang, C. A. Wilkins, P. K. Wilkinson, E. Williams, J. B. Williams, K. E. Wilson, J. S. Wood, J. W. Wooden, H. B. Woodruff, M. Woods, M. F. Woods, L. A. Zimmerman, D. Zink.

References

Albers-Schonberg, G., Arison, B. H., Chabala, J. C., Douglas, A. W., Eskola, P., Fisher, M. H., Lusi, A., Mrozik, H., Smith, J. L., & Tolman, R. L. (1981). Avermectins: Structure determination. *Journal of the American Chemical Society, 103,* 4216–4221.

Aziz, M. A., Diallo, S., Diop, I. M., Lariviere, M., & Porta, M. (1982). Efficacy and tolerance of ivermectin in human onchocerciasis. *Lancet, 2,* 171–173, 1456–1457.

Blair, L. S., & Campbell, W. C. (1978). Trial of avermectin B_{1a}, mebendazole and melarsoprol against pre-cardiac *Dirofilaria immitis* in the ferret (*Mustela putorius furo*). *Journal of Parasitology, 64,* 1032–1034.

Blair, L. S. & Campbell, W. C. (1980a). Suppression of maturation of *Dirofilaria immitis* in *Mustela putorius furo* by single dose of ivermectin. *Journal of Parasitology, 66,* 691–692.

Blair, L. S. & Campbell, W. C. (1980b). Efficacy of ivermectin against *Dirofilaria immitis* larvae in dogs 31, 60 and 90 days after infection. *American Journal of Veterinary Research, 41,* 2108.

Burg, R. W., Miller, B. M., Baker, E. E., Birnbaum, J., Currie, S. A., Hartman, R., Kong, Y.-L., Monaghan, R. L., Olson, G., Putter, I., Tunac, J. B., Wallick, H., Stapley, E. O., Oiwa, R., & Omura, S. (1979). Avermectins, new family of potent anthelmintic agents: Producing organism and fermentation. *Antimicrobial Agents and Chemotherapy, 15,* 361–367.

Campbell, W. C. (1983). Progress and prospects in the chemotherapy of nematode infections of man and other animals. *Journal of Nematology, 15,* 608–615.

Campbell, W. C. (1989). *Ivermectin and Abamectin.* New York: Springer-Verlag.

Campbell, W. C., Bartels, E., & Cuckler, A. C. (1978). A method for detecting chemotherapeutic activity against *Schistosoma mansoni* in mice. *Journal of Parasitology, 64,* 69–77.

Campbell, W. C. & Blair, L. S. (1978a). *Dirofilaria immitis:* Experimental infections in the ferret (*Mustela putorius furo*). *Journal of Parasitology, 64,* 119–122.

Campbell, W. C. & Blair, L. S. (1978b). Efficacy of avermectins against *Dirofilaria immitis* in dogs. *Journal of Helminthology, 52,* 308–310.

Campbell, W. C., Fisher, M. H., Stapley, E. O., Albers-Schonberg, G., & Jacob, T. A. (1983). Ivermectin: A potent new antiparasitic agent. *Science, 221,* 823–828.

Chabala, J. C., Mrozik, H., Tolman, R. L., Eskola, P., Lusi, A., Peterson, L. H., Woods, M. F., & Fisher, M. H. (1980). Ivermectin, a new broad-spectrum antiparasitic agent. *Journal of Medical Chemistry, 23,* 1134–1136.

Chiu, S. L., & Lu, A. Y. H. (1989). Metabolism and tissue residues. In *Ivermectin and Abamectin* (W. C. Campbell, Ed.), pp. 131–143.

Clark, R. (1984). *J. B. S.: The Life and Work of J. B. S. Haldane.* Oxford: Oxford Univ. Press.

Drummond, R. O. (1984). Control of larvae of the common cattle grub (Diptera: Oestridae) with animal systemic insecticides. *Journal of Economic Entomology, 77*, 402–406.

Eckholm, E. (1989). Conquering an ancient scourge. *New York Times Magazine,* January 8, 20–27, 58–59.

Egerton, J. R., Birnbaum, J., Blair, L. S., Chabala, J. C., Conroy, J., Fisher, M. H., Mrozik, H., Ostlind, D. A., Wilkins, C. A., & Campbell, W. C. (1980). 22,23-Dihydroavermectin B_1, a new broad-spectrum antiparasitic agent. *British Veterinary Journal, 136,* 88–97.

Egerton, J. R., Brokken, E. S., Suhayda, D., Eary, C. H., Wooden, J. W., & Kilgore, R. L. (1981). The antiparasitic activity of ivermectin in horses. *Veterinary Parasitology, 8,* 83–88.

Egerton, J. R., Ostlind, D. A., Blair, L. S., Eary, C. H., Suhayda, D., Cifelli, S., Riek, R. F., & Campbell, W. C. (1979). Avermectins, a new family of potent anthelmintic agents: Efficacy of the B_{1a} component. *Antimicrobial Agents and Chemotherapy, 15,* 372–378.

Egerton, J. R., Suhayda, D., & Eary, C. H. (1988). Laboratory selection of *Haemonchus contortus* for resistance to ivermectin. *Journal of Parasitology, 74,* 614–617.

Fisher, M. H. (1985). Recent advances in the chemistry of insect control. In *Royal Society of Chemistry Special Publication* (N. F. Janes, Ed.), 53, p. 53.

Fisher, M. H. & Mrozik, H. (1984). The avermectin family of macrolide-like antibiotics. In *Macrolide Antibiotics* (S. Omura Ed.). New York: Academic Press, pp. 553–606.

Fisher, M. H. & Mrozik, H. (1989). Chemistry. In *Ivermectin and Abamectin* (W. C. Campbell, Ed.), pp. 1–23.

Fritz, L. C., Wang, C. C., & Gorio, A. (1979). Avermectin B_{1a} irreversibly blocks postsynaptic potentials at the lobster neuromuscular junction by reducing muscle membrane resistance. *Proceedings of the National Academy of Science, 76,* 2062–2066.

Greene, B. M., Brown, K. R., & Taylor, H. R. (1986). Use of ivermectin in humans. In *Ivermectin and Abamectin* (W. C. Campbell, Ed.), pp. 311–323.

Halasz, Z. (1963). Cited in Moss, R. W. (1988). *Free Radical.* New York, Paragon House.

James, P. S., Picton, J., & Riek, R. F. (1980). Insecticidal activity of the avermectins. *Veterinary Record, 106,* 59 (only).

Lankas, G. R. & Gordon, L. R. (1989). Toxicology. In *Ivermectin and Abamectin* (W. C. Campbell, Ed.), pp. 89–112.

Leaning, W. H. D. (1984). Ivermectin as an antiparasitic agent in cattle. *Medical Veterinary Practice, 65,* 669–672.

Lo, P. A., Fink, D. W., Williams, J. B., and Blodinger, J. (1985). Pharmacokinetic studies of ivermectin: effects of formulation. *Veterinary Research Communications, 9,* 251–268.

McCall, J. W., Dziminanski, M. T., Plue, R. E., Seward, R. L., & Blair, L. S. (1986). Ivermectin in heartworm prophylaxis: Studies with experimentally induced and naturally acquired infections. In *Proceedings of the Heartworm Symposium, 1986* (G. F. Otto, Ed.). Washington, D.C.: American Heartworm Society, pp. 9–13.

Miller, T. W., Chaiet, L., Cole, D. J., Cole, L. J., Flor, J. E., Goegelman, R. T., Gullo, V. P., Joshua, H., Kempf, A. J., Krellwitz, W. R., Monaghan, R. L., Ormond, R. E., Wilson, K. E., Albers-Schonberg, G., & Putter, I. (1979). Avermectins, new family of potent anthelmintic agents: Isolation and chromatographic properties. *Antimicrobial Agents and Chemotherapy, 15,* 368–371.

Miwa, G. T., Walsh, J. S., VandenHeuvel, W. J. A., Arison, B., Sestokas, E., Buhs, R., Rosegay, A., Avermitilis, S., Lu, A. Y. H., Walsh, M. A. R., Walker, R. W., Taub, R., &

Jacob, T. A. (1982). The metabolism of avermectins B_{1a}, H_2B_{1a}, and H_2B_{1b} by liver microsomes. *Drug Metabolism and Disposition, 10,* 268–274.

Mrozik, H., Chabala, J. C., Eskola, P., Matzuk, A., Waksmunski, F., Woods, M., & Fisher, M. H. (1983). Synthesis of milbemycins from avermectins. *Tetrahedron Letters, 24,* 5333–5336.

Mrozik, H., Eskola, P., & Fisher, M. H. (1982). Partial syntheses of avermectin B_{1a} and ivermectin B_{2a}. *Tetrahedron Letters, 23,* 2377–2378.

Mrozik, H., Eskola, P., & Fisher, M. H. (1986). Mercuric acetate oxidation of avermectin A_{2a} as a route to the selective cleavage of the allylic C-5-methoxy group. *Journal of Organic Synthesis, 51,* 3058–3059.

Mrozik, H., Eskola, P., Reynolds, G. F., Arison, B. H., Smith, G. M., & Fisher, M. H. (1988). Photoisomers of avermectins. *Journal of Organic Chemistry, 53,* 1820–1823.

Nallin-Omstead, M., Kaplan, L., & Buckland, B. C. (1989). Fermentation development and process improvement. In *Ivermectin and Abamectin* (W. C. Campbell, Ed.), pp. 33–54.

Ostlind, D. A., & Cifelli, S. (1981). Efficacy of thiabendazole, levamisole hydrochloride, and the major natural avermectins against *Trichostrongylus colubriformis* in the gerbil (*Meriones unguiculatus*). *Research in Veterinary Science, 31,* 255–256.

Ostlind, D. A., Cifelli, S., & Lang, R. (1979). Insecticidal activity of the antiparasitic avermectins. *Veterinary Record, 105*(8), 168.

Paul, A. J., Tranquilli, W. J., Seward, R. L., Todd, K. S., & DiPietro, J. A. (1987). Clinical observations in Collies given ivermectin orally. *American Journal of Veterinary Research, 48,* 684–685.

Pulliam, J. D. & Preston, J. M. (1989). Safety of ivermectin in target animals. In *Ivermectin and Abamectin* (W. C. Campbell, Ed.), pp. 149–161.

Sano, M., Terada, M., Ishii, A. I., & Kino, H. (1981). Effects of avermectin B_{1a} on the mobility of various parasitic helminths. *Experientia, 37,* 844.

Stapley, E. O. & Woodruff, H. B. (1982). Avermectins, antiparasitic lactones produced by *Streptomyces avermitilis* isolated from a soil in Japan. In *Trends in Antibiotic Research* H. Umezawa, A. L. Demain, T. Hata, & C. R. Hutchinson, Eds.). Tokyo: Japan Antibiotics Research Association, pp. 154–170.

Stretton, A. O. W., Campbell, W. C., & Babu, J. R. (1987). Biological activity and mode of action of avermectins. In *Vistas on Nematology* (J. A. Veech, & D. W. Dickson, Eds.). Hyattsville, Md.: Society of Nematologists, pp. 136–146.

Turner, M. J. & Schaeffer, J. M. (1989). Mode of action of ivermectin. In *Ivermectin and Abamectin* (W. C. Campbell, Ed.), pp. 73–88.

Wang, C. C. & Pong, S. S. (1982). Actions of avermectin B_{1a} on GABA nerves. In *Membranes and Genetic Disease* (J. R. Sheppard, V. E. Anderson, & J. W. Eaton, Eds.). New York: Liss, pp. 373–395.

Wilkins, C. A., Conroy, J., Ho, P., O'Shanny, W. J., & Capizzi, T. (1981). The effect of ivermectin on the live mass, period of attachment and percent control of ticks. In *Tick Biology and Control* (G. B. Whitehead & J. D. Gibson, Eds.). Grahamstown, South Africa: Rhodes University, pp. 137–142.

Wilkins, C. A., Conroy, J. A., Ho, P., O'Shanny, W. J., Malatesta, P. F., & Egerton, J. R. (1980). Treatment of psoroptic mange with avermectins. *Amercian Journal of Veterinary Research, 41,* 2112–2113.

IV | THE LOGIC OF INVENTION

What kind of thinking does invention involve? There can be no doubt that its "logic" has to go beyond humdrum convergent thinking, making room for leaps of insight and fundamental revisions in our ways of doing things.

Robert Weber helps us to understand the logic of invention by examining a simple model case, the knife. As he moves between the Stone Age knife and the Swiss Army knife, he reveals how a number of somewhat systematic processes can transform older inventions into newer, more sophisticated and powerful ones. Along the way, a number of powerful heuristics for invention are extracted and shown to have broad generality.

Strangely, the Swiss Army knife and the Soil Biotron are close first cousins, a bit under the skin. As with the biotron, the Swiss Army knife is a building-block invention. It takes previously existing blades (inventions or instruments) and combines them into a meaningful package. The problem here is to formulate principles for which things to combine and how to combine them.

David Perkins offers a complementary perspective on the "logic" of invention. Adopting a metaphor from the Alaskan gold rush, he shows how inventors make discoveries by searching around in conceptual "Klondike Spaces" of possibilities. Klondike Spaces have characteristic pitfalls and opportunities; how well inventors invent depends on how artfully they dodge the one and seize the other.

Because Klondike Spaces are rather like looking for a needle in a haystack, inventors go to great length to translate them into Homing Spaces, search spaces with more or less continuous gradients along which they can move with confidence and partial rationality. Perkins is our tour guide as we move through both types of space, and as he gives us some hints for how to translate Klondike Spaces into Homing Spaces.

Jacob Helfman outlines a systematic strategic approach to invention, even now helping engineers to solve stubborn design problems. He shows how the "logic" of this approach deliberately cultivates creative insight into the nature of the problem and its possible solutions. He forthrightly claims that we can train people to become inventive.

The idea of training people to invent more effectively is surely an important one. In a way, it is the idea of inventing invention. Whether we can now do this provokes disagreement, but surely it is one of invention's holy grails.

12 | Stone Age Knife to Swiss Army Knife: An Invention Prototype

ROBERT J. WEBER

Every discipline needs a model system to study. That system should be both simple and complex: simple enough to understand and readily manipulate, and complex enough to embody important phenomena of interest. Genetics has *Drosophila,* or fruit flies (Morgan, 1926), and medical research has tissue cultures and mice. Cognitive psychology has candidate *Drosophila* in the form of various tasks devoted to problem-solving: the pendulum problem (Maier, 1931), the Tower of Hanoi problem, the cannibal/missionary problem, anagram problems, crypt-arithmetic problems (Newell & Simon, 1972), and finally chess problems (Chase & Simon, 1973). While all of these tasks are suitable for the study of various problem-solving facets, they do not readily lend themselves to the study of invention. Either they are not sufficiently open-ended or they do not deal with the physical world of device, process, and effect. In the context of invention, they fall short of either the simplicity or the complexity standard: they are not really simple enough to understand and manipulate, or they do not seem to embody the complex requirements of invention—something that is new, useful, and unobvious (U.S. Department of Commerce, 1985). A better candidate model system, a *Drosophila* of invention and creativity, is all about us. It is the simple hand tool as revealed in forms like needles, knives, forks, hammers, and shovels (Weber & Dixon, 1989; Weber & Perkins, 1989). The simplicity of the hand tool is obvious, but there is an underlying complexity also. Any given hand tool embodies function, structure, human interface and grip, actions, internal materials (what it is made of), and external materials (what it operates on). In microcosm the hand tool links our intentions to our actions via means; it must fit the mind, the hand, the world of action and effect, and the world of material, design, and construction. It is both simple and complex.

As such, the hand tool involves many of the categories that the cognitive scientist is interested in, and it does so in relatively understandable form. Underscoring the importance of the hand tool is its long history; many particular forms have existed for centuries if not millennia (Bordes, 1968). In this chapter I consider one interesting specimen of the hand tool, the Swiss Army knife, and show how the principles that underlie it and its ancestors serve as prototypes of invention. In particular, I identify at least four distinctive forms of invention embedded in the Swiss Army knife.

Before going further, we should contrast the approach to invention through the hand tool, a common everyday object, with another recent treatment of everyday objects. Norman (1988), in his book *The Psychology of Everyday Things,* describes the pathology of artifacts. For example, he details numerous problems associated with badly designed door handles, illegible or confusing visual displays, and phones that fail to give a user adequate feedback as to their state and functioning. All told, a sorry record of bad design is extensively documented. Norman's approach is important, but the approach taken here is the opposite. Rather than drawing attention to *pathology,* I will document some of the *hidden intelligence* that resides in invented everyday things. Hand tools will serve as the prototype.

This study of invention raises two fundamental questions: Can we describe inventions in a general way? And can we extract principles of invention from particular cases that have some generality across inventions? Our plan for answering these questions is, first, to describe an integrated hand tool, a typical form of the Swiss Army knife, and, second, to analyze it for invention principles and heuristics. There are numerous advantages to symbolically describing inventions. The descriptions can be more readily manipulated than the real thing, abstraction from description becomes possible, and finally numerous paths of generalization may be suggested by a good description. Processes such as manipulation, abstraction, and generalization can be captured in part with heuristics—procedures or strategies for generating ideas that are often useful, although they do not produce guaranteed results. As I unpack the complexity of the Swiss Army knife, I will draw attention to important heuristics that are seemingly embodied in its construction. My method of unpacking is a retrospective analysis. It is retrospective in a deep sense: the original inventors of the main components of the Swiss Army knife are unknown and long since dead. Nonetheless, it is argued that such an analysis can lead to a rich set of invention principles.

The descriptive scheme I use is based on a frame analysis (Minsky, 1975), a form of description that has previously served for the study of invention (Weber & Dixon, 1989; Weber & Perkins, 1989). Everyone is familiar with the concept of *frame.* It is an abstract structure, skeleton, or framework on which to hang things, in particular slots or components. The slot is a generalization on the idea of a variable. Each slot is a place on the skeleton; each slot or place may be single or multivalued and contains structures, actions, or procedures, and each slot may have other embedded frames as well. For example, a tax form is a frame; it involves slots (Name, Social Security Number, Number of Dependents) and associated "values": John Smith, 526-96-1234, and 3. In addition, those values may be more complex; they may be calculated based on other slots (lines) in the form, they may be hierarchical (based on another form or frame that is attached), and so on. I will describe a frame structure for the Swiss Army knife, with slots shared by many hand tools. Then I will show several forms of invention embodied in the Swiss Army knife. Those forms are: *joining,* in which previously independent tools are combined or integrated to form a single tool; *adding slots,* or features, to increase functionality; *fine-tuning,* or refining those features to make for better overall functioning or for a better fit between tool and a particular environment; and finally *using an abstract element* on which spatial transformations and heuristics operate.

A Frame Description

The Swiss Army knife comes in a variety of forms.[1] A common one has the following "blades" or components, shown in Table 12.1 in the form of a frame description (Weber & Dixon, 1989; Weber & Perkins, 1989). For this particular case of the Swiss Army knife, a frame description has a series of slots like "Blade," "Edge,"

TABLE 12.1. Frame description of a Swiss Army knife's blades/components

Blade/ Component	Edge	Function	Action for Function	Grip[a]
Large knife blade	Point	Penetrate	Stab, bore	PO, F
	Edge	Cut	Slice, whittle, slash, scrape	PO, F
Small knife blade	Same as above	Same	Same, specialized by size	Same, PR
File	Flat file	File	Reciprocal to-fro	PO
	Saw	Saw	Same	F
	Point	Pry, clean	Leverlike	PO, PI
Fish blade	Serrated scaler	Scale fish	Scrape	PO
	Forked tip	Remove hooks	Leverlike	PO
	Back/ruler	Measure	Lay beside object and read markings	?
Scissors	Two levers	Cut	Shearing	PI
Phillips screwdriver	Point	Screw	Rotate screw	PO
Magnifying glass	Face	Magnify	Bend light rays	?
Can opener	Can opener	Open cans	Up-down movement	PO
	Small blade tip	Screw	Rotate screw	PO
Bottle opener	Side	Open caps	Lever upward	PO
	Large blade tip	Screw	Rotate screw	PO
	Notch	Strip wires	Remove insulation	PO
Corkscrew	Point/coil	Pull corks	Push, rotate, pull	PO
Long-blade screwdriver	Blade tip	Screw	Rotate screw	PO
Awl	Sharp tip/side	Penetrate	Rotary drilling	PO
Toothpick[b]	Point	Clean teeth	Penetrate, pry	PR
Tweezers[b]	Points	Pick up things	Pincer action, opposing levers	PI
Approximate totals for distinct entries:				
14	23	18	20	4

[a]PO = power; PR = precision; PI = pincer; F = forefinger.

[b]A case join, so strictly speaking not a blade in the same sense as the others.

"Function," and each of these slots has one or more "values" such as "large knife blade," "sharp edge," "cutting function." In all, the frame description of Table 12.1 indicates that there are fourteen "blades," twenty-three working edges, and about eighteen standard functions for this model of the Swiss Army knife. The functions are fewer than the working edges because, for example, there are a number of different-sized screwdrivers of different lengths, and we count them all as one function, with specializations. Associated with the functions and actions are four different grips. A *power grip* calls for the hand to be completely wrapped around the handle, as with a baseball bat; a *precision grip* requires coordination of thumb and forefinger, as in writing with a pencil; a *pincer grip* involves pulling thumb and fingers together, even though they may not meet, as in using tweezers; and a *forefinger grip* is when we stretch the forefinger along the back of a tool edge, such as the back of a knife when we are slicing bread. Each of these grips emphasizes different characteristics, such as power, leverage, or control; and each allows for different actions, such as stabbing, slashing, and whittling.

Table 12.1 also can be viewed in another way, by examining a *tool schema* and the corresponding tool space that it generates. By "schema" I mean a pattern of tool surfaces and behaviors required to accomplish a given function. Instead of starting with a specific tool and its components, we may start with a function and describe a general tool schema.

$$\text{Function} = \text{tool edge} + \text{grip} + \text{action}$$

According to the tool schema, to achieve a given function of the Swiss Army knife, one selects a tool edge and then a grip, and finally executes an action. Thus the function of penetration might involve using the blade point, applying a power grip, and then engaging in the action of stabbing. Similar analyses for other functions reveal the underlying schema of edge, grip, and action, in each case.

The tool schema suggests another concept. If we wished, we could construct a *potential use space.* We do this by multiplicatively combining all distinctive forms

$$\text{tool edges} \cdot \text{actions} \cdot \text{grips}$$

The corresponding numbers are shown by the approximate totals at the bottom of Table 12.1, using only distinctive forms. The resulting product, depending on how fine-grained we make our actions, yields approximately:

$$23 \text{ edges} \cdot 20 \text{ actions} \cdot 4 \text{ grips} = 1840 \text{ potential functions in the space}$$

Of these 1840 functions, only about 18 are realized because we do not distinguish all the cases: the small and large blade are lumped together; the several sizes of screwdriver are not distinguished; and not all of the combinations are possible or useful, for example, a stabbing motion with the flat side of a file blade. By any estimate of this nature it is clear that a great deal of structure, constraint, or lawfulness is focused on reducing the potential use space of 1840 possible functions to the *realized use space* of 18 functions. Only about 1 percent of the potential functions is realized. This finding of massive constraint must have implications for any theory of creativity or invention.

Inventing with Joins

When we combine entire, separately existing inventions or their frame descriptions, the result is a *join*. Thus, a claw hammer is the join of a striker head and a claw that share a common handle. (In a join, overlapping redundancies, such as two handles, are usually removed.)

So far, nothing is new here. Indeed, a common view of creativity is that it involves combining or joining together simpler objects or ideas. Thus Koestler (1964) speaks of bisociations, the unconscious coming together of previously disparate ideas. The problem is that without qualification such notions explain too little and too much, at once. On the side of too little, we know less about the unconscious than we know about the conditions of creativity, so the unconscious tells us too little. For this reason, we will avoid further discussion of unconscious processes, while acknowledging that a rich theory of unconscious processes would change that decision. On the side of too much, we recognize that a form of creativity is to combine ideas, but without rules of combination, we are faced with a combinatorial explosion. Indiscriminate combination provides too many possibilities. Let us dwell on this latter point.

Joining Fuels the Combinatorial Explosion

Combinatorial explosion is the result of promiscuous idea association. With free rein, the number of possible pairs of different idea or object combinations in the world is

$$\frac{n(n-1)}{2} = \frac{(n^2 - n)}{2}$$

Thus the first of n possible ideas can be selected in n ways and the second different idea can be selected from any one of the $(n-1)$ remaining ideas; multiplying these together gives us the numerator $n(n-1)$. If we do not care about the order, then we divide by 2. As the number of ideas n increases, the number of possible pairs increases as Order (n^2)—a value larger than the number of ideas in the universe. If we combine ideas r at a time, then the order of r-tuples increases as Order (n^r), a number that becomes very large very fast as the separate elements or parts in an invention increase. What this means is that if we are going to explain invention or creativity as the combination of ideas, we shall need constraints on the way in which elementary things can join or combine. Otherwise we are confronted with an exploding universe of combinations.

One argument holds that combinatorial explosion is the nature of creativity: anything can go with anything else, and in any way. I do not want to argue this point on a general plane, so I will confine myself to a limited domain—hand tools. I have already shown that hand tools in fact are restricted in the ways that they can join together: the realized functions are far fewer than the potential functions. Underlying those restrictions, in turn, are important heuristics of combination that trim the tree of possible combinations.

Furthermore, for any given join of separate tools, there are a number of levels at which the join can take place. These levels of joining provide additional structure. A classification of joining levels allows us to systematically examine combinations and provides for some limited order in the way things come together.

To hold down the combinatorial explosion of joins between different things, we may employ the *complement heuristic: Combine only those tools or ideas that are used in the same context.* For example, any of the tools used by a carpenter are fair game for joining, because they occur in similar contexts or settings involving construction. A particularly useful join would be the carpenter's square combined with a ruler; one is used for angular layout and the other for size or distance layout. In contrast, we would not be inclined to combine a surgeon's scalpel with a shovel, because they do not occur in the same work contexts—with the possible exception of malpractice cases. Similarly, the same heuristic can be used for farm tools: combine only those tools used for harvesting. In fact, there is such a device that goes by the intriguing name of the *combine.* The complement heuristic may be too broad or too narrow. If it is too broad, then the explosion of possible joins is too large to work with. But as I now show, further containment is possible. A more specific form of the complement heuristic is the *inverse heuristic: Combine only those tools or ideas that are inverses of one another.* The claw hammer is an example. What the striker part of the hammer will do, the claw will undo, and vice versa.

Probably the inverse heuristic is too narrow for some purposes. On occasion, even the complement heuristic will miss some striking joins of potentially great importance. An example is Gutenberg's possibly apocryphal combining of a grape press and royal seals to create movable type and a printing press (Burke, 1978; Usher, 1954). But that is the nature of all heuristics: they are not guaranteed to work, yet at their best they are very helpful. If we are worried about the narrowness of the complement heuristic it can be expanded to include tools with overlapping or shared characteristics to form the *overlap heuristic: Join only those tools with partially overlapping parts, properties, or functions.* Their joining can then serve to eliminate redundancies and integrate functions. For example, if a number of different-sized knife blades are joined together in a pocket knife, we have eliminated redundancy by having them all share a common handle. In fact, the Swiss Army knife has some "blades," such as the magnifying glass and the corkscrew, that have little more in common than sharing the overlapping feature of a common handle, or occasionally sharing complementary work environments: after you have opened a bottle of wine with the corkscrew, you use the magnifying glass to look for your contact lens that fell out after you drank too much of the wine.

What this discussion illustrates is that when joining things or ideas, the combinatorial explosion can be arbitrarily focused in range to suit our interests. The focus is achieved through the choice of a suitable heuristic, like applying the complement, inverse, or overlap principles. Although some disagree (Koestler, 1964), the use of these heuristics flourishes when their application is conscious and deliberate, as opposed to letting the unconscious do our work for us. For systematically exploring combinations, the more deliberation the better.

Levels of Joining

Just as we think the combinatorial explosion of idea or object combinations is under control, another facet of idea promiscuity manifests itself. Once two inventions are selected, they still can be integrated with one another in a variety of ways, in crude analogy to different forms and strengths of chemical bonding. However, for mechanical inventions we have no metric of join strength; instead, we refer to *levels of joining.*

Again to provide focus, I concentrate on joining simple hand tools, without internally moving parts. In each case I relate the level of join to the Swiss Army knife. Once more the problem of combinatorial explosion is averted, because the ways in which such hand tools may join together forms a relatively small set of meaningful categories. Also, I note that a higher level of joining or integration does not necessarily mean "better." The question of what constitutes the best level of joining two tools X and Y is not addressed here. Instead, I turn to the nature of the joins, a topic that is best illustrated by examples, ranging from weak to strong integration.

UNRELATED ASSEMBLAGE.   Strictly speaking, this and the next category are null joins, but just as zero is a number or the null set is a set, so too are these categories a level of joining. The weakest form of joining is an *unrelated assemblage,* a collection of miscellaneous items. A junk drawer full of diverse and unconnected items serves as an example. Clearly, the Swiss Army knife is more than an unrelated assemblage. Its separate blades and functions are connected to one another, and they are designed to produce a tool kit of complementary functions. Of course, the number of complementary functions varies with the model of the Swiss Army knife; less expensive models have fewer functions. Nonetheless, the impression is the purposive combination of blades and features.

RELATED ASSEMBLAGE.   This is a somewhat stronger form of joining or integration, an assemblage of *related* tools that are *separate* from one another. An example is a set of wood-carving knives or perhaps a toolbox that has a rational design behind it to allow for many different tool functions building on and complementing one another. The Swiss Army knife is not a related assemblage because its various components share a common handle or case. Related assemblages are often based on the complement heuristic: Bring together those tools used in a similar setting. The complement heuristic is heritable; it applies as well to the higher levels of integration that follow.

CASE JOINS.   Here several different tools are joined with a common handle, and that handle also serves as a case. Survival knives operate this way; the handle may unscrew to include a snakebite kit, matches, and a cyanide capsule. The Swiss Army knife's toothpick and tweezers are examples of a case join. Case joins are driven by the *multiple function heuristic: Find multiple functions for the same part.* A particular example is the case doubling as a handle. Combining the case and handle saves space, material, and weight; all of this makes for increased portability. The notions of multifunctionality, economy of resources, and portability are also heritable; they apply to all higher levels of joining.

ATTACHMENT JOINS. This is a still stronger form of integration. A central unit has specialized attachments that fit with it in a modular way. One example is the vacuum cleaner and its attachments; another is the oxyacetylene torch with separate welding and cutting heads that may be alternately attached and removed from the main unit. The Swiss Army knife is not an example of attachment joins; it does not work like a vacuum cleaner and its attachments. However, attachment joins for knives do exist. The X-acto knife consists of a main unit and a number of different blades that can be attached, much like the attachments of a vacuum cleaner. Attachment joins are driven by economy and by the *specialization heuristic: Allow for different specific blades as part of the same overall tool to maximize the fit between tool and task.* Although the Swiss Army knife does not use attachment joins, it is interesting to speculate on how they would work. The separate blades (like those in an Xacto knife) could be kept in the handle (a case join). But space probably is not sufficient for a cylinder chuck to hold the working blades; the handle must be kept flat for the storage of other blades.

LOOSELY BONDED JOINS. A stronger form of integration occurs when different tools are permanently attached to one another, say, at a handle. An example is a set of measuring spoons on a metal ring. The Swiss Army knife also fits this category because it has a common handle to which most of the blades are physically and permanently attached by a pin or hinging mechanism. (The exceptions are the toothpick and tweezers, which may be physically separated from the handle and are at the case join level.) With loosely bonded joins, a selection of function requires some setting or "dialing" to get out the right working blade. Loosely bonded joins are driven by the *compacting heuristic: Join components tightly, so they are in a package and will not become separated or lost.* The *switching avoidance heuristic* is also at work: *Cut down on the dead time between uses that results from having to look for a related tool and then switch to it.* Both of these heuristics are heritable.

MODERATELY BONDED JOINS. In this level of integration, the different edges of the *same* tool or "blade" have different functions. We simply need to change the working edge of the blade, perhaps with a different grip, to change functions. Examples include the claw hammer (both claw and hammer) and a graduated square (measures or assesses both linear distance and angles.) For the Swiss Army knife, one blade has both a can-opener edge and a screwdriver edge. We can open a can or drive a screw simply by using the different edges of the same blade and somewhat different hand actions. No new heuristics seem to be at work here; we are continuing along the path of greater compaction and multiple functionality, with a minimum of materials.

TIGHTLY BONDED JOINS. An even stronger integration occurs when the same tool edge has more than one function, and the only distinction among functions involves the grip or action. For example, the blade of a shovel is used for digging, scooping, chopping—with the different functions determined by the hand or foot grip on the shovel and the actions of the body on the tool. The Swiss Army knife's screwdriver is an example. The same blade is used for both inserting and removing screws, depending on the direction of rotation of the grip. Again, we are simply continuing on the same path of compaction and multiple functionality.

The classification of joins just put forth reveals a good deal of hidden structure in hand tool invention. Indeed, the classification, once constructed, becomes a vehicle for systematic tool design, and it helps us deal in another way with the combinatorial explosion. Earlier the number of joins formed from n items was stated to be $n(n - 1)/2$. If we include the fact that each join may take place at a number of different levels of integration, the correct value is more like $mn(n - 1)/2$, where m is the number of levels of joining for a given class of inventions. If anything, m is likely to get larger as we get more sophisticated in drawing distinctions among different forms of joining. Even though the overall number of joins is large, if we focus on a particular tool combination and use the inverse or complement heuristics, the combinatorial explosion still can be contained.

Some Reasons for Joining at Different Levels

When integration of tools is at a low level, different tasks require different tools, and batch processing is pushed on us. To avoid costly switching operations, we must do all of one kind of activity before doing any of another. For example, writing text and drawing graphics on many older microcomputers has to be a batch process. Separate programs are required, and one must be shut down before another is operated. Further, there may be no way of incorporating both text and graphics in the same document file. But on some newer computers, it is now easy to cycle back and forth between text and graphic modes. This allows an individual idea to be built from the core out instead of in batch mode, one aspect at a time. Thus we can do text and related illustrations close together in time as linked ideas, instead of all text ideas and then all graphics ideas, each in batch mode.

The two examples of the Swiss Army knife and the computer implementation of text and graphics suggest some reasons why tools should be joined or integrated:

- To achieve greater portability. The Swiss Army knife is much more portable than would be the separate tools of a related assemblage with the same capability.

- To achieve economy and nonredundancy of materials. For example, the handle of the Swiss Army knife serves as the case for blades when they are not in use.

- To avoid the irresistible push toward batch processing made by low levels of tool integration. Effort and time are lost in switching between different tools (Weber & Dixon, 1989). We can escape these switching costs by resorting to batch processing. Or we can integrate our tools at a higher level. The Swiss Army knife is an example of the second path. Because most of the Swiss Army knife's joins are at the higher levels of integration, little time is lost in switching between functions.

These are reasons for a join. When should tools not be joined?

- To achieve greater specialization. For example, a related assemblage of wood-carving knives of different shapes provides the ultimate flexibility in cutting: small blades, large blades, curved and straight; the combination is large indeed. To combine them all into one integrated tool is not practical.

- To achieve ease of manufacture. Usually, more skill and manufacturing capabilities are needed to produce a highly integrated tool than several individual tools that are simpler. For example, compare the complexity of constructing the Swiss Army knife with that required for constructing individual knives and screwdrivers.

The Swiss Army knife involves integration at several levels of joining. Is one level of joining better than another? Under what circumstances? For highly specialized functions such as wood carving—where compactness and portability are not important—a related assemblage of separate knives provides the greatest flexibility. For general-purpose use—where compactness and portability are important—high levels of joining may be best. High levels of joining also minimize switching times between functions. This switching is not just physical but also involves the different mental routines involved. Henry Ford in designing the auto assembly line was aware of both physical and mental switching problems of alternating between tasks (Ford, 1925; Weber & Dixon, 1989). One of his primary objectives was to eliminate or hold down those switching activities.

Does switching time always vary systematically and inversely with the degree or level of integration? Probably not. If our set of wood-carving knives is in front of us, we can switch from one knife to another more rapidly than we can, say, insert new blades in an Xacto knife, which is at the higher level of an attachment join. But this situation presumes that all the knives of the wood-carving set are laid out in front of us, ready to go, or that we have them with us when we travel. Accordingly, when general use and portability are emphasized, level of join and switching time are probably negatively correlated in many contexts.

This concludes my preliminary examination of the complex topic of joining separate inventions. I now turn to another way of inventing that is embedded in the Swiss Army knife.

Invention by Adding Features: The Point and the Handle

In addition to joining existing inventions, we can add *slots* or *features* to the invention frame. To see this form of invention, we will concentrate on a particular blade, the knife, and show the allied development of an important human interface, the handle.

Figure 12.1 shows a *rational progression* of the knife. By this I mean a progression that uses steps that are part of the archaeological record and that are ordered from simple to complex. No suggestion is made that all cultures went through each successive stage in the development of a knife. A given invention has many potential sources, ranging from rational development to cultural borrowing to finding useful models in nature shaped by random processes. All that is attempted here is to provide a systematic and simple sequence that is rich in conceptual principles of invention.

A. ROUNDED BLADE

B. POINTED BLADE

C. TOP-SHOULDERED BLADE

D. BOTTOM-SHOULDERED BLADE

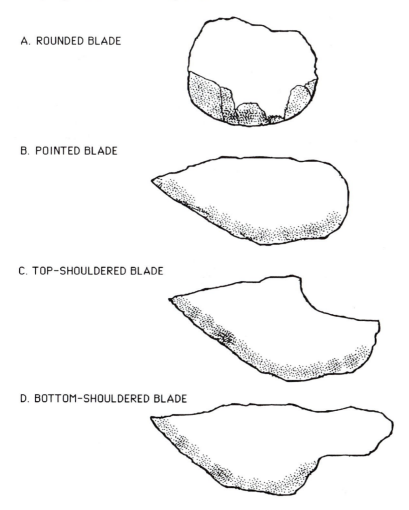

FIGURE 12.1. A conceptual account of the knife's development. The addition of features (A–D), and the slow movement toward a longer and sharper cutting edge (not illustrated).

The rounded stone blade (Leakey, 1971), as shown in Figure 12.1A, dates to approximately 2 million years ago. The ridges indicate a chipped or sharpened edge. The exact form of use is not clear; there are no user manuals. But scraping, chopping, and primitive slicing are certainly possible.

The addition of a point to the rounded stone blade (Leakey, 1971), Figure 12.1B, is like adding a slot or feature to an invention's frame description; normally, points do not exist in isolation, so they are viewed as features.[2] Undoubtedly, the point greatly increased the range of the blade's functioning. Notice that a handle is also missing; somehow the idea of a human interface as a separate feature was slow to come. The blade of Figure 12.1B must have been gripped from above with less than a power grip; there is no way to wrap the entire hand around the sharpened blade. Clearly, this is not a good human interface.

The top-shouldered blade, Figure 12.1C, introduces another new slot, the handle. The top shoulder represents an explicit attempt to construct an interface for the hand, with the grip from the top. It is present in Upper Paleolithic times (probably between 20,000 and 40,000 BC) and may have been developed earlier; examples have been found at the Kostenki I site in Russia (Semenov, 1964). Notice that the positioning of the hand behind the blade's shoulder will allow for greater force and a more comfortable grip than the handleless knife forms of Figure 12.1A and B. However, the top-shouldered blade still does not allow for a power grip, with the entire hand circling the handle.

The bottom-shouldered blade (Bordes, 1968), Figure 12.1D, is a great advance. For the first time a complete power grip is allowed; the entire hand can fit around the handle, allowing more power, comfort, and control for many knife actions. A further refinement in the interface between blade and hand is wrapping of the handle part with leather or the lashing of it to wood. Both would increase the fit or comfort of the human interface between hand and blade.

In comparison, the Swiss Army knife obviously has a handle that allows for a full power grip for those blades that need it, and its handle allows for different grips for other blades, as indicated in the last column of Table 12.1. Its handle differs from that of the stone knife in another way—it can also function as a case. But the essential form of the knife is present from the early Stone Age.

Several background heuristics are suggested in this conceptual progression of stone knives. The *slot addition heuristic* says: *Increase functionality by adding features like a point and a handle.*[3] The *packing heuristic* says: *Pack as much functionality as possible into the same structures and space.* Packing both a blade and a point together increases functionality and portability, and it also conserves resources. The *interface heuristic* says: *Develop a human interface, like the handle, that is comfortable and that will enhance leverage and control.*[4]

We can see these same heuristics at work in the various blades of the Swiss Army knife. For example, the "fishing blade" has a rough edge for scaling fish, a forked tip for disgorging fishing hooks, and a spine or back with a ruler. One side of the spine is graduated in inches and the other in centimeters. This one blade, then, has three different slots added and packed together—scaling, disgorging, and measuring. The particular combination of functionality constitutes a complementary package, because a person fishing might well wish for all of these functions in a short period of time. Finally, the human interface for the blade is of course the shared handle.

The separate edges of the bottle-opener blade are not so rational. This blade has three edges: bottle-opener edge, screwdriver, and wire stripper. Conceivably, the screwdriver and the wire stripper are bound together because of complementarity. The bottle opener is not, unless part of the context is drinking on the job.

Even less clear in rationale is another blade, the combined can opener and screwdriver. Such a combination of edges is probably based on the *opportunity heuristic: Here's a place that we can add a function, so let's do it.* However, even functions and edges put together under the opportunity heuristic have intelligence behind them. To see this, think of what might have been done. The screwdriver tip could have been put on the end of a knife blade. This is a dangerous combination, if the other hand is holding the screw, and it is a physically bad combination since the knife blade is long and flexible and a screwdriver should be rigid. An even more bizarre combination is a pairing such as the corkscrew and the magnifying glass; no obvious way suggests itself for packing them together on the same blade.

In brief, adding features and functions is a very old enterprise in invention and design. The rationale can vary from clear, to opportunistic, to Rube Goldberglike. The edges and functions of each blade in the Swiss Army knife have been packaged in the range from clear to opportunistic, probably a good range to be in.

Invention by Refinement: Fine-Tuning

We now introduce a third form of invention found in the Swiss Army knife and its precursors, the fine-tuning or optimizing of functionality. Semenov (1964), in his study of Stone Age tools, points out that the stone knife evolved along several historically driven evaluation criteria, notably a sharper cutting edge and a longer cutting edge. To Semenov's criteria, we also add easier maintenance and greater strength.

What these developments mean for an invention path is plain. An inventor should find the direction that evaluation criteria move in, and try to anticipate the next steps. This is seemingly obvious, but in the early stages of invention it may not be. If we lived midstream in the evolution of Paleolithic stone knives, and if we extracted historical evaluation criteria, we might look for a way of manufacture that provides for longer, sharper cutting edges and easier maintenance, a method of manufacture different from the flaking off of small pieces of stone. In fact this was done, by moving to a technology of grinding. Grinding allows for greater control of the edge, both in length and sharpness; it allows for new varieties of stone to be worked, those with a grain that is less homogeneous than flint; and it allows for easier maintenance. This last point is easily made if we consider the expertise needed to sharpen a stone knife precisely by microflaking at the edge versus the operation of simply grinding it, something that anyone can do without much skill at all.

The idea of progressive refinement along an evaluation criterion is very common. Often it makes the difference between an interesting idea and a successful invention. It is the stuff of slow historical progress or of large-scale development teams and corporate programs. A more modern example than stone knives is the development of audio recording, starting with the first primitive recordings of Edison (1878) and moving up to compact disks. Historically the evaluation criteria have been clear: better fidelity, lower cost, longer play, and so on. For each successive method of recording—mechanical, electrical, electronic, and digital electronic—a longer or shorter period of development follows in which variables are optimized in order to climb similar evaluation criteria. (However, the shifts from one method of recording to another, mechanical, tape, CD, is much more than a matter of fine-tuning.)

The Swiss Army knife also shows its own set of evaluation criteria: pack more blades and functions into the same or smaller space, while holding down weight. Unfortunately, these criteria are seemingly incompatible (Weber, Moder, & Solie, 1990). As the Swiss Army knife takes on more functions, its human interface is breaking down also. A fully equipped Swiss Army knife is really too heavy for a pocket, so there is a special belt-loop case. Not to waste space, the belt case also has a honing rod for sharpening the blade (a case join). In addition to being heavy, the feel of the knife is beginning to be awkward also. A long session of carving will leave the hand sore. The solution is to cut down on the number of blades, or to use some of the new materials that are lighter and stronger than steel. These include metals like titanium and the new synthetics, like graphite, that may work for some of the functions. Whatever the successful material, it should lead to a lighter and thinner knife, if it is to follow the evaluation criteria that apparently have guided the development of the Swiss Army knife.

Invention by Abstraction and Transformation

The fourth method of invention suggested by the Swiss Army knife involves the abstraction of a building block and subsequent spatial transformations of that building block to produce different blades and blade edges. To be sure, this is not the way the pointed knife and other tools were invented. Instead, it is an after-the-fact rationalization and systematization of hand tool inventions that is very powerful. We begin with one blade, the knife, and then consider other related blades or tools.

The idea of the knife is based on the wedge: to focus forces that are applied over a broad range (by hand, wrist, arm, shoulder) to a very narrow wedge-shaped blade or point region, thus resulting in a tremendous amplification of pressure. The most extreme amplification of pressure results for a point. In fact, the fundamental element of abstraction that underlies the knife is the point or tooth, which itself may be regarded as a wedge; it is shown in Figure 12.2. We now apply different spatial transformations to that abstract tooth to generate a variety of tools, many of which are part of the Swiss Army knife, some that are not but could have been, and some that go beyond the Swiss Army knife for reasons to be noted.

The Awl. The most simple use of a tooth-shaped tool is to punch or bore holes, as with an awl (not shown in Figure 12.2). The awl is essentially the tooth of Figure 12.2 with a handle. Simply push and rotate with the wrist to produce a hole in leather, wood, or some other material. Not surprisingly, the Swiss Army knife contains an awl.

The Saw. If a tooth element is spatially transformed by iterating and punctuating it along a straight line, in one dimension, with a space between each tooth, what is the result? Figure 12.2 shows a saw, requiring a to-and-fro action. Notice that this is essentially a one-dimensional transformation, with the tooth iterated along a line. The Swiss Army knife contains a saw.

The Blade and the Pointed Knife. When the tooth is iterated in a very densely compacted or continuous straight line, a blade edge results. The blade edge allows

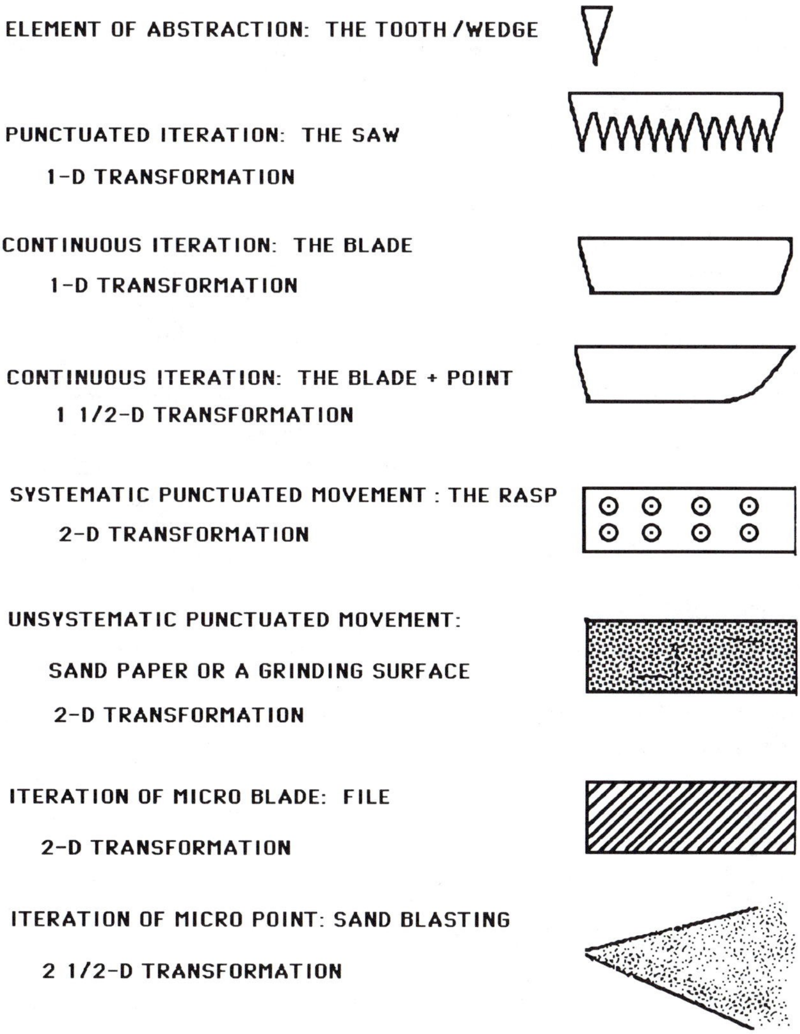

ELEMENT OF ABSTRACTION: THE TOOTH /WEDGE

PUNCTUATED ITERATION: THE SAW
   1-D TRANSFORMATION

CONTINUOUS ITERATION: THE BLADE
   1-D TRANSFORMATION

CONTINUOUS ITERATION: THE BLADE + POINT
   1 1/2-D TRANSFORMATION

SYSTEMATIC PUNCTUATED MOVEMENT : THE RASP
   2-D TRANSFORMATION

UNSYSTEMATIC PUNCTUATED MOVEMENT:

   SAND PAPER OR A GRINDING SURFACE

   2-D TRANSFORMATION

ITERATION OF MICRO BLADE: FILE

   2-D TRANSFORMATION

ITERATION OF MICRO POINT: SAND BLASTING

   2 1/2-D TRANSFORMATION

FIGURE 12.2. The tooth as an element of abstraction. How simple transformations applied to the tooth give rise to several common tool forms.

new modes of action, separate from those of the tooth. Examples include scrapping, whittling, or slicing. This long and dense iteration of a tooth along a straight line provides a blade without a point. However, if the tooth is rotated upward toward the end of the spatial transformation, a point also results. If the action mode is a slow pull across the surface of work, then the knife point and blade in combination act as an etching tool that can carve in relief, something that neither component is good at individually. In short, we have emergent functionality produced by the parallel action of the two components, point and edge. Notice that the generation of the simple pointless blade from the tooth is a one-dimensional transformation because the tooth slides along a line. But the pointed blade is a one-and-one-half-dimensional transformation because the tooth iterations wrap around into part of a second dimension to form the point. The Swiss Army knife has several different pointed blades that vary primarily in size, a dimension readily varied through the one-and-one-half dimensional transformation.

The Rasp and the Grinder. What if a set of teeth is arrayed in two dimensions? If the teeth are relatively large and separate, a rasplike tool results. If they are small, densely packed in no special pattern, a grinding or sanding surface results. Neither the rasp nor a sanding surface is part of the Swiss Army knife, but both could have been included. In fact, a grinding surface does get in as an option, through the honing rod that comes with the leather case.

The File. If a knife blade is made very small and then iterated many times at the correct angle, a file results from a combination of microblades. The file is an interesting tool in our classification because it builds on a blade, a higher-order element than the tooth, and it involves more spatial organization than grinding teeth, since the microblades are at a fixed distance from one another and they are at angles with respect to the work in order to let waste cuttings escape. The action of the microblades is in parallel, each one doing its own work. The microblade array is two dimensional. The Swiss Army knife has a file with a point.

The Sand Blaster. Can the tooth be extended to form tools with dimensionality greater than two? Yes, two-and-one-half dimensions are possible. So far we have assumed that the teeth were fastened to a surface. But if we were to allow the teeth to decrease in size to a micro scale and were then to "throw" them at a surface, we would have sand blasting, a technique that allows us to cut in the picture plane in front of us and also in the depth plane extending away from us. The blasting would not be fully three dimensional because it would not be directed at all sides of an object at once; hence the description of two-and-one-half dimensions. Clearly, sand blasting is not available with the Swiss Army knife, and for good reasons. Nonetheless, it belongs in the same family as many of the Swiss Army knife blades.

Thus the knife, and other tools as well, can be viewed as generalizations of the tooth that result from a relatively small group of spatial transformations. Many of the tools that can be created by these transformations also are blades or blade edges in the Swiss Army knife.

What has been done here is both simple and powerful. The *abstraction heuristic* was used to arrive at the tooth or sharp point as the building block for the knife, and then there were *iterating* and *packing heuristics* applied to that tooth, in one, one-and-one-half, two, or two-and-one-half dimensions, while the tooth's size scale was changed. Thus the tooth is the abstraction behind the various tools; and that abstraction, together with heuristic principles of simple spatial transformation, generated other tools and tool edges.

A question may be raised over using spatial transformations of the tooth to generate tools. Were we not just taking a geometric abstraction, the point, and showing that it can generate any structure in three-dimensional space? No, we were dealing with a real form, the tooth, which operates on a real physical principle, the wedge. This principle is not sufficient to produce all tools, not even all the blades and edges of the Swiss Army knife. For example, the bottle opener does not operate on the principle of the tooth or wedge; instead it is an example of the lever. Likewise the Swiss Army knife's scissors do not work on the basis of the wedge; the scissor "blades" are really levers with a common fulcrum that work through a shearing action. Clearly, the tooth is different from a geometric point.

Another comment is in order. As appealing as this exercise has been, it should be pointed out that fairly general heuristic principles of invention must yield to specific problems. The idea of a saw is more than a line of punctuated teeth. Serious cutting quickly reveals that such a saw binds. Additional refinements are required to free the saw from binding and make it a viable cutting tool. The teeth must be staggered or "set." In other words, very delicate and precise relations are often needed as refinements or fine-tunings to a basic idea to make a tool work well. The difference between an idea that works and one that does not can be the presence of a single nut and bolt in the right place. Nonetheless, tens of thousands of years separated the development of these different tools that, joined together, form the Swiss Army knife, each blade with its marvelous integration of parts, action, and human interface. That long path of development makes it tempting to think that the invention processes could be more rapid, if moderately powerful invention heuristics were employed.

Conclusion

Our study of the Swiss Army knife as an invention prototype gives rise to several findings and qualifications.

- Multiple ways of inventing are revealed. We can invent in different ways: by joining, by adding slots, by traveling along evaluative criteria to provide refinement or optimization, and by building from an abstract element, such as a tooth, to which simple spatial transformations can be applied.

- Heuristics are uncovered and generalized on. The heuristics suggested by the Swiss Army knife are moderately general and are shown by illustration to apply to a number of tools.

- Training methods are suggested. For example, by having a scale of integration for joining tools, methods for generating alternative designs can be taught. The potential for systematically generating more ideas is thereby increased. If more systematic ideas are available, better ideas may follow.

Some caveats remain. The levels-of-joining classification was useful, but we can wonder about its completeness. The same comment can be made about invention via spatial transformations. What is most needed is independent evidence that the concepts and heuristics developed here have generality beyond the immediate examples from which they are drawn.

Three forms of independent test are suggested, from strongest to weakest. The strongest test requires us to produce new and useful tools by the application of the heuristics set forth in this chapter. A more immediate test is that the concepts developed for hand tools have generality beyond that immediate domain. A third test is that the concepts simply be useful for thinking about tools, that they perhaps allow for classifications and organizations not previously considered.

Of these tests, the first one, to generate new and useful tools, is an acid test. We must admit that we are not ready to meet it, yet. The other two tests warrant more immediate effort. Obviously, the weakest requirement, a new way of classifying and organizing tools, is satisfied. If other forms of validation fail, certainly the concepts provide a conceptual scheme for organizing tools that appears to be novel and rich in its texture. This is true for both the way in which tools may be joined with one another and the way spatial transformations applied to an abstract element generate other tools.

The remaining test of validation, the intermediate claim that the concepts developed have generality beyond their immediate origins, is now examined, first for joins and then for transformations. Do the join concepts found in our model system of hand tools scale up in the sense that they help us understand more complex inventions? For example, do concepts like *complementarity, inverses,* and *levels of join* have counterparts in the camera? Yes. For example, earlier cameras were frequently used in conjunction with separate light meters and flash devices; all three were required in the work environment for photographically recording images. The separate components were part of the same tool kit, at the level of a related assemblage based on complementarity. Now many cameras have a built-in light meter and a built-in flash. The level at which these devices are joined with the camera differs among models. The flash in some models must be manually engaged (by pulling it up) or disengaged (by pushing it down); this makes it a loosely bonded join that requires user action to set. In other cameras, with more automation, when the light level reaches a certain level, the flash automatically and simultaneously comes into use, a form of parallelism that we might refer to as the automated level of join, a category not found in simple hand tools. The 35-mm camera with multiple lenses that can be attached or removed is a join at the attachment level. A zoom lens is an adjustable join (combined with an attachment join on a removable lens camera).

What about inverses? We cannot undo results on film, but video cameras allow us to erase, certainly a form of inverse. As long as we are talking about video recorders, we should mention the camcorder. It is a join of a camera and a recorder. The camcorder, a highly complex system, also has its share of automatically related joins that are not found in hand tools. All this suggests that the join scale established for hand tools also has applicability to another quite different domain involving complex systems such as cameras. But the join scale established from hand tools is not yet complete; it needs further extension, as shown by the automatic couplings of the camera, light meter, and lens adjustment.

Validation is also needed for invention by transformative operations. Here we have the inner logic of transformations applied to an abstract system, often independent of invention based on practical need. This violates many people's concept of invention. A common view is that invention is propelled by need. No doubt many inventions are so directed. But I want to argue here that other avenues to invention are also possible, in particular that transformations applied to one invention (or its frame description) can yield other inventions. The following quote from Robert Fulton, an early designer of successful steamboats, is illuminating:

> As the component parts of all new machines may be said to be old ... the mechanic should sit down among levers, screws, wedges, wheels, etc. like a poet among the letters of the alphabet, considering them as the exhibition of his thoughts; in which a new arrangement transmits a new idea to the world. (Quoted in Philip, 1985, frontispiece)

Fulton seems to be saying that invention can result from the inner logic of arranging a series of components. In a similar way, a polymer chemist may explore systematically properties of a substance, such as strength and flexibility, without having in mind particular applications. In both cases, form takes on a life of its own. Of course, after generating an interesting form, one must find applications for it to have a practical invention. While this may seem like invention turned on its head, interviews with a number of inventors indicate that it is a more common practice than one might suppose. Certainly, when we apply systematically the different spatial transformations to a tooth, we may have no goal in mind more specific than trying to invent another hand tool. At a slightly less abstract level, we may want to design a more efficient cutting tool. Still more specifically, we may want to design a knife that does not need frequent sharpening. Clearly, the idea of need comes in various levels of abstraction, and for all intents may not be present in any practical sense at all.

Another conceptual issue requires comment. None of the methods of invention described here, nor any of the related heuristics, will mechanically or computationally produce inventions. Human judgment is very much required. The disadvantage of relying on such judgment is the vagueness that comes with it. The advantage, as discussed in Weber and Perkins (1989), is that quite general heuristics may suffice to generate ideas, heuristics that would be completely unpalatable to computers and artificial intelligence. At this stage in the study of invention, that is a reasonable trade-off.

Enough of conceptual rambling. Let us return to the palpable comforts of the Swiss Army knife. The complete form of the Swiss Army knife is beginning to have limitations. Because of all the blades and functions that it encompasses, it is becoming excessively heavy and bulky for a pocketknife; it is developing baroque tendencies. This is dealt with in an immediate way by having available a leather carrying case with a belt loop. But there are other problems. For example, the handle is bulky and is not suitable for a small hand or for protracted use by a larger hand. This partially negative evaluation suggests an as yet untaken step in the evolution of the Swiss Army knife: Find another material that is lighter than steel but even tougher, so that the blades and handle can be thinned out and the weight decreased.

Notice that this is a problem very similar to what must have confronted the evolution of the stone knife—find better materials. Indeed, rapid changes in the frame description of the knife have often taken place in the materials slot, allowing for a more maintenance-free sharp edge. Those changes include the movement from the brittleness of stone to the more flexible metals: copper, bronze, iron, and steel, each tougher and more maintenance free. If that development is extrapolated, what can we expect next in the future of the knife? Undoubtedly, even now some manufacturer is figuring out how to apply a vaporized diamond coating to knife blades to allow life-long sharpness and complete freedom from maintenance (Browne, 1988). Perhaps other new materials are being considered to bring down the weight and bulk of the Swiss Army knife. But materials changes are not the only direction of change. An even more radical step is to use a different principle of cutting, such as the laser. Whether the surgeon's laser knife will ever become a home product remains to be seen. But a Swiss Army knife with its own low-powered laser beam for small-scale cutting may not be as much of a science fiction fantasy as it seems.

The study of other artifacts undoubtedly will reveal still other methods of invention, other modes of description, and other heuristics. But our original questions may now be answered with some confidence. It is possible to describe inventions at a fairly general level using framelike concepts. The methods of invention and the heuristics uncovered are validated by both the richness of the conceptual scheme they give rise to and by their applicability to domains foreign to their origin. The hand tool has generated a rich set of concepts; it does function as the *Drosophila* of invention.

Notes

1. More complex versions of the Swiss Army knife are now available. For a history of the Swiss Army knife, see Page and Hoffman (1989). A rough trend in that history is to incorporate ever more functionality by adding blades and blade edges.

2. Another interpretation is possible here: the pointed blade may also be viewed as the join of a blade and an awl (Weber & Perkins, 1989). That several different routes take us to the pointed blade should not be surprising. There is no one way to invent.

3. We may also invent by *slot deletion*. The original Sony Walkman did not have a record function—it was dropped from a tape recorder to reduce weight, size, and cost.

4. I am not asserting that the knife's path of development involved a series of *deliberate steps*. As Perkins (1988) has argued, even evolutionary processes based on variation, selection, and retention can produce complex inventions. Even if the knife's development is similarly devoid of intention, we can extract principles that seem to capture its development. Nature does not deliberately use differential equations, but it is very useful for humans to do so (Weber, 1993).

References

Bordes, F. (1968). *The Old Stone Age*. New York: McGraw-Hill.
Browne, M. W. (1988). New diamond coatings find broad application. *The New York Times*, October 25, pp. 19, 23.
Burke, J. (1978). *Connections*. Boston: Little, Brown.
Chase, W. G. & Simon, H. A. (1973). Perception in Chess. *Cognitive Psychology, 4*, 55–81.
Edison, T. A. (1878). Phonograph or speaking machine. U. S. Patent 200,521.
Ford, H. (1925). *My Life and Work*. New York: Doubleday and Page.
Koestler, A. (1964). *The Act of Creation*. New York: Dell Publishing.
Leakey, M. D. (1971). *Olduvai Gorge, Vol. 3*. Cambridge: Cambridge Univ. Press.

Maier, N. R. F. (1931). Reasoning in humans. II. The solution of a problem and its appearance in consciousness. *Journal of Comparative Psychology, 12,* 181–194.

Minsky, M. (1975). A framework for representing knowledge. In *The Psychology of Computer Vision* (P. H. Winston, Ed.). New York: McGraw-Hill.

Morgan, T. H. (1926). *The Theory of the Gene.* New Haven, Conn.: Yale Univ. Press.

Newell, A. & Simon, H. A. (1972). *Human Problem Solving.* Englewood Cliffs, N. J.: Prentice-Hall.

Norman, D. A. (1988). *The Psychology of Everyday Things.* New York: Basic Books.

Page, J. & Hoffman, C. (1989). Switzerland's jackknife of all trades. *Smithsonian, 20,* No. 7, 106–116.

Perkins, D. N. (1988). The possibility of invention. In *The Nature of Creativity* (R. J. Sternberg, Ed.). pp. 362–385. Cambridge, England: Cambridge Univ. Press.

Philip, C. O. (1985). *Robert Fulton: A Biography.* New York: Franklin Watts.

Semenov, S. A. (1964). *Prehistoric technology* (M. W. Thompson, Transl.). New York: Barnes & Noble.

U. S. Department of Commerce. (1985). *General Information Concerning Patents.* Washington, D. C.: U. S. Government Printing Office.

Usher, A. P. (1954). *History of Mechanical Inventions.* Cambridge, Mass.: Harvard Univ. Press.

Weber, R. J. (1993). *Forks, Phonographs, and Hot Air Balloons: A Field Guide to Inventive Thinking.* New York: Oxford University Press.

Weber, R. J. & Dixon, S. (1989). Invention and gain analysis. *Cognitive Psychology, 21,* 283–302.

Weber, R. J. & Perkins, D. N. (1989). How to invent artifacts and ideas. *New Ideas in Psychology, 7,* 49–72.

Weber, R. J., Moder, C. L., & Solie, J. B. (1990). Invention heuristics and mental processes underlying the development of a patent for the application of herbicides. *New Ideas in Psychology, 8,* 321–336.

13 | The Topography of Invention

DAVID N. PERKINS

In the mid-fifteenth century, books, and especially the Bible, were not widely available for lack of an efficient technology of printing. It was then that the metalworker Johann Gutenberg began his systematic search for an approach to mass printing of the Bible. In Gutenberg's day, a handcraft of printing already existed: Wooden plates were carved and used to print a number of copies of a page. However, the plates were laborious to prepare and printing a page took some time, because it involved placing the paper against the inked wooden plate and rubbing it until a good impression resulted.

Gutenberg set out to solve both these problems. Seeking efficient page composition, Gutenberg explored an analogy with stamps and seals that embossed their marks on paper. This notion would evolve into movable type. However, for rapid printing, Gutenberg realized that he needed a source of enormous pressure to impress an entire inked array of type at once onto a page of paper.

Escaping from his dedicated quest for wide-scale reproduction of the Bible, Gutenberg participated in a festival celebrating the wine harvest. There by chance, amidst the flowing wine and high spirits, he encountered another piece of technology that gave him the clue he needed: the wine press, used to extract the juice of the grapes. On viewing this device, Gutenberg immediately saw within it the source of the great pressure he needed (Koestler, 1964).

This episode resembles many others in the history of science and technology, where individuals have made connections across barriers of context, custom, and convention to come to an important discovery. Another classic case is Charles Darwin's formulation of the principle of natural selection after many months of effort, in response to reading Malthus's "Essay on Human Population" (Darwin, 1911; Gruber, 1974). Yet another is the probably apocryphal tale of Archimedes who, needing to find a way to measure the volume of an irregular object, conceived the principle of displacement of water while lowering himself into a bath and noticing the water overflow the sides (Koestler, 1964).

Such episodes are favorite points of departure for scholars of invention. To many, they seem to encapsulate what is most fundamental about creative thinking, the moment of discovery. They foster a view of inventive thinking that might be called *invention as heroic quest*. This vision of invention, part and parcel of a tendency to elevate inventors to epic hero status (see Friedel, Chapter 1 in this volume, for a further critique), includes at least these key ingredients:

1. *Heroic persistence.* The inventor persists for a considerable period with little progress.
2. *Unexpected encounter.* The inventor eventually encounters a subtle clue from an unexpected direction.
3. *The gift of insight.* The inventor has the insight to seize on the clue and make something of it to complete the quest.

It is easy to feel uneasy about the heroic quest model of invention. For one thing, the story line seems altogether too pat. Surely events do not always or even often unfold according to this epic pattern. For another thing, the model does not explain as much as we would like to understand. What is this gift of insight that equips the inventor to catch the significance of the subtle clue? Why does the clue appear at all? If the clue showed up in the normal course of the persistent search, one could say that it was due. However, the clue typically comes from an unexpected direction. Indeed, the connotation of the heroic quest model is more that the clue is a reward for, rather than the direct consequence of, persistence.

Finally, if we believe that invention is something that can be cultivated, the heroic quest model is singularly unempowering. True, it encourages us to persist, certainly good advice if not carried into fruitless perseveration. However, it does little to reassure us that the subtle clue will eventually show up, and little to guide us in homing our gifts of insight in preparation for the clue.

With these shortfalls in mind, a rather different view of invention is developed in these pages. It's argued that the heroic quest model should give way to what might be called a *smart foraging* model. The smart foraging model acknowledges the roles of a lengthy search and unexpected clues. However, it also emphasizes the importance of a search well-tuned to the "topography of ideas" involved, and the role of a prepared mind in detecting the significance of clues. The central concept in this account of invention is an idea of some importance in contemporary cognitive psychology—the notion of a "problem space."

Problem Spaces

Complex cognitive processes such as invention, decision-making, planning, problem-solving, and more have always challenged psychologists to find adequate frameworks for analyzing them. One particularly useful tool was elaborated by Alan Newell and Herbert Simon in their 1972 book, *Human Problem Solving,* the notion of *search in a problem space.*

The general idea of a problem space is easily described. Addressing any problem, a person begins in some initial state, the point of departure. The person's goal is to attain any of a set of target states, solutions to the problem (there may be no, one, or many solutions, and hence, no, one, or many target states). The person travels from the initial state in search of a target state by a series of transformations that change the person's position in the logical structure of the problem space.

Formally defined tasks such as playing chess or doing algebra give us especially clear examples of problem spaces. Suppose, for example, that you are solving a set of algebraic equations with two unknowns, x and y. The initial state, your point of departure, consists of the given equations. Legal state-changing moves are defined by the rules of algebra. You move to a new state by deriving a new expression, for instance by transposing a term or subtracting one equation from another. A target state is any state you can reach by legal algebra operations that isolates each unknown on one side of the equation: $x =$ such-and-such and $y =$ so-and-so, where such-and-such and so-and-so do not have the terms x and y in them. Your task, then, is to find a path of transformations from the initial state to a target state. The process of seeking this path constitutes search in the problem space.

It is worth noting that people often solve problems by searching in more than one problem space at the same time. For example, the algebra problem-solver, besides manipulating equations on paper, may think ahead in qualitative ways about the best approach to take. This thinking ahead occurs in a "planning space," a schematic abstraction from the precise business of formal algebra, in which the person tries to anticipate the broad consequences of alternative plans. Other problem spaces might be involved as well.

While the notion of a problem space seems to suit rather formal contexts such as chess play or algebra problem-solving, does it apply to the fuzzy situation of innovative thinking? Yes indeed. Just as the algebraist has a point of departure, an "initial state," so does the inventor: whatever knowledge and other resources are at hand as the inventor addresses the design problem. The inventor has end-states too: whatever states of knowledge constitute a fairly well-worked-out solution to the design problem.

Like the algebraist or chess player, the inventor has moves to make, albeit moves not so crisply defined as those that occur within formal systems. These moves are discernible and distinctive acts such as generating conjectures, seeking particular pieces of information, running mental simulations, attempting actual mockups or prototypes, and so on. As the inventor undertakes such moves, the inventor advances "position" in a problem space of accumulated knowledge and insight, including knowledge of dead ends explored and rejected as well as promising leads needing investigation (Perkins, 1981, 1990).

The greatest misgiving one might have about this picture concerns the target states of the problem space. It is commonly the case that the end states are not very sharply conceived at the beginning of a process of inventive thinking. An inventor may begin with a relatively unfocused problem—or perhaps no problem at all other than the general challenge to invent something—and refine a vision of the goal even as he or she pursues the task. The best way to reconcile this point with the problem-space perspective seems to be to acknowledge it. It is simply a fact about inventive process that the target states are not always closely circumscribed at the outset but evolve while the person searches in the problem space. The notion of "position" in the problem space expands to include current specification of target states, which changes with time (cf. Perkins, 1990a).

The problem-space framework has proved very useful in close-grained analyses of solving formal problems (Newell & Simon, 1972). Whether it can function in a more qualitative way to illuminate phenomena of thought and discovery in less formal contexts is another question. In the pages to come, a positive answer is suggested. The concept of problem spaces provides a tool for characterizing broadly some important features of human invention and challenging the oversimple picture of inventive thinking sketched earlier.

Klondike Spaces and Homing Spaces

Suppose you were searching for gold in the Alaskan Klondike at the end of the nineteenth century. The governing principle of your search would have to be, "Gold is where you find it." You would look here, there, everywhere you could. You would be persistent, try different areas, and hope for the big strike.

You would know a good deal about how to look, of course. You would know what kinds of rocks might bear ore. You would have a sharp eye out for the glint of gold in river gravel. You would search upstream from sites that showed some traces, in hopes of finding the mother lode. Despite this savvy, however, you would still find that most of your time was spent in searching rather than in systematically homing in on a find.

Your search for gold is, of course, a special case of problem-solving. You are searching in the physical space of the Klondike, shifting from one position to another, exhausting dead ends, seeking new and promising terrain. Indeed, it's useful to generalize the characteristics of this "Klondike Space," because many other problem situations not so geological and geographical in nature have essentially the same *logical* topography. Many problem spaces, that is, involve punctuate targets with sharply defined boundaries (see Figure 13.1A), like a needle in a haystack or a few large nuggets or a hominid bone in a stratum. In such circumstances, it is difficult to move systematically toward a target. Rather, you find yourself casting about a lot.

Very often, problems we think of as calling for invention display this character. Consider Gutenberg's problem, for example. He knew he needed a way to apply great pressure over a wide area. But he did not know quite how to go about it. He lacked any systematic method of deriving the structure of such a device from any set of basic principles. So he cast about, with the problem on his mind even as he went on with other matters, such as the wine harvest. And he struck it lucky.

Of course, we should not dismiss Gutenberg's perspicacity in seeing the significance of the wine press for his problem. Many others working on the same sort of problem might have made no connection between the wine press and their own needs. They might display "functional fixedness," seeing things only in their usual roles. Gutenberg's perspicacity is somewhat analogous to the hunter for gold knowing the look of gold-bearing rocks, even if to you and I they just appear to be ordinary rocks. However, that granted, we also have to recognize that Gutenberg, like many inventive people, was casting about in a Klondike Space that afforded him no systematic way to home in on a target state.

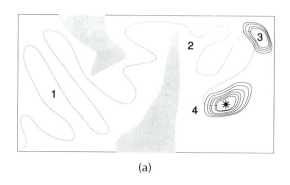

(a)

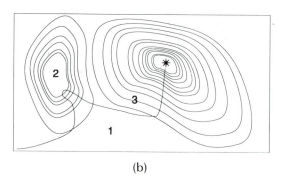

(b)

FIGURE 13.1. Two types of searches. A. Search in a Klondike Space: 1. Large clueless regions. 2. Easily overlooked regions. 3. False targets. 4. Clues only close to the target. B. Search in a Homing Space: 1. Small clueless regions. 2. False targets. 3. Large clued regions that lead to the target.

In contrast with Klondike Spaces, one might speak of "Homing Spaces"—problem spaces that support homing in on solutions. Homing Spaces involve not punctuate targets but a *target gradient* that leads toward the target itself (see Figure 13.1B), like an increasing proportion of gold particles in a streambed leading toward the mother lode. Conventional algebra problems, for example, submit to a fairly straightforward and systematic methodology that will produce solved equations. The structure of algebra allows you to examine the equations you have, discern the gaps between these and a solution state, and take a variety of actions to reduce the gaps. This is a basic "homing" pattern embodied in some computer programs that attack a variety of problems with a general problem-solving approach (e.g. Ernst & Newell, 1969).

To be sure, there can be some tricky aspects to an algebra problem: Perhaps isolating the unknown is not so straightforward. You may need to attempt a variable substitution, or square both sides of the equation to eliminate a radical, thus running the risk of introducing spurious roots. Nonetheless, these complications are of limited scope. You may have five or ten methods at your disposal, but have a sense of direction—elements of the expression to reduce or eliminate. You are not faced with the extreme punctuate character of a Klondike Space.

What Makes Problems Hard?

This contrast between Klondike Spaces and Homing Spaces is certainly rather crude. Realistically speaking, many problem spaces involve a mix of Klondike and Homing characteristics. Nonetheless, the notion of the two spaces with their different topographies permits formulating some broad generalizations about what makes problems hard.

Problems in Klondike Spaces are difficult because of the lack of gradient in their topography and the consequent wide-ranging search that they call for. It's all too easy not to search widely, but to confine your exploration to a narrower region, perhaps not even recognizing the importance of looking over the next hill or down the next valley. As noted earlier, invention requires making unexpected connections across boundaries of habit and convention. Yet it is all too common only to cast about in the familiar regions. Besides that, there is a challenge of systematicity: managing the exploration of the large Klondike problem space so that you cover much of it without repeating yourself unduly, with a fine enough grid not to miss opportunities, but with a coarse enough grid to be efficient and not spend all your time in one small region. In other words, Klondike Spaces call for a kind of art of expansive search.

Homing Spaces offer a rather different set of challenges. The homing opportunities of a Homing Space do not help much unless one can take them with some precision. In some domains, they require a good deal of technical proficiency, for instance with symbol systems such as algebra. Mistakes in the homing process—such as an algebra error—may take one down a primrose path to a mistaken resolution that one may not even recognize as such.

Another characteristic trap of Homing Spaces is that not all "homing signals" are reliable. Sometimes, what appears to be a promising line of attack plays out poorly. Sometimes a procedure that seems to bring the problem-solver close to a solution leaves an unbridgeable gap. This is commonly called the difficulty of "local maxima" in a problem space—the problem-solver gets as close as possible to a solution along one path, but the path simply does not lead all the way to a solution. So the problem-solver has to back out of the cul-de-sac and find another path taking quite a different approach. This backing out is often hard to do when the solution seems so close (cf. Perkins, 1981, Chapter 4).

These remarks characterize the difficulties of Klondike Spaces and Homing Spaces as though they were matters entirely separate. But that is not quite the case. Indeed, Klondike Spaces have Homing Spaces inside them. Once the searcher in a Klondike Space gets close to a solution—catches the glint of gold, so to speak— what then ensues is like homing in a Homing Space: digging where the glitter is, to find the gold. In effect, a Klondike Space has spotted within it small Homing Spaces. These Homing Spaces may of course present all the hazards characteristic of Homing Spaces—fool's gold, for instance.

Likewise, problem spaces that are predominantly Homing Spaces may have within them subregions—subproblems—that have Klondike Spaces. While systematically pursuing a problem up to a point, the problem-solver may encounter a kind of plateau that requires casting about here and there for a way to proceed until a path finally opens up.

Insight and the Topography of Problem Spaces

The notions of Klondike Spaces and Homing Spaces provide the conceptual tools for revising the overly pat heroic quest model of invention mentioned at the outset. To be sure, often moments of punctuate discovery occur in the course of invention. However, the following explanation for them has some advantages over the heroic quest model:

1. *Klondike Space.* The search is conducted in a Klondike Space, else there would be no reason for punctuate discovery instead of steady progress in the first place.

2. *Well-adapted search.* The search is well-adapted to the character of Klondike Spaces and the particular space in question (appropriate grain size, etc.), else no discovery would be likely.

3. *Probable encounter.* The well-adapted search makes an encounter with a relevant clue probable, presuming that a solution exists.

4. *The prepared mind's detection of promise.* The clue is detected by the "prepared mind" (what this involves will be discussed shortly).

5. *Discrimination of potential.* Simply detecting a promising clue is not enough; because of the "fool's gold" problem, the inventor must be able to sort out true potential.

6. *Effective pursuit.* Finally, ultimate success involves good follow-through in the Homing Space signaled by a solid clue.

Considerably more complex than the heroic quest model, this model captures some of the features of the former in a transformed way. Heroic persistence has a place, but simply as one facet of a search well adapted in other ways as well to a Klondike Space. Subtle clues are important, but are expected to show up one place or another because of the well-adapted search. The gift of insight is no gift, but a matter of a mind prepared to discern the significance of clues.

The new model adds two other considerations as well: discrimination of potential and effective pursuit in the discovered Homing Space. To put a name to the entire conception, we might call it a *smart foraging* model, a way of acknowledging that wide-ranging search with little moment-to-moment progress is involved while emphasizing the intelligence that figures in the good conduct of the search, the detection of clues, the discrimination of potential, and the follow-through in the Homing Space.

With all this said, one aspect of the smart foraging model needs further comment: the nature of the prepared mind. The phrase is drawn from Louis Pasteur's famous remark that "chance favors the prepared mind." But what prepares a mind?

Immersion in the problem plainly is one factor. Along with prior experience in the field in question, extensive wide-ranging search in a Klondike Space saturates the mind with the considerations of the problem, making more likely the recognition of significant clues.

Still, mere immersion does not seem likely to be sufficient. Many technically well-versed individuals in the history of science and engineering have missed important discoveries. Surely if the problem space in question were a straightforward Homing Space, these individuals would have found their way.

What else, then? One important characteristic discernible in the case of Gutenberg and many other cases is *abstraction of the problem* from its superficial contextual trappings. Gutenberg, for example, seems to have realized that he needed a means of applying great pressure, analogous to that applied when a seal is stamped into paper but suitable for an entire page of type. This is quite an abstract formulation of conditions, well suited to see the significance of the wine press during a chance encounter.

In summary, the smart foraging model offers a conception of punctuate invention both more sophisticated and more empowering than the heroic quest model. Its greater sophistication lies in accommodating in a transformed way several characteristics of the heroic quest model and in adding several others. Its empowerment lies in its laying down broad conditions for discovery that we can strive to attain.

Problem Spaces Are Partly What You Make Them

It would be easy to presume that the nature of the problem space—Klondike, Homing, or some mix—gets determined by the nature of the problem. For example, perhaps the rules and methodologies of algebra imply a certain problem space. But the matter is not so simple. Often, the very same problem can present a Klondike Space or a Homing Space, depending on the knowledge the problem-solver brings to the task, whether, for example, the problem-solver knows the tricks of the algebra trade.

There is a simple puzzle that demonstrates this point: Take ten matches and arrange them to form two squares of different sizes. No breaking of matches or other "tricks" are allowed. Some readers may want to try this problem themselves before continuing.

The correct solution is shown in Figure 13.2. Note that the solution involves placing one square inside the other. Many people, when they first attempt the problem, make the assumption that the squares should be separate, or perhaps touching at the corners or along one side. This premise has to be rejected to solve the problem.

How do people escape the entrapping assumption and solve the problem? There is a Klondike way and a Homing way. In the Klondike way, you take ten matches (or sketch on paper) and try different arrangements. Gradually, you begin to eliminate parts of the problem space, noticing that certain approaches lead nowhere. Eventually you conjecture that some configuration that shares many matches between the two squares might work. This starts you off on a homing process that quickly leads to a solution.

However, if you adopt a different perspective on the problem, the initial "casting about" phase is unnecessary. You can home in deductively on the solution. There are ten matches in all. If there are to be two squares of different sizes, one

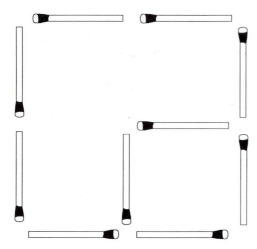

FIGURE 13.2. Two squares of different size made out of ten matches.

square must have one match on a side and the other two matches on a side, because a size-three square would use up more than ten matches just in itself. Now, completely separate squares of size one and two would require twelve matches, so, to get the number down to ten, the squares have to share two matches. To be part of a small square, the matches shared with the big square must make up a corner. So take a corner of the big square and build a little square on it.

Or consider this example from the world of everyday experience rather than from the world of puzzle problems. A friend found himself with his family in the French countryside, prepared for a picnic with bread, cheese, wine, and even the most likely thing to be missing—a corkscrew. But nothing to cut the cheese. How did he resolve the dilemma? After a moment of thought, he drew out his credit card and cut the cheese with it (Perkins, 1990b).

But how did he arrive at this clever solution? He explains that he reflected on the requirements: something thin and stiff—and the credit card came to mind. This is a "homing" solution by way of generalization from a knife. One can easily imagine someone else arriving at the same solution by an extended search, rummaging through pockets, glove compartment, trunk of the car for something that might serve as a knife. Perhaps, coming across his credit card, such a person would notice its potential. But my friend adopted a more direct approach, abstracting the needed characteristics and retrieving from memory an object that fit them. In effect, he treated what might have been a Klondike Space as a Homing Space.

What in general transforms a Klondike Space into a Homing Space? Several factors seem important.

Reasoning and Abstraction Can Build a Homing Space

The straightforward moral of the credit card story is that reasoning and abstraction can often turn what otherwise would be a Klondike Space into a Homing Space.

This does not always work, of course. When Gutenberg characterized his needs abstractly, that did not immediately tell him how to meet them. But it is a powerful heuristic.

Accumulation of Discipline-Specific Knowledge Can Build a Homing Space

Reasoning and abstraction are not the only activities that convert Klondike Spaces into Homing Spaces. Learning the ins and outs of a discipline has the same effect. For example, consider again the problem-solver faced with an algebra problem. To the novice, with only a fuzzy sense of the subject matter and a few techniques fragilely grasped, solving an equation may involve a Klondike Space: the novice has to cast about widely to gain some purchase on the problem. With persistence, the novice may find a successful path.

As the novice masters the domain, how different sorts of problems should be approached becomes clearer. The novice learns ways of homing in and the problem space becomes a Homing Space, with, of course, its own characteristic traps.

However, this does not imply that experts deal only in Homing Spaces. As a generalization, solving *novel* problems in a familiar domain involves mixed problem spaces. Evidence on this point comes from some research conducted by John Clement (1991), who presented unconventional physics problems to individuals well versed in physics. Clement found that his subjects adopted mixed tactics, sometimes proceeding systematically when they could apply their well-tuned physics knowledge and at other moments resorting to analogy, extreme-case arguments, and other tactics to gain purchase on the problem. During episodes of the one kind, we could say that the subjects were navigating through Homing Subspaces, whereas during episodes of the other kind they were navigating through Klondike Subspaces. The successful subjects won through by shifting back and forth between the "Klondike" mode and the "Homing" mode, working effectively in each.

Heuristic Frameworks Can Move Klondike Spaces toward Homing Spaces

Also important are efforts to define heuristics for inventive thinking. For example, Robert Weber (Chapter 12 in this volume; Weber & Dixon, 1989; Weber & Perkins, 1989) offers a heuristic analysis of inventive thinking based on the cognitive science concept of schemata. Weber identifies a number of heuristics for invention, such as *joining*—combining two or more inventions with related functions. Often a *join* combines functions that are inverses of one another. An example is the claw hammer, with the hammer part for nailing and the claw part for removing nails. Weber also emphasizes the importance of *evaluation functions*—general conceptualizations that give a sense of the direction for improving something before the means are apparent. For example, before the invention of the compact disk, it was clear that lower background noise and greater scratch resistance were desirable.

For another example, Jacob Helfman (Chapter 14 in this volume) offers a systematic heuristic approach to improving inventions, beginning with an analysis of the causal factors that most immediately yield the desired effect. For instance, the maximum illumination from an incandescent light bulb depends directly on the filament being as hot as possible without vaporizing. Now, light bulbs are not usually designed this way because it leads to a short filament life. However, one of several key heuristic principles in Helfman's model says that key causes should operate optimally: The filament should indeed be as hot as possible. The focus of invention becomes how to resolve the paradox and create an incandescent light with a very hot filament that nonetheless lasts a long time. Much of the method consists in deliberately creating and then striving to resolve such paradoxes.

In general, Weber's and Helfman's approaches replace broad casting about for ideas with some specific steps that seem likely to help. Their analyses of invention in terms of joins, evaluation functions, optimizing of immediate causes, and so on, disclose more structure in the *general* character of invention search spaces than one might have thought was there. Although their frameworks certainly do not transform the Klondike Spaces of invention into pure Homing Spaces, the whole process becomes somewhat more hominglike.

What Is Creativity?

The revisionary view of discovery presented so far challenges typical concepts of the nature of creativity. First off, the romantic notion of invention as heroic quest gets replaced by the more technical notion of smart foraging. But beyond that, effective navigation not just in Klondike Spaces but in Homing Spaces takes on considerable importance. This seems much less the kind of thinking we usually call creative. It seems too, well, systematic.

We could of course say that search in Homing Spaces is not creative thinking. Paradoxically, in transforming a Klondike Space closer to a Homing Space, the inventive individual has actually made the enterprise less creative, albeit perhaps improving chances of success.

However, let me suggest a different view. Let us take as the gauge of creative thinking not the processes employed or the topography of the problem spaces, but the transcending of boundaries. When Gutenberg conceived the printing press with movable type, or the fellow on a picnic in France cut cheese with his credit card, each made connections he could easily have missed because of conventional patterns of thinking. Accordingly, if search in a Homing Space transcends relevant boundaries that might reasonably have entrapped a less agile thinker, it should count as creative thinking.

Another way to put the matter turns to the traditional vocabulary of "divergent" versus "convergent" thinking. Divergent thinking occurs when the mind ranges widely, sampling possibilities including unexpected possibilities—as Klondike Spaces require. Convergent thinking occurs when the thinker works systematically toward a distinctive solution more or less entailed by the problem space—as happens in Homing Spaces. Ordinarily, we identify divergent thinking with creative thinking and convergent thinking with uncreative, albeit often very useful, thinking.

On the present view, this is simply a mistake. Just as divergent thinking can lead to the transcending of boundaries in Klondike Spaces, so artful convergent thinking can lead to the transcending of boundaries in Homing Spaces. It is neither divergent nor convergent thinking in itself that makes thinking inventive, but what each of these accomplishes.

Of course, to say that either style can be creative neglects the point that typical inventive thinking appears to demand a generous helping of both. And one does not always find both in a person. Some people seem to have a flair for search in Klondike Spaces but not in Homing Spaces. They explore widely, challenge assumptions, and find homing opportunities. But they do not so readily take those homing opportunities, pushing through with logic and technique to a solution. And they are easily fooled by false homing signals into paying too much attention to "local maxima." They do not discriminate "promisingness" well. This is, of course, partly a matter of expertise in the domain in question. But it also seems to me to be partly a matter of cognitive style: Some people do not take well to the homing style.

Other people seem to have a flair for search in Homing Spaces but not Klondike Spaces. Given a well-defined problem, they can turn the crank of logic and technique to find a solution. But they flounder around in, and even avoid, Klondike Spaces. Also, when logic and technique within the Homing Space ask them to challenge a boundary of habit or custom, they may quail and retreat.

In contrast, inventive people are mode shifters, comfortable and adroit in either kind of space as they encounter it and ready to bridge boundaries by flexible casting about in a Klondike Space or by following the thread of logic wherever it may lead in a Homing Space. Also, they will convert a Klondike Space into something closer to a Homing Space by adroit abstraction, reasoning, and the use of heuristics.

This viewpoint might seem somehow to wring the creativity out of creativity, reducing it to too much of an algorithmic homing enterprise. But not likely. First of all, we are speaking of a mix, not pure homing. Second, search in a Homing Space is not likely to bridge the barriers of convention and habit unless driven by a kind of adventurous faith in seeing where the logic goes. Third, turning a Klondike Space into something more like a Homing Space is itself a creative activity. And fourth, to the extent that creative thinking can be pursued more systematically, the greater creative reach would lure inventive folks to try to stretch even further, leading them on to new Klondike wildernesses.

References

Clement, J. (1991). Nonformal reasoning in physics: The use of analogies and extreme cases. In *Informal Reasoning* (J. Voss, D. N. Perkins, & J. Segal, Eds.). Hillsdale, N.J.: Lawrence Erlbaum.

Darwin, C. (1911). *The Life and Letters of Charles Darwin,* Vol. 1 (Francis Darwin, Ed.). New York: D. Appleton.

Ernst, G. W. & Newell, A. (1969). *GPS: A Case Study in Generality and Problem Solving.* New York: Academic Press.

Gruber, H. (1974). *Darwin on Man: A Psychological Study of Scientific Creativity.* New York: E. P. Dutton.

Koestler, A. (1964). *The Act of Creation.* New York: Dell.

Newell, A. & Simon, H. (1972). *Human Problem Solving.* Englewood Cliffs, N.J.: Prentice-Hall.

Perkins, D. N. (1981). *The Mind's Best Work.* Cambridge, Mass.: Harvard Univ. Press.

Perkins, D. N. (1990a). Problem theory: In *Varieties of Thinking* (V. A. Howard, Ed.). New York: Routledge, pp. 15–46.

Perkins, D. N. (1990b). The nature and nurture of creativity. In *Dimensions of Thinking and Cognition Instruction.* (B. F. Jones & L. Idol, Eds.). Hillsdale, N.J.: Lawrence Erlbaum, pp. 415–443.

Weber, R. J. & Dixon, S. (1989). Invention and gain analysis. *Cognitive Psychology, 21,* 283–302.

Weber, R. J. & Perkins, D. N. (1989). How to invent artifacts and ideas. *New Ideas in Psychology,* 7(1).

14 | The Analytic Inventive Thinking Model

JACOB HELFMAN

Analytic Inventive Thinking is a practical model designed for scientists, engineers, and technicians to use in creating original and easy-to-implement solutions across the broad spectrum of technology. It provides an organized, systematic approach and efficiently shortens the problem-solving process. This teachable model has been developed in the Open University of Israel and is briefly outlined in this article. The university is continuing to investigate and develop the model and offers teaching, training, and consultation in its use. To date, about 1250 students representing most of the major industries in Israel have participated in fifty in-house courses based on the model.

The basic theory and method of this thinking model can be taught in a course of about twenty-five hours. About sixty more hours of training are needed for practice and application of the methods and techniques. In the last three years, the Open University of Israel has run extensive basic and advanced courses on the Analytic Inventive Thinking model. The main emphasis of the courses is not to provide students with new basic knowledge, but rather to give them a systematic way to use effectively the knowledge they already possess.

Graduates of the course have already invented original, elegant, and efficient solutions to practical problems at work in such places as the military industries, civil aviation, electronic and electrooptic industries, Raphael R&D Research Institute, the Israeli Air Force, the Israeli National Train System, Tnuva Food Industries, and the Israel Atomic Energy Center.

The Model's Background

The development of the model was begun in the 1940s by G. S. Altshuller (1973) in the Soviet Union. His idea was to find the essential characteristics of known inventive solutions and to replicate them in an intentional approach to new questions, so creating new inventive ideas. To develop this systematic method, Altshuller and his colleagues analyzed tens of thousands of inventive solutions in different technological areas. As a result of this analysis, it became clear that under-lying completely different problems may be found the same types of paradoxes and that there are, thus, some basic tactics to overcome them. Types of paradoxes (con-tradictions) and tactics for overcoming them were discovered. For instance, a pol-ishing disk is poor at processing a product with a complicated shape. The standard contradiction would be "The outer layer of a disk should be firm in order to polish the product, and should be not firm in order to adapt to its curvature."

The continuing research focused on finding general and abstract principles to serve as a common basis for different contradictions, different devices, and the rela-tions between them. The principles were formed and explained as basic universal laws, understood to determine and direct the evolution of every technological sys-tem. According to this deterministic approach, the analysis of a problem must find what evolutionary stage the given system has reached and thereby how it must be changed according to these universal evolutional laws. This deterministic approach dictates an algorithmic path of solution.

Parallel to this research, intensive research on this subject was started three years ago at the Open University of Israel. In this work (Helfman, 1988) we came to the conclusion that the development of a technical system is not a deterministic, evo-lutional process but rather is carried out by meshing goals and the difficulties. By this approach, the principles of searching for inventive ideas are not based on any independent universal laws, but are logical principles based in engineering design.

Applying the logic of analysis to the problem often results in a logical-physical paradox. The inventive solution frames the changes in the given situation in such a way that the same logical-physical demands will cease to be in conflict. This approach develops a heuristic path of solution.

Example: The Incandescent Light Bulb

A dramatic episode in the history of technical inventions is the story of the electric light bulb. A seemingly insoluble problem stood for a long time in the way of its development: how to improve the quality of light (and carry it close to that of sun-light), and the efficiency of radiation (energy in the visible spectrum vs. other radi-ation).

Scientists knew that the incandescent filament of the electric bulb radiates nearly as a "black body." That implied that raising the temperature of the filament to as close as possible to its melting point would result in radiation more similar to that of the sun itself and would increase efficiency. The only obstacle to heating the filament is the more or less gradual evaporation of the material it is made of. This attrition, with the consequent eventual break, restricts the filament's efficiency. By using tungsten (the most widely used filament) near its melting point, the radiation efficiency in the visible spectrum could be 52 lumens per watt (Lu/W), but because of the physical limitations mentioned before, 22 Lu/W is the highest practical radi-ation efficiency for incandescent lamps (Encyclopedia of Science and Technology, 1977).

How could this problem be solved by the model in a creative manner? Let us apply the nine-stage model to the problem situation. We begin the problem-solving process by focusing on aims to be achieved rather than on detail of existing structure, processes, or constraints and limitations on problems. According to our approach, the lamp and the given form and behavior of every one of its elements were designed to accomplish a predefined goal. In approaching this goal, the purpose (objective) and the accompanying physical action (performed by specific parameters) are important. The first aspect (the "why?" question) is completely in the designer's mind, whereas the second ("how?") is indeed in the designer's hands but is controlled by laws of nature.

Purposes and physical characteristics together constitute the function of an element. In our opinion, the functions are the essential knowledge for the understanding of the whole system (get the forest before getting lost in the trees). The function of the filament, for instance, is to emit light by the incandescence process, that of the bulb to contain the gas, and so forth.

From the problem situation, alternative thinking directions may be drawn. We asked students at the beginning of the course, qualified engineers in different areas, to list some of their spontaneous ideas. We then arranged part of their listing in the following order:

1. How to get an unbreakable new incandescent filament
2. How to create an inner environment that will prevent the existing filament from evaporating
3. How to change the supports so that the filament wouldn't vibrate and thus avoid the last sudden cut in its thinner section
4. How to reduce the heating losses of the filament
5. How to improve the gas pressure or vacuum conditions inside the bulb
6. How to supply less current at the beginning (gradually increasing current), and how to stabilize it, preventing physical shock to the filament
7. How to improve the electric contact of the current and to avoid sparks and extra heating

Every one of these alternative problems was derived from the same problem situation, but different possible physical reasons may have led to the filament's evaporation or breaking. They may be placed in a hierarchy of problems in accordance with the hierarchy of functions. For instance, one problem is the light-filament function—changing the physical parameters of the filament. Another problem is the glowing filament–inert gas function—creating a physical environment that prevents the filament from breaking.

These and many other alternative problems raise a practical question: What is the right problem to start with? Or, in our model, where in the functional hierarchy would we tackle the problem first? After drawing the functional hierarchy, the next step is to examine the *ideal state,* a functional state that successfully provides the required result of every component and then supplies the suitable conditions for performing it. For an ideal state, every function is performing at its best; the required result has been achieved.

Let us examine the filament–light functional link first. The given filament has many "good" parameters, such as conductivity, strength, durability, and worka-bility (tungsten may be formed into very thin coils). But the essential parameter for best performance (in accordance with the required results) is the temperature T. Increasing T improves the results. Accordingly, a temperature like $T = T_{max}$, the melting point, is used. This is the maximum temperature that remains true to the concept of solid incandescent filament and guarantees a feasible, relatively imme-diate, and inexpensive solution. Later on, theory reveals that we may still increase T higher and deal with "ion conduction," which is another possible level of solu-tion. T_{max} makes it possible to produce light that meets the required results (effi-ciency radiation of 52 Lu/W and whiter light). Although this temperature brings a drawback, as it causes loss of atoms and shortens very quickly the life of the fila-ment, we should supply it; so $T = T_{max}$. We made here a decision: in the ideal state the temperature of the filament will be T_{max}. The drawbacks this produces, as you will see, should help us to steer the analysis toward a contradiction that will evoke the desired inventive idea. Overcoming the contradiction (conflict) would turn the disadvantage of the drawback (here, the rapid evaporation) into an advantage.

Next consider the electric current. The current should be of a magnitude that makes possible a constant $T = T_{max}$, and thus the parameter of current intensity $I = I(T_{max})$. There is no problem in meeting this requirement. At the ideal state we thus decided that the current intensity would be $I(T_{max})$. The explicit requirement for whiter light and increased efficiency was translated to the explicit goal $[T_{max}, I(T_{max})]$.

These decisions supplied us with some explicit goals to be achieved and new information about our target: the ideal system. There the filament temperature and the current would be T_{max} and $I(T_{max})$, and according to our model, as if by magic, there would be no drawbacks. So we have the first links in the chain of solution: goals and a target. The new information (even though partial) about our target makes it possible to use a very powerful and systematic problem-solving strategy, working backward.

Through working backward from the ideal desired-end system, we would be able to find out the logically necessary conditions for performing our goals in sequence, not only in the ideal system but in reality (facing physical conditions). At the end of the process our real system would become the ideal working one.

In general, applying the ideal system principle to all components produces a system in which all the relevant components are functioning with the required result. On paper, the above is an ideal light bulb, and the goal was attained—but in reality we have a physical deficiency, evaporation! The previous equilibrium between the system and the environment was broken. A new equilibrium must be found in accordance with the new explicit goals.

At this stage every physical deficiency is formulated in detailed relationship with both the physical parameters and the physical causes that produce the phenomena. In our example the very high temperature of the glowing filament causes its metal to evaporate (atoms escape from the filament), and the filament gets thinner. This effect causes its resistivity and therefore its temperature to be further heightened, and the filament breaks more rapidly.

Sometimes we can make an X-ray depiction comparing the structure of param-eters in the shortcoming and in the ideal system, enabling us to identify the opposed demands at this stage in the manner that may be seen in a *contradictions formulation*. In our example, the opposed demands can now be seen immediately. To get high quality of illumination (whiter and more efficient), the temperature of the filament has to be very high, but to get the long-life filament, the temperature has to be low. How can the filament temperature be very high and also low at the same time? A parametric conflict is revealed, and we should try to overcome it by applying the following stages.

Now we turn to problem-finding. The product is the incandescent filament, the only element in the shortcoming structure. In the theoretical part, below, we deal with cases in which multielements appear in the shortcoming.

Looking from the desired end state (working backward) we can now ask, What is required of the product so that the shortcoming should disappear? The conventional, and usual, answer is that the metal atoms should not escape from the filament even when the filament reaches the high temperature required. However, the right decision at this stage would be to use the *open product principle* to generate nonconventional alternative requirements and seek a promising one. For methodological reasons, to introduce one of the many loops in our model we will continue the process with the above (conventional) requirement and later come back to use the right decision.

From our present scientific knowledge it does not seem possible for the product to meet the requirements by itself unless something is added to perform them. The purpose of that added element would be to prevent the escape of metal atoms from the glowing filament. This element is called a "tool." A tool is a simple element (as opposed to a device or system) that may influence the product by one of its parameters.

How can we find a concrete tool that fulfills the requirement of the product? We continue to work backward by finding first a subgoal: the necessary conditions imposed on the function of the tool. We ask, What preceding state could have led to the desired position of the product? Or, what are the necessary conditions to reach that preceding state? The specific tool that meets these conditions would be our final goal (the solution) and we would continue to find the unknown conditions with small yet concrete steps.

The function of the tool can be examined and visualized using the concept of "elves at work." These "elves" are capable of performing simple physical actions. They can see, speak, run, understand, and so on. By visualizing and simulating a situation in which elves perform the function of the unknown tool, we make it more obvious and simple to understand at the micro level (micro viewpoint). In one possible version, each elf performs the task of holding a metal atom in its place, preventing its escape from the filament. Applying force from inside (attraction) can be one version, from outside (push) can be another version, from inside and also from outside (push-pull) can be still another one.

The visualization and simulation may illuminate certain conditions relevant to the desired function. In this instance, the following conditions logically become apparent:

- The tool should deal with the product at the level of separate atoms, and should therefore be active at the same (atomic or molecular) level.

- The tool may act from inside the filament (attracting the atoms), or from outside the filament (pushing the atoms back).
- The tool should create a force acting on the atom to prevent its detachment and escape.
- The tool function should overcome (if possible) the temperature conflict.
- The elves should not interact with the glass or other materials that exist in the light bulb.
- The function should be accomplished by a simple physical operation.

Now we need to find a specific, concrete tool that would adapt its physical behavior successfully to the logical necessary conditions. Because we found the physical contradiction above, we can go directly to seeking ideas to solve it.

What are the physical effects and phenomena that can aid and support us in trying to achieve the functional requirements? What are the forces available? How can they meet these logical conditions, and who can carry them out? The forces may be, for example, mechanical, electrical, magnetic, and chemical.

Mechanical force does not seem to be applicable because the force should act on individual atoms. Chemical bonds seem unsuitable in the high temperature on the filament's surface. It does not seem feasible for a magnetic force to be applied to separate atoms instead of to a whole mass of atoms. Electric force is theoretically suitable, but its use in this situation does not seem applicable. (From similar reasoning one can show that the hydraulic and pneumatic forces are not applicable.)

We may spend more time on checking alternatives, but as a methodological example we have chosen to stop at this stage.

The above analysis suggests that the model for the function of the tool does not lead to a principal solution: we have reached an insoluble path and we have to abandon it.

At this stage we have gained some experience with the model and we can try to understand some of the theory more deeply and become more familiar with the model's loops before continuing the problem-solving process.

Stage 1: Physical Elements

This list includes all the physical elements (both matter and fields) relevant to the functional system (defined as an assemblage of elements working together toward some common objective) and its environment (elements that remain outside the system but are physically interrelated with it) (see Figure 14.1.)

By contrast, the essence and focus of the next step is on the objectives to be achieved rather than on details of mechanism or existing problems.

Stage 2: Functional System

According to our approach, each element of a man-made functional system exists for the sole aim of carrying out a clearly defined function. Together, the purpose of producing light and the physical action of incandescence performed by the filament are light bulb's function. The physical action changes specific parameters according

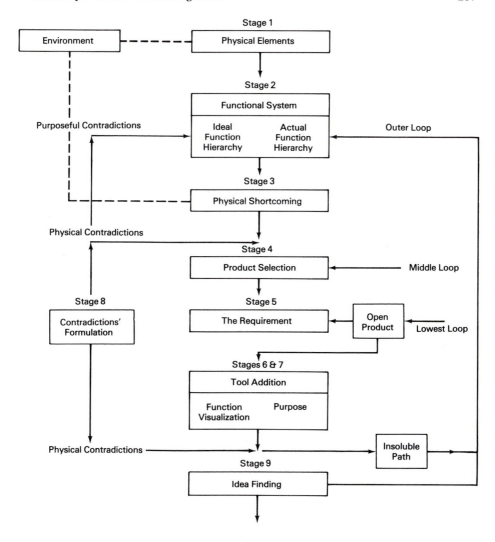

FIGURE 14.1. The nine-stage model and its loops.

to the required purpose of the action. This is done by changing operating temperature or by changing the spectrum in the visible part. At this stage we are not interested in the object itself (substance, dimensions, strength, workability, etc.), but only in its purpose and its relevant parameters. One leaves aside all the attributes of the system's elements apart from those that have significant potential for further functional development. This step emphasizes those parameters.

The main product (light) is the interface between the system (inner environment) and the outer environment. When the system successfully attains its goal it is through an adaptation of the inner parameters to the outer environment in accordance with the designer's calculations (Simon, 1969).

The functional hierarchy of every functional system may be represented by an inverted tree, with the individual functional elements as nodes and the functional connections made by physical action as arrows. The top node represents the main product of the whole system and every terminal intermediate node represents the product of an intermediate system.

Formulation of a purpose is usually in the most general and abstract terms (verb and noun only). That is, it excludes hints or indications that may prejudice the solver toward a possible fulfillment of the function that prematurely excludes other alternatives.

This takes us to an important question: What are the main benefits of using the system functional analysis?

1. The analysis describes the essence of a system's relationships in a general, compact, and graphic way. The problem-solver gets the whole picture without getting lost in detail. The amount of data collection is limited to general knowledge (excluding processes, numbers, and values), which keeps it relatively simple to digest and clear to start with. For instance, we are not interested in the quantum-mechanical processes by which the filament produces light, or how the gas decreases the evaporation of the filament.

2. The general and abstract nature of the purpose formulation enables the problem-solver to escape from his or her specific subjective conception, as well as from the problem limitations, and be more flexible and open to other interdisciplinary perceptions unrelated to the old design. In our example, heating (a metal) might be accomplished in many alternative ways—bombardment by accelerated particles, alternating electromagnetic field, and so on.

3. Purpose expansion (dividing the problem into hierarchy levels) enables the problem-solver to examine independently many alternatives, thus enlarging the problem–solution space and ensuring that the right issues will be addressed.

4. Dealing first with system functional analysis restrains the spontaneous and natural tendency to prejudge and commit oneself prematurely to a course of action that is often very difficult to change. The ideal systems approach plays an important roll in the model; it strives for a far-reaching target. Among the various systems levels, the ideal system is the practical one.

The contemporary ideal systems are divided into two classes. The first generates easy-to-implement and relatively inexpensive solutions—by using most of the available components in the existing system. An example is when we increased the temperature of the filament to produce better requested results and stopped near the melting point. It enabled us to keep the existing incandescent filament in the system. Increasing the temperature further would prevent our using a conventional filament and bring us to the second class, perhaps a new conception for producing light by ionized moving particles.

In this chapter we deal only with the first class of contemporary ideal systems. Their ideal structure is generated using the ideal final state. Accordingly, each component in the functional hierarchy should be represented as a functional state that provides the required successful result (at any required time, place, and position), regardless of demands of other parameters or components (local principle). According to this principle every parameter value of any component that is important for the direct physical performance of the purpose gets its "best" quantitative level. No quantitative compromises are made, and even extreme values are taken. In the ongoing process one is not interested in the other parameters of the component but only in the functioning parameters and only in their most effective values (T_{max}, melting point).

This decision-making procedure for inventing or gaining some data on the ideal system may lead to opposing demands (paradoxes, contradictions) or drawbacks within the actual system. In our example, one such problem is how the lamp can sustain a long life despite the very high filament temperature that burns out the bulb. However, in the ideal system there should not exist drawbacks or contradictions. For the purpose of further analysis, even though we don't know how the ideal system would actually perform, we "act" as if our goals were accomplished somehow (as if by magic) and none of the drawbacks or contradictions existed. In the ideal lamp the temperature and current would be T_{max} and I_{max}, the required light would be produced, and no drawbacks would exist. For the present, we accept as our main target to realize the ideal system—to find out how it works, from the real frame of reference.

Knowing the ideal system enables us to work backward and find the path to a solution in a systematic way. In the steps to follow, we would try to find the conditions that have to be fulfilled in order to realize the ideal system. The ideal system serves as a long-term guide (a beacon) to reach our desired destination; it enhances the innovation process and fosters creativity no matter how many obstacles are encountered along the way.

One ostensible obstacle is the contradiction. In general, contradictions may have two aspects: the purposeful (conflicts among objectives) and the physical (related to physical properties and explained in the following stages). In the lamp example, after the ideal system principle was applied there were no purposeful aspects in contradiction. Every one of the required objectives was accomplished by the desired parameters.

Speaking generally, the purposeful aspects of contradiction must be solved at this stage. We do this by using operations such as *functions separation* and *dynamization*. Consider two examples.

Suppose that after applying the ideal system principle to the filament's supports we find that in the ideal state the supports cannot be produced from conductive materials. A contradiction is at hand. The previous two purposes (hold and conduct) cannot be performed anymore by the same functional element. A function separation is needed in which the main function (to hold) is performed by the supporters and a new tool is added to the system to perform the new required function: to conduct.

Another way of resolving conflicts is through dynamization. The essential parameter of the functional link has to be changed in time, but the present function can respond steadily to only one state. According to the ideal system requirement, the purpose cannot be accomplished. A dynamization of the parameter must be done by application of some of the model techniques (e.g., ordinary sunglasses vs. self-adjusting photogray sunglasses that darken in proportion to the sun's intensity).

What are the main benefits of developing the ideal system approach?

1. It translates the needs of the external world (clients, users) to a system's functions. The desired explicit aims of the client (for instance, a whiter and more efficient spectrum of light) become implicit goals for the physical system, and they are translated to system functioning explicit goals (T_{max}, I_{max}, etc.).

2. The ideal system approach provides information about the desired-end state that serves as a long-term guide to stimulate our imagination, gives us a far-reaching target to work toward, and enables us to work backward in a systematic way.

3. The method provokes contradictions and provides the first hints of possible directions to overcome them.

4. The approach fosters creativity, enabling the problem-solver to free himself or herself from past problem limitations, to break through the existing perception, to overcome psychological inertia, and to widen the choice of alternatives (entertaining even utopian and futuristic ideal systems).

5. Every objective is taken tentatively and is checked carefully; nothing is taken for granted and compromises are prevented.

6. It encourages us to take risks.

We now move toward the outer loop for future alternatives. The analysis continues with the maximal structure; the structure includes all the relevant functional elements of the existing system that are able to perform their complete function. Later on, after it has passed through all or most of the stages, and other inner loops, the problem-solving process returns to this stage (outer loop), and different functional elements according to their hierarchic level will then be canceled and new problem situations created.

For instance, we may eliminate electric current as the physical subsystem that accomplishes the purpose of heating, replacing it with other conceptions for heating. By working through the following stages of the model, a new inventive idea may be explored, for instance a point light source, in which a point filament is bombarded by ions of gas. The ions are accelerated by an electric field that concentrates at the point filament. The field comes from the bulb surface, which is covered with a very thin (microns) layer of metal and acts as an electrode. This particular inventive solution falls into the second class of contemporary ideal systems.

Stage 3: Physical Shortcomings

The ideal system is a black box, so for the light bulb example it is one meeting the conditions [T_{max}, $I(T_{max})$]. We can analyze the ideal system from the base of our present scientific knowledge and come to some conclusions. A situation like this one, in which all functional elements are in their complete functionality, yet still constitute a problem, demonstrates that the issue is of a physical nature and not one of reaching an objective (purpose). At this stage we formulate the physical shortcoming in detail with respect to the physical parameters of the element(s) and to the physical causes that produced the unwanted physical phenomena. Here we need as much specific, detailed, and precise information as we can get.

The shortcoming we examine at this stage usually would be different from the original one not only in its physical nature, but also due to changes that our formulation of purposeful contradictions may have introduced into the initial system structure. These changes in our problem representation across the previous stages leave us more ready to find the right problem to deal with.

Sometimes, the analysis of a parameter's structure and its role in the shortcoming may lead us directly to the physical contradiction (Stage 8), as we have seen in the lamp example (see allusion above in Stage 3, contradiction formulation); in other cases it is developed later on.

Function formulation is complete when one develops the ideal functional hierarchy and identifies the physical shortcomings. The elements that remain in the description of the shortcomings are those that are necessary and sufficient to establish the physical contradictions. Focusing on these elements ensures that the solver will concentrate on the right element and will have a worthwhile payoff. The next step therefore would be to apply the minimal problem criterion and so to select the right element.

Stage 4: Selecting the Product

To eliminate the shortcoming, identified in the above work, the state of one (or more) of the physical elements mentioned as elements of the shortcoming must change. Selection of an element to start with (the product) is done by the minimal problem criterion, which determines the branch and level of the functional hierarchy at which the problem will be addressed.

The minimal problem criterion determines how the shortcoming can be overcome in a way that will permit most of the system to function as it is. If such a solution exists, it does not demand any major changes and so may be efficient, easy to implement, and relatively inexpensive. Usually, the component of the lowest subsystem is chosen, and thus the system and the supersystem remain unchanged.

Once one has analyzed and solved (as far as possible) the problem by changing the state of the first chosen element, one may return to the other potential elements that appear in the shortcoming and repeat the process on each.

These possible specific selections make up the middle loop for alternative directions of analysis but continue to focus on the same mentioned shortcoming. By contrast, when we cancel a selected element in the outer loop, new situations and new shortcomings are created.

Stage 5: The Requirements of the Product

The question, What must happen to the state of the chosen product for the shortcoming to disappear?, relates strictly to the physical parameter associated with the shortcoming—that is, what sort of change in the state (parameter) of the product should be implemented so that the deficiency can disappear? For instance, to prevent the tungsten atoms from escaping from the filament, changes in the atoms' motion was the requirement made.

As was mentioned before, people's accustomed thinking is to struggle against the harmful properties or phenomena that cause the unwanted shortcoming. The model approach is different. According to the ideal aspect of our method, the deficiency has to yield profits. To turn the disadvantage into an advantage, one has to leave the narrow and limited thinking approach mentioned above and turn to the *open product principle*. This principle produces many alternative ways of formulating functional requirements (divergent thinking) by which the shortcoming may be resolved.

The open product principle is a process of guided practical imagination, used to define alternative problems. To generate requirements, one applies the various principles of the open product principle (namely, fractionation and unification, past and future states, reversal state, "go to the extremes," and all their possible combinations) to a given product, using them as a base from which to free-associate toward a target, one that is clear and obvious.

In the reversal operation, for instance, the shortcoming situation should be examined from viewpoints opposed to the routine view; things are taken as they are and then turned around, back to front, inside out, upside down, and so on. A fishing net may be viewed as a lot of holes linked together; background becomes image and image becomes background. If the routine process is to change state A of the product to state B by specific requirements, then the new starting state in the reversal operation may be, for example, anti-A. As a result, a new requirement in sharp opposition to the original one appears. Instead of heating, for example, examine cooling; instead of firm links among atoms (solid state), try weak links (liquid) or free atoms (gas state), and so on. In the light bulb, for instance, how can we apply the reversal method? At first sight it is not clear how turning things upside down would be of use, but if the starting point of the product is defined as the opposite of the existing state (solid → liquid → gas), firmly linked atoms would change to a liquid filament or even to free atoms. A solid filament will turn into a liquid or gaseous one, and the problem becomes how the new phase can fulfill the requirements. Below we will use the past and future operations to solve the lamp problem.

If one of the previous requirements can be achieved immediately, the problem may be solved in the lowest loop, the one for alternative problems with the same product. The other requirements lead us to formulate additional problems, and any plausible and promising ones should be dealt with.

Stage 6: The Tool's Purpose

How can the requirement to change the state of the chosen product be fulfilled? In the ideal system, we left it to be fulfilled as if by magic, imagining elves to accomplish it. In real life, a tool, the simplest functional component that performs a simple physical action toward a purpose, needs to be added. Hence, our present main goal is to invent a specific, concrete tool, or tools, to do the work the black box does in the ideal system. In the steps that follow, the ideal viewpoint (elves) and the scientific approach complement each other toward attaining the main goal.

Up to this point, to find the specific tool we had started from the known product (in its ideal environment) and worked backward to find the first subgoal, the unique requirement. Now we begin with the present subgoal. We determine the tool's purpose and how it relates to our subgoal. For instance, the purpose of the additional tool in the lamp was to "stop the escape" of tungsten atoms in the almost-melting filament. Tools (solutions) that might possibly accomplish the needed purpose are many. In this stage we open the way to divergent, interdisciplinary thinking. The many options may come from any discipline. The finding of the logical necessary conditions for their realization, and thence the proper tool, is left to the next step. One seeks a tool, not a device or apparatus (this is a micro, not a macro, orientation). If a device (a complete system consisting of some tools) is needed, the model will build the special, suitable device, by repeating use of the model's loops, step by step, producing tool by tool, without any unnecessary or irrelevant extra function. Instead of selecting devices from catalogues, we invent a specific one for a unique demand. We generally assume that every problem is unique and is best solved by a unique solution in a unique path. Therefore, our approach adapts itself to the unique situation instead of forcing the situation to conform to a given approach.

Stage 7: The Tool's Functional Visualization and Simulation

A tool has to accomplish the required purpose by performing a physical action. The analysis at this stage goes very gradually from the tool objective to its physical realization, that is, to finding the object that best answers the functional conditions. The tool's function is determined by analyzing the logical and physical aspects of the elves' operations. These help us to understand the necessary conditions for our present subgoal attainment: to find the physical action of the tool.

The next subgoal is to find a specific, concrete tool that will adapt its physical behavior to these conditions. Elves may assist us here. The elves can see, think, fly, and so on, and perform simple physical actions (at the level of a tool, not a device). By using the elf principle, one may make the required function visible, obvious, and simple to understand at the micro level. Conflicting requirements may be viewed from the physicist's or chemist's perspective in a popular and effective way. Sometimes the elves' perception makes a task easier for our reasoning to manipulate, and thus helps to resolve the conflicting demands by rearranging or reconstructing the relative performances. These manipulations may be translated to physical, chemical, or technological new effects in the forefront of science, which help us to overcome contradictions. The elves may come from any discipline, and therefore they represent an interdisciplinary approach. Different minimodels of the elves may yield alternative ways for solutions. Employing elves requires us to delay our judgment and makes us concentrate on the important general physical aspects of performing the function in an interdisciplinary approach. This micro tendency, when combined with our previous general macro ideal system, provides the micro view and macro design of man-made systems, placed in an interdisciplinary framework.

As long as a tool can operate in accordance with the ideal principle, it is a fine tool in our model. Even if it has some physical (nonpurposeful) drawbacks, that is not a reason to turn immediately to seek another tool. Instead, we proceed to develop and to change the existing tool in order to overcome its shortcoming.

What are the main benefits of the tool concept and its application?

1. The tool, the smallest functional component that operates by a single and simple physical action, enables us to focus locally and deal with the highest available resolution of the system structure (e.g., the atomic structure in the bulb example).

2. The tool concept enables the problem-solver to create the minimal device needed to carry out the inventive idea without adding anything extra or superfluous. The device is not something from a catalogue, adapted to fit, but a device invented tool by tool for a specific purpose.

3. The tool is developed very gradually by visualizing the performance of the needed purpose without the use of an object; thus, all options are open and the solver does not jump immediately to conclusions.

4. Visualization and simulation by dwarfs of the poorly understood function can easily guide our thinking process by helping us picture the function. It provides original new information and guidance to physical effects and new technology in the forefront of science as a creative aid to realize the inventive ideas.

5. The elfs' viewpoint frees our mind from the old design (one discipline) and the limitations that existing attitudes impose. Using means of microvisualization and simulation, it broadens the frame of reference to embrace new, active, and dynamic interdisciplinary options and possibilities.

Stage 8: Contradiction Identification and Formulation

If the contradiction could not be identified before, it would be identified now. The difficulty that prevents the physical application of the solution is defined and analyzed to determine which of two types of contradiction exists. The two sorts of contradictions can follow from the two aspects of the ideal system principle that govern the improvement and development of system components. The first aspect requires that the functional component possess the attributes that ensure the complete performance of its required function. If those properties cannot exist in the real system, parametrical contradictions crop up. If the need to change a parameter by one requirement, for example, is obstructed by other requirements and as a result the accomplishment of the function cannot be reached, a contradiction should be eliminated.

In the lamp, the ideal filament temperature should be very high, but this need is disturbed by the other requirement for long life, which imposes a low temperature need. The requirement for a simultaneous low and high temperature is a parametrical contradiction. The conventional engineering thinking is to make a compromise: not too low (1000°K) but not very high (3500°K)—something around 2000°K.

The second aspect of the ideal system principle suggests that the component should not possess (at any time, or place) qualities that are not essential for its function. For instance, our eyes perceive pulses of light at a frequency of 24 pulses per second as continuous light (as in film shooting and projecting). Thus, the lamp does not have to emit light all the time; twenty-four brief fractions of pulses (each perhaps lasting only thousandths of a second) would be enough. Thus the temperature of the filament and the current need not be very high all the time in order to fulfill their functions. The recommendation would be to use very short pulses of electric current. This new direction may open a way to overcome the contradiction and produce a longer-life bulb.

However, adding a tool to the system involves the introduction of parameters not necessarily relevant to its function. The addition, for instance, may entail difficulties in installation and maintenance; it may cost more in time and money. Furthermore, the presence of a given tool may make the system heavier, more noisy, more expensive, or more difficult to handle and thus produce phenomena that disturb each other and conflict with the ideal system. Some sort of compensation has always to be made for the presence of a tool in a functional system. The shortcomings required for the presence of the tool in the system are evidence of an existing contradiction. In the case of existing contradictions, conventional engineering thinking is to compensate for the required result (sacrificing energy, time, substance). The ideal approach, however, fights against this tendency; there should be no "payment," but the objective should be obtained; there should be no substance, but the physical action should be accomplished. One should keep in mind this ideal tool approach: it is necessary that a new tool be there yet not be there. How can this be done? For instance, one may utilize one of the coexisting components or change a variant of it so the previous component in its new state can fulfill the required function without a new tool at all.

In general, when a conventional approach is used and the problem-solver reaches such logical contradictions, he or she changes direction, gives up, backs away, or tries to find a compromise. Our approach requires us to overcome contradictions. Conflicts provoke our thinking process and focus our thinking effort on the right issue to work on.

Stage 9: Idea Finding

How can we escape from contradictions? Conventional thinking is based on dichotomous reasoning, the reasoning of "is . . . or is not." According to that approach, consistency is an absolute requirement of rationality, and violation of the "law of noncontradiction" destroys any possibility of rational thought, producing logical anarchy. The human brain by means of words enables us to judge consistency or inconsistency. But words or statements are incomplete representations of real nature and words never express all the relevant details. Because different eyes present different pictures and meanings of phenomena, a word's meaning is not in the word but in our mind. The projection of a film that our brain may perceive as a continuous process is actually a series of individual pictures. Thus pulses of light (24/second) produced by peaks of electric current may be enough for full illumination. This new frame of reference can help us to escape from the filament contradiction; it could allow, perhaps, a very high temperature for very short periods and a low temperature in between.

Therefore a willingness to doubt and to accept statements as tentative to varying degrees enables us to be flexible, innovative, and ready to examine their credibility—sometimes even to change the frame of reference in order to overcome contradictions. Consider how this paper may be asserted (truly) to be at rest and at the same time to be moving: the paper is at rest from your point of view but is moving from any other frame of reference that is not at rest relative to you (a moving car, the moon, and others). Such observations show that, in a sense, two contradicting tendencies can prevail simultaneously and that the clash of the two may vary with spatial or temporal location. What overcomes the contradiction is not space and time alone—they have no such effect—but the differences between different parts in space and the changes that occur in the same part.

From our point of view there is a close connection between time, change, and contradiction on the one hand and between space, difference, and contradiction on the other hand. Our taking into consideration different points in space and time, in the framework of our real four-dimensional world, can help us to escape from contradictions. The inventive solution for a light bulb, described in the following section, illustrates this.

Analyzing the contradiction brings us a step closer to the solution—we would know the physical conditions necessary for the solution. A small creative leap is now needed, and with the help of the model's tactical operations and analogical examples one can connect the situation to a related situation with the same source of contradiction and design the inventive idea for a technical solution.

In the analytic thinking model, three techniques are used to eliminate contradictions:

1. Transposing the real, actual system to an ideal, desired-end system by means of the ideal system principle and applying operations such as dynamization that eliminate the purposeful contradiction.

2. Using elves to allow us to examine and reconstruct the conflicting actions, as will be demonstrated in the lowest loop of the light-bulb section in the next section.

3. Applying by analogy a system of spatial-temporal operators that are generalizations of results based on a large repertoire of case studies.

In practice, Analytic Inventive Thinking is not the pedantic step-by-step method that the above description may suggest. Each real problem situation is unique and requires a unique approach toward its solution. One of the basic strategy aims is to tailor a specific approach to a specific problem so as to create a specific solution and not adapt or force the problem to fit into available general solutions. In practice, heuristic decisions are taken during the solving of various phases, so steps may occur out of accustomed sequence and may also be used repeatedly, thus reflecting the value of looping through the process. In the lamp example, a right heuristic decision would be to apply the open product principle at Stage 5 for alternative requirements and not to fight against the shortcoming, as was wrongly done. As the next section shows, proceeding through the lowest loop would repair the wrong decision.

A Detailed Solution

Let us now return to the lowest loop of the light-bulb problem and try to find a detailed solution.

The application of the open product principle on the metal atoms may develop some alternative requirements toward the product. Dealing with the atoms in the filament before the filament is heated answers the question, What should have been done to the product in the past so that the present problem would not arise? This direction was considered (attracting the atoms from inside or pushing them back by externally applied forces) but did not seem to lead to an inventive solution.

What about the future-state direction of the principle? Dealing with the atoms in the filament after they escape from it and answering the question, What other problems will we have to solve in the future, if we don't solve the present one?, the answer becomes how to retrieve the atoms (not, as in the initial state, avoiding their escape). This does seem a promising alternative—recycling the metal!

We may spend more time on creating alternatives (and normally do), but as an example of method we have chosen to solve the future-state problem first. What is required of the product for the shortcoming to disappear in its future state? The metal atoms are to return to the filament and rejoin it after having "run away." This amounts to recycling the metal. Is the "right" problem, then, how to recycle the tungsten? Framing the question this way, we are not fighting against the physical cause of the shortage; instead we try to gain from it, to harness the "harmful" phenomenon to our benefit.

The tool's purpose is to return the metal atoms to the filament. The next step would use the elves to demonstrate it. The elves exert force on the atoms; for example, they stick to metal atoms that have escaped from the filament; they hold it; they move with it; they return it, or with it, to the filament; and they separate from it. Since elves are capable of performing only simple physical actions (not being a device or system), this whole process has to be done in a simple way.

What are the requirements of an elf's function?

- The elf adheres to the atom somewhere off the filament (but before it reaches the bulb wall).
- The elf and atom move together and have to cross to the filament.
- The elf separates from the atom it has brought back to the filament, and hovers off the filament, ready to repeat its job again and again.
- The tool function should overcome (if possible) the temperature conflict (high for the good qualities of light and, at the same time, low for the long-life duration).
- The elf should not interact with the glass or other materials that exist in the light bulb.
- The function should be accomplished by a simple physical operation.

Examination of even these partial requirements makes it clear that a bond must be created between the tool and the atom somewhere off the filament. The tool should be of atomic effect, and its link with the atom should be at the interatomic level (a chemical, external magnetic, or electric bond) almost all over the bulb volume (maybe gas?). How can the tool catch the atom somewhere off the filament and release it (or move with it) on the filament surface? What is the difference between the two separate states where the atoms are caught and released? Is there any link to the temperature spatial change inside the bulb? As the temperature of the glowing filament is considerably lowered as a function of the distance, it seems that a chemical bond can be created off the filament. Such a bond seems possible between the tungsten atom (T), and a gas atom that may be inside the bulb. Let us consider a "gas," X, that is to stick to the T atom to form a TX molecule away from the glowing filament where the temperature is low. The separation of T from X close to the filament may follow by itself as a natural result of the very high temperature on the filament surface.

How would the TX molecules hit or come near the glowing filament? The movement of TX toward the filament, and of X away from it, follows by itself as a result of the statistical law of equalization of gas concentrations. Many TX molecules would be produced "far" from the glowing filament (near the bulb), and according to the above-mentioned law they would spread all over the volume and also toward the filament. Whenever a TX molecule hit or came near the glowing filament, it would separate as desired. On the other hand, nearest to the filament the concentration of X would become greater, causing X to diffuse again toward the bulb. There, where the temperatures are much lower, X would again fulfill its job.

Thus an inventive idea for the uninterrupted function of the tool has finally been found. The inventive idea of recycling the tungsten metal can be accomplished by an unknown (as yet) gas whose basic characteristics we know. The problem was in electricity but the solution came from chemistry.

Halogens turned out as suitable gases, and the inventive idea was implemented and produced as tungsten halogen lamps. We can look now at the filament (Figure 14.2) as a big cylinder consisting of a "cloud" made of tungsten atoms and halogen, with a metal tungsten coil at the center. Along the radius of the cylinder there is a gradient of temperature from almost the melting point at the center down to several hundred degrees near the surface. This new filament is simultaneously at a very high temperature in the center and at low temperature at the surface! The conflict has been overcome.

There are many alternative loops in the model that were not used in this example. The analysis should now continue to develop more alternative requirements in accordance with the open product principle (Stage 5) and then continue to higher levels of hierarchies, options that would not be included in this paper.

Conclusions

This chapter concerns a practical model and methods to teach engineers, scientists, and technicians improved thinking skills toward fostering systematic creativity. The mystic idea that creativity can only be prayed for is substituted with a deliberate and practical approach for combining systematic thinking with insight to produce inventions. The model can be learned, practiced, and used; it can readily be dissem-

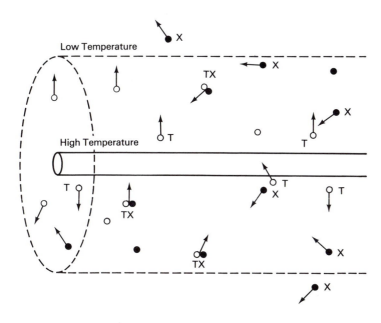

FIGURE 14.2. The interaction of tungsten atoms (T) and gas atoms (X) at low and high temperature.

inated widely. It is possible to acquire skills in use of the Analytic Inventive Thinking model just as it is possible to acquire skills in physics. This enterprise is very important in a world characterized by growing complexity, rapid change, and vastly expanding knowledge.

In our view, the model provides a rationale and methodology for generating inventive solutions in a systematic and organized manner, with prescriptions general enough for use in a broad spectrum of technological fields. Teaching the model, we feel the close interrelation between existing general theoretical knowledge and its practical application. On the one hand we use an overview structure of ideal performance using a means-end analysis, a purpose-oriented approach, and a prescriptive systems outlook as a conceptional basis. These combine with local strategies including working backward, replacing a given difficult goal by subgoals as steps toward achieving the main goal, and macro-micro analysis. On the other hand, we have a set of practical tools for implementing its conceptual basis; the ideal system technique that strives for far-reaching targets; shortcomings that bring benefits; paradoxes that provoke original thinking; elves as a scientific micro model to foster creativity, and so on.

My colleagues and I feel very strongly that we are on the right track in attempting to teach an interdisciplinary technological course in creative problem-solving. We still have a long way to go, but with the enthusiasm, dedication, and commitment of our staff we hope to make it.

References

Altshuller, G. S. (1973). *The Algorithm of an Invention* (in Russian). Moscow: Mos Rabochy.

Helfman, J. (1988). *The Analytic Inventive Thinking Model.* Tel Aviv: Open University of Israel.

Encyclopedia of Science and Technology. (1977). Vol. 7, p. 56, Incandescent lamps. New York: McGraw-Hill.

Simon, H. A. (1969). *The Sciences of the Artificial.* Boston: MIT Press.

V | THE SOCIAL CONTEXT OF INVENTIONS

The pursuit of invention has changed as its social context has changed. One way that the twentieth century differs from the nineteenth is in the presence of large corporate laboratories. There is a creative tension between the free-wheeling flights of human imagination and the financial constraints of producing a marketable product. That tension is nowhere more present than in the contest between individual and corporate goals. How this plays out is discussed here. A still broader context for invention is provided by a social invention, the patent system itself.

David Hounshell takes a close look at the famous Pioneering Research Laboratory of the Du Pont Fibers Department between 1928 and 1968. He discusses tensions between the director of the laboratory and the higher management. Through persistence and imagination, sustained innovation came despite somewhat conservative policies among the DuPont management.

Hounshell also presents an interesting insight on how the nature of a search target can change. An example of radical restructuring was the movement at the Pioneering Lab from duplicating natural properties like woolliness to the very different target of reaching beyond natural fiber to super fibers like Kevlar and Nomex that offer strength and fire retardation greater than that of any natural fiber. Finally, of particular interest here is the comparison of the account by Hounshell, an historian of technology, with the earlier account of Morgan, a chemist in the Pioneering Research Lab.

If since the explosion of the Challenger you have always wanted to know how O-rings work, here is the background of that exquisitely simple and effective invention. George Wise paints a shifting portrait of invention inside and outside industrial laboratories—with a good deal of conflict along the way. His examples, from the braking of streetcars to the development of the O-ring, emphasize how the many very different social configurations can feed invention.

Another aspect of invention highlighted by Wise is the very human drama of conflict between the individual inventor and the giant corporation. That conflict plays out its course not only in strained relations but in the courtrooms of the land.

Donald Quigg discusses the role of an important social invention that many believe provides the cultural climate for technological invention. It is the patent system itself, designed to protect intellectual property and at the same time to make completely public the basis of an invention so that others may build on it. He emphasizes how streamlining of the U.S. patent system and worldwide collaboration in patenting standards are creating a fertile milieu for creative initiative in technology.

Quigg then gives us a glimpse of what the U.S. Patent and Trademark Office is doing to promote the study of invention by children. Perhaps the most important technological invention of all is the human organization and social context of custom and law that facilitate the acts of individual invention.

15 | Invention in the Industrial Research Laboratory: Individual Act or Collective Process?

DAVID A. HOUNSHELL

The primary question this chapter explores is whether invention in the industrial research laboratory is an individual act or a collective process. The chapter also addresses the issue of whether the inventive act occurs in a discrete moment or in a more continuous process. These questions will be examined by focusing on the "inventions" of one particular industrial laboratory, the Pioneering Research Laboratory of the Du Pont Company's Textile Fibers Department in the period 1928 to 1968. Even in 1928 when this laboratory was established, the diversified, decentralized Du Pont Company had at least a dozen research laboratories; by 1968, the Textile Fibers Department alone had half a dozen laboratories, including four in the Wilmington, Delaware, area and others in Waynesboro, Virginia, and Kinston, North Carolina.[1] The Pioneering Research Laboratory's mission was to do just what its name implied—to conduct longer term and more basic research and to invent new products and processes within the Textile Fibers Department's areas of business. This laboratory was extraordinarily productive during this period, especially after 1941, and therefore it provides an excellent vehicle through which to explore the inventing mind. Readers should compare and contrast this chapter's analysis, which reflects the work of an historian of technology, with that of Dr. Paul Morgan (Chapter 10), who was one of the Pioneering Research Laboratory's distinguished chemists during a good part of the period under consideration and who is rightfully to be considered an important inventor of the twentieth century.

Creation of the Pioneering Research Laboratory

Du Pont became a manufacturer of rayon (viscose cellulose, a "man-made" fiber as opposed to "synthetic" fiber because it is derived from the natural polymeric substance cellulose) in 1921 as part of its aggressive diversification program. This program had been implemented in 1916 to make the company less dependent on its explosives business, which executives knew would collapse with the end of World War I. Rich in cash but lacking in fiber-making know-how, the firm established the Du Pont Fibersilk Company, a joint venture with a factory in Buffalo,

New York. In return for 49 percent of the new company's equity, a French rayon manufacturer provided the technology and know-how; Du Pont assumed all the capital and start-up costs for its 51 percent share. The company found it necessary to establish a research and development organization around its newly acquired technology in order to rationalize and improve both the rayon product and its manufacturing process. Hence the establishment of what was called the Technical Division in 1924, which complemented the new company's marketing and manufacturing divisions. Soon the Technical Division would also work on cellophane film and cellulose acetate fibers, products that Du Pont also began to manufacture after buying French technology. By 1929, seventy-three researchers worked in the Technical Division of the now wholly Du Pont-owned Du Pont Rayon Company. (Du Pont's total R&D personnel numbered 572 that year.)[2]

Two years earlier, Leonard Yerkes, the president of the Du Pont Rayon Company, proposed to his Board of Directors that "our position in the industry [i.e., rayon] has so improved and the capital we have invested in it [is] so great, it seems to us to justify some consideration to Pioneering Research on Rayon, which we may attempt to describe as being a search for new compounds which could be used in the manufacture of rayon."[3] Heretofore, the Rayon Company's technical efforts had been so closely tied to the immediate problems of getting the rayon plant up and running and the French technology rationalized in the Du Pont way that no medium- to long-term research work had been done. All efforts were short range. This worried Yerkes now that the business had begun to earn profits (exceeding 30 percent return on investment). He wanted to protect his capital investment; that was what Yerkes always had in mind when he talked about pioneering research. Yerkes's Board concurred, and he was allowed to spend about $50,000 per year on pioneering/defensive research. The total R&D budget of the Du Pont Rayon Company was about $450,000 at this point.[4]

Immediately after this Board meeting, Ernest Benger, who was the research director of the Rayon Company, departed for Europe to find a first-class cellulose chemist to head the new pioneering effort. Benger thought he could hire someone really good for $1000 per month, which was quite an extraordinary sum for 1928 dollars (the average starting salary for Ph.D. chemists at Du Pont was about $2500 to $3000 per year). But as Benger soon learned, the chemists he sought asked for no less than $5000 per month, or more than the total sum of money the company wanted to spend on pioneering.[5] Benger came home empty-handed. He then offered the job to William Hale Charch, the outspoken young chemist who had recently succeeded in short order in moisture-proofing cellophane, thereby making it one of the most profitable products in the company's history.

Had it not been for Benger's secretary, Charch would probably not have joined the Du Pont organization. Having written his doctoral dissertation in physical chemistry on chemical control of gaseous detonation in the internal combustion engine, Charch was hired by General Motors' Charles Kettering and Thomas Midgley to work on the internal combustion engine's knock problem that threatened development of the automobile industry. Ironically, Midgley's discovery of tetraethyl lead and Du Pont's major achievement in developing safe processes for its manufacture rapidly undermined Charch's ability to contribute to General Motors' research, so in 1925 he was fired. Without immediate luck in finding employment,

Charch took a job teaching French in Ohio. Nevertheless he placed a "situations wanted" ad in a chemical industry trade journal, and to his delight he received a reply from Benger asking him to come to Buffalo for an interview. Benger's secretary had read Charch's appeal and, despite much protest from Benger (who said the company never hired anyone taking out a "situations wanted" ad), convinced her boss to sign a letter she composed inviting Charch for an interview. As it turned out, Benger liked Charch and hired him.[6]

Charch made immediate and lifelong contributions to the company. Assigned to work on cellophane, within a year and a half or so he came up with a way to moisture proof the new film, thereby earning for himself a very handsome bonus on which he could have comfortably retired had he been so inclined.[7] Charch then worked at the Old Hickory, Tennessee, rayon plant where he contributed to the development of a dry-cake rayon-manufacturing process. Immediately before Benger offered him the job of directing a pioneering research effort in rayon and cellophane, Charch had toured European rayon plants with Ernest K. Gladding, Benger's boss.

Once offered the job of supervising pioneering research—Charch being a clear second choice as far as Benger was concerned—Charch began to rattle some cages. Benger had envisioned that "pioneering research" meant employing "the scientific method of attack on the problem[s]" faced by rayon and cellophane, but Charch saw it differently. As Benger reported to the head of the cellophane division, "Dr. Charch has considered as pioneering research any kind of experimental or research work which is directed toward the development of a comparatively radical new type of Cellophane or ordinary Cellophane by a radically new process." Moreover, Charch argued that he would employ "any method designed to produce those [radical] results."[8] In other words, Charch would pursue an entrepreneurial strategy rather than a purely methodological one in his direction of Pioneering Research. The same held true of Charch's views on pioneering research on rayon. Thus from the very outset—and to his last breath in 1958—Charch maintained that Pioneering Research would bring about radically new products or processes by any means necessary. He was absolutely consistent in this philosophy.

Charch's ideas soon ran afoul with those of Yerkes and the heads of his rayon and cellophane divisions. These men were interested in protecting the company's capital, not in developing radically new products to displace the company's existing cellophane and rayon. Therefore, Charch and his handful of pioneering researchers were confined to research in cellulose chemistry. In 1930, Benger and Charch sought Gladding's permission to undertake research on synthetic resins, apparently without success.[9] Dissatisfied, Benger left the Du Pont Rayon and Cellophane companies to accept a position as assistant director of the Du Pont Company's Chemical Department under Elmer K. Bolton.[10]

The Climate for Invention in a Bureaucratic Organization

Thus far, the narrative suggests that the environment within the Du Pont Rayon and Cellophane companies was not conducive to the kind of research and development that Hale Charch wanted to pursue in his Pioneering Research program. Surely the *climate for invention* that exists within a bureaucratic organization (and one can expand this to a nation and indeed to an entire culture) must be a critical factor in explaining that organization's (or nation's or culture's) rate and nature of invention. In the case of the Du Pont Rayon and Cellophane companies, the climate for invention—or at least radical invention of the type Charch envisaged—was bad. The companies' leaders had created a supposed pioneering research organization but then put it in a straitjacket. Hale Charch believed that the real opportunities for radical invention in fibers and films lay outside cellulose chemistry in the area of synthetic resins, which were just beginning to appear on the horizon. Given this negative climate for invention, what kind of performance might be expected from the Pioneering Research Laboratory in particular and the Technical Division in general?

Charch's Pioneering Research Laboratory came up with precious little during the period that its mission was so severely circumscribed. This fact gnawed at Charch throughout the 1930s.

The Technical Division as a whole produced few significant product developments during this era. Cordura tire cord, a high-tenacity rayon filament yarn, was perhaps the most important product developed during these years. Du Pont, however, found that Cordura could not be adequately protected by patents, due largely to the strength of a British patent and the research of Goodyear Rubber Company, which had worked with Du Pont on Cordura's development.[11] With respect to developments in process technology, economist Samuel Hollander found that the bulk of contributions to productivity improvements emerged from in-plant, trial-and-error engineering work rather than from research laboratories.[12]

Changing the Departmental Climate for Invention

How did the climate for radical invention change in the Du Pont rayon organization? Essentially, change was forced on the organization by developments *outside* the organization. Even then, change came slowly.

In the larger Du Pont Company's central research department (known then as the Chemical Department), an important revolution was taking place in the late 1920s and early 1930s in the laboratory of Wallace H. Carothers. Carothers had been hired in 1928 to lead an organic chemistry group within a small, elite program of fundamental research designed to compete with the very finest academic research organizations. Within two years Carothers had presented a massively documented case that polymers—what he called macromolecules—were simply chains of regularly occurring molecules held together by either single or double bonds. In addition to carrying out this first-rate scientific work, Carothers and his group had discovered—"invented"—two things in the same month. First they had discovered the first wholly synthetic rubber, developed during the 1930s as neoprene. Second, having synthesized an aliphatic polyester with a molecular weight in excess of 12,000, they had also spun and demonstrated the technique of cold-drawing (or orienting the molecular chains of) the first wholly synthetic fiber. By

1934, Carothers had laid out a synthesis route to the first of the polyamides, polymers that would become known generically as nylon. Carothers and his group—
and especially Charch and others in the Rayon Department's[13] Pioneering Research
Laboratory–knew that nylon would become a revolutionary fiber because it melted
at a relatively high temperature, demonstrated great tenacity and extreme abrasion
resistance, had the same strength when wet as when dry (a property possessed by
no natural or man-made fiber), and had the appearance of silk.[14]

As early as 1930, Carothers began communicating his group's results to Charch,
seeking Charch's expertise on matters of fibers and films.[15] Carothers' work convinced Charch more than ever of the need for the Pioneering Research Laboratory
to be undertaking research on synthetic polymers. But, as noted, change came
slowly. Unlike Benger, however, Charch remained in the Rayon Department.
Moreover, he continued to ask for permission to move beyond cellulose chemistry.
Yerkes and Gladding repeatedly denied his requests despite suggestions from the
vice-chairman of Du Pont's Board of Directors, Irénée du Pont, that Yerkes's
department broaden its horizons on textile research to include synthetics.[16]

In the fall of 1933, Charch vented his dissatisfaction in a long letter to his superior Gladding:

> In some ten years [of] rayon experience, we have in but two cases bent any part of our
> research program in a direction other than one relating directly to the most immediate
> manufacturing and selling problems. . . . In only one case have we pioneered in the field
> of new technical knowledge—otherwise we have been working within the classical tech-
> nology which is more or less known and generally available to all interested. . . . We ques-
> tion whether this policy has not become outgrown. Both rayon and cellophane have for
> practical purposes grown up. Unless we concede that there will be no radical departures
> in the synthetic fiber (or film) industry in the next ten years, then it must be concluded
> that our technical program falls short in its more radical and forward looking aspects.[17]

Charch sought more latitude. "Our ultimate objective," he suggested, "would
be to produce something new and unique in the fiber field which might represent
some basic new industry, such as for instance, the development of a wool substitute,
a fur substitute, or bristle substitutes, or special fibers for a multitude of industrial
uses."[18] All he needed to achieve these goals was permission and money to initiate
a broad-based, long-term research program on synthetic fibers. Once again, he was
rebuked.

Not even the discovery and development of nylon changed things immediately
in the Rayon Department. In fact, not until Gladding moved to a different position[19] and not until the Executive Committee forced Yerkes to broaden the department's research horizon—not until mid-1939—did Charch begin to gain the latitude that he had sought for more than a decade and that Pioneering later came to
enjoy and use so effectively to the company's benefit. In response to Executive
Committee pressure, Yerkes brought back Ernest Benger to head the Technical
Division of the Rayon Department and gave him a mandate: the "Technical Division is to be strengthened and built up to perform its research and experimental
duties in a more thorough, systematic [sic] and broader manner than has ever been
possible in the past."[20]

Even then, however, Charch had to struggle to realize the charter he sought for
Pioneering. The instant success of nylon led many in the department, especially

Yerkes, to see nylon as the be-all and end-all fiber. Consequently, they tried to keep Pioneering's work limited to the older products and nylon. In 1941, Charch asserted his belief that other synthetic polymers would wind up in the fibers market:

> We believe that it would be a gross mistake for any Pioneering-Nylon program to over-look the possibility of a competitive fiber from some other base than a polyamide. As a matter of fact, we consider vigilance along this line a major responsibility. . . . Potential fiber forming materials are being synthesized at a great rate and I think it can be stated with almost complete certainty that polyamide polymers are not the last super-polymers which the world is going to see in the form of threads and fibers. Therefore, in connection with a Pioneering-Nylon Program, we feel that we should have sufficient latitude to give attention to this competitive field . . . and to know something about the properties of other polymers which may be competitive with nylon. We ought to know what they will do in the form of threads, what their properties are, something about their spinnability and a lot of other things. It is work and vigilance along this line that we also have in mind to pursue under the broad exploratory project [being proposed].[21]

Climate for Invention in Pioneering Research under Charch

As the decade of the 1940s began to unfold, Charch's Pioneering Research Laboratory entered one of the most productive eras in the company's history, a time in which both the genius of individual inventors and the power of collective activities flowed forth. The critical factor in this transformation was the climate for invention that Charch established in his own laboratory even before the overall departmental climate changed for the better.

As early as 1933 Charch had suggested that the "development of a wool substitute, a fur substitute, or bristle substitutes, or special fibers for a multitude of industrial uses" were appropriate targets for his laboratory.[22] Charch always wanted his laboratory to invent and develop products for markets he perceived as potentially important. The case of a wool substitute provides an especially good example.

From the early 1930s, Charch closely followed the work of the Rayon Division's Fabric Development Section. In report after report, members of this section pointed out the critical need to build a more wool-like feel into fabrics made from the company's rayon fibers. Pioneering Laboratory researchers attempted to make a more wool-like fiber, although they were, as noted, limited to cellulose chemistry. However, even if they could have worked on synthetic polymers, they lacked some of the intellectual tools they needed to understand precisely what makes wool "woolly."

During the late 1930s Charch and his staff groped toward correlating "woolliness" in fibers and resilience. By the time World War II broke out, Charch had tumbled to the conclusion that the critical step in developing a wool substitute was to gain a fundamental understanding of wool's properties, particularly its resilience.

Yet the war prevented Charch from assigning researchers to tackle this problem. Not until very late in the war, when certain wartime restrictions on research projects were lifted, was he able to begin in earnest research on resilience. At this time, he wrote that "resilience is [the] key property to add to all crimp[ed] fibers" and concluded that "synthesizing specifically for resilience" was the key to entering the wool market with a synthetic.[23] The problem, of course, was that neither Charch nor anyone else knew in a fundamental way what resilience is and what makes wool possess woolliness. Du Pont's competitors were also seeking to develop wool-like fibers, and many of them spent considerable sums of money trying to make what Charch called a Chinese copy of wool.[24] That is, they tried to synthesize the natural wool polymer, or they tried to fabricate related polymers into the physical form of wool, crimped and complete with its microscopically visible scales.

In August of 1944, Charch lectured his fellow research directors in the Rayon Department's Technical Division about the need for great precision in property determination, including resilience. Quoting General Electric's Nobel Prize-winning physical chemist, Irving Langmuir, Charch said that "the progress of modern science depends largely upon (1) giving to words meanings as precise as possible; (2) definition of concepts in terms of operations; (3) development of models (mechanical or mathematical) which have properties analogous to those of the phenomena which we have observed."[25] Charch stressed that his laboratory would pursue the study of resilience in the manner prescribed by Langmuir.

During the next five years or so, Pioneering Research effected a profound understanding of fiber properties, thanks largely to the impressive efforts of R. M. Hoffman, L. F. Best, L. G. Ray, H. J. Kolb, C. E. Black, and Andrew Pace, among many others (almost all of whom were physical chemists). Hoffman's recognition of the critical role of the time element in determining fiber behavior was especially noteworthy. Pioneering's intensive resiliency studies yielded enormous results. Resilience did prove to be the principal factor in imparting woolliness to wool, and importantly, it was something that could be identified and indeed built into a wholly synthetic fiber. Moreover, additional studies equipped Pioneering with the powerful tool of being able to predict fabric properties based on data of individual fiber properties and eventually to deduce fiber behavior from knowledge of polymer structure.[26] The importance of this work cannot be overemphasized if we are to understand the inventive activities of Pioneering Research Laboratory personnel in the 1940s and beyond.[27]

The Rayon Department's development of Orlon acrylic and Dacron polyester fibers rested squarely on Charch's desire to develop a wool-like fiber and on the Pioneering Research Laboratory's resiliency studies, polymer structure/fiber property research, fiber spinning and drawing capabilities, and general scientific and technical know-how. The history of these two fibers suggests how we might look at "invention" in a broader light than is customarily done and begin to see invention as a process involving actors who do not necessarily perceive what is being created in the same way, thereby producing very different views of what has been "invented."

Orlon Acrylic Fiber

Orlon emerged from Pioneering researcher Ray Houtz's 1941 discovery of how to spin polyacrylonitrile into a fiber possessing a high melting point and good chemical stability. Houtz made his discovery while carrying out a research program that had been formulated by Hale Charch to improve the wet strength and resilience of rayon—part of his wool-like fiber campaign. Charch had observed the outstanding tensile properties of partially oriented polyvinyl alcohol films and initiated a search for vinyl polymers with which to work. He and Houtz chose polyacrylonitrile because of the potentially low cost of its intermediates and because of its resistance to degradation by heat. Houtz pursued several ways to use it to improve rayon's resilience, including trying to cross-link rayon and polyacrylonitrile molecules and polymerizing acrylonitrile in situ in rayon fibers. Soon, however, he became convinced that polyacrylonitrile by itself might be spun into the much-sought-after resilient fiber.

Polyacrylonitrile, a polymer first synthesized by Herman Mark in the late 1920s, is a highly intractable substance. It does not melt; rather, it simply falls apart at a specific temperature. Moreover, chemists knew of no solvents that would dissolve the polymer and then leave it tractable when the solvent evaporated. Houtz's contribution to Orlon's development was to find such a solvent and then spin the polymer solution into a fiber that possessed some interesting properties depending on how highly the molecules were oriented (i.e., depending on the extent to which the fibers were cold-drawn).[28]

Houtz demonstrated that when left undrawn or only slightly drawn, polyacrylonitrile fibers possessed wool-like properties (as imperfectly as those properties were understood in 1941). When drawn more—six to ten times their length when spun—the fibers looked and felt like silk. Houtz had, in effect, "invented" a wool-like fiber and a silklike fiber. Subsequent study and testing of the fiber produced yet another conception of it: fibers with moderate draw ratios possessed excellent resistance to light, chemicals, and bacteria. These fibers had no counterparts in nature.

During the next ten years, managers in the Rayon Department battled, sometimes vehemently, over the development program for these three very different polyacrylonitrile "inventions." Space constraints prohibit even the barest outline of this struggle. The important element in this drama, however, was Hale Charch's steadfast conviction that polyacrylonitrile was an almost-ideal wool substitute if it were produced in a crimped staple form with no or low draw ratios.[29] Indeed, Charch's convictions grew ever stronger as his researchers' resiliency studies and fiber characterization/fabric properties studies yielded highly useful tools for fiber analysis. For a long time, Charch's superiors were so keen on other development paths for the fiber that he was essentially forced to take his wool-substitute program underground. Only when the market rejected the other forms of the fiber, as developed in other Rayon Department laboratories, did the department's top managers listen to Charch. As he had written earlier, "the idea of this Fiber A [the code name for Orlon] staple has been slow to soak into people's heads, I think largely because our idea of 'staple' is a 25¢-per-pound product of the viscose rayon type. We have overlooked the unique properties of Fiber A as a curly staple which would bring it into the very high price wool field such as vicuna, cashmere, and a lot of fancy wools selling for upwards of $5.00 per pound, and some even higher."[30]

Orlon succeeded as a product when made into wool-like, crimped staple, which could be blended with wool for suiting material or used alone in knitted wear like socks and sweaters. Particularly in this latter market Orlon's economic performance was outstanding, and by the mid-1960s it was the third leading earner for the Du Pont Company as a whole.[31]

Dacron Polyester Fiber

The history of Dacron polyester fiber development parallels that of Orlon to a remarkable degree. Polyethylene terephthalate (commonly known as polyester) fiber was the discovery (in 1940) of two British chemists employed by the Calico Printers Association.[32] The emergency conditions surrounding World War II severed Du Pont's normal information channels, but in 1944 Pioneering researchers learned secondhand that the British were at work on a fiber called Terylene. A consultant to Du Pont, Herman Mark, told them that the mystery fiber's very name and the fact that it could be melt-spun suggested what it was made from. With this information, Pioneering researcher Emmette Izard synthesized polyester terephthalate and spun it into a fiber with attractive properties.[33] Those attractive properties, however, were obvious only to those who knew what they were looking for. As Pasteur once said, chance favors the prepared mind.

Once again, Pioneering's resiliency studies allowed the laboratory to recognize quickly that polyester could be spun and drawn in such a way as to achieve a highly resilient fiber. Charch rapidly concluded that his laboratory could develop an ideal wool-like synthetic out of polyester. Seeing close parallels in X-ray diffraction patterns between wool and Fiber V (as the new fiber was code-named in those days), Pioneering researchers stressed that "we have not yet begun to scratch the surface of making yarn properties to ordered specifications."[34] Pioneering researchers learned that the properties of polyester fibers could be manipulated almost at will by not only changing the molecular weight of the polymer and the draw ratios of spun fibers but also by varying the shape of the cross section of the fibers and by altering their morphology through such techniques as applying air or steam to polyester filaments as they emerged from the spinneret. As the laboratory gained experience in modifying the characteristics of polyester fibers, this knowledge was fed back into its Orlon work and contributed substantially to Charch's efforts to make Orlon a wool substitute.[35] His goals for Orlon did not, however, deter him from his conviction that polyester could also become an ideal wool substitute because one could easily build resilience into the polyester fiber.

But once again, Charch's superiors ignored his ideas about how polyester should first be developed. Over strenuous objections by Charch, the department's managers decided that polyester would first be a tire cord. These men were attracted by polyester's high tenacity and modulus (measures of strength and stiffness, respectively), and they ordered the Technical Division's Nylon Research Section to shut down all work on nylon tire cord as soon as possible to devote all its time to polyester tire cord. Within a year, however, this strategy failed. Initial and subsequent tests of polyester-reinforced tires made by the rubber companies showed that much more research would have to be done on the fiber.[36] Only then did management listen to Charch. Skeptics remained, however. Not until about 1948 did the power of Pioneering's resiliency studies become evident to the department's Development Section. By this time, Church was running his own development program, geared to developing a wool-like polyester, in conjunction with the Lowell Textile Institute, which possessed woolen and worsted machinery and expertise not available in the Du Pont Company. Ultimately, Church's strong views of polyester as a highly resilient fiber became the basis for Du Pont's great success with Dacron polyester fiber, which was commercialized in 1953.[37]

Even with the significant success of Dacron, Church was always haunted by the fact that Du Pont had to license Terylene from the British in order to commercialize Dacron. He believed that the Pioneering Laboratory never received the recognition it deserved for making polyester into a successful commercial product long before the British. As he wrote in 1952, "Dacron's position in the textile world is largely the result of the wool-like properties that were deliberately built into it. In this form there is no conflict whatsoever with British findings or discoveries. The wool-like form and processes therefore are a 100% Du Pont contribution."[38]

"Inventing" a New Fiber

Did the "invention" of acrylic and polyester fibers occur at the moment that their base polymers were first synthesized and spun into filaments? Emphatically not. In both instances the products that ultimately emerged from the Pioneering Research Laboratory and that were eventually introduced commercially had literally to be "constructed" within the laboratory itself.[39] The process of constructing these two important fibers was mediated by Hale Church's single-minded pursuit of a wool-like artificial fiber—that is, a fiber possessing many of the same physical properties as, and to a more limited extent some of the same appearance as, wool (i.e., a fiber that could perform like wool). Church's support for fundamental research projects aimed at understanding such questions as what made wool woolly and the relationships between polymer structure and fiber properties and between fiber properties and fabric qualities provided the Pioneering Research Laboratory with the tools to carry out its construction of wool-like fibers. Lacking these basic tools, the laboratory would almost certainly have failed in its attempt to invent wool-like fibers. Pioneering's versions of Orlon and Dacron were not the only acrylic and polyester fibers ever made by Du Pont. Indeed, with Dacron polyester, the company now makes literally dozens of types of products. But the commercially successful large-scale manufacture of both fibers rested initially on Church's unaltered conviction that crimped acrylic and polyester fibers possessing resilience comparable to wool's would sell well in staple form.

1948: Pioneering Studies the Future

In 1948, even before Orlon and Dacron were commercialized, Hale Church led the Technical Division in a study of the future. This study grew out of the stock-taking that the various research managers had carried out on the occasion of the Technical

Division's twenty-fifth anniversary. Looking at the Rayon Department's current and anticipated product line, these research directors concluded that comparatively low profitability in the rayon and cellulose acetate businesses made it impossible to justify any further expenditures for research and development on these cellulosic fibers. In fact, these research directors were so bold as to urge management to withdraw immediately from their manufacture. The future, they argued, lay in synthetics like nylon, acrylics, and polyesters.[40]

Church argued that Du Pont was but at the beginning of a "synthetic textile revolution" and that with greater fundamental knowledge of fibers and fiber properties, it could dramatically expand the revolution. "As our basic knowledge of fiber properties is enlarged," he stressed, "we are truly approaching the time when we can deliver fibers to predetermined specifications. This can only mean greater and greater diversification in the uses for synthetics which, in turn, means ever broader market opportunities."[41]

Earlier, Church had asked the Pioneering staff, from his assistant director down to the laboratory's clerical workers, to describe the future ten, fifteen, and even twenty-five years out. What role would fibers play in that future?, he asked them to contemplate. What would fibers look and feel like? Where would they be used?[42] Such questions and the answers submitted to him allowed Church to address the future and Pioneering Research's specific role in it in a full staff meeting.

Church opened his presentation by giving his view of Pioneering's place in the department. He maintained that Pioneering's function was unique and thus far different from the industrial research sections. Pioneering possessed great freedom in that its programs encompassed the "whole field outside" the areas covered by the industrial research sections. Pioneering could design its own programs and not be tied down "by *current* economics, sales needs, [or] process troubles." Rather, Pioneering always had to look to the future ten to twenty years hence. "If we know our objective and function," said Church, "we should know better where to work than management." Such freedom, he argued, carried responsibilities. "We must produce," he said:

> We do not exist for ourselves—but [we] must see that our produce is bro[ugh]t to [the] attention of others. Pioneering must never become ingrown or become an end in itself. [Pioneering] must exist for broader purposes. In [the] last analysis, we ourselves can do nothing about any of our discoveries. This emphasizes [the] necessity for spreading and opening our results freely all over the Co[mpany] to see that they reach others and do not fall through [the] cracks.[43]

What did Pioneering actually produce?, asked Church rhetorically. Four things, he answered: new polymers, new processes, new products, and fundamental knowledge, "which will help lead to discoveries."[44] During 1948 and subsequent years Church outlined for his staff what kinds of new products they should be striving for. He argued that developing another really big-tonnage fiber like nylon, Orlon, and Dacron would be very difficult, so he suggested that emphasis be placed on the development of what would later be termed specialty fibers.[45] Unlike nylon, Orlon, and Dacron, these projected specialty fibers would be aimed not at duplicating the properties of natural fibers but transcending them. In particular, Church saw the need for an elastomeric fiber that would be superior to cotton-covered rubber elastic; for fibers that would perform in high-temperature environments and that would even be flame resistant; for fibers that would be very high strength; for synthetic leather; for synthetic paper; and for entirely nonwoven fabrics. Such products would come about only through application of the correct pioneering research formula, he argued.[46]

Charch steadfastly resisted a powerful movement within the Du Pont Company at this time, which was to emphasize the primacy of fundamental research. Under another leader, Pioneering Research could easily have become devoted almost exclusively to fundamental research and isolated from the long-term market considerations that had driven the organization.

Charch was a believer in fundamental research, but he stoutly resisted the idea of turning Pioneering into an exclusively fundamental research laboratory. In fact, given the new corporate culture of the early 1950s, Charch had constantly to remind others outside his organization that Pioneering was not just a house full of starry-eyed scientists doing only fundamental research. With the world needing such things as synthetic fibers with improved properties, Pioneering could not afford to devote itself entirely to fundamental research. Rather, Charch sought a balance of approaches to R&D, including fundamental research, scouting, problem-solving, and development of discoveries.[47]

This, then, was the climate for invention that Hale Charch had firmly established in Pioneering Research in the late 1940s and early 1950s. When the Pioneering Research Laboratory moved from Buffalo into its new, spacious facilities at the Experimental Station in Wilmington in 1950, its researchers could not have hoped for a better situation. With major achievements under its belt, with excellent resources, with growing sophistication in understanding fiber properties and their correlation with both polymer structure and fabric performance, with rapidly mounting expertise in polymer chemistry, and with leadership that had clearly articulated major targets at which to aim yet allowed ample freedom to pursue new ideas, the Pioneering Research section was poised for one of the most productive eras in its history. This was the context in which distinguished chemist inventors, such as Dr. Paul Morgan, worked and flourished. This was the context in which what might have appeared as a small discovery in some laboratories became the basis for the invention and development of major products—products like Kevlar and Nomex aramid fibers. Here I am alluding specifically to the 1950 discovery of what became known as low-temperature, interfacial polycondensation. Discussed at greater length in Morgan's chapter in this volume (Chapter 10), this discovery and those that followed from it opened up the possibility of synthesizing literally tens of thousands of new polymers that were impossible to prepare using existing polymerization techniques. Under Charch's management, this discovery was pursued at many levels, which together proved to be critical to the laboratory's success. These levels included seeking to understand in a fundamental way the observed phenomena, synthesizing polymers to achieve specifically targeted fiber objectives, trying to apply low-temperature polycondensation techniques to the manufacture of existing products, and attempting to broaden and simplify the new polymerization method.[48] Throughout this whole process, the targets that Charch had so clearly laid out in 1948 mediated the creative energies of the Pioneering Research Laboratory staff; from this process emerged products like Lycra spandex fiber, Nomex high-temperature aramid fibers and papers, and Kevlar high-strength, high-temperature aramid fiber. As Church told his staff in 1948 when they were charting the future in Pioneering and in the world of synthetic fibers, "If you go hunting for small game, you don't shoot elephants."[49]

Conclusions

So what does this case add up to? Was invention in the Pioneering Research Laboratory an individual act or, rather, a collective process? I believe that there was something of both in this case, a position that is not very different from the general theory of invention that the economic historian Abbott Payson Usher articulated in his chapter on "The Emergence of Novelty in Thought and Action" in his *History of Mechanical Inventions* (2nd ed. 1954, pp. 56–83). Usher was loath to accept what he termed the "transcendentalist position" that all invention is an "inspiration of genius" or the "mechanistic determinism of the sociologic theories" that stresses the necessity of invention, thereby minimizing or negating "the significance of individual effort and achievement" (pp. 60–61).

Addressing the strengths and weaknesses of both positions, Usher offered what he called a gestalt psychology-inspired model of invention that possessed a "genetic sequence" of four steps:

1. *Perception of a problem,* in which "an incomplete or unsatisfactory pattern" in need of resolution is recognized
2. *Setting the stage,* in which "all data essential to a solution" is found either through "pure chance" or "the mediated contingency of a systematic effort to find a solution by trial and error"
3. *Act of insight,* "by which the essential solution of the problem is found"
4. *Critical revision,* in which a solution is fully explored and revised and even open to new acts of insight (Usher, 1954, p. 65).

As argued above, the director of Pioneering Research, Hale Church, perceived a problem in the 1930s—how to attain rayon that would exhibit wool-like properties in woven and knitted goods. His department's marketing personnel presented him with this problem because "the market" (i.e., Du Pont's customers, who were textile manufacturers) told them this is what they needed. Church's individual contribution, among his other contributions at this stage, was to communicate this problem throughout his entire organization (in the words of cognitive psychologists, to provide his organization with a heuristic). Indeed, throughout the second half of the 1930s and the entire decade of the 1940s, Church preached a gospel of woolliness. He preached as passionately in the period after 1948 about the need to develop fibers that had no counterparts in nature—fibers with radically superior strength, fibers that are fire retardant, high-temperature fibers, and so on. In this later period, Church's problem identification seems to have possessed a more entrepreneurial than organizational flavor.

The second step of invention in Pioneering Research—setting the stage—was a far more complex process than Usher probably ever anticipated. Moreover, it was a *collective* process punctuated all along by individual acts of insight. Pioneering's researchers struggled to find a solution to the problem of making rayon more wool-like but were largely unsuccessful in spite of knowing a lot about cellulose chemistry. Nevertheless, in their quest, they posed the critical question of what made wool wool-like. Fundamental research on wool itself did not ensure an answer. But through a process of abstraction, they identified resiliency as the critical factor in wool's performance in a woven fabric—as the key property to build into an artificial fiber. Here, of course, was a major act of insight. But even then, the researchers had to correlate perceived resiliency in a fiber with real properties. They had to develop a general model of fiber resiliency—no small feat because it required many years of work by chemists and physicists with very good minds. Thus the boundaries between Usher's second and third steps are not so distinct in this instance; the process was far more fluid than lockstep. Pioneering's researchers had to develop many tools before the ultimate problem could be solved, and many acts of insight, both collective and individual, were necessary before they could be developed.

Even after Pioneering's researchers had worked out their brilliant resiliency model and had gone beyond it to correlate the structure of polymers with their performance in woven fabrics (yielding a more rational process for fiber development), Pioneering would never have succeeded in solving their original problem (a wool-like rayon) because that problem space was too narrowly bounded to find an adequate solution. Had Pioneering Research's problem space continued to be restricted to cellulosic chemistry (as Charch's superiors had wanted), the laboratory would have fallen well short of its goals. Only through external pressure—a contingency in Usher's view—was the laboratory able to explore a larger problem space (synthetic polymers) in which solutions, such as Orlon acrylic and Dacron polyester fibers, could be found.

Yet, as noted, wool-like Orlon and Dacron were not "discovered." They were really "invented" or "constructed." Charch's superiors believed that polyacrylonitrile and polyester possessed properties that made them more suitable for other applications. But Charch, working within a gestalt or frame of wool substitution, pushed his researchers to bring out fully the woolliness in these new fibers. Eventually he succeeded in convincing those above him that Orlon and Dacron should be commercialized as resilient fibers that could be substituted for wool (and in the case of Dacron, for cotton as well). Proponents of the Usher model might describe these events as critical revision, but this term is probably inadequate to capture fully the Orlon and Dacron stories.

Pioneering Research Laboratory's history during this period suggests very strongly that invention can be a collective process. But it also underlines the importance of individuals from the bench level (such as Ray Houtz, who decided to try to spin polyacrylonitrile by itself instead of cross-linking it with rayon, or Paul Morgan, who advanced the art of low-temperature polycondensation and laid out synthesis roots to important products) to the head of the research organization. Hale Charch played a critical role in the invention of the products mentioned in this chapter by identifying and communicating problems to his researchers. Problem selection is no easy matter. The best entrepreneurs, it seems, always choose the best problems, and Charch was among them. He also kept his researchers' work focused on the solution to the problems he had identified. Finally, he served both as cheerleader and integrator of his staff's ideas.

Thus, with modifications and qualifications, the Usher model can be useful in understanding invention in the industrial research laboratory.[50] As Usher argued, the four-step process of cumulative synthesis allows room for individual acts of genius and collective processes as well, an account of invention that is certainly required when discussing the inventive fruits of industrial research and development laboratories.

Invention in an industrial research laboratory is seldom a discrete moment; it is a process. Invention is dependent on establishing the right kind of environment in which creativity can flourish—in which problems can be recognized and then pursued both individually and collectively.

Notes

1. These facilities included the Pioneering Research Laboratory and the Nylon Research Laboratory, located at Du Pont's Experimental Station in Wilmington; the Textile Research Laboratory at the company's Chestnut Run research complex in Wilmington; the Christina Laboratory near the Port of Wilmington; the Acetate and Orlon Research Laboratory in Waynesboro, Virginia; and the Dacron Research Laboratory in Kinston, North Carolina. From its creation in 1928 until 1950, the Pioneering Research Laboratory was located in Buffalo, New York.

2. For more information on the establishment and subsequent history of the Du Pont Fibersilk Company, see David A. Hounshell and John Kenly Smith, Jr., *Science and Corporate Strategy: Du Pont R&D, 1902–1980* (New York: Cambridge University Press, 1988), pp. 161–182. Research personnel figures are from page 290 in this book.

3. Minutes of the Board of Directors, Du Pont Rayon Company, November 15, 1927, reproduced in Marian C. Lepper to Alma O. Cohn, "Pioneering Research on Rayon," April 17, 1930, Records of E. I. du Pont de Nemours & Co., Textile Fibers Department, Pioneering Research Laboratory, Hagley Museum and Library, Wilmington, Delaware. This collection of records is hereafter cited as Pioneering Research Records.

4. Minutes of the Board of Directors, 1927. The R&D budget figure is for both rayon and cellophane research. See Hounshell and Smith, *Science and Corporate Strategy*, 1988, p. 288.

5. E. B. Benger to E. K. Gladding, January 24, 1928, Records of E. I. du Pont de Nemours & Co., Series II, Part 4, Box 98, and E. B. Benger to Hamilton Bradshaw, February 21, 1928, Accession 1784, Records of E. I. du Pont de Nemours & Co., Central Research and Development Department, Hagley Museum and Library, Wilmington, Delaware.

6. Robert E. Ellsworth, Personality: W. Hale Charch, *Modern Textiles Magazine, 34* (July 1953), 44.

7. See Hounshell and Smith, *Science and Corporate Strategy*, 1988, pp. 174–176, for a discussion of moisture-proof cellophane.

8. Ernest B. Benger to J. E. Hatt, July 18, 1928, Pioneering Research Records, File P-1, 1926–1927 (see Note 3).

9. Ernest B. Benger to Ernest K. Gladding, May 16, 1930, Pioneering Research Records, File P-3, 1930. W. H. Charch to E. K. Gladding, May 19, 1930, Pioneering Research Records, File P-3, 1930 (see Note 3).

10. Ernest B. Benger to Hamilton Bradshaw, January 28, 1930, Accession 1784 (see Note 5).

11. For more information on Cordura's development, see Hounshell and Smith, *Science and Corporate Strategy,* 1988, pp. 167–169.

12. Samuel Hollander, *The Sources of Increased Efficiency* (Cambridge, Mass.: MIT Press, 1965).

13. In 1934, for legal reasons, the Du Pont Company converted its wholly owned Du Pont Rayon and Cellophane companies into the Rayon Department of the Du Pont Company.

14. For more information about the discovery of nylon, see Hounshell and Smith, *Science and Corporate Strategy,* 1988, pp. 221–248.

15. See, for example, W. H. Charch, "Review of Dr. Carothers' Rough Draft of Patent Application on Fibers From Synthetic Polyesters (Carothers Case 5)," October 24, 1930, Pioneering Research Records, File P-3, 1930, and W. H. Charch to W. H. Carothers, October 24, 1930, Pioneering Research Records, File P-1, 1930 (see Note 3).

16. See, for example, Walter S. Carpenter to L. A. Yerkes, November 5, 1930, Records of E. I. du Pont de Nemours & Co. Series II, Part 2, Box 818 (see Note 5).

17. W. H. Charch to E. K. Gladding, "Discussion of Basic Study for New Fibers, Fiber Materials, and Solutions," September 21, 1933, Pioneering Research Records, File P-9, 1933 (see Note 3).

18. W. H. Charch to E. K. Gladding, September 21, 1933, Pioneering Research Records, File P-9, 1933 (see Note 3).

19. Ironically, executives selected Gladding to head the newly created Nylon Division of the Rayon Department!

20. Maurice du Pont Lee to G. P. Hoff, July 7, 1939, Records of E. I. du Pont de Nemours & Co., Series II, Part 2, Box 963 (see Note 5).

21. W. Hale Charch to G. P. Hoff, August 7, 1941, Pioneering Research Records, Box 110195 (see Note 3).

22. W. H. Charch to E. K. Gladding, September 21, 1933, Pioneering Research Records, File P-9, 1933 (see Note 3).

23. W. H. Charch, "For File PD-1," March 1944, Pioneering Research Records, Box 180177 (see Note 3).

24. W. H. Charch, marginal notation on H. J. Kolb, "Resilience Program," November 13, 1946, Pioneering Research Records, Box 180184 (see Note 3).

25. W. H. Charch to G. W. Filson, August 4, 1944, Pioneering Research Records, Box 180177 (see Note 3).

26. These studies were also important because they lowered fiber development costs. At a time when chemists were synthesizing an increasing number of polymers, each of which had to be screened for its potential as a commercial fiber, the resiliency and polymer structure/fiber property studies carried out by Pioneering Research provided its researchers with the tools to weed out quickly many new polymers without having to go through the very expensive process of making a lot of polymer, spinning it into fibers, weaving the fibers into cloth, and only then evaluating its performance.

27. In 1951, when Charch proposed awarding financial bonuses to the researchers who had successfully conducted the fundamental research on resiliency mapping, he stressed that his laboratory's efforts to build resiliency into fibers had been "fruitless" and "unprofitable" until these resiliency theories had been developed. W. H. Charch to Lester Sinness, July 3, 1951, Pioneering Research Laboratory History Files, Du Pont Experimental Station, Wilmington, Delaware. For more information on the laboratory's research on resiliency, see Hounshell and Smith, *Science and Corporate Strategy,* 1988, pp. 392–394.

28. Houtz's success owed something to the suggestion made by one of Du Pont's consultants, Carl Marvel of the University of Illinois, to try dimethylacetamide as a solvent. Also, Houtz later learned that G. H. Latham of Du Pont's Central Research Department had demonstrated how polyacrylonitrile could be dissolved in dimethylformamide, the solvent that Houtz had finally succeeded with.

29. Du Pont was manufacturing rayon in both continuous filament and staple forms. Charch believed that the new fiber could best serve as a wool substitute if manufactured with a crimp and cut in lengths comparable to wool staple.

30. W. H. Charch to R. M. Horsey, May 24, 1944, Pioneering Research Records, Box 180179 (see Note 3).

31. The *development* of Orlon (as distinct from its *invention*) posed some severe and interesting problems for the Textile Fibers Department. For a fuller treatment of this history, see Hounshell and Smith, *Science and Corporate Strategy,* 1988, pp. 394–407.

32. For two accounts of polyester's discovery by one of its discoverers, see J. R. Whinfield, "Textile Fibers: Variations on Some Familiar Themes," *Chemistry and Industry,* March 14, 1953, 226–229; J. R. Whinfield, "The Development of Terylene," *Textile Research Journal, 23* (May 1953), 289–293.

33. Prior to the news from Herman Mark, Du Pont's researchers had developed a mind set, based on Wallace Carothers' work going back to 1930, that any polyester would have a low melting temperature and would easily hydrolyze (i.e., fall apart in the presence of water). For more information on this mind set, see Hounshell and Smith, *Science and Corporate Strategy,* 1988, pp. 407–411.

34. This statement derives from either a monthly or quarterly report from W. H. Charch to E. B. Benger, July 24, 1946, which is quoted in *History of Fiber V in Pioneering Research,* typescript compiled by R. M. Hoffman and edited by W. H. Charch, in Pioneering Research Laboratory History Files, p. 33, Experimental Station, Wilmington.

35. See Charch's comments on this process of feeding information gained from manipulation of polyester's properties into the Orlon project in *History of Fiber V,* Pioneering Research Laboratory History Files, p. 24 (see Note 34).

36. The primary problem with using polyester as a tire cord was lack of a good adhesive owing to the fiber's extreme hydrophobic nature. Consequently polyester-reinforced tires suffered problems of ply separation.

37. For more information on the development of this fiber, see Hounshell and Smith, *Science and Corporate Strategy,* 1988, pp. 407–420.

38. Comment of W. H. Charch, in *History of Fiber V,* Pioneering Research, Laboratory History Files, p. 23 (see Note 34).

39. Here the reader should contrast my use of the word *construct* with that of the social constructionists as represented in Wiebe E. Bijker et al., *The Social Construction of Technological Systems* (Cambridge, Mass.: MIT Press, 1987). See in particular the essay by Trevor J. Pinch and Wiebe E. Bijker, "The social construction of facts and artifacts: Or how the sociology of science and the sociology of technology might benefit each other, pp. 17–50.

40. On the research managers' desire for Du Pont to pull out of cellulosic fibers manufacture, see Hounshell and Smith, *Science and Corporate Strategy,* 1988, pp. 421–422.

41. W. H. Charch to W. W. Heckert, October 27, 1948, Pioneering Research Records, Box 180187. See also Charch to A. E. Buchanan et al., "Research and the Future," January 14, 1948, Pioneering Research Laboratory Library Authors' Files, Du Pont Experimental Station, and Minutes of Special Staff Meeting, January 16, 1948, Pioneering Research Records, Box 180187 (see Note 3).

42. See F. K. Signaigo, "The Future," August 15, 1947, Pioneering Research Records, Box 180185 (see Note 3).

43. W. H. Charch, notes of presentation to Pioneering Research Laboratory staff, January 1948, in Pioneering Research Laboratory Library Authors' Files, Experimental Station, Wilmington.

44. W. H. Charch, notes of presentation, January 1948, in Pioneering Research Laboratory Library Authors' Files, Experimental Station, Wilmington.

45. W. H. Charch, miscellaneous notes on fundamental research, Pioneering Research Laboratory Library Authors' Files, Experimental Station, Wilmington.

46. Charch consistently made these arguments in his presentations to his staff and to other Technical Division research directors, as is well documented in his notes, which are located in the Authors' File, Pioneering Research Laboratory Library, Experimental Station, Wilmington.

47. Throughout the late 1940s and early 1950s, Charch offered a consistent agenda for research work in Pioneering while maintaining that the various approaches to research had to be balanced. His most fully developed statement about fundamental research is W. H. Charch to G. D. Graves, "Basic Research," March 22, 1957, Pioneering Research Records, Box 191130 (see Note 3).

48. For a more extensive discussion of the discovery and development of low-temperature polycondensation methods and products at Pioneering, see Hounshell and Smith, *Science and Corporate Strategy,* 1988, pp. 425–432.

49. Charch, notes of presentation, January 1948, in Pioneering Research Laboratory Library Authors' Files, Experimental Station, Wilmington.

50. I would also suggest that George Basalla's discussion of the continuity of artifacts in his book, *The Evolution of Technology* (New York: Cambridge University Press, 1988), is applicable to any discussion of invention in industrial research and development laboratories.

Bibliography

Basalla, G. (1988). *The Evolution of Technology.* New York: Cambridge Univ. Press.

Bijker, W. E., et al. (1987). *The Social Construction of Technological Systems.* Cambridge, Mass.: MIT Press.

Ellsworth, R. E. (1953). Personality: W. Hale Charch. *Modern Textiles Magazine, 34* (July), 44.

Hollander, S. (1965). *Sources of Increased Efficiency.* Cambridge, Mass.: MIT Press.

Hounshell, D. A. & Smith, J. K., Jr. (1988). *Science and Corporate Strategy: Du Pont R&D, 1902–1980.* New York: Cambridge Univ. Press.

Usher, A. P. (1954). *The History of Mechanical Inventions.* Cambridge, Mass.: Harvard Univ. Press.

Whinfield, J. R. (1953). Textile fibers: variations on some familiar themes. *Chemistry and Industry,* March 14, 226–229.

Whinfield, J. R. (1953). The development of Terylene. *Textile Research Journal, 23* (May), 289–293.

16 | Inventors and Corporations in the Maturing Electrical Industry, 1890-1940

GEORGE WISE

It was the wedding of the year in Cleveland in 1929, but not for the usual reasons. On the full page in the Sunday supplement devoted to the marriage of Charles Young and Esther Christensen, the pictures of the fathers were bigger than those of the newlyweds.

Charles' father, Owen D. Young, was chairman of the board of General Electric, a renowned "industrial statesman" who had just led the U.S. delegation that had negotiated an apparently definitive settlement of the vexing World War I debt issue. The feat would help make him *Time* magazine's "Man of the Year" and a strong dark-horse candidate for the 1932 Democratic presidential nomination (Case & Case, 1982). Esther's father, Niels Anton Christensen, was a well-known inventor. He was on his way to becoming a great inventor, if you are willing to define that term as someone who *twice* in his life invents the world's best way to do something important. Thirty years earlier he had invented the best way to stop streetcars. Three years after the wedding, the father of the bride would become the father of the O-ring.

The term *O-ring* refers not just to the donut of hard rubber itself, which had been around long before Christensen. It refers to putting that rubber donut in a square-sided groove with length greater than, and width slightly less than, the ring's cross-sectional diameter (Figure 16.1). O-rings serve many purposes, most notably as seals for pistons sliding in a cylinder under the pressure of a fluid. That combination, which Christensen patented, ranks with the safety pin, paper clip, and zipper on the short list of humankind's simplest, most useful, most ubiquitous, and most elegant inventions. There are dozens of O-rings in every home and car, and they have been applied to everything from fountain pens and soap dispensers to hydraulic presses and bomb-bay doors. Total usage measures in the billions. In 1986, their misapplication in the space shuttle Challenger contributed to a tragedy and focused national attention on this essential element in modern industrial life.

The Sunday supplement headline caught yet another side of the wedding: "Law Suit Bride's Introduction to Electrical World" (*Milwaukee Journal*, 21 June 1929). For Niels Christensen was nearing the end of a twenty-five-year pursuit of one of

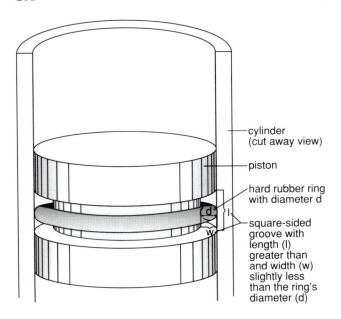

FIGURE 16.1. O-ring seal.

those drawn-out patent infringement suits that regularly bedevil the U.S. patent system. "Like the famous Jarndyce versus Jarndyce (in Charles Dickens's novel *Bleak House*), the suit seems to go on forever" the newspaper noted. The case had already outlived one judge, gone through three appeals, and was now before the Supreme Court. Its motif was classic. On one side, an immigrant inventor who had made good by inventing a superior electric railway braking system. On the other, the people whom, he claimed, had illegally used and gained the financial payoff from his invention: the business giants of the electrical industry, of which Owen D. Young was a prominent representative.

Christensen's quarrel was more directly with Westinghouse than with GE. But, more generally, his quarrel was with the system that Young personified: a system of giant corporations working hand in hand with big government as stewards of the "balanced best interest" of consumers, shareholders, workers, and citizens. In 1929, in defense of his first major invention, Christensen was embattled with the big business side of that combine. In the 1940s, in defense of the O-ring patent, he would take on the big government side. His battles would dramatically illuminate an important aspect of national technology policy: the role of the independent inventor in a world of giant institutions. It was widely assumed during Christensen's lifetime that first big business and then big government were taking over the job of technological innovation from the independent inventor. But was that actually possible or desirable? Did the giants offer the superior technical skill of armies of employed engineers and scientists, or just the financial power to take over, copy, or appropriate the work of those independents?

Independents such as Christensen often needed to work with giant private and public institutions. Yet they found it difficult to do so without losing control of both their inventions and the right to profit from them. On their side, the institutions found that even their growing complex of laboratories and their giant engineering forces needed the stimulus of the new ideas that often only the independents seemed able to provide. Yet corporate and government officials often found the independents stubborn, egotistical, and unwilling to make practical compromises. The tension that resulted could wear down and discourage the independent; but it also could become a spur to further invention.

No single inventor's story is typical: after all, invention means transcending the typical. But Christensen's story can serve as a framework for looking at the role of the independent-minded inventor in the maturing electrical industry: roughly speaking, from the emergence of the modern giant industrial corporation in the 1890s to the Second World War, when government accelerated its role as a prime supporter of advanced technical work in the United States.

The focus here will not be on the mental processes of the inventor, but on the external conditions encouraging or constraining the exercise of those processes. A spectrum of inventors contributed to the electrical industry in that era, some remaining independent, some becoming corporate employees. Consider a sample of five, each of whom was born in the 1860s and continued his professional career into the twentieth century: on the independent wing, Christensen, who battled corporations, and Elmer Sperry, who retained his independence and launched a corporation of his own that eventually became a giant; on the corporate employee wing, Charles P. Steinmetz, and William LeRoy Emmet, leading General Electric inventors in the areas of alternating current electricity and power generation; square in the middle, William Stanley, who helped create both the Westinghouse Electric and Manufacturing Company and GE's electric power business, and also battled both corporations (Emmet, 1940; Hughes, 1989; Kline, 1989; Passer, 1953; Wise, 1988, 1989).

These men, and others like them, represented a spectrum, not an opposition. The "outside" inventors were more dependent on, and the "inside" inventors were more independent of, corporate policies and choices than previous accounts have depicted. Their choice of targets, the marshalling of support, the use of resources and information, differed in degree, not in kind. The era when corporations matured left vacuums within the organization that insiders exploited. At the same time, tactics apparently aimed at suppressing progress in fact promoted progress by driving outsiders toward fruitful new areas where they could once again pioneer.

This approach helps reconcile two lines of historical inquiry that have added greatly to understanding of the climate for invention. One line, pursued by such diverse scholars as Alfred D. Chandler (1982) and David Noble (1979), emphasizes the ability of the corporation to replicate within its organization the institutions that previously had remained outside: marketing, apprenticeship, information gathering, and research, for example. Chandler updated Adam Smith, describing how the "visible hand" of managerial coordination replaced the invisible hand of the market. This opened up the possibility of institutionalizing invention itself. The corporation, argued Noble, could control technology and therefore its future, and in the process supersede the independent inventor as the principal source of new technology.

Yet even before Chandler and Noble wrote, the economists Jewkes, Sawyers, and Stillerman had shown in their classic work *The Sources of Invention* (1969) that this had not happened in the twentieth century to anything like the degree that its prophets expected. At least as late as the 1960s, the independent still remained a major contributor of important inventions, from the ball-point pen to the jet engine. Subsequent developments, in such realms as computer hardware and software and biotechnology, have, if anything, strengthened the case.

A second line of historical inquiry, to which the leading contributor is Thomas P. Hughes, built on this insight. It distinguishes between a creative era of an industry, in which the independent inventor dominated, and an era of consolidation, in which corporate inventor-engineers and researchers tied up the loose ends. Independents, in Hughes' (1989) view, make the radical inventions that define systems. Corporate employees make the evolutionary improvements that remove the roadblocks that rapid emergence of those systems have left behind.

Yet this view too is incomplete. For consider some inventions that by any reckoning must be considered radical: television, nylon, and the transistor. All were made within corporations. While the stories of these particular inventions, and the laboratories where they were invented, have been well told by such historians as David Hounshell and John Smith (1988), Margaret Graham (1985), Albert Abramson (1989), and Lillian Hoddeson (1981), less attention has been given to the work that went on earlier in industry but outside laboratories. This work was important both in its own right and in setting the stage for later achievements.

A closer look at that transitional period indicates that Hughes's distinction is too stark. Corporate inventors can make radical inventions. And they can do so because Chandler and Noble's assertion is too sweeping. Corporations did not so quickly create such an ordered and organization-charted internal world as Chandler and Noble depict. The combination of a measure of internal corporate chaos with effective corporate use of economic strength and the legal system enabled both internal and external invention to flourish in unexpected ways. It enabled, for example, an insider such as Steinmetz to create a research laboratory that was sufficiently isolated from day-to-day corporate needs to spawn major inventions and Nobel Prize-winning research. Even the intimidating effect corporate power had on independents had a beneficial side. For it drove outsiders into new fields of invention: Sperry into stabilization, guidance, and control; and Christensen into the realm of the O-ring.

To understand how this is possible, let's look at the inventor's career, focusing again on Christensen, with the others as corroboration and background. Christensen is the focus not because he is more important than the others, but because his story has not been told before. The others are included to help filter out the individual elements and see the shaping forces exerted by the times. We will consider six stages: family roots; formative experiences; early invention; clash and compromise with corporations; changing focus; and later fruits.

Family Roots

Niels Christensen was born in 1865, on a farm in Toerring, Jutland, Denmark, that had been in the family for fifteen generations. His father, a staunch royalist, Lutheran, and landowner, had ventured off the farm to help defend Denmark from Prussia in the short and unsuccessful Schleswig-Holstein war. Otherwise his interests do not appear to have extended far beyond the boundaries of the family property. Within those boundaries, young Niels found a blacksmith shop and a woodworking shop. There he built a spinning wheel, a windmill that actually ground wheat (using a coffee grinder he borrowed without permission from his grandmother), a working gyroscope, and much more.

At age 14 he apprenticed to a machinist in Viele, Jutland. At 18 he became a journeyman machinist and draftsman in a series of Danish shops. He helped to make Denmark's first Maxim gun, and to draw the plans for its biggest lighthouse. He qualified as a marine engineer, and joined the Danish navy, where he sailed a desk in a design office. He was chosen as one of a group of young technically trained sailors to tour the machine shops of Britain and bring back technology. On the tour, "he jumped ship," as his family puts it. A Danish friend named Jens Moller, who emigrated to Texas to run a shipping company, provided a letter of introduction that got Niels a job as draftsman in a marine engineering firm on the Tyne River in Northern England, then the world's center of advanced-power engineering. He perfected his English by signing on as a merchant marine officer under the British flag and taking a four-month voyage. A succession of drafting jobs in the Liverpool area followed, accompanied by night-school courses in mechanical engineering which he first took, then taught.

In late 1891, Moller provided him with passage money to America and a letter of introduction that gained him the job of "leading draftsman" at Fraser and Chalmers in Chicago, a manufacturer of machinery for industry and transportation. "I was almost sorry to leave my last place in England," he wrote a British friend. "Still it was not a place that will ever rise to anything very big." Fraser and Chalmers would (it would soon merge with Allis of Milwaukee to form the Allis-Chalmers company), and moreover had doubled his last British salary (Christensen, 1891).

The backgrounds of the other members of our sample were also solidly in the middle class. They were sufficiently well to do that they could experiment with education and independence rather than settling down early into the role of breadwinner. Yet they were not so wealthy to be tempted into the position of gentleman inventor or amateur. The poorest of them, Elmer Sperry, nevertheless had ties in his upstate New York community that allowed him easy entry into factories and workshops, and enabled him by the age of 23 to create a company capitalized, nominally at least, at $1 million (Hughes, 1972). Steinmetz was the son of a minor official of the German state railways, but able to attend the University of Breslau, an opportunity available to few (Kline, 1989). Stanley, the son of a lawyer, dropped out of Yale after a semester. He went to New York and apprenticed himself to electrical pioneers Hiram Maxim and Edward Weston (Wise, 1988). Emmet's father was a business executive fallen on hard times. But though family fortunes declined, family connections got him into the Naval Academy (Emmet, 1940).

So all of them got a good start. Family connections and ambition were more important than great wealth or academic degrees. Emmet was the only college graduate in the group. Yet all absorbed the skills and knowledge they needed, and followed that start with a period of occupational experiments, at times sought, at times involuntary, but in all cases looked back on as crucial.

Formative Experiences

For Christensen, casting loose from a secure job came sooner than expected. Within a year of joining Fraser and Chalmers, "certain rearrangements that were peculiar to large syndicates," as he wrote without elaborating, cost him his job. He was undiscouraged. Draftsmen and designers with his level of skill and training were in short supply in Chicago. "I have now got a free hand," he wrote. "I am free to act according to my own judgment" (Christensen, 1892). Already he had chosen a patent agent and was completing the application for the first of what would be some 200 U.S. patents. A series of temporary jobs, such as helping install the electrification in the "Tower of Light" for the upcoming Columbian Centennial Exposition, or drafting plans for sewer systems, helped tie him into the network of machine shops and engineering offices where prototypes of inventions could be built. He also became part of the local Scandinavian immigrant community. At a debutante party of that community he would meet a young woman from the North Cape of Norway, and marry her after a whirlwind courtship.

Thus, being a young man with no permanent position in 1893 at the depths of what was until then the greatest depression in U.S. history did not faze him. He looked around for a focus for his inventive talents, a problem that could be productively attacked by a person with no college degree but extensive hands-on experience in the machine shop and at the drafting table. He found such a problem in newspaper headlines about a major crash of a streetcar in Oak Park, Illinois.

The other inventors in the sample had similar detours on the road to fame and fortune. Sperry moved to Chicago, installing himself in the same network of technical skill and knowledge that nourished Christensen, and sought to make a go in the arc lighting business. But his company never quite caught on (Hughes, 1972). Stanley bounced from one inventive apprenticeship to another, ending up back at his home laboratory before allying his electrical expertise with railroad machinery and natural gas magnate George Westinghouse (Wise, 1988). Steinmetz was run out of Breslau by Bismarck's police because of his socialist convictions (Kline, 1989). Emmet was discharged from the Navy during a period of defense economies, and spent time as a railway clerk and salesman of patent lathing. "All of this was somewhat humiliating to a man of twenty-nine who had led the life of a naval officer and stood quarter deck watches on a Man of War" (Emmet, 1940, p. 69), he recalled later. Yet for each, the knocking around was beneficial, not destructive. In the large cities, particularly New York, Pittsburgh, and Chicago, a network of factories and shops, and a mixture of ambitious ingenious Yankees in from the farm, and equally ambitious capable foreigners, often with superior shop or school training, created an inventive ferment that intoxicated a newcomer with the possibilities of an inventive career.

Early Inventions

That newspaper story Christensen read in 1893 put him on the track of a major inventive opportunity. From the late 1880s through the 1890s, the street railway was the principal growth element of the U.S. electrical industry. As street railways departed from their horsecar past, they had retained the horsecar's increasingly unsatisfactory hand-braking system, dependent on the mechanically amplified muscle power of the conductor. The succession of streetcar accidents caused by brake failure in the early 1890s indicated that the bigger and more powerful cars of that decade needed a new source of power to force the brakes against the wheels.

There were many candidates. An obvious one was compressed air, already used to brake railroad trains. Other inventors chose more experimental methods; electric or magnetic brakes, for example, or storing the energy of the streetcar's motion mechanically, as the spinning of a flywheel.

Christensen correctly judged that those rival methods, though intriguing, would not soon be practical, and stuck to compressed air. That created another choice: how to power the compressor. Here he initially went along with those who argued for a mechanical compressor carried beneath the car and driven mechanically from an axle. But, quicker than most (quicker than the engineers at the big electric transit car companies), he concluded that this method would not be efficient or reliable enough. So he jumped directly to driving the compressor with its own electric motor, driven by the same current that powered the car. This would result, before the end of the decade, in the first "independent motor compressor for air brake service" (Christensen, 1905).

The choice was controversial. The electric motor was already the most unreliable component of the streetcar. Why add more trouble by adding another one? To meet these objections, Christensen designed a combination of compressor and motor totally enclosed in a metal case, the moving parts of the compressor bathed in a bath of oil, and the combination made simple, reliable, and of high-quality components. Setting a tone for his entire career, he sought not a low-cost, marginally satisfactory solution but a solution offering markedly superior performance at a somewhat higher cost. In this case, he judged that the costliness of an accident due to brake failure justified the extra expense of a top-quality system. He designed such a system, built prototypes, and in 1895 and 1899 secured patents on its key elements: his particular form of sealed-in motor–compressor combination and a special "triple valve" for controlling the flow of compressed air (Christensen, 1899).

Meanwhile, he went looking for financial backing. The first two partners with whom he joined forces did not deliver the money needed to start a business (Christensen, 1893). He moved to Milwaukee and took a job with the E. P. Allis Company. In that city, in 1895, it looked like he had found the right backers, two Milwaukee brothers-in-law, one of them a bank president. They organized the

Christensen Engineering Company to produce and market the braking systems. Christensen began manufacturing the system in Milwaukee, and went on the road, to equipment manufacturers and street railway companies, to sell it.

Confident of its superiority, he asked only the opportunity to put it to the test against rival approaches under ordinary service. Gratifyingly often, his system won. Word began to reach the leaders of the industry. A breakthrough came in 1897 when Frank Sprague, the street railway industry's most successful entrepreneur, chose Christensen braking systems for use on the innovative "unit trains" he was building for Chicago's South Side Elevated. Success in Boston followed (Passer, 1953).

So by the end of his first decade in America, it looked like Christensen had successfully followed in the footsteps of the leading inventors–entrepreneurs of the new industrial age, such as Edison, Westinghouse, Sprague, Brush, and Thomson. Sales were booming. His company moved into a brand new ten-acre Milwaukee works, where some 600 people worked in long, high bay peak-roofed, red brick "cathedral shops" that marked a major manufacturing company. He toured Europe to secure overseas orders and license patents, and climaxed the trip with a triumphant return to Denmark. Back at home, his face adorned the cover of the September 1901 edition of a magazine called *Successful Americans.*

The other inventors had similarly turned that rough early going into a gratifying rise from obscurity. Sperry took on the same problem as Christensen, braking electric streetcars. His solution was technically inferior to Christensen's. His electric brake did not hold when the car stopped on a grade. But he incorporated it in a full system and proved superior to Christensen both in finding backing and in negotiating with the corporations that were just becoming giants (Hughes, 1972). Stanley, backed by Westinghouse, established a laboratory at Great Barrington, Massachusetts, and there, in 1886, perfected a major invention originally made in Europe, the transformer. He went on to break with Westinghouse and, in the 1890s, create his own company to pioneer in high-voltage power transmission (Passer, 1953; Wise, 1988). Steinmetz, within two years after arriving at Ellis Island tired, poor, huddled, and yearning to breathe free, had established himself as one of the leading electrical engineers in the United States. In his post as chief assistant to a successful industrialist–inventor branching out into the electrical industry, Rudolf Eickemeyer, he made the first of some 200 patented inventions (Kline, 1989). Emmet, once he found his feet, rose quickly through the ranks of the electrical industry working for traction pioneer Frank Sprague and a couple of street railway companies, and then in 1890 went independent with some of his trolley-related inventions (Emmet, 1940).

The 1890s, the years of the emergence of all of these inventors, were also the years of the emergence of the modern corporation. Chandler (1982) has told the story well: how the cornucopia of production outran the capabilities of distribution; how the firms therefore decided to bring under their control activities from invention to sales that had previously been left to the market; how the electrical industry was a pioneer in this emergence.

But what Chandler leaves out is also important. The electrical manufacturers grouped their factories into giant works, composed of dozens of buildings and tens of thousands of workers. Within the works, pockets of invention and innovation emerged. They either did not show up on the organization chart, or showed up in misleading ways. In GE, the leader of an inventive team might be labeled a shop superintendent, as were such prolific GE inventors as Henry Geisenhoner or Christian Steenstrup; or a consulting engineer, as were Emmet and Steinmetz; or simply a mechanical engineer, as was Sanford Moss, for forty years from 1903 on the resident gadfly of the Lynn, Massachusetts, Works. His championing of the gas turbine resulted decades later in GE's entry into the jet engine business. These people did not necessarily occupy lofty levels in a hierarchy. Rather, they enjoyed the patronage, support, and protection of a high-level executive. For example, Edwin W. Rice, GE's Vice President of Engineering and Manufacturing, was the patron of Steinmetz and Emmet. So the turn-of-the-century corporate climate provided opportunities for what Gifford Pinchot III (1985), a business consultant, would later label "intrapreneurship": playing the role of the entrepreneur within the corporation.

Meanwhile, as the inside inventor used the patron's clout to keep his options open, the outside inventor sometimes found his freedom blocked by corporate actions.

Crisis and Corporation

Suddenly, in 1901, Christensen found he was not really in control of his own empire. His new manufacturing works had more capacity than needed to serve the needs of electric railway companies. Christensen proposed diversifying into other compressor applications. But his backers had a more ambitious plan: enter the electrical industry, going head to head against the giants, GE and Westinghouse. The backers held the majority interest, so their view prevailed. In 1902, Christensen resigned, accepting $400,000 in preferred stock and a 5-percent royalty on sales of his patented brake in exchange for his share of the company.

The name of the company was changed to National Brake. Here, too, it followed a trend. Across U.S. industry, companies named for individuals—Edison, Thomson, Sprague, Brush, Vandepoele, Bentley, Knight, Wood—were disappearing into combinations with generic labels like "national" or "general." George Westinghouse held out. But his independence was purchased at the expense of an 1896 treaty with General Electric. The two companies pooled their patents in the electric power and electric railway fields, and set up a "board of patent control" to allocate license fees and prosecute independents that infringed patents the giants controlled (Passer, 1953, pp. 331–334).

Christensen had already been a target of that combination. His "triple valve" patent became the subject of a Westinghouse infringement suit. That company owned a rival patent on the same idea. (Two patents covering the same subject are not supposed to make it through the patent office, but occasionally do.) It took a five-year battle to establish Christensen's clear priority. His experience was not unique. As another independent inventor, William Stanley, put it, those drawn-out legal battles were used by the corporation against the independent "to annul his usefulness, discourage his endeavors, disgust him with surrounding conditions, and finally remove him from the land" (Stanley, 1903). Both Stanley and Frank Sprague had the experience of having their own inventions, which they had sold to the giants, used against them in patent suits (Wise, 1988).

Though removed from the company that his inventions had created, Christensen at least retained ownership of his patents and that lucrative royalty arrangement with National Brake. But the unwise policy of the new owners drained the brake business to support the unsuccessful electrical lines. And then, on Easter Sunday 1905, the Milwaukee papers exploded with a dramatic story. The bank president who also controlled National Brake had been caught with his hand deep in the bank's till. He had borrowed a million dollars without authorization, to support his son's role in a syndicate trying to corner wheat on the Chicago Board of Trade. The scandal brought down National Brake. It went bankrupt, and Christensen's apparently secure stock and royalty payments became worthless creditor's claims.

He created a new Christensen Engineering Company and tried to buy back the brake business. But the giants again forestalled him. An agent with Westinghouse connections got control of the claims of the company's creditors and sold the business to a syndicate that kept it, though nominally independent, in the Westinghouse orbit. That reorganized company, National Electric and Brake, went back to making the product Christensen invented, but without recognizing the validity of his patents (Christensen, 1905).

Christensen could have compromised with the giants, perhaps selling his patents to Westinghouse or GE, as many independents such as Nikola Tesla and Frank Sprague had done. But this was not his nature. "I won't say that Grandpa Chris didn't know what compromise was," says his grandson, John Young. "But if he thought he was right, that was the end of it" (Young & Young, 1989). Christensen took his patents to another competitor, Allis Chalmers, and offered an exclusive license under the condition that a patent infringement suit be prosecuted against National Electric and Brake. Thus, in 1905, the thirty-year court battle began.

National Electric and Brake was the nominal defendant. But the Christensen family tradition leaves no doubt who the real enemy was. "Fight Westinghouse— do not give up," is how John Young recalls his mother putting it. George Westinghouse became the family devil. Family tradition depicts an occasion when he passed Niels Christensen on the way into the courtroom, sidled up to him, and hissed, "We'll get you yet, you little Dutchman!" (Young, 1989). Historically, the incident is doubtful: George Westinghouse died in 1914, before the long case had really heated up. The story is worth more as an indication of the view the Christensen family held of the corporate opponent, and more generally, of the domination of the street railway industry by Westinghouse and GE. Together, claims Christensen, Westinghouse and GE got involved in one of the numerous reorganizations to which Allis Chalmers was subjected, and effectively eliminated that company as a competitor in the street railway equipment industry.

Meanwhile, back in court, the defendants did not contest the originality or value of Christensen's work. They rested their defense on an incredibly flimsy legal pretext. The first time Christensen received a patent on his compressor–motor combination, the Patent Office had mistakenly included a drawing from another patent. In the course of fixing this administrative error, the patent was issued again under a new number. This, the opponents charged, was "double patenting," and therefore invalidated the patents. That defense was maintained through a twenty-five-year struggle. In 1918, newspapers carried stories of an all but completed settlement under which Westinghouse would pay Christensen $2 million. But it never happened. It took until 1930 for the verdict to come in: total victory for Christensen. He got a $325,000 payment and total control of his patents. But by then they were long expired, the trolley age was over, and the Great Depression had begun.

The victory hardly compensated the inventor for the losses the campaign against him had cost him. "We read in the daily papers that some poor devil who has helped himself to a loaf of bread for his starving wife and children is sent to jail in 24 hours," he wrote in 1928. "Why not let the same law apply to those who, while hiding behind a corporate charter, have been found guilty of a more vicious offense: destroying the incentive for progress" (Christensen, 1905).

Here Christensen's experience contrasts with that of the other inventors in the sample. Sperry early sold out his street railway company to GE, which went on marketing it under the Sperry name. The inventor signed a lucrative consulting agreement with GE, and went on developing electrical equipment for the mining industry that GE could sell (Hughes, 1972). Stanley found his company successful in the field but short of capital, and besieged by Westinghouse and GE. The giants used his own patents on the transformer (long since assigned to Westinghouse and administered by the Board of Patent Control). After that newspaper blast at the giants, he too sold his company to GE and signed a lucrative consulting agreement with that company that included GE setting up a lab for him to pursue new inventions (Wise, 1988).

Steinmetz also came to GE by acquisition, when that company bought up Eickemeyer's street railway motor patents. By 1900 he was GE's chief consulting engineer, but by no means was harnessed to the corporate routine. Rather, he had an amount of freedom rarely granted anyone inside or outside the corporation. He received dozens of patents on equipment ranging from a new electricity distributing system to street lights to a battery charger for electric automobiles. He taught electrical engineering at Union College. He created three different laboratories, including the GE Research Lab, the first industrial laboratory in the United States to be devoted at least in part to doing scientific research and publishing the results. Far from being a strategic initiative by the company's chief executive, creation of the research lab was an extension of the previous informal effort by inside inventors such as Steinmetz to preserve pockets of inventive effort from control by the organization (Wise, 1985).

Emmet, too, quickly traded his independent role for a GE staff position, where he earned a substantial degree of inside independence. As a consulting engineer, he roamed the organization chart: spearheading GE's successful attempt to break Westinghouse's grip on the hydroelectric generation business at Niagara Falls; taking over a faltering program to develop a steam turbine based on the original ideas of the independent inventor Charles A. Curtis, and making several supplementary inventions, including changing the axis of the turbine from horizontal to vertical, that ensured its success; and then moving on to other projects, such as electric drive for ships, and eventually a would-be revolution in power generation—the use of mercury vapor in place of steam as a working fluid (Emmet, 1940).

Summing up all these experiences, and abstracting out the purely personal, what remains? Unquestionably, as David Noble has stressed, giant corporations wanted to dominate their industries, and tame competition. To do so it was sometimes necessary to bring inventors into line. But Noble and others fail to recognize that intent does not guarantee success, and control does not require predation or destruction.

At GE, for example, policies from its founding in 1892 until the 1920s were shaped by Charles A. Coffin, its first president. A former shoe company executive, he had built the Thomson-Houston Company, the least original of the initial trio of electrical giants, into perhaps the most broadly successful by 1890. He masterminded its union with the faltering Edison interests in 1892 to form GE. In doing so, he recognized that absorbing outstanding technologists was preferable to merely buying or capturing their companies and leaving the inventors free to compete again. So, time, and again, he made independents offers they couldn't refuse. Such inventors as James J. Wood, Charles Vandepoele, Charles S. Bradley, and Walter H. Knight became either permanently or for crucial periods part of the Thomson-Houston or GE technical forces. Others, such as Frank Sprague and Elmer Sperry, became, temporarily, crucial consultants and allies. Even so prickly an independent as Stanley ultimately came on board.

Christensen was not alone in choosing to fight. Such other independent inventors as Charles Van Choate and Peter Cooper Hewitt saw their patents either brought into interference or violated, waged long court cases with the giants, and won Pyrrhic victories that did not prevent their technology or company from being absorbed by the giants. But much more often, corporations and independents reached a mutually agreeable compromise.

Meanwhile, both outside and within the corporations, what became of the inventiveness of the inventors?

Staying Creative

That thirty-year legal struggle had hardly annulled Christensen's usefulness or discouraged his endeavors. After the crash of his first company, he started a smaller one that achieved a few years of modest success with gasoline engines for farm use. Again, his trademark was high quality. He continued to turn out a stream of inventions, all based on the theme of hydraulic or pneumatic power for starting and stopping things. He came up with a pneumatic automobile starter, an airplane starter, and various pneumatic and vacuum braking systems for automobiles and trucks. None of them quite became commercially successful. He had some near misses. One promising backer went down on the Titanic; an opportunity for his airplane starter vanished in World War I defense procurement scandal.

Still, his licensing and consulting fees were sufficient to support his family in comfortable, if not captain-of-industry, style and to feed an unfortunate habit of buying stock in not very successful mining companies. But he retained his most precious asset: his ability to pick out crucial problems and visualize, draw, build, and test elegant and functional solutions, usually in the form of high-performance hydraulic and pneumatic power equipment.

The 1929 union with the Young family was not much help. From this era only a single exchange of letters with Owen D. Young survives. Christensen points out that he has a new braking system for automobiles. Can Young, a director of General Motors, bring it to the attention of that company's management? Young replies formally that he can do nothing. The name of the president of GM is Alfred Sloan. If Mr. Christensen has information for that company, it should be directed to that gentleman (Young, 1929).

Young and his employer GE were at the same time seeking to convince the public that the world of technology had changed since the days of Edison. Corporate teamwork had replaced the independent; science was replacing invention. Progress (not yet, but soon, to be labeled GE's most important product) was more likely to come out of research laboratories like GE's "house of magic" in Schenectady than out of the independent's workshop. The publicity left discreetly unmentioned the fact that GE itself had been principally built on patents purchased from such independents as Edison, Thomson, Stanley, Sprague, Brush, Vandepoele, Bradley, and Curtis.

Christensen himself, by 1930, might seem to personify the declining independent inventor, drifting placidly toward retirement, a 65-year-old with skills now thirty years out of date. But that was anything but the case. His greatest invention still lay ahead. For the skills and knowledge he had started learning in a four-year apprenticeship, ripened in the machine shops of Copenhagen and on the Tyne, and matured battling corporate giants while earning his living with his hand and brain were not something that was being taught in American engineering schools.

American engineers got a more theoretical training. It was suited to the emerging high-tech industries of the first third of the twentieth century, such as alternating current electricity and radio. But when it came to mechanical systems, the European-born, shop-trained craftsmen–engineers still designed rings around their college-trained yankee rivals. GE, for example, held in 1925 a competition between two engineering teams to design the cooling system for the refrigerator that would launch its appliance business. A Danish-born mechanical superintendent at the GE Schenectady Works, Christian Steenstrup, was called on for consulting help. His training in European and American machine shops and lack of formal education had paralleled Christensen's. So did his temperament and determination. Rather than merely consult on the project he designed his own refrigeration system and got it included in the competition. It won an easy victory over both candidates of the college-trained engineers, and became the basis for the GE "monitor top" refrigerator, a design classic and phenomenal commercial success.

So, though they were in their 60s in a depression era, the skills of the likes of Steenstrup and Christensen were scarce and still in demand. Midland Steel Products had brought Christensen to Cleveland in 1926. In 1930, even after the stock market crash had dampened the daring of would-be innovators, that company paid Christensen a $25,000 advance on future royalties and a guaranteed $5000 per year consulting fee until 1941 to develop new types of automobile and truck brakes (Christensen, 1933).

The other inventors in the sample also sustained their creativity. As he matured from youthful inventor to middle-aged engineer, Elmer Sperry found the ideal form for his talents: as the principal in a development company that licensed patents to others. Though he, like Christensen, Stanley, and Steinmetz, argued that the patent system unduly favored money and legal maneuvering over invention, he got bogged down in no long court campaigns (Hughes, 1972). Stanley mellowed in his last years (he died in 1916), using his lab to pioneer a new area: heating devices and insulating materials (Wise, 1985).

Steinmetz's independence increased with age. He returned to socialism and ran successfully for local office. He extended his own work further afield, to such areas as electrical stimulation of plant growth, man-made resins, and studies of lightning, and created yet another laboratory (Kline, 1989). Emmet turned turbines back to the turbine engineers, and flourished as an intrapreneur. He assembled backing, carried ideas from the concept stage to hardware, got prototypes built and necessary research and testing done, and secured customers willing to try out the new idea. He did it first for his electric ship propulsion system. The customer, the U.S. Navy, permitted him to use a collier, the U.S. Jupiter, for a successful trial. Before too long, putting electric drive on warships was a growing GE business. With three wins under his belt, Emmet took up the intrapreneur's role again, this time with the more challenging task of replacing the steam turbine, now well entrenched, with the mercury vapor turbine (Emmet, 1940).

So the originality of the inventors, whether inside or outside the corporation, did not diminish with age. In fact, it is for their late efforts that they are best remembered.

Crowning Achievements

It was in the Midland lab, in 1933, that Christensen decided to do something about a problem that had bothered him throughout his long career of using fluids to actuate the movement of pistons in cylinders: lack of a simple reliable seal that let the piston slide easily while blocking the flow of the fluid.

He does not appear, either then or later, to have written down the detailed steps by which he arrived at his solution. Certainly rubber rings had been tried for sealing before. Their weakness was a tendency to wear, leading to early failure. The new synthetic rubber materials coming along had ameliorated somewhat but not really solved this problem. Niels Owen Young recalls a later comment by his grandfather that experience with ship propeller shafts mounted in blocks of hard rubber suggested that the wearing problems of rubber could be overcome.

For whatever reason, in 1933 Christensen took a piston and cylinder for a hydraulic brake, cut a square-sided groove around the piston, and inserted in that groove a hard rubber ring with a circular cross section. The ring's cross-sectional diameter was slightly greater than the distance from the bottom of the groove to the cylinder wall (so the cross section would be slightly compressed when squeezed between piston and cylinder). The groove's length was about one and a half times the diameter of that ring cross section (see Figure 16.1).

Arriving at those dimensions no doubt took some unrecorded trial and error. But the first prototype to be photographed and talked about shows all the earmarks of the modern O-ring. It also showed a remarkable performance. "Packing ring tested for 2,790,000 1/2″ strokes at 600 psi. and 2,790,000 strokes at atmospheric pressure," Christensen wrote. "The packing never leaked and is still tight" (Christensen, 1945).

One might expect Midland Steel to have been delighted with this breakthrough. But the manager of that company's lab had his own ideas about hydraulic seals, and they did not include O-rings. Christensen's treatment of those he felt had made technical errors may not have helped at this juncture. "He'd cut them down to nothing and then jump on the bloody remains," John Young recalls (Young, 1989). In 1934, Christensen received a letter from the president of Midland: "We do not desire you to dedicate any of your time to the uses of Midland." The next year another letter arrived: "It has come to my attention that you are again visiting the Midland plant. I insist that you refrain" (Midland, 1934).

Christensen made an abortive attempt to interest a Cleveland maker of aircraft equipment. A few machinery makers tried the new idea, as much out of curiosity as anything else. "It is fantastic to think that one ring of synthetic rubber could seal 900 lbs. pressure in a hydraulic shock absorber," responded one. "I'm willing to try it just to prove that you are wrong" (Allen, 1946). Christensen was not wrong. The applications worked. But commercially, the O-ring went nowhere for most of the 1930s. Christensen did submit a patent application in 1937. The patent office, as is customary, challenged its originality. Patents on using hard rubber rings of circular cross section went back well into the nineteenth century. As is usual in these cases, Christensen and his attorney honed their application to focus in on the particular original combination for which they were seeking protection.

The legally binding part of every patent is the set of claims, a series of repetitively worded statements at the end explaining precisely what is unobvious, original, and useful about the invention. The key to Christensen's patent was Claim 5, which specified "the combination of a cylinder and piston, of a resilient elastic packing element therebetween having normally approximately circular cross section of a groove having a flat bottom portion spaced from the cylinder wall a distance less than the normal radial dimension of the ring, whereby when the ring is in the groove in operative position, is compressed into somewhat ellipsoidal cross section, and the width of the groove being greater than the axial dimension of said compressed ring by a fractional part of said axial dimension" (Christensen, 1939; see Figure 16.1).

That long complex sentence is worth struggling with, for it expresses the essence of the O-ring. Fortunately for Christensen, the inventor does not have to know why his invention works. For the opening paragraphs of his patent suggest very strongly that he did not. He speaks of the ring being "continuously kneaded or worked to enhance its life," as if the rubber ring could get stronger through exercise, like a human muscle. This is, if anything, the opposite of what actually happens.

Here's why the O-ring actually works (see Figure 16.2). That groove slightly

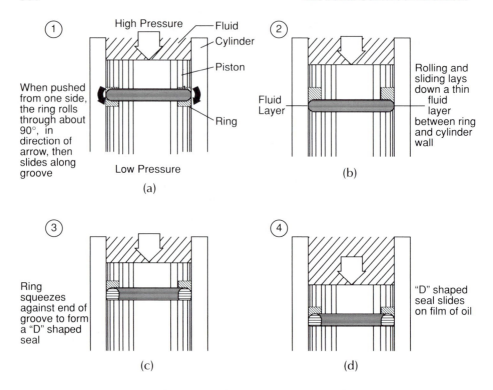

FIGURE 16.2. Operation of O-ring seal on moving piston (side view).

longer than the diameter of the ring's cross section allows a brief rolling motion of the ring. When it is pushed from one side, the ring rolls through about 20 degrees. That lays down a very thin (maybe 1/10,000th of an inch) layer of the hydraulic fluid between the rubber and the cylinder wall. This lubricates the subsequent slide of the ring as it first squeezes against the end of the groove to form a D-shaped seal, and then slides along with the piston. This lubrication protects the ring from wear and lengthens its life.

The groove length of between one and two times the diameter of the ring cross section is crucial. If the groove is too short, no rolling and no lubrication of the ring will occur. If the groove is too long, too much rolling and flexing of the ring will occur, and the ring would also wear out too fast.

All of this was later ingeniously proved with transparent plexiglass cylinders and slow-motion photography by researchers at Vought-Sikorsky and Lockheed Aircraft. But not by Niels Christensen. He was not a man with a consuming interest in why his inventions worked. His "research" was of the most direct and unsophisticated possible. His grandson Niels Owen Young recalls watching him at work in his Cleveland home:

He worked in the cellar, and coal dust was all over everything. He had a closet full of neoprene rings of all sizes; I know it was neoprene because the stuff had the most awful smell. He'd put a ring through a test, then look at it under a magnifying glass to see where it was scratched. No complicated analysis at all. (Young, 1989)

The other inventors also had late career surprises. Elmer Sperry's invention of the gyrostabilizer and gyrocompass launched a great corporation named after the inventor (and now absorbed in Unisys). Stanley's name never persisted on transformers as he had hoped. But it lives on a brand of thermos bottle still sold in the 1980s in hardware stores across the country. (That thermos was a spin-off of his late inventing efforts in the field of electric stoves, which to use electricity efficiently had to be well insulated.) Steinmetz made major headlines (though only minor technical contributions) with a high-voltage generator that mimicked the power of lightning. Emmet, in a technological tour de force, pushed his mercury vapor system far beyond what either economics or safety would justify. Efficiency gains proved ephemeral, mercury boilers leaky, and mercury in the environment a hazard more serious than anticipated. But the boldness of the effort at least inspired parallel and far more successful efficiency-increasing innovations by his steam turbine rivals.

Meanwhile, all the inventors (except Stanley) were finding a new patron for their efforts.

A New Patron and New Problems

By the end of 1939, Christensen had his patent, and Europe was at war. Franklin D. Roosevelt told the nation to hunker down behind its ocean barrier and build tens of thousands of airplanes for coastal defense. Each airplane would have retractable landing gear and control surface actuators, and many would have bomb-bay doors or cargo doors, too: hundreds of thousands, perhaps millions, of hydraulic shafts to be sealed.

Niels Christensen wrote the Army Air Corps for an interview, loaded his car with O-rings, and drove across Ohio to Dayton's Wright Field (now Wright-Patterson Air Force Base). There, among many other things, the Army Air Corps tested and specified standards for shaft seals.

Among the men to whom Christensen showed the new seal were a pair of engineer–administrators in charge of hydraulic seals. "Mr. Christensen was the father of the O ring," writes the ring's historian, Robert E. Allen. "His two sons were Nicholas Bashark and Ellsworth M. Polk" (Allen, 1946). They did not shout "eureka" or otherwise get excited at that first exposure. Their pictures and their later testimony indicate that they were not eureka-shouting types.

But they immediately agreed to give the O-ring a test. They put some on the worn, rusty hydraulic landing gear on a Northrup A-17A airplane, and the seal held up through some eighty-eight bumpy landings. They built a special machine for more controlled, quantitative tests, and the results were just as good. Polk and Bashark were not eureka-shouters, but they were decisive. Within just two years, the O-ring had been specified as the seal of choice in virtually every Army Air Force hydraulic sealing application to which it could be applied. And the specification clearly called for a combination of square-sided groove and rubber ring fitting the description given in Christensen's patent (Bashark, 1955).

So a 75-year-old man, written off by the technical community and his employer, had come to the Army Air Corps field with an invention that met a pressing need of the entire aviation industry and materially advanced the U.S. war effort. Government accounts estimate that the O-ring saved the U.S. taxpayer more than $5 million over the next ten years by simplifying and making longer lasting the seals on hydraulic systems, not to mention any lives that may have been saved by more reliable aircraft controls and landing gear. And that was just the beginning of a technical success story that made the O-ring ubiquitous. It would not have seemed out of line for a grateful nation to give that inventor a medal and a million dollars. Instead, it gave him a hard time, forcing him into another legal struggle, one that outlived him by twenty years.

That, however, is another story. The essential point for this story is the shift of patrons. Other members of the sample also experienced that shift. Sperry had, in World War I, led the attempt to develop a primitive, propellor-driven guided missile. By that time, the U.S. Navy had become Sperry's main customer. As Hughes (1972) has shown so well, Sperry's work for the government is a prototype for the relationships later summed up under the much over-used label "military industrial complex." Steinmetz, blocked from participation in one World War I defense effort because of alleged pro-German sympathies, found other government projects to which to contribute, such as an early effort to make a proximity fuse. After the war, he modified his socialism into an evolutionary variety he labeled simply "cooperation" and sought to shape energy, labor relations, and environmental policy until his death in 1923. And Emmet's ship propulsion program had been, like Sperry's work, a pioneering link between industry and government.

Conclusions

The story of Niels Christensen confirms again the insight of Jewkes, Sawyers, and Stillerman. The decline of the independent inventor in the twentieth century has been exaggerated. Particularly in the realm of mechanical equipment, hands-on shop training, mechanical intuition, and an independence honed through many technical and legal battles are more than a match for formal education and corporate affiliation. Translating that talent and stubbornness in the shop into business success can depend more on selecting the right partners and lawyers than on the intrinsic worth of the inventions.

But that story also suggests that at least one independent was able to sustain his inventive drive in spite of struggles against the system. Niels Christensen kept up a steady stream of inventions during both of his battles. And, in the brief time between them, he achieved the peak of his creativity and fathered the O-ring.

The system, in unintended ways, had worked. The inside inventors preserved their independence from total corporate control. The outside inventors took advantage of corporate policies and choices, whether by licensing and consulting agreements, or by turning bitter adversity to sweet new inventions. The inventors excelled at choosing the right targets (with occasional overreaches like Sperry's electric brake and Emmet's mercury turbine). They learned how to gain support from patrons, whether they did it on the inside or the outside. On the inside, that meant inventing a new role, the intrapreneur: the creator of new institutions in the case of Steinmetz, or of new products in the case of Emmet. On the outside, it often meant being driven by the dominant giants into new fields far off the beaten path. In such fields Sperry found his gyros, and Christensen his O-ring. Some, such as Stanley, managed to have it both ways, accepting a salary and serving on the Technical Advisory Council of GE while independently developing his thermos bottle.

So what? What suggestions does this story of a vanished era make about the present and the future? One is the value of organizational inefficiency. It is possible that corporations, when less efficiently organized than today, were more effective at innovation. Strategy indeed, as Chandler demonstrated, shapes structure. But formal strategies and rigid structures can be dangerous to innovation. Both outside and inside inventors escaped that rigidity and secured a measure of isolation from day-to-day pressures. Some did it by going it alone on the outside; some by finding an executive patron, or securing the invisibility of a mislabeled post, on the inside.

This suggests that the perfection of "professional management" may work against innovation. The apparently inefficient organizational structures, such as were found in early U.S. industry (and more recent Japanese industry), might be more conducive to invention and innovation than the more polished and rational decentralized structures of the 1960s and 1970s, with their discouragement of dirt-under-the-fingernails degreeless inventors and their facile identification of innovation with a research laboratory.

Another suggestion concerns the real role of the patent system. Study after study has shown it to be hardly the simple mixer of the fire of genius and the fuel of interest that Abraham Lincoln labeled it. As interpreted in the courts, the system tends to swing between extremes. At times courts narrow the concept of invention and undercut the value of patents, as happened between the late 1930s and the 1950s. At other times, the patent system largely serves to protect established interests, as happened during most of the period covered by this chapter. Yet even that protection of corporate interests played the positive social role of forcing independents into the unoccupied and speculative regions where they can do the most good.

Whether all inventors are basically alike is something for the psychologists to determine. But all climates for invention are clearly not alike. In different industries, and in different eras, inventors have faced radically different social and economic environments. From 1890 until 1940, inventors of electrical technology dealt with maturing corporations in terms neither of total enmity, nor total subordination. Bitter struggles occurred and attempts to exert the corporate will could be heavyhanded, as Christensen's story shows. But over all, the connection between inventor and corporation was something like the union of the Christensen and Young families with which this account began. Independent and corporation circled each other warily, more like in-laws than like outlaws, unable to live with each other, but just as unable to live without each other. Much of the technology we use in our daily lives descends from that uneasy but never dissolved marriage of the inventive brain and the visible hand.

References

Abramson, A. (1988). *Vladimir Zworykin.* Unpublished.
Allen, R. E. (1946). High pressure packing development. In *Conference on Hydraulic Machinery,* 23 Oct 1946.
Allen, R. E. (1969). *O-Rings Make History.* Dayton: Otterbein.
Bashark, A. N. (1955). Testimony, Appendix, *U.S. Court of Claims #432-55.*
Case, J. Y. & Case, E. (1982). *Owen D. Young and American Enterprise.* Boston, Mass.: Godine.
Chandler, A. D. (1982). *The Visible Hand.* New York: Knopf.
Christensen, N. (1891–1953). Personal Papers, in possession of Niels O. Young, Boise, Idaho. (Subsequent Christensen references are all in this collection.)
Christensen, N. (1891). To H. W. Culliford, 3 June 1891.
Christensen, N. (1892). To Mr. Jussey, 19 November 1892.
Christensen, N. (1893). To S. W. Walker, 12 January 1893.
Christensen, N. (1905). *Synopsis of Development of Brakes for Electric and Cable Railways.*
Christensen, N. (1899). U.S. Patents 621,324, 635,280.
Christensen, N. (1933). License Agreement with Midland Steel Products Company, 25 August 1933.
Christensen, N. (1937). To [illegible], President, Midland Steel Products, 15 July 1937.
Christensen, N. (1939). U.S. Patent 2,180,795.
Christensen, N. (1945). *In Retrospect: The O-Ring Development.* Unpublished.
Emmet, W. L. R. (1940). *Autobiography of an Engineer.* Albany, N.Y.: Fort Orange.
Graham, M. B. W. (1985). *RCA and the Videodisc.* New York: Cambridge Univ. Press.
Hoddeson, L. (1981). The emergence of basic research in the Bell Telephone System, 1876–1915. *Technology and Culture, 22,* 512–544.
Hounshell, D. & Smith, J. K. (1988). *Science and Corporate Strategy.* New York: Cambridge Univ. Press.
Hughes, T. P. (1972). *Elmer Sperry, Inventor and Engineer.* Baltimore: Johns Hopkins Univ. Press.
Hughes, T. P. (1989). *American Genesis.* New York: Viking.
Jewkes, J., Sawyers, R., & Stillerman, C. (1969). *The Sources of Invention.* New York: Norton.
Kline, R. (1989). *Charles Proteus Steinmetz.* Unpublished.
Milwaukee Journal (1929). 21 June.
Noble, D. (1979). *America By Design.* New York: Knopf.
Passer, H. (1953). *The Electrical Manufacturers.* Cambridge, Mass.: Harvard Univ. Press.
Pinchot, G. (1985). *Intrapreneuring.* New York: Harper & Row.
Reich, L. (1985). *The Making of American Industrial Research.* New York: Cambridge Univ. Press.
Stanley, W. (1903). The inventor and the trust. *Electrical World and Engineer,* 28 March.
Wise, G. (1988). William Stanley's search for immortality. *American Heritage of Invention and Technology, 2,* 42–49.
Wise, G. (1985). *Willis R. Whitney.* New York: Columbia Univ. Press.
Wise, G. (1989). "Father of the O-ring." Unpublished.
Young, N. O. & Young, J. P. (1989). Interview with George Wise. Unpublished.
Young, O. D. (1929). To Niels Christensen, 21 August 1929.

17 | Technology on the Move: The Role of Patents

DONALD J. QUIGG

Inventive Force

It is well occasionally to examine the trends in inventive activity that are likely to change the way we live—and perhaps how long we live.

The rate of patenting is generally accepted as an indicator of national and international technological trends. A look at patenting activity in the U.S. patent system tells us a lot. It's clear that microelectronics, telecommunications, computers, robotics, and biotechnology continue to be among the fastest growing areas.

Deep within the research labs of companies, both big and small, and in private labs and workshops throughout the land, is the real creative resource—the inventor. We still depend heavily on the lone inventor and on the patent attorney who helps to bring inventions to the marketplace. Many large companies sprang from an inventor's single creative thought.

Too many of us take for granted the miracles that inventive activity can bring. The prices of groceries tend to divert attention from the amazing laser scanner that reads the bar-coded price labels at the checkout counter. People are so happy to talk to a loved one on a distant continent that they forget about the complex satellite communications network that carries their messages. They are so relieved at the capture of the dreaded nightstalker of Los Angeles that they ignore the computerized scanner that reviewed more than 300,000 fingerprints in less than a half minute to come up with that incriminating match from the police files. Technological change—one does take it for granted.

In terms of budding industries, there is little if anything more exciting to watch than the booming genetic engineering areas of biotechnology. Estimates are that more than $200 million a year are being spent on research and development of genetically engineered products.

A major factor encouraging this activity is that those investing in this technology are able to protect the inventions resulting from their efforts. The celebrated Diamond V. Chakrabarty decision[1] by the Supreme Court (1980) opened the door of patent protection for genetically engineered microorganisms. In April 1987, another landmark decision was announced. It, too, opened doors.

In Ex Parte Allen (April 3, 1987),[2] the U.S. Patent and Trademark Office Board of Patent Appeals and Interferences held that the subject invention, a polyploid oyster, was a non-naturally occurring manufacture or composition of matter under the patent laws.[3] In reaching this position, the Board relied on the opinion of the Supreme Court in Chakrabarty as controlling authority that Congress intended statutory subject matter to "include anything under the sun that is made by man." Yes, animals are patentable!

It seems ironic. For centuries, inventors were encouraged to come up with a "better mousetrap"—but what did we get? A "better mouse," and one that went to Harvard no less!

One loses perspective if attention is given only to American inventors. An increasing amount of U.S. patenting activity comes from foreign shores—around 48 percent of the more than 85,000 utility patents granted by the Patent and Trademark Office in 1988. (Twenty years ago that figure was around 20%.) Of the top twenty companies receiving U.S. patents, three-fourths are foreign!

This has both positive and negative implications. On the one hand, U.S. scientists can be glad for the new foreign technology contributed to our wealth of knowledge. More than 115 nations are represented in the U.S. Patent and Trademark Office inventor index. It has been estimated that more than a quarter-million new inventions occur annually worldwide, and it is important to know about each one. That will happen, of course, since U.S. patents can issue only upon full disclosure of the new technology.[4]

On the other hand, some people are troubled by the fact that foreign nationals hold proprietary rights to so much of this new technology. Foreigners' quests for patent grants in this country signal an intent to enter our markets. That means competition! Foreign-origin inventors are entitled to the same protection of industrial property as our own nationals.[5]

Trade Concerns

We don't need to be reminded of our overall trade deficit. The United States has depended heavily on high-technology products in its trade relations—such products as computers, optical and medical instruments, electrical equipment, drugs and medicines, plastics and synthetic materials, engines, turbines, scientific instruments, and so on. Until 1988 the United States held only a narrow lead in those areas. Now that too is slipping.

There is a terrific resurgence of interest in patents throughout the world. During the 1970s there appeared to be a strong chance that the U.S. patent system might not survive the negative attitude taken to patents here. Congress, the courts, and industry had little or no faith in the system.

The U.S. Patent and Trademark Office was underfunded and understaffed to such an extent that it was taking about twenty-six months between the filing of an application and its final disposal (either grant of a patent or abandonment of the application, referred to as pendency). That pendency was increasing about 10 percent per year.

That situation changed in 1981 when Congress saw fit to raise the fees so that adequate staffing could be obtained in the office. Since that time, emphasis has been placed on improving the quality of patents being issued and on shortening the pendency. By the end of September 1989, average pendency had been reduced to 18.4 months and it was still going down. The Patent and Trademark Office met a goal set nine years ago.

In 1983, Congress formed the U.S. Court of Appeals for the Federal Circuit. That court was given the responsibility for all appeals dealing primarily with patents. The benefits of that court were apparent almost immediately. Before creation of the CAFC, patent appeals were handled by eleven courts of appeals, with widely divergent positions. The new CAFC gave coherency to the interpretation of the patent laws. The combination of the new court and increased attention to quality within the Patent and Trademark Office began to get the attention of industry.

In 1981 and 1982, the filings of patent applications in the U.S. PTO were running about 107,000 per year. In fiscal year 1989, they were filed at the rate of about 152,000. If things continue at that rate of increase, by the turn of the century the PTO has projected that filings will be between 300,000 and 500,000. Sounds great?! Wrong!! There is a slight problem. You see, there is another prediction. The availability of scientifically trained personnel is going to decline rather markedly. A tremendous number of new examiners will need to be recruited and trained. What can we do about that problem?

Another Concern

For the past twenty-five years we have watched as foreigners obtained a larger and larger share of the patents issued by the U.S. Patent and Trademark Office each year. This would indicate that we are not doing enough to ready our players for the growing competition. America has done too little for too long in preparing our youth for the competitive challenges they will face in the coming years.

Outreach

In the last few years, the Patent and Trademark Office has been very concerned about how this country will go about the task of developing people to be tomorrow's thinkers and innovators—our problem-solvers and inventors. The Office has become involved through a very special outreach program.

In 1983, the Office became aware of a pilot program in a school in Buffalo, New York, that seems to hold some intriguing possibilities for a long-range solution to the problem. In fact, it has tremendous possibilities for giving the future managers of our corporations better capabilities to manage.

Working with the teacher from Buffalo who had installed the pilot program, the PTO began to spread the idea of teaching teachers, from kindergarten up, to teach creative and analytical thinking on a daily basis. A Commissioner's Education Roundtable was organized. Initially there were twenty-five members. The number has now grown to more than ninety. It includes university professors, teachers from all grade levels, school administrators, parents, patent attorneys, and others too numerous to mention. At meetings of that group, strategic planning for the program is carried out.

Great strides have been made in the outreach efforts to foster national competitiveness by encouraging analytical thinking and problem-solving skills among America's youth. That program is called Project XL. The program has four major goals:

- To generate awareness among educators, parents, businesses, government agencies, educational associations, and professional societies of the importance of applied thinking skills.
- To motivate educators to use their inventive processes as a vehicle through which students apply their skills of inquiry and critical thinking to real-life problem-solving experiences.
- To identify and, where possible, provide the tools needed to accomplish these educational goals.
- To establish a network of information, communication, and support for persons interested in participating in the Project XL vision.

Project XL has been introduced to several thousand teachers across the country. We are seeing impressive results as students who were first exposed to this training in the lowest elementary grades progress through higher grades utilizing similar training.

In June 1988, a third national conference on this subject was held in Dallas. More than 800 participants were on hand to learn from a workshop faculty that read like a "Who's Who" of analytical and creative thinking experts. The PTO co-sponsored the Fourth National Creative and Inventive Thinking Conference in Portland, Oregon on October 27 and 28, 1989. A fifth national conference was held in Toledo, Ohio in November 1990.

A regional conference was held in Ohio in September 1989. Participating were the Inventor's Hall of Fame, University of Ohio, East Ohio Gas, the U.S. Departments of Commerce, Energy, Labor, and Agriculture, and the Small Business Administration. That conference will be used as a prototype for additional regional conferences around the country.

Project XL is spreading across America like a prairie fire. The PTO is coordinating and nurturing its progress, but it's not just another government program—it's a grand national partnership that involves corporate officials, educators, trade and professional associations, parents, as well as every level of government.

Copies of the PTO publications, the *Inventive Thinking Curriculum Project*, the *Inventive Thinking Resource Directory*, and *Black Innovators in Technology* are now being disseminated.

Worldwide Concern

The increasing work load referred to earlier is not a problem that is confined to the United States. The European Patent Office is experiencing the same type of growth. However, the Japanese Patent Office is in the worst shape of all. It has a backlog of about 2.5 million unexamined applications. Unfortunately it has about the same size staff of examiners as the U.S. Patent and Trademark Office had in 1981. With the projected shortage of scientifically trained personnel in years to come, it is obvious that steps must be taken now to find a solution before the crisis arrives.

For the last five years, the U.S. Patent and Trademark Office has been spending a great amount of time trying to negotiate with other countries a harmonization of the patent laws. The PTO has exchanged examiners with the European Patent Office and the Japanese Patent Office in an attempt to find ways in which they can search the prior art and examine applications in the same way.[6,7] If the patent laws and examination procedures can be standardized, it should be possible to file a patent application in any participating country and receive a patent that would be the same, regardless of country.

That would be a great step forward. However, it would provide only two legs to support a three-legged stool. The third leg would be to provide a means to ensure uniformity of interpretation and enforcement of a patent in each participating country. One possibility would be to establish an International Court of Patent Appeals, similar to our own Court of Appeals for the Federal Circuit.

The suggestion of that combination of steps as a possible solution for the anticipated future problem has tended to elicit a considerable amount of mirth and comment to the effect that such a result is a long way off. The logical answer is that unless we set some objectives now, the day of crisis will arrive and we will not be ready. That could cause chaos in the intellectual property community. The objective of the three-legged-stool approach is simply this: an applicant could file an application in any country, get a patent, and have it enforceable in any of the participating countries, all for the work and expense of a single application. What a savings in time and expense! It's time to set objectives.

Optimism

From the above, one might draw the conclusion that the sky is falling. Not so! At present, the U.S. patent system is probably the best system in the world. And to make things more interesting, the system is getting better.

Genetic engineering is not the only technology capturing the world's imagination. Exciting developments in high-temperature superconductivity have resulted in the filing of an increasing number of related applications. As of June 1, 1989, the PTO had 1000 applications involving disclosures of high-temperature superconductor technology filed in the office.

Another technology capturing the world's attention is cold fusion. Because of the potential of this technology, all cold fusion applications are being identified to ensure uniform and consistent examination. Well over fifty cold fusion applications have been filed from a variety of sources.

Good News

There was an exciting development in the PTO's patent statistics at the end of fiscal year 1989. During the 1970s, patent statistics painted a picture of slipping U.S. technology while the number of utility applications filed by foreign applicants increased over 30 percent. The Japanese accounted for the biggest portion of foreign-origin applications, and the number of U.S.-origin applications dropped 16 percent. That was a dramatic drop for U.S. interests, especially when compared with the increased foreign filing during the 1970s.

During the 1980s, that picture changed significantly in many respects. Though the number of foreign utility applications continued to rise, the U.S.-origin utility applications also rose by more than 24 percent. This represents a significant turn-around from the disastrous 16 percent drop in the 1970s. Furthermore, U.S.-origin filings in five key foreign countries rose by an astonishing 79 percent during the 1980s.

It appears that a turnaround in the U.S. versus foreign filing ratio has finally taken place. The percent of utility application filings in the United States from U.S. inventors increased in 1988 (there was also a substantial increase in overall filings in the PTO). This is the first time that an increase in the ratio of U.S. versus foreign filings has taken place in over sixteen years. The trend continued into the first part of 1989. Also in 1988, a dramatic increase occurred in U.S.-origin filings in three of the five key foreign countries. This is not to say that the United States should relax its concerns. But a move is being made in the right direction with increasing strength.

Other notable facts are the substantial filings in European countries that are filed through the European Patent Office rather than directly in the national patent offices, and the substantially increasing use of the Patent Cooperation Treaty[8] everywhere. The European patent system has become the dominant vehicle for patent protection in Europe. Similarly the Patent Cooperation Treaty is rapidly becoming the key vehicle for patent filing in several countries.

As we approach the bicentennial, the world has certainly awakened to the value of intellectual property. More important, the United States has come around dramatically in the 1980s from the depressed patent picture of the 1970s.

George Bernard Shaw wrote something, often repeated by others, that is appropriate here. He said, "You see things and say, 'Why?', but I dream things that never were, and say 'Why not?'"

Notes

1. Diamond v. Chakrabarty, 447 U.S. 303; 206 U.S.P.Q. 193 (1980).
2. Ex Parte Allen et al. 3 U.S.P.Q. 2d 1425.
3. 35 U.S. Code 100, 101.
4. 35 U.S. Code 112.
5. Paris Convention for the Protection of Industrial Property of March 20, 1883 (revised).
6. Journal of the Patent and Trademark Office Society, Vol. 70, No. 7 "JPO-USPTO Examiner Exchange Program Final Report (Part I)," pp. 449–485.
7. Supra Note 6, (Part II), pp. 561–596.
8. Patent Cooperation Treaty (PCT) of June 19, 1970 (Revised).

CONCLUSION
Effable Invention

DAVID N. PERKINS AND ROBERT J. WEBER

Especially when creativity is the topic, one hears more about the ineffable than the effable. The word *effable* really exists, literally meaning "sayable"—that which can competently and properly be said, named, described, talked about. Creativity has the reputation of being ineffable, not something one can say much about, and perhaps not something one *should,* as though the curious prods of the investigator might offend the gods.

Without question the essays in this book would insult Olympus. They individually and emphatically reach for the effable, trying to probe the nature of human invention. Looking back at them taken together, the question inevitably arises: How effable did invention turn out to be? What do these diverse contributions say?

One thing they surely teach us concerns why invention so often seems ineffable. Looking from chapter to chapter, we get a rigorous lesson about the hazards of overgeneralization. Plainly, invention is *diverse.* It takes one form here for this quest, another form there for that quest. Of course, diversity is not ineffability. But it makes the phenomena of invention look slippery, and that can easily slide into an impression of ineffability.

However, despite the diversity, strong trends emerge as well. One thing we will try to do in the pages that follow is to mark out where trends dominate and where diversity holds sway.

Diversity aside, another reason emerges for invention's reputation of ineffability. Substantive invention is never routine. It is never a matter just of good laboratory technique or turning the crank of any other craft. Substantive invention breaks boundaries—sometimes conceptual, sometimes technical, but boundaries that stand in the way and challenge the ingenuity of the inventor.

To generalize, significant invention is never *mere* anything. For example, it is not *mere* persistence in examining possibilities, nor *mere* inference from subtle clues, nor *mere* technical teamwork. On the other hand, it often involves them in crucial ways. Sometimes invention depends very much on persistent search through a large number of options, or inference from subtle clues, or adroit technical teamwork.

Such intricacies go far toward explaining the reputation of invention for ineffability. However, they do not justify it. Quite the opposite, they cast a vote for the broad understandability of human invention, providing we take into account both diversity and trend, and both the features that figure importantly in invention and the caveat that invention is not *merely* any one of them.

So let us get on with "effable invention." As outlined in the introduction, we find it useful to look at invention in three ways: the *search perspective,* which views invention as a matter of effective search for ideas in a space of possibilities; the *psychological perspective,* which asks what psychological attributes equip and motivate such searches; and the *social perspective,* which asks what social patterns and institutions support inventive search. While we certainly do not presume that all the contributing authors would subscribe to the following conclusions, here is how it looks to us—our forthright, but we hope not brash, gesture toward proving invention effable.

The Search Metaphor: From Haystacks to Sherlock Holmes

We can think of invention as a search through a number of possibilities to find one that serves well. The target may be a way of making artificial diamonds, a procedure for using sound effectively to probe body tissues, a device for magnifying images with electron beams, or anything else.

The search metaphor has several appeals. First of all, it has served well in a history of efforts to unravel the puzzles of human thinking. Newell and Simon (1972) based their classic *Human Problem Solving* on the notion of search in a "problem space," and many investigators since have extended the Newell and Simon conception.

Second, search affords a powerful metaphor for recasting in more familiar terms the esoterica of seeking antibiotics, devising a "biotron," or cracking petroleum more efficiently. We all search: for good used cars, pretty shells on the beach, a lost pin on the floor. And many of the factors that figure in the success of everyday search count just as much in the quests of inventors: persistence, looking in the right places, questioning assumptions about where to look, being efficient about it, and so on.

The search metaphor also allows stripping away the particulars of different tales of invention and seeing the logical bones. How does the searcher go about finding a workable idea among the many possible ideas? Obviously not by considering them all, not even all possible ideas in the general neighborhood. As has been pointed out by many authors, a basic challenge to the inventive mind lies in the "combinatorial explosion" of possibilities. Effective search must pare down dramatically the ideas actually investigated. How this happens yields fundamental insight into the nature of discovery, no matter who does the discovering or in what kind of a social setting.

Finally, besides its promise in other respects, the search metaphor serves well because of its flexibility. Far from saying that invention is one thing, the search metaphor allows characterizing an impressive range of patterns of search "from haystacks to Sherlock Holmes." Sometimes invention has very much the character of looking for a needle in a haystack. The inventors scrutinize innumerable possibilities, looking for what they want. In contrast, sometimes invention wears the persona of "Holmesian deduction." From a variety of clues, inventors piece together what must be the way to go. And, of course, one finds mixed forms between the haystack and Holmes.

With this general rationale in mind, let us put the search metaphor to work to see how effable it can make the subtle turns of human invention.

Trends within Diversity

As emphasized earlier, human invention earns its reputation of ineffability partly through sheer diversity. For example, the stories of invention told in this book are not all alike, not even when highly abstracted. Nonetheless, looking across the variety, one finds significant trends that deliver telling messages about the character of invention. Here are several that seem especially revealing.

The Length of Search

Virtually all these cases teach us that significant invention is a long haul. Ideas and artifacts evolved not even over several months but over several years, sometimes decades, as in the case of the technology of ultrasound. The notion of the inventive genius whipping up something in the basement overnight gets little encouragement here. While such things may happen, they appear to be far from the norm.

The Grain of Progress

Popular writings on creativity cherish the "breakthrough." Saturated in the problem, the creative individual finally arrives at the moment where everything falls into place. Perhaps a chance observation triggers this moment, as with Darwin's famous reading of Malthus, or Gutenberg noticing the power of the wine press at a wine festival and seizing its principle for the printing press. Whatever the character of the particular epiphany, everything pivots there. Before is preparation. After is mopping up.

In none of the stories told in this book do we see any such thing. While pivotal episodes certainly occur, there are typically several of them rather than one. Everything does not fall together at once; rather, one aspect gets sorted out, another emerges, a problem erupts, gets solved, a new direction suggests itself, and so on.

Indeed, we suggest that the grain of progress has a "fractal" character. Just as coastlines are wiggly at all grain sizes, so is progress toward an invention. There are little leaps forward, big leaps forward, and all sizes in between. The one big leap with preparation beforehand and mopping up afterward is simply a statistical anomaly.

The Object of Search

It is important to recognize that in principle the course of invention does not always involve searching for a thing to serve a purpose. Sometimes it involves searching for a purpose to fit a thing. A classic case is the development of the popular Post-Its. These came about when researchers in a 3M laboratory found themselves with a substance that might have been an adhesive, but did not prove sticky enough. What to do with the stuff? Post-Its!

Certainly the thing-in-search-of-a-purpose situation needs to be acknowledged. Still, the trend of the present cases lies in the opposite direction. Many involved very clear goals from the first: find a process to create artificial diamonds, use catalysts to make petroleum cracking more efficient, translate from theory into practice the notion of an electron microscope. In other cases, the purposes began broader and gained more focus as the project evolved: develop artificial fibers for good uses, including good uses that suggest themselves along the way. Seek active antibiotic agents; for exactly what maladies? . . . whatever looks promising. Develop the potentials of ultrasound for probing body tissues; toward diagnosis of what? . . . whatever looks promising.

As we step back, we do see a possible variant on the Post-It pattern of finding a purpose. A new scientific instrument not only solves old problems better; it also creates new problems that it may solve. Some of this has no doubt occurred among the users of the electron microscope, the microprobe analyzer, ultrasound instrumentation, and the biotron. The new capabilities of these instruments and labs create new problems and in doing so offer new purposes. This business of finding new purposes is intriguing, a gray and shady area that needs analysis. But it is possibly very important. To find a new purpose for an existing invention is to serve up the freeist lunch that technology has to offer!

The Role of Chance

Chance figures frequently in our cases in one way or another: a conversation, an article read by happenstance, an experiment that did not turn out as hoped but taught the investigators something else.

On the other hand, we see nothing like *mere* chance. As urged earlier, invention is not *mere* anything. Pasteur wrote that "chance favors the prepared mind." So it does and did in some of these cases. However, the purest cases occur when the mind is just generally prepared, as in Alexander Fleming's discovery of penicillin through noticing how mold accidentally growing on a bacterial culture killed the part of the culture near it. Fleming was not even looking for antibacterial agents.

Here we find little of this. While chance from time to time fed the inventive searches examined here, chance did not generally provide the one critical connection or even most of the several critical connections. These were projects and programs under way, pursued with persistence and ingenuity. Chance opportunities were seized along the way, much as were many other resources that might forward the quest. Persistence as well as the prepared mind routinely raised the odds that useful chances would eventually present themselves. It is not that chance is irrelevant, but that it makes little sense to view the process of invention as typically dominated by chance, dependent for success on the lucky happenstance.

The Role of Formal Methods

Formal methods—solving differential equations to find a solution, for example—constitute a resource for the inventor almost opposite to that of chance. Where chance by definition presents itself haphazardly, formal methods are always there, with their cranks ready to be turned, should they prove useful.

Given that formal methods stand opposite to chance, it is interesting to find that virtually the same thing can be said about their role: they figure in a secondary way. Certainly formal methods are employed. For example, the basic parameters for the electron microscope are given by electromagnetic theory. James Hillier and his colleagues had to develop the electron microscope with attention to those boundary constraints. Nonetheless, solving equations certainly did not dissolve the challenges of engineering such a device, which included the subtle influences of innumerable factors that impaired the quality of the image.

The role of theory should not be underestimated of course. In some cases at least, it was an important presence. A quest for an electron microscope would make no sense at all without the buttressing theory. Even if the notion were proposed, one would hardly know how to begin without a theory to define the basic constraints. Likewise, without a theory of materials, states of matter, and crystallization, the quest for artificial diamonds would make little sense. Again, one would hardly know how to begin. But in other cases, theory did not seem to be very important at all. George Wise tells us that the inventor of the O-ring was simply mistaken about his theory of why it worked. But he focused on testing its functioning in practice, and work it did.

For our inventors, it is fair to say that formal methods never seem to do more than *inform* invention, laying down boundary conditions and rough guidelines. Most of inventors' time certainly is not spent manipulating the machinery of theory—more likely the machinery they are trying to fashion hands on. Like chance, formal methods sometimes figure importantly but do not dominate the picture.

Styles of Search

While the previous section focused on commonalities across cases, we emphasized earlier that diversity marks the cases of invention examined in this volume. A good part of that diversity lies in the different styles of search.

In fact, we can define a spectrum of styles of search that classifies some of our cases and helps to explain why search occurs the way it does.

1. *Sheer chance.* What was not particularly sought is stumbled on by an active searcher poking into all sorts of matters.
2. *Cultivated chance.* The searcher deliberately exposes himself or herself to wide semi-

random input, expecting that occasionally useful connections will get made to the objectives.

3. *Systematized chance.* The searcher undertakes a systematic survey of a sizable number of possibilities within a defined set, looking for ones with the desired properties.

4. *Fair bet.* The searcher prototypes a possibility (or two or three) with reasonable expectations that it will serve with modifications. If it does not, other possibilities are explored.

5. *Good bet.* The searcher prototypes from principle and experience something that probably will work.

6. *Safe bet.* The searcher derives by formal methods something that almost certainly will work.

The Popular Styles

The earlier comments on trends already tell us that there is very little of either (1) or (6), a minor role for both sheer chance and "safe bet" formal methods. Evidently and understandably, neither speaks powerfully enough to the essential dilemmas of invention to serve centrally, even though it contributes on the side.

Our authors frequently give limited evidence of (2), cultivated chance. Some of the inventor–participants noted that they deliberately browsed in the library or held side conversations with people from other fields, fishing for the interesting connection. At the same time, cultivating chance cannot be viewed as a mainstay.

Most of the action occurs between (3) and (5), from systematized chance through the good bet. As we move from one to the other, the style of search changes radically. Indeed, our earlier metaphors of the haystack and Sherlock Holmes help to characterize this shift.

How would you search for a needle in a haystack should you have to attempt this apocryphal task? Not, presumably, by examining straws at random until you find the needle. You would employ systematized chance. You would systematize your search, seeking to make it more efficient. At the least, you would set straws aside after examining them, to be sure that you did not look at anything more than once (unless some redundancy was needed for reliability). Further, you might sweep through the hay with a powerful magnet to catch the needle. You might shake the haystack so that the heavier needle would fall to the bottom, where a search of just the bottom layer would turn it up. You might toss the haystack up in the air a handful at a time in front of a powerful fan, so that the fan would blow the hay away, leaving the needle behind. Any of these strategies could miss, of course. But all are systematized search.

It would be easy to identify Sherlock Holmes with formal methods. But this goes too far. Holmesian reasoning falls closer to the fair bet and good bet categories. Holmes's analytical insight constitutes something more subtle and certainly less reliable (despite his success) than activating the inexorable engine of deductive logic. One of the most famous quotes from the Holmesian oeuvre makes the point well: "When you have eliminated the impossible, whatever remains, however improbable, must be the truth" (from *The Sign of the Four,* Doyle, 1890). So does another quote, in a different way. Watson asks how Holmes discerned the culprit. Holmes explains, "the curious incident of the dog in the nighttime." Watson protests: " 'The dog did nothing in the nighttime.' " " 'That was the curious incident,' remarked Sherlock Holmes" (from *Silver Blaze,* Doyle, 1894).

In other words, the logic we see when invention takes this path works through following out likely implications, often implications that challenge the obvious and capitalize on subtle clues. Such logic stands far from "Aristotle is a man; all men are mortal; now what would you conclude?" In fact, our inventors' logic is usually based on heuristic or plausible reasoning (Polya, 1954), but more of this later.

With haystacks and Sherlock Holmes in mind, what do we discover from the essays here? One of the surprises of this inquiry concerned how much systematized chance appeared. As we learn from Bernard Carlson and Michael Gorman, systematized chance was one of Edison's tactics, something he called a "draghunt" for the right substance or device. William Campbell tells us that the search for antibiotic agents that yielded ivermectin involved over 40,000 samples. The zeolite catalyst for more efficient petroleum cracking emerged from Edward Rosinski's testing program in a search that examined several dimensions of varying conditions. Theory and experience said that the conditions could be relevant, but exactly what configuration would serve required a long series of experiments.

At the same time, other cases followed more a Holmesian pattern of inference to a "fair bet" or "good bet," prototyping one or two things and testing them. For example, John Wild's development of clinical ultrasound can be seen as a series of prototype devices trying one thing and another, each leading on to refinements and to ideas for new devices altogether. Each prototype ranged from a fair to a good bet.

Finally, it is hardly surprising that many of these sagas of invention involved a mix: some episodes of systematized chance examining, if not hundreds, at least tens of possibilities, and other episodes of more confident prototyping. The development of the electron microscope, for example, invited prototyping of an overall design and particular parts. At the same time, a bewildering number of influences figured in the quality of the image, and these required painstaking search as well as considerable ingenuity to sort out. The ultimate masters of mixed search forms may well be the Wright brothers, who in Tom Crouch's account moved adroitly across all of our styles of search, from a little bit of sheer chance to a little bit of safe bets, with most of their work in between.

Compressing Search

Why do we see the patterns of search that we do, and why do they vary? Part of the answer is that inventors—like problem-finders and -solvers in general—seek to compress the search. They strive to search without searching; that is, to find the one item among the many without actually looking at the many one by one.

For example, when you shake the haystack to bring the needle to the bottom, or sweep the haystack with a magnet, you are compressing the search, reducing the amount of time and probes needed to find the needle. Even more so, when you infer, as Sherlock Holmes does, that something is a likely bet, you save yourself the trouble of testing a multitude of possibilities.

The dilemma is that some searches compress only up to a point. William Campbell and the other developers of ivermectin devised automated machinery and other means to seek what they wanted. But the very nature of the enterprise—fishing for antibiotic agents—meant that large numbers of samples would need to be tested, however efficiently. In the development of the zeolite catalyst, as just emphasized, theory and experience left a residue of indeterminacy: one simply could not say what combinations would serve optimally. They had to be tried to find out.

Indeed, this point helps to clarify the role of chance in invention. Reliance on chance, even systematized chance, is the residue after inventors have squeezed the most that they can out of theory and experience. As emphasized by David Perkins in his discussion of Klondike Spaces, Homing Spaces, and intermediate varieties, artful invention tends to transform Klondike Spaces into Homing Spaces—that is, to transform the problem to make it more amenable to homing in on a solution rather than engaging in far-ranging search.

Expanding Search

Fine as far as it goes, this leaves out another important part of the picture. While inventors seek to compress search for the sake of efficiency, they often find it important to *expand* search toward ensuring that good solutions actually lie within the range being searched.

Of course, expanding search does not always mean adding large numbers of possibilities. By opening up a new approach through challenging an assumption, one may find it possible to prototype a fair-bet or even good-bet solution of a different kind, rather than adding dozens or hundreds of options.

Among our cases, we see Faraday expanding the range of electrical phenomena by deliberately looking for its connections with magnetism, chemistry, and light. We see a related expansion as people add features to electron microscopes and ultrasound scanners, and even more so when people join together previously existing devices to produce the biotron and the Swiss Army knife, thereby attaining ever higher levels of integration and inclusion. As Robert Weber argues in his chapter, often these feature additions and joins are governed not by randomly combining and borrowing, but by simple heuristics based on complementarity: putting together things that are used separately in similar settings.

The moral of the tale is that the styles of search we actually find reflect each inventor's resolution in each situation of the thrust toward efficiency, which tends to push toward safe-bet search (6) along our spectrum of styles, and the thrust toward breadth, which tends to push toward sheer chance (1). That we see little of (1) and (6) reflects the fact that (1) generally gets too big even to attempt, while the available formal tools rarely suffice to make (6) work. So most of the action sways back and forth between systematic probes of the haystack and Holmesian inference. All our inventors try to be Holmes as much as the circumstances allow, and tolerate the haystack as much as they have to.

A Psychology to Sustain Search

Besides the abstract logical perspective of invention as search, we also seek to examine invention from the psychological perspective: What kinds of abilities, attitudes, proclivities, and so on, fuel invention? Here the search perspective is not to be lost. The demands of search for inventions establish boundary conditions on the psychology of people who can play that game well. While there are no doubt many ways of functioning inventively, those ways must all lend themselves to sustaining the haystack-to-Holmes range of search required and to handling effectively the twin needs of search compression and expansion and the tension between them.

Invention being invention—by definition a pursuit that reaches beyond boundaries—it would be natural to expect some surprises about the nature of inventors. Curiously enough, the surprise is that there were fairly strong trends and not very many surprises. Of course, most of the inventors past and present did not fit the classic mold of Thomas Edison, the acquisitive self-made culture hero, building his own independent empire of invention. But Edison is so much of a figure, a veritable Paul Bunyan of the world of invention, that one would hardly expect them to. If we instead glean our anticipations from the extensive history of research on the creative persona, drawn from studies of architects, painters, musicians, writers, and scientists (Perkins, 1981,1990), what we find here varies little from what one would anticipate.

Cognitive Characteristics

Of inventors, one would certainly expect intelligence, ingenuity, and articulateness (remembering that inventors have to persuade others of the worth of their enterprises). Such traits were abundantly apparent. Indeed, they shine through in the essays written by the inventor–participants.

In keeping with other research on creativity, we find that often visual imagery and analogy figure prominently in the stories of invention. Evidently, here as in other forms of creativity, these are resources for encoding the less familiar in terms of the more familiar and for making fertile connections between one domain and another. No better example can be found than in Edward Rosinski's striking metaphor that his zeolite catalysts capture and hold long petroleum molecules for cutting "like a snake caught in a rathole." There were other examples as well. Bell conceived of the early telephone by analogy with the inner workings of the ear. No matter that the analogy was rough; it served to move him forward.

In keeping with the contemporary work on expertise, it is hardly surprising to find that, by and large, our inventors past and present display thoroughgoing expertise in their fields of inquiry. It seems most appropriate to speak of something that goes well beyond academic expertise, something like a "sense of the medium," conceptual and physical, in which they work. Partly this manifests itself through visual imagery, as already mentioned. For example, Bernard Carlson's and Michael Gorman's discussion of the evolution of the telephone highlights the "mental models" that Bell and Edison developed, closely yoked to prototypes embodying their concepts. Robert Wentorf, in developing artificial diamonds, emphasized the importance of envisioning what happens under conditions of high temperature and pressure in the chamber where artificial diamonds might form.

One especially interesting symptom of this sense of the medium emerged in a happenstance observation made by one of the inventor–participants that provoked echoes from others. Several noted that they, unlike many of their colleagues, had had considerable hands-on machine shop experience early in their careers, where they personally had crafted devices. Of course, we cannot say whether there is a genuine correlation with inventiveness, and certainly not whether it is a contributing cause or simply another effect of an already inventive mind seeking outlets. But we can certainly say that the inventors themselves felt it to be important to their sense of the medium. While the predominant trend was toward high expertise in their disciplines, in a couple of cases we find inventors virtually creating technical fields as they move along. A historical case in point is Tom Crouch's account of the Wrights, two brothers who in essence composed the science of aerodynamics even as they worked toward powered flight. A contemporary case is John Wild's development of ultrasound technology; his medical background certainly did not equip him straightforwardly for the enterprise, but he learned what he needed as he went along.

Attitudinal and Affective Characteristics

In many ways, a broad attitudinal profile of the contemporary inventors also yields what one might expect. First of all, we see ample signs of aesthetic sensibility, humor, and playfulness. One regret about the compendium of chapters in this book is that they cannot in any way convey the high spirit and good humor of the conference that gave the book birth. We remember those days with special pleasure— jokes around the dinner table, stories about talking with children to get across some abstract idea from engineering, expostulations about the fascinating pattern of some physical phenomenon.

This picture is more difficult to confirm concerning the historical inventors. To be sure, Faraday's involvement with the aesthetics of his ideas seems plain from Ryan Tweney's account. However, this is a harder call in the case of the Wright brothers, Edison, and Bell; and we simply do not see that much about such things as sense of humor, which after all is less likely to be preserved in laboratory notes.

Whatever the case there, the one attitudinal trait prominent without question right across the board is persistence, often remarkable persistence. As discussed in the context of search, virtually all of the inventions, historical and contemporary, required not weeks or months but years of development through many twists and turns. Persistence of a high order fairly plainly is a crucial survival trait for the inventive mind.

If we see Edison as the aggressive self-made entrepreneur, this does not seem to be the median profile of inventors past and present. Few amassed anything like a fortune from their work, much of which after all occurred in corporate contexts where the corporation benefits more than the individual. A diversity of motives combined to drive these inventive minds: the need for concrete solutions, the joy of risk, the puzzlingness of puzzles, the tedium of business detail, curiosity, publications, esteem.

In general, there is a tendency to think of highly creative individuals as "outgroup" people, restless characters on the fringes. Robert Friedel tells us of this as he shows inventor stereotypes in transition, from eccentric genius to technological expert. In a way, Edison and the Wright brothers give currency to the stereotype. However, it cannot be sustained in terms of the inventors represented in this volume.

The context of invention needs remembering here. Especially as technology has become more complex, invention is inherently a highly social enterprise (a theme visited more fully in the next section), involving teams of individuals, requiring leadership, benefiting from good social relations, and calling for the finesse to promote ideas with both colleagues and superiors. In keeping with this, at the conference itself the inventors (and indeed the participants in general) were very sociable creatures, easy to get along with, articulate, entertaining. This is not just a nice thing but an adaptive trait valuable for the successful inventor in an inherently social setting.

The Relation to Search

As promised, we have offered few surprises about inventors' psychological characteristics, especially if one's expectations are governed less by the romantic image of creativity than by the technical literatures on creativity and expertise (Perkins, 1981,1990). Indeed, the broad generalization is rather easy to come by. Above all, the strong traits of our inventors are *adaptive* for the work of invention.

Specifically, they are adaptive to the demands imposed by the need for effective search for inventions. Inventors' playfulness and ingenuity help them to expand the search, drawing in solutions where otherwise none might be found. That same ingenuity and their deep sense of the medium within which they work allow them to compress search, staking out realistically explorable ranges of options, operating frequently in fair- to good-bet prototyping mode rather than with systematized chance, and handling systematized chance with technical efficiency when it is necessary. Their good humor, curiosity, and persistence help them to put up with the whole thing for long enough to get something done.

The tension between the needs for search expansion and search compression makes effective invention something of a balancing act. Lean too far toward expansion and you have an unmanageable option set. Lean too far toward compression and chances are you have squeezed out the powerful solutions that lead on to other things. Walking the tightrope requires immense commitment and mental agility; it comes down to that.

Search in a Social Context

Invention does not take place in isolation (Bijker, Hughes, & Pinch, 1987). There is a coarse continuum of social contexts and settings, from the basement workshop of the independent inventor, to university lab, to corporate lab, and to the broader social setting of law and patent system (Westrum, 1991). We can place our inventors roughly on that continuum. At the independent position we have Bell and to some extent Wild; then we have Edison in his own lab; at the university lab we have the biotron and Hillier's early development of the electron microscope. The development of the electron microscope moves into the corporate lab with Hillier; and firmly in the corporate lab we have Morgan and the development of Kevlar, Wentorf and the synthesis of diamond, Rosinski and catalytic cracking.

In the broader social context, we have Jacob Helfman working out of a university setting, teaching the idea of heuristics to practicing engineers. At a still more general social level we have Donald Quigg administering the workings of the U.S. Patent and Trademark Office, using law, policy, and agency to further the idea of intellectual property. Of these social structures, the corporate lab and the patent system are themselves social inventions, not mechanisms as such but systems of social organization for the nurture and perpetuation of invention.

Let's look more closely at some of the points on the continuum. Often people think of Edison's lab as the first real industrial laboratory. But, as Robert Friedel shows us, it was really a different creature. Except for not being part of a larger institution, it seems more like a modern university lab, with a single prime motivator and a number of technicians to carry out his bidding. In another way, in its grounding more in craft than in science, it is different from a university lab. Edison's "lab" was a workshop on a grand scale. One hand—the craftsman's—is in the past, and the other hand is reaching in the direction of the corporate lab.

But the corporate lab as social invention is still beyond his grasp. Its modern form is devoid of a meteoric personality like Edison, its funding is internal rather than external, and it is likely to be more formed by science. For these reasons it institutionalizes, sustains, and produces invention on a reliable basis. The corporation provides stability and resources not readily available elsewhere. To be sure, men and women of great talent are sought, but rarely does the existence of the lab and its funding depend on any one person. This marks it in contrast to the workshop of the independent inventor and the university lab of the professor, both of which tend to be dominated by individuals. The corporate lab is a large stride to a different model.

But the corporate lab is not monolithic. Within it, we find a continuum of styles. These range from the visible hand of management exercising strong control; to the supportive protective manager, with some sanctioned independent activity; to the corporate skunkworks where people bootleg resources behind the back of management in order to work on projects that they believe in—all because their managers would believe otherwise.

David Hounshell's account of the Pioneer Lab at Du Pont shows the oscillation between the first two styles. Paul Morgan's informal comments indicate that it is a tension that is sometimes helpful and at other times not. Our inventors were evidently not involved in a skunkworks, but these informal social structures are widely known.

The power of the corporate lab when focused is a thing to behold. Bill Campbell's account of ivermectin's development tells a story of vast resources and the importance of dedicated people up and down the line—not just the biologist-chemist inventors but the management and the technicians, who all come together in such a way as to produce success or failure. Had one person in the field not picked up a promising sample, the microorganism responsible for ivermectin would not have been found. Social support and organization is especially important for big searches.

Often corporate research is slammed for a lack of innovation. While our sample is certainly biased, we have no doubt that the corporate inventors here did the real thing. Whatever the norm, ivermectin, synthetic diamond, Kevlar were big creative inventions. Indeed, the development of ivermectin proceeded from the deliberate intention to jump out of the grooves and try something very different.

Not to slight the individual inventors, the work of Faraday, Bell, the Wrights, and Wild was largely outside of any structure remotely resembling a corporate lab. This comparison illustrates that important invention can take place in a variety of settings.

While our stories of contemporary inventors are by and large "big science," that should not be surprising. We chose people who have produced a sustained impact on technology. Perhaps other generalizations would have emerged if we had talked about the invention of paper clips and thumbtacks. In contrast, the work of our inventors provided sustainable building blocks for technology, in contrast to one-shot inventions like thumbtacks. Another point: Almost all the stories of our contemporary inventors are collaborative in some sense. Even Wild, the most independent of the contemporary inventors, frequently used the engineering and electronic expertise of others. However, one has the impression that he knew what he wanted before he brought in other people.

Invention as a Distinctive Kind of Creativity

It is time to contrast invention with other forms of human creativity. We do this with trepidation because almost certainly it will be possible to find counterexamples to any broad generalizations we make. Nonetheless, thinking begins with distinctions, and it is time to make some. The domains to contrast are invention, science, and the arts, three forms of human activity and knowledge that most everyone will agree contain supreme acts of human creativity.

A good beginning is to say that invention is not just applied science with a dash of art added. Invention, as we mentioned in the introduction, has a much longer history and a more universal appearance than science. It begins with stone tools, whereas science begins with Greek philosophy. It makes its appearance in every culture, whereas science does not. The appearance of art is commonly dated to the Cro-Magnon culture, when decoration first made its appearance on implements. So art is much younger than invention but much older than science. In cultural universality, art approaches the generality of invention.

The search path of invention may differ from that of science. Invention often begins with simple components and then builds complexity from these components. This is apparent in many of the tales told by inventors in these pages. The development of the biotron, related by James Teeri, offers an especially clear case in point: an intricate and ingenious assembly of devices each in itself not necessarily technically challenging. Science often starts with complexity and then unbuilds that complexity in order to understand its fundamental building blocks. In this respect, invention and art are much more similar, because art often follows the same search path, from simple components to complexity.

However, there are apparent exceptions to invention starting with simple components and ending with complexity. The Sony Walkman is a simplification in some ways. To make it portable, the early version had no speakers and no record function. Another apparent exception is that a large part of more routine invention consists of trying to do the same thing with fewer parts and less resources. Perhaps this can be characterized as a search for efficiency or yield? Probably both science and art sometimes do similar things, seeking more for less?

The "why" of the contrast between invention and science is not hard to fathom. Inventors accept complications to solve the practical problem at hand, whereas scientists pare them off with conceptualizations like ideal gases and frictionless planes, abstract denizens of unreal worlds. The inventor cannot deal with an ideal world; he or she must accept the world for what it is and work within it.

Another contrast about search distinguishes invention and science on the one hand from other inventive pursuits. We really do not encounter massive search outside the sciences and technology. People in the arts and humanities craft their products with relatively modest searches; for the most part it is search at levels (4) and (5). Of course, the occasional author may produce ten or fifteen drafts, but that is unusual and it is still small-scale tweaking compared with what went into ivermectin. The Wright brothers' four-year path to powered flight may not have been longer than it takes to write a great novel, but we would guess that the Wrights' fundamental revisions were far more frequent than those of a gifted novelist, even though the invention of both might require comparable effort.

Another apparent distinction lies in product, the target of the search. For invention it is likely to be a concrete workable form. For science it is often abstract symbols conveying descriptions, laws, models, explanations, and theories. For the arts the target is likely to be a sensible form that communicates esthetic or dramatic effect. While invention in its more visible forms often embodies beauty, that is not its primary emphasis. Often, crude workability will do nicely. Usually it is well toward the end of the invention process before designers are brought in to make artifacts beautiful or elegant.

Still another contrast: It is more difficult to break up a work of art into independent components than to similarly parse an invention. Our historians of invention and our inventor participants have given several examples of teamwork. But what would it mean to assign a musical composition team to work on the different themes and movements of a symphony, with the end result being #9 by a group whose last-name first letters produce the acronym BEETHOVEN? Somehow, it just wouldn't be the same as Beethoven. The parts of a great symphony are too closely related in texture and mood to allow for a successful parsing or carving into independently developable parts. Many inventions, even complex ones like the first airplane, allow for just such divide and conquer strategies.

A final contrast is in order. The names of great inventors are less likely to be household words than the names of great scientists and artists. At least that is true for the inventors of this century. Two of our contemporary inventors are members of the Inventor's Hall of Fame—arguably more difficult to get into than it is to receive a Nobel Prize; one is the recipient of the Japan Prize, that country's principal honor for technological achievement; and the others have received a host of honors. Yet none of these shapers of the modern world is widely known outside his own field. For whatever reason, being a modern inventor does not lead to the public acclaim prevalent in the sciences and arts.

With these contrasts in mind, let us tie up some loose ends. Where do applied science and engineering fit into the scheme of things? We would say most often halfway between science and invention. Where does design fit? At the intersections among invention, science, and art, with a dash of economics added. It has been argued that design and invention are on a continuum, with invention concerned with new forms and design concerned with fitting existing forms into constraints (Weber & Dixon, 1989). So a free-standing dwelling, as distinct from a cave, was once a great architectural invention because it was a new form. But now most conventional architecture is toward the design end of the spectrum because the architect is trying to fit an existing form into spatial, temporal, and economic constraints.

Invention as a Normative Endeavor

Can we think in terms of recommended practices—strategies or heuristics to facilitate the process of invention? This question provoked one of the more spirited debates at the conference. People like Helfman, Perkins, and Weber took the "yes" position. Helfman's paper explicitly promoted the idea of teaching invention. Quigg lies implicitly if not explicitly in this camp. He was a prime mover while Commissioner of Patents and Trademarks in setting up Project XL, an invention program for children. In contrast, several of the historians, Hounshell and Friedel among others, were strongly opposed to the idea.

The royal opposition, the skeptics, rightly objected to some of the more trivial attempts in the social sciences at explaining real and complex creativity. They felt that the work of a genius was by definition beyond the reach of explanation. They thought that generalizations about inventive processes missed the fine grain of invention, that the right nut and bolt in the right place could mean the difference between a successful flight or never getting off the ground. If the fine grain is that important, how could big generalizations possibly fly?

The believers agreed that many prior explanations of creativity are trivial, but they were more optimistic about future accounts. While agreeing that the fine grain of invention is undoubtedly important, the believers did see significant generalizations across many inventions, principles that can be helpful. Depending on one's goal, those principles might simply facilitate an appreciation for invented forms, or show their hitherto unknown relations to one another, or even help people invent more effectively. It is regarding this last goal that the heat was most intense.

As we contemplate the record of the conference and reflect on the beautiful frictions that arose, we have decided to take the horned end of the bull and present the case for instruction. Right or wrong, here is the argument.

Heuristics of Search

Because so much of search is in the middle range (3) to (5), neither statistical methods for dealing with chance nor logical-mathematical methods for dealing with certainty are applicable. In their place we find heuristics—methods and strategies that deal with these middle-range searches. We see heuristics as the normative basis for invention: how to overcome the perils of chance and the limitations of formal methods. The idea of heuristics or strategies is not new (Polya, 1954), but their role in invention may not be widely appreciated. Here are some of the more important ones that we have abstracted.

- *Organize search by parsing.* Parsing is the division of a problem into meaningful components that can be attacked at least semiindependently. It is especially important for large group efforts—sending up a space ship or writing a computer operating system. The Wright brothers' key idea may have been the parsing of flight into three semiindependent components—lift, control, and power. This parse enabled them to attack each aspect of the problem more or less in isolation. James Hillier used a related approach when he assumed that the sources of distortion in his electron microscope images were independent. Even though he had no way of knowing this in advance, it was a good working assumption.

- *Find the boundaries, like Faraday, and cross them.* Instead of looking for independent divisions of a problem, search out connections between things. Although this is somewhat opposite to the parsing idea of divide and conquer, there is no contradiction. Both strategies can take place on the same problem. In general, a nice thing about heuristics is that one need not worry about contradiction.

- *Attain goals through a backward search, especially when a forward search does not work.* This is the rationale for using invention models found in nature. For example, as David Hounshell recounts the activities of Du Pont's Pioneer Lab, a large part of the effort was aimed at artificial fibers with many of the properties of real wool or silk. That problem turned out to be too difficult, so the researchers settled for something less than an exact copy, although their searches were certainly guided by the real thing. Another example is Robert Wentorf's goal of producing a synthetic diamond. Here the effort was fully successful. In each case, by starting with a natural material and then trying to synthesize it, one has a precise definition of the search target and an existence proof that it can be produced. But there is a catch to using natural products as a target. Backward search presupposes a science sophisticated enough to mimic nature—a recent attainment for many fields.

- *Do not be constrained by nature.* Paul Morgan's development of Kevlar and the development of other synthetics indicates that it is often possible to go beyond nature's inventions. The Kevlar fiber, on a weight basis, is much stronger than steel.

- *Minimize search by using a theory or a metaphor or a mental model to work from.* There is a trade-off between search and theory: the better the theory, the less one has to engage in big searches. The same sort of trade-off occurs when we use mental models and metaphors. Thus Bell's ear model served to direct his efforts toward a telephone, and Edward Rosinski's snake metaphor guided his search for a cracking catalyst.

- *When all else fails, do a systematized big search.* This is the strategy behind the development of ivermectin. It is also Edison's draghunt strategy for finding suitable materials for microphones and light filaments. While heroic searches are to be avoided if possible, sometimes a problem is important enough to warrant rolling up your sleeves and getting on with it. But we want to do it efficiently so that we do not repeat our steps, always on the lookout for smarter ways of searching—like applying a magnet to the haystack instead of sifting through it a handful at a time.

There are many other broad heuristics that could guide invention. Rather than go on and on, we will simply list out several others more briefly, to convey the character of the heuristic tool kit.

- Re-represent the problem in different ways. Evidently, this was one of Bell's strong suites (Carlson and Gorman).
- Deliberately move away from an old path, as in the search behind ivermectin (Campbell).
- Look for building-block inventions; the screw idea used by the Wrights for wing warping and for an early propellor analogy, the tooth for forming hand tools.
- Borrow the desirable properties of many things and try to integrate them (Teeri and the biotron). To hold down the number of combinations, look for different levels of integration: feature additions and joins (Weber and tools).
- Look for conflicts and resolve them. This is Helfman's strategy.
- Sustain motivation and persistence by building in large chances for small successes (several people).
- If something works, use it again. This is what the Wright brothers did when they applied their knowledge of wing aerodynamics to the design of a propellor; a propellor is just like a wing that is rotating.
- Try to translate discrete processes into continuous processes. This is what Morgan did when he introduced the Nylon Rope Trick to pull a continuous polymer strand from the interface of two compounds.

Many of these ideas are quite vague. They certainly would not get one very far in a computer simulation of invention. Nor do we propose that they could be applied very effectively in a rote fashion by individuals lacking a "sense of the medium," that precious corpus of imagery and feel that seems to make a technical domain a familiar place for those who work within it.

On the other hand, immersion in a technical area and familiarity with its ins and outs do not in themselves yield artful handling of the balancing act of invention—search neither too narrow nor too broad. Heuristics logically should help. And in fact they seem to. As we have argued elsewhere (Weber & Perkins, 1989), heuristics like those described above appear to figure in human invention. And, while they are weak in isolation, they pick up power rapidly when applied in combination. Gains build on one another—as in the haystack search, where a magnet *plus* shaking the stack to move the needle toward the bottom is likely to be much more efficient than use of magnet or shaking alone.

Heuristics at the Social Level

While the heuristics mentioned above deal with the artful handling of search, other heuristics concern more how to set the social stage for motivating and supporting effective search. Our participants suggested a number of ideas along these lines. For example:

- *Back winners with support and latitude.* Several of the inventors thought that a good way to move the inventive frontier was to fund individuals who had demonstrated their creativity. The best way to do this, they maintained, is to have very little management control over their work.
- *Encourage intrapreneuring.* Again, several inventors felt that the corporation could do a better job of fostering the intrapreneurial spirit. One way of accomplishing this is to institutionalize the skunkworks. Anyone at a certain level of expertise should be a part of some freewheeling activity, with little required, other than an occasional report of what is going on.

- *Foster the interdisciplinary spirit.* Undertaking this effectively is easier said than done. It is not enough for management to simply assign people to teams; those teams must mesh in terms of problem and personalities. One mechanism to encourage interdisciplinary thinking was suggested by John Wild. He talked about a practice at Cambridge University in the 1930s where he was a student. Five nights of the week a student had to invite to his college for dinner someone from another college—or be the dinner guest of someone else. The rules of engagement were simple. No one could talk shop, which meant talking to someone in your own discipline about that discipline. So physicists could not talk to physicists, but it was perfectly permissible and encouraged for the physicist to talk to a biologist about physics, and vice versa. Violators of this rule were "sconced": they were required to buy a gallon chalice of ale for the table. Wild credits these dinners at Cambridge with providing his interdisciplinary interests, and ultimately his approach to clinical ultrasound.

A second mechanism for encouraging interdisciplinary thinking comes from the development of the Sony Walkman (Nayak & Ketteringham, 1986). Honorary Chairman Ibuka had recently retired as the head of Sony. He may have been at loose ends, because he spent most of his time wandering between labs and just looking around. One lab was working on ultralight headphones, another on a super-light and portable tape recorder, with neither lab aware of the other's projects. Ibuka suggested putting these ideas together to produce the Walkman, a portable tape player with headphones instead of speakers. The really important part of this may not be the Walkman as product but the social invention of having a senior, respected individual walking between labs in order to integrate their activities (Weber, 1993).

Can we institutionalize these two practices—sconcing and walking integrators—making them applicable across a range of invention settings?

- *Consider changing the philosophical basis of the Patent Office.* This topic came up after the conference in some private conversations. There are two contrasting views on how the Patent Office should be set up. The present one makes it self-supporting; the people who use it finance it with patent and service fees. Alternatively, one might treat the Patent Office as a national investment, making it easier and cheaper to get patents instead of harder and more expensive. In addition, this latter view says that there should be extramural funds for research into the invention process. The idea relates to the arguments of Jacob Rabinow (1990), who first brought machine recognition of printed characters to the Post Office. Rabinow urged that institutions with the scope of the Post Office ought to actively engage in research and its sponsorship, that to do so is both prudent and cost effective. The same logic applies to patenting and the Patent Office. Of course, there is merit to both perspectives. In any case, the matter should be debated more publicly than it seems to have been.

- *Do a better job of educating about invention.* We as a society evidently do not effectively educate people about the invention process. Some recent steps have been taken toward improvement. Thus Project XL of the Patent Office has formed a partnership with *Weekly Reader* to provide for children's invention contests around the country. Some curriculum materials have also been developed. While the materials are a good first step, they are not deeply based on principles—because the principles of invention are largely unknown. At a more advanced level, engineering curricula certainly include material on design, a close relative of invention. But design is only likely to be emphasized late in training, as a capstone course (Accreditation Board for Engineering and Technology, Inc., 1986). The rationale is that students need to know a great deal of technical information involving science and math before they can begin to design. This is surely false, since many of history's great inventions occurred well before formal engineering curricula (Weber, Moder, & Solie, 1990).

All of this leads one to ask what an invention curriculum might be? Surely it should start early by teaching children to see the hidden intelligence of simple things around them, things like pencils, forks, and tools, about which there has been some analysis (Perkins, 1987; Weber & Dixon, 1989; Weber & Perkins, 1989). Suitable curriculum materials could then be introduced to different grade levels and courses. These materials should emphasize both important historical cases and the principles that can be extracted from them. For each principle, there should be exercises to show its generality beyond a particular case. Above all, the idea of invention should be better integrated with science, math, history, and the business world. The materials might be part of a thinking skills unit, or they might constitute a topic of their own.

At a more advanced level, high school or the university curriculum, more complex cases could be introduced. Students could learn to extract principles such as the kind of search followed in a given case and the heuristics used to cope with it. Special projects and field work could be introduced. Oh, yes, this should be for more than engineering students (Perkins, 1987). Social science and humanities students would also profit from seeing invention in their worlds and their fields, because much of the world we live in is an invented or designed world.

Looking Ahead

We believe that the great strength of the conference and this book lies in the synergy—and occasional tension—of perspectives among inventors, historians, and cognitive psychologists. More is known about invention than one might think! Striving to assemble a coherent mosaic, we are surprised at the structure and rationality of invention's many forms as we catch occasional glimpses of its underpinnings. We had not anticipated the organization that we have ultimately imposed. The levels of search and the heuristic approaches to dealing with them were discovered as we went along. The social continuum that sustains, encourages, and sometimes thwarts invention also emerged from the cutting-room floor (Mokyr, 1990).

With these ideas in mind, in closing we touch on two broad implications—invention as a focus for education and invention as an area of inquiry in itself. As to the first, students' understanding of mathematics and science has never seemed so disappointing, or so urgent, as in recent years. Yet, in efforts to help learners toward a better understanding, the importance of technology has been slighted. After all, technology is what directly impacts our lives. Technology surrounds us, supports us, empowers us, and sometimes even backfires and endangers us. The effects of science and mathematics, while profound, touch most people's lives much less directly, and then through the vehicle of technology.

Therefore, we suggest that technology in general, and invention in particular, could be an ideal subject for bringing together considerations of science, mathematics, history, and technology itself in a coherent and motivating package. Moreover, such an approach would create a forum for cultivating students' appreciation of, and perhaps abilities at, inventive thinking, even as it strengthens and broadens their understanding of key subject matters.

As to the second, invention as an area of inquiry, certainly much remains to be known about the invention process, and no better national investment could be made than to study that process systematically. There is just enough structure behind the diverse activities and processes that we call invention to suggest that serious study will reveal important truths.

It is time to return to the haystack metaphor. What if Sherlock Holmes were searching the haystack not for a needle but for the essence of invention? What would he say about his search and his target? No doubt he would say that there is more to invention than one simple target like a needle. Instead, invention is a shadowy form with multiple pieces, some of those pieces have very irregular shapes, and their boundaries are not sharp. Nonetheless there is form, and it begins to make sense as Holmes pulls the straw away. He is confident that he is on to something, that the essence of invention is at least moving toward the effable. Just the kind of target and search that can provide great yield!

References

Accreditation Board for Engineering and Technology, Inc. (1986). Criteria for accrediting programs in engineering in the United States.

Bijker, W., Hughes, T. P., & Pinch, T. (1987). *The Social Construction of Technological Systems: New Directions in the Sociology and History of Technology.* Cambridge, Mass.: MIT Press.

Doyle, Arthur Conan, Sir. The Complete Sherlock Holmes. Garden City, New York: Doubleday, 1960.

Mokyr, J. (1990). *The Lever of Riches: Technological Creativity and Economic Progress.* New York: Oxford Univ. Press.

Nayak, P. R. & Ketteringham, J. M. (1986). *Breakthroughs!* New York: Rawson Associates.

Newell, A. & Simon, H. A. (1972). *Human Problem Solving.* Englewood Cliffs, N.J.: Prentice-Hall.

Perkins, D. N. (1981). *The Mind's Best Work.* Cambridge, Mass.: Harvard Univ. Press.

Perkins, D. N. (1987). *Knowledge as Design.* Hillsdale, N.J.: Lawrence Erlbaum.

Perkins, D. N. (1988). The possibility of invention. In *The Nature of Creativity* (R. J. Sternberg, Ed.) pp. 362–385. Cambridge, England: Cambridge University Press.

Perkins, D. N. (1990). The nature and nurture of creativity. In *Dimensions of Thinking and Cognition Instruction* (B. F. Jones & L. Idol, Eds.). Hillsdale, N.J.: Lawrence Erlbaum.

Polya, G. (1954). *Mathematics and Plausible Reasoning* (2 vols.). Princeton, N.J.: Princeton Univ. Press.

Rabinow, J. (1990). *Inventing for Fun and Profit.* San Francisco: San Francisco Press.

Weber, R. J. (1993). *Forks, Phonographs, and Hot Air Balloons: A Field Guide to Inventive Thinking.* New York: Oxford University Press.

Weber, R. J. & Dixon, S. (1989). Invention and gain analysis. *Cognitive Psychology, 21,* 283–302.

Weber, R. J. & Perkins, D. N. (1989). How to invent artifacts and ideas. *New Ideas in Psychology, 7,* 49–72.

Weber, R. J., Moder, C. L., & Solie, J. B. (1990). Invention heuristics and mental processes underlying the development of a patent for the application of herbicides. *New Ideas in Psychology, 8,* 321–336.

Westrum, R. (1991). *Technologies & Society: The Shaping of People and Things.* Belmont, Calif.: Wadsworth.

Biographical Sketches

WILLIAM C. CAMPBELL is a Fellow of the Charles A. Dana Research Institute, Drew University, Madison, N.J. and adjunct professor of New York Medical College and the University of Pennsylvania. He was senior director of basic parasitology at the Merck Sharp and Dohme Research Laboratories during the development of ivermectin. He has been president of the American Society of Parasitologists, president of the International Commission on Trichinellosis, and member of the Steering Committee of the World Health Organization's Onchocerciasis Control Project. He is a recipient of the Discoverer's Award of the American Pharmaceutical Manufacturers Association, the Distinguished Veterinary Parasitologist Award of the American Association of Veterinary Parasitologists, and the Medal for Microbial Chemistry of the Kitasato University, Tokyo. Dr. Campbell is the editor of four books and author of 150 scientific papers.

W. BERNARD CARLSON is assistant professor of humanities in the School of Engineering and Applied Science at the University of Virginia. A historian of technology, he specializes in nineteenth-century American inventors and the electrical industry. He has received fellowships from the Harvard Business School, the Smithsonian Institution, and the Institute of Electrical and Electronics Engineers. He is author of *Innovation as a Social Process: Elihu Thomson and the Rise of General Electric, 1870–1900* (Cambridge University Press, 1991).

TOM D. CROUCH is currently serving as chairman, Department of Aeronautics, National Air and Space Museum, Smithsonian Institution. A native of Dayton, Ohio, he holds a B.A. degree from Ohio University (1966), an M.A. from Miami University (1968), and a Ph.D. from Ohio State University (1976). He has written or edited seven books and a score of articles on the early history of flight technology. His publications include: *A Dream of Wings: Americans and the Airplane, 1875–1905* (1981); *The Eagle Aloft: Two Centuries of the Balloon in America* (1982); *Bleriot XI: The Story of a Classic Airplane* (1900); *The Bishop's Boys: A Life of Wilbur and Orville Wright* (1989); and *Charles A. Lindbergh: An American Life* (1977).

Dr. Crouch has been honored with the major book prizes offered by the American Institute of Aeronautics and Astronautics and the Aviation/Space Writers Association. He received a 1989 Christopher Award for *The Bishop's Boys.*

MICHAEL E. GORMAN is associate professor of humanities in the School of Engineering and Applied Science at the University of Virginia. A psychologist, he has published half a dozen experimental studies of scientific reasoning, including "Error, Falsification, and Scientific Inference: An Experimental Investigation" (*Quarterly Journal of Experimental Psychology,* 41A(2): 385–412, 1989). In a forthcoming book, *Simulating Science* (Indiana University Press), he fits this experimental work into a larger philosophical, historical, and sociological context.

ROBERT FRIEDEL is associate professor of history at the University of Maryland, College Park. He was previously director of the IEEE Center for the History of Electrical Engineering and a historian at the Smithsonian Institution's National Museum of American History. His books include *Pioneer Plastic: the Making and Selling of Celluloid* (1983) and *Edison's Electric Light: Biography of an Invention* (1986).

JACOB HELFMAN is currently director of the Inventive Thinking Center in the Open University of Israel. He has a M.Sc. degree in physics. He is involved in developing and teaching a practical model of systematic approach to inventions, designed for engineers and technicians.

Dr. Helfman is the author of *Analytic Inventive Thinking* (Open University Publishing House, 1988) and of several self-instruction books in physics. From 1975 to 1985 he was director of the Adult Education and Overseas Division in the Open University of Israel.

JAMES HILLIER was first recognized for his pioneering development of the electron microscope, his invention of the electron microprobe microanalyzer, and development of their many applications (University of Toronto 1937–1940 and RCA 1940–1953). He is the author of over 100 technical articles, holds forty-one patents, and is co-author of *Electron Optics and the Electron Microscope* (1945). His many awards include the Albert Lasker Award (1960), two honorary doctorates, and induction into the National Inventors Hall of Fame (1980).

Dr. Hillier's second career, until retirement, was in research management. He became the chief technical officer of RCA, in charge of the David Sarnoff Research Center and functionally responsible for RCA's 5000 scientists and engineers. He is the author of about fifty articles on research management. His several awards in this field include the Medal of the Industrial Research Institute, and election to the National Academy of Engineering.

DAVID A. HOUNSHELL, Henry Luce Professor of Technology and Social Change at Carnegie Mellon University, has published widely in the history of technology. His book, *From the American System to Mass Production, 1800–1932* (1984), received the 1987 Dexter Prize of the Society for the History of Technology, and his study (co-authored with John Kenly Smith, Jr.), *Science and Corporate*

Strategy: Du Pont R&D 1902–1980 (1988), won the 1990 Newcomen Book Award in business history.

Professor Hounshell holds a B.S. degree in electrical engineering from Southern Methodist University and an M.A. and a Ph.D. from the University of Delaware. He has taught history at Harvey Mudd College in Claremont, California, and the University of Delaware and has held fellowships at the Smithsonian Institution and the Graduate School of Business Administration, Harvard University.

PAUL W. MORGAN retired as a senior research fellow from the Textile Fibers Department of the E. I. Du Pont de Nemours and Co., Wilmington, Delaware. He is the author of a book and numerous articles and patents on polymer chemistry and applications. He is a member of the National Academy of Engineering and the recipient of many awards recognizing his work, such as the Potts Medal of the Franklin Institute, the Swinburne Award of the Plastics and Rubber Institute (London), the Carothers Award of the American Chemical Society (Delaware Section), and the Midgley Award of the American Chemical Society (Detroit Section).

DAVID N. PERKINS is a senior research associate at the Harvard Graduate School of Education and co-director of Harvard Project Zero, a research group that since 1968 has been investigating the development of cognitive abilities and their application to education. He has written and spoken widely in the United States and abroad about the teaching of thinking, teaching, and learning for understanding, and related themes. Dr. Perkins is author of *The Mind's Best Work, Knowledge as Design,* and *Smart Schools: From Educating Memories to Educating Minds,* and coauthor of *Block: Getting Out of Your Own Way; The Teaching of Thinking;* and *Teaching Thinking: Issues and Approaches.*

DONALD J. QUIGG has forty-five years of varied experience in the patent and trademark field. He is a partner in the intellectual property law firm of Roper & Quigg, with offices in Chicago and Washington, D.C. He is a former Assistant Secretary of Commerce and Commissioner of Patents and Trademarks, Deputy Commissioner of Patents and Trademarks, and a staff attorney, Assistant Manager Patent Division, and General Patent Counsel for Phillips Petroleum Company. He was the 1990 recipient of the prestigious Jefferson Medal Award by the New Jersey Patent Law Association.

EDWARD J. ROSINSKI retired as senior research associate from Mobil Research and Development Corporation after thirty-seven years of catalyst research and development. During this period he invented and co-invented some 107 patents covering catalyst compositions and applications. A number of these patents were also issued in foreign countries. One of the patents led to his induction into the Inventors Hall of Fame in 1979 along with his co-inventor Charles J. Plank.

JAMES A. TEERI is professor of biology at the University of Michigan and the director of the University of Michigan Biological Station. He received his Ph.D. from Duke University and then spent fifteen years on the faculty of the University of Chicago. He moved to Michigan in 1987, where his research addresses the extent to which the rising level of atmospheric carbon dioxide is likely to alter the growth and development of the green plants of the world.

RYAN D. TWENEY received his B.A. degree at Chicago and his Ph.D. at Wayne State University, both in experimental psychology. He is professor of psychology at Bowling Green State University. He is the co-editor of three books: *On Scientific Thinking* (with M. Doherty and C. Mynatt, 1981), *Wundt Studies* (with W. Bringmann, 1980), and *Michael Faraday's "Chemical Notes"* (with D. Gooding, 1991). His interests in the cognitive bases of scientific thinking have resulted in a number of articles and book chapters.

ROBERT J. WEBER is professor of psychology, Oklahoma State University.
    Dr. Weber became interested in invention while on sabbatical at Harvard, where he and David Perkins spent many long lunches probing the conceptual basis of invention. His publications include "How to invent artifacts and ideas" (*New Ideas in Psychology 7:* 49–72, with David Perkins, 1989); "Invention and gain analysis" (*Cognitive Psychology 21:* 283–302, 1989, with Stacey Dixon); and *Forks, Phonographs, and Hot Air Balloons: A Field Guide to Inventive Thinking* (Oxford University Press, 1993).

ROBERT H. WENTORF, JR. was strongly attracted to mechanical and electrical things at a very early age, and his father, an engineer, found it necessary to lock up most of his tools and keep a sharp eye on electrical outlets. Robert Jr. began studying chemistry in grade school and maintained a small home laboratory, which was soon moved to a shed far from the house. He also spent time reading all the technical books he could get his hands on, whether he understood them or not.
    Dr. Wentorf earned a B.S. in chemical engineering in 1948 at the University of Wisconsin. He then switched to physical chemistry for a Ph.D. in 1952. Most of his so-called working life was spent at the GE Research Laboratory in Schenectady, New York, where he concentrated on high-pressure phenomena and superhard materials. These activities yielded many patents, prizes, and publications. Since his retirement from GE in 1988 he has been a research professor at Rensselaer Polytechnic Institute in Troy, New York, where he teaches various aspects of chemical engineering.

JOHN J. WILD received degrees in natural sciences, medicine, and investigative medicine at Cambridge University, England. His major work was the discovery of ultrasonic soft-tissue echoing, including differential ultrasonic properties of neoplastic tissue. In May 1953 he produced the first ultrasonic image in real time of a cancer within the living breast. He actively promulgated the results of his scientific research in diagnostic ultrasound both in this country and abroad. His work was done in Minneapolis in a series of local institutions: the Wold-Chamberlain Navy Air Base, the departments of surgery and electrical engineering, University of Minnesota; Saint Barnabas Hospital; and the Minnesota Foundation. He received the Pioneer Award of the American Institute of Ultrasound in Medicine, was elected honorary member of the British Institute of Radiology, and was awarded the 1991

Japan Prize for Medical Imaging. He continues his work toward objective detection of neoplastic growth in the breast and lower bowel as director of the Medico-Technological Research Institute in Minneapolis.

GEORGE WISE is communications specialist at the GE R&D Center, Schenectady, New York. He has published the book *Willis R. Whitney, General Electric, and the Origins of U.S. Industrial Research* (Columbia University Press, 1985) and several articles on the history of science and technology. He received a B.S. degree in engineering physics from Lehigh University, an M.S. in physics from the University of Michigan, and a Ph.D. in American history from Boston University. He has worked for GE since 1973.

Index